Leninism

Leninism

Neil Harding

DUKE UNIVERSITY PRESS
DURHAM, N.C. 1996

First published 1996

Published in the USA by
Duke University Press
Durham, North Carolina
and in Great Britain by
Macmillan Press Ltd

Printed in Malaysia

Library of Congress Cataloging-in-Publication Data
Harding, Neil.
Leninism / Neil Harding.
p.   cm.
Includes bibliographical references and index.
ISBN 0–8223–1875–X (alk. paper). — ISBN 0–8223–1867–9 (pbk. :
alk. paper)
1. Communism—Soviet Union.   2. Communism.   3. Lenin, Vladimir
Il'ich, 1870–1924.   I. Title.
HX311.5.H37   1996
335.43—dc20   96–3874
                                                          CIP

To

Alexander Macleod
Gareth Videon
Marcus Daniel
Benjamin Lloyd
Quentin Thomas
              five of the best

Contents

Acknowledgements

Practically and organisationally, to Phyllis Roberts who treats with compassion and high professionalism my primitive manu (that is, handwritten) scripts. Intellectually, to the late John Collwyn Rees, teacher, colleague and friend, who taught me how to read a text and who proposed, many years ago, a joint book on Leninism.

NEIL HARDING

Introduction

In October 1917 the Bolshevik Party, under the leadership of V. I. Lenin, staged a successful revolution that was to transform the politics of the twentieth century. It is generally accepted that, without the presence of Lenin, and the pervasiveness of his ideas in key strategic sectors of Russian society, this extreme polarisation, first of Russian politics and then of world politics, would not have occurred. Until that time, Leninism as a body of ideas, as an ideology or world view, was virtually unknown outside the struggles of Russia's socialist groupings and insignificant European factions opposed to the First World War. Without success in Russia, it would doubtless have joined the great repertoire of implausible socialist scenarios whose leading men had faded into petulant obscurity. Some six months earlier it had seemed to many (even those politically close to him) that this was to be Lenin's fate also. His ideas were too extreme even for extreme left socialists in Russia and Europe, and his financial and organisational resources were negligible. He himself hardly disposed of the oratorical prowess or conventional charisma of a born leader. This stocky, reserved man in shabby overcoat, who had spent the war years in lonely exile in Swiss public libraries, hardly seemed cut out to lead a revolution in the world's largest empire, still less to threaten the bases of the established world order.

From the time it burst upon the world scene with the Bolshevik Revolution in October 1917 until the collapse of communist power in Eastern Europe and Russia itself in the late 1980s and early 1990s, Leninism constituted the most comprehensive alternative to global capitalism and every variant of bourgeois ideology. It was, from first to last, an ideology that was grounded in the view that a whole historical epoch, a mode of life and a civilization had finally forfeited, with the First World War, its historical right to exist. Its epoch was at an end. It had brought death into the world on a scale unprecedented in human history. A civilization and an epoch was

1

sounding its obscene death rattle in the blood and mud of Flanders. Capitalism, according to Lenin, had long ceased to be competitive and progressive; it had become monopolistic and militarised, oppressive within and despotic abroad. The Bolshevik Revolution that he inspired was not therefore an anti-tsarist revolution concerned with sweeping away the remnants of autocracy and the feudal landlords. It was not conceived of as a provincial side show – a catching up with Europe. It was, rather, an anti-bourgeois, anti-capitalist revolution for the creation of a new time; a new epoch in human history that was, at last, to put an end to exploitation, inequality and war. It proclaimed war on the values, institutions and practices of the bourgeois world. And when it said war, it *meant* war – revolution and civil war as the only means of transforming men so as to begin the construction of a wholly new order of things and a new structure of values. It was a militant and separatist body of ideas that constituted one of the ideological poles of the bipolar world that was the dominant feature of the international politics of our century.

Leninism was also the theory of communism in power, whose policies and actions were invariably justified by reference to its hallowed texts, organisational practices, and strategic injunctions. It promised to create an entirely new pattern for the allocation of material rewards, power and status that would put an end not only to the exploitation of man by man but, eventually, to all domination and subordination within society. It was a programme for the end of scarcity and, therewith, for the end of politics.

This book sets out to examine critically the constitutive elements of Leninism as a world view, as a way of comprehending the economic, social, and political realities of the modern world. My main objective is therefore to give an account of the mental map that Leninism provided to its followers through which they orientated themselves, came to recognise friends and were impelled to mobilise and organise themselves against their perceived enemies. The business of modern ideologies is, after all, to locate and target a constituency and to move that constituency to alter (or to preserve) an existing order. To accomplish this, ideologies have to present their potential constituents with a plausible account of who they are, how they came to be in their present situation and through what concrete strategies they might transform (or preserve) their prospects.

A necessary condition for the emergence of Leninism as a distinctive ideology was that it had to distinguish its particular character, and the basis of its appeal, from all competitor ideologies. It not only had to distinguish itself from all bourgeois ideologies that were broadly supportive of existing allocations of wealth and power, it also had to distinguish itself from all other varieties of socialism and Marxism and show them all alike to be in error. Like all ideologies, Leninism, as it emerged, had to demonstrate the errors of all competing ideologies by appeal to philosophical, sociological, economic and historical analyses.

Broadly-based ideologies, with a considerable prior history and extensive geographical spread are, on the whole, little concerned with the consistency or coherence within and between these different moments of their theoretical base. The eclecticism of ideologies such as liberalism, conservatism and socialism partly reflects the diversity of their origins, and is partly a function of their felt need to appeal to a broad constituency. They constitute an (often elusive) unity in diversity. Leninism, by contrast, pretends to a tight consistency binding every aspect of its discourse and every moment of its philosophical, sociological, economic and historical analysis. It was able to project itself as internally consistent ('moulded from one block of steel' as Lenin put it) because it was developed by just one man in less than a decade after 1914. Most of its leading ideas were indeed developed in the period 1914–17. Part of the case of this book is that Leninism did indeed have a considerable internal coherence, but that this was bought at the price of being fixed in a time-frame whose extraordinary contours formed the projection for a fixed map of the world.

As will become clear in what follows, the manner in which an ideology defines itself, its history and its relations with all competitors, is fraught with very large practical consequences. The manner in which it resolves these issues frequently has a decisive impact upon the way in which institutions are structured; groups, classes and individuals are treated; and the business of public life is conducted. Ideologies have, and are intended to have, large entailments for political practice – they do not walk innocently in the world, and for this compelling reason they require careful scrutiny and criticism. In no other ideology of the modern world is the transformative intent so emphatic as in Leninism; its responsibilities are, therefore, commensurately large. It aspired, after all, to restructure radically all human relationships – economic, political, social, legal, aesthetic and personal – in a manner without precedent in history.

It was the success of the October Revolution of 1917 that gave the communists the opportunity to implement their transformative programme, and the difficult task of adapting it to a rapidly changing environment. Abstract theorising had now to be rendered as the policy directives, concrete programmes, legislation and executive orders of a government in power. Part of our concern will therefore be to explain and to criticise the practical implications of Leninism as an operative ideology and as a structure of power.

It may already be apparent to the reader that I have made a whole number of assertions that are themselves hotly disputed in the literature on Lenin and Leninism. I have, for example, invited the reader to assent to the propositions that Leninism was, in 1917, an integrated ideological system of thought in the sense that it provided its followers with a comprehensive world view – an economic, social and historical account of who they were and how they came to be in their present condition. I have also maintained that Leninism, as a distinctive ideology of this sort, was formulated principally in the period 1914–17 and did not exist before this time. Revolutionary ideologies also, of course, explain to their constituents how they may get from a despised present to a desired future – they formulate strategies of transformation. I am supposing that that too had already been elaborated in Leninism. Above all, I have suggested that this more or less integrated and consistent body of ideas *did* inform Lenin's actions, formed the basis of his appeal to the Russian people (and to the peoples of the world), and had a decisive impact on the institutions and practices of the Soviet state. I will go on to maintain, in almost every chapter of this book, that Leninism was a much more authentic (if modified and updated) reading of Marxism than most commentaries allow. I maintain that Leninism was a tightly theorised species of doctrinaire Marxism (though I emphasise at this point that I do not necessarily consider that to be a mark of approbation). Both its considerable strengths and its considerable weaknesses were derived almost wholly from Marxism.

The general interpretative line of this book should by now be clear, but it may serve to orientate the reader if, at this point, some of the main alternative and competing interpretations of Lenin and Leninism are outlined.

The dominant interpretative line (let us call it the 'basic position') has it that the nature of Lenin's genius consisted in his ability to grasp the potentialities of a concrete situation. As a practitioner of revolutionary politics he was without peer; as a theorist, however, he was inconsistent, unorthodox and mercurial in his changes of stance and, by these tokens, unimportant. The history of how this basic position was articulated and hallowed by repetition in the work of successive generations of prominent scholars has been explored elsewhere.[1] It has a number of variants and subsidiary arguments, but here we may take Edmund Wilson's early formulation as typical:

> The theoretical side of Lenin is, in a sense, not serious; it is in the instinct for dealing with the reality of the definite political situation that attains in him the point of genius. He sees and he adopts his tactic with no regard for the theoretical positions of others or of his own theoretical position in the past; then he supports it with Marxist texts.[2]

As with the man, so with the doctrine. As Lenin is presented as an adroit power-seeking opportunist, so Leninism is conceived of as an organisational code – a set of organisational precepts and mobilising devices presided over by a centralised and disciplined political party. The general tenor of Western commentary maintains that Leninism was the first modern ideology to grasp the potential of new means of mass mobilization. Modern media of communication, skilfully manipulated by professional agitators and propagandists, were to mould and radicalise public opinion. The grievances of the most diverse groups, from national minorities to land-hungry peasants, were to be exploited and canalised by party-controlled front organisations. It is hardly surprising that this conception of Leninism neatly complements totalitarianism as the prevalent mode of understanding communist regimes and their ideology. Pride of place is again given to the control mechanisms made available to dogmatic party/states by modern technology, to mould the thoughts, mobilise, direct and police the activities of their citizens. Leninism is here presented as precocious totalitarianism and it is consequently to Lenin's early account of party organisation (written in 1902) that most commentators turn in their quest for the origins of Leninism.

A parallel and supportive view has it that Leninist ideas on party organisation and revolutionary mobilisation, though wholly at odds with political practice in contemporary Europe, were a natural product of the backward Russian environment that produced them. The history of the Russian revolutionary movement has been combed assiduously to produce 'precursors' such as Zaichnevsky, Nechaev and Tkachev[3] who, it is maintained, provided Lenin with the model of how to transform society. The historical process could, they argued, be transformed by the purposive intervention of a dedicated, disciplined and ruthless minority resorting, when necessary, to terror, to accomplish their aims. Some warrant for this view could, in the eyes of some commentators, be extrapolated from the fiery writings of Marx himself in the heady period of European revolution and reaction, during 1848–51. It was the 'voluntarist' Marx, a Marx reflecting on the desperate measures needed to put down the anti-democratic reaction in Europe – a Marx desperate to unleash socialist revolution in backward Germany – that Leninism allegedly appropriated. The more mature and determinist Marx who emphasised the necessity of a lengthy historical phase in which new forces of production eventually produced new class relations; where the contradictions and instability of capitalism would be exposed increasingly as it moved towards its full maturity; this Marx, it is frequently maintained, had little impact upon Lenin and Leninism.[4] Leninism is, in this light, a politics of backwardness that appropriated some of the vocabulary and rhetoric of Marxism, but fundamentally distorted its mode of analysis and traduced its means for realizing socialism. Thus we have the frequently cited divide between Eastern Leninism and Western Marxism and, in this way, the benign, academic and methodological aspects of Marx's thought can be appropriated as part of the seamless web of the Western intellectual tradition.[5]

This book questions all these widely current versions of the nature of Leninism. It finds that Leninism was authentic Marxism; that it did indeed revitalise Marxism as a doctrine (and practice) of class war and revolution. It should not, however, be supposed that closeness to Marxism carries with it any positive recommendation. On the contrary, one of the themes of this book is that Leninism replicated the dogmatic and intolerant themes of Marxism itself. The dramatic contrast between Marxism and Leninism has, in short, been sustained only by counterposing a hypostasized and sanitized Marx to a mythic Lenin.

I should, perhaps, at this point make the obvious (but often overlooked) point that the Marxism accessible to Lenin was different from that accessible to us today. Marx's early writings, concerned as they were with the themes of man's alienation and the possibilities of transcending it, were no part of the public ideology of Marxism at that time (and ideology is, after all, an expressly *public* discourse). These early writings were never published by Marx, and he resisted the promptings of his disciples to bring them into the public arena. I have argued elsewhere that he had sound reason to be cautious. He recognized (as did subsequent Leninists) that their message of inclusive socialist humanism was radically at odds with the divisive class war analyses of his mature ideology that received its only comprehensive (if succinct) expression in *The Manifesto of the Communist Party*.[6] The point to be made is that since Marx's early writings were published for the first time in the 1920s in Riazanov's edition of the Marx/Engels *Gesamtausgabe* and, subsequently, in Russia in 1956 (*Iz rannikh proizvedenii*), it would be quite anachronistic to upbraid Lenin for failing to assimilate them. It is, in any case, clear that Marx himself never intended them to be part of his publicly accessible doctrine.

The assessment that follows locates the origins of Leninism, as a generalised ideology, in an authentically Marxist response to the First World War, and its mobilising appeal in a plausible (but fatally frozen) analysis of the degeneration of contemporary capitalism. Its intellectual bona fides were set out in the beguiling certainties of a philosophical scheme that contended that its methods and conclusions were in every respect superior to all bourgeois philosophy. Its historical analysis added a final convulsive phase to the Marxist account of the development of capitalism – the phase of monopoly or finance capitalism. This was the historical terminus of capitalist civilisation in which all its contradictions would be raised to the highest degree and which simultaneously contained all the conditions necessary for the transition to socialism on a global plane. It should by now be clear that we are dealing with a complex and highly theorised ideology that pretended to be a total explanatory system of ideas – all things, past, present and future, fell within its purview and were, in principle at least, explicable in terms peculiar to its thought structure. It prided itself upon its separateness and self-sufficiency – it had no need for bourgeois science.

A large part of the appeal of Leninism was that it provided not only a comprehensive critique of the economics and politics of contemporary capitalism, but also an integrated alternative. To many who, for varied reasons, felt themselves disadvantaged, deprived, alienated, exploited or marginalised by a capitalist-dominated national or international market, it offered explanation for their grievances, and inspiration and organisation to motivate them to remedy their situation. To exploited workers it promised an end to wage slavery; to poor peasants the end of landlordism; to the oppressed nations of the colonies it held out the hand of brotherhood in the common struggle with international imperialism; to guilt-stricken philanthropists and intellectuals it promised the quickest route to the elimination of injustice, and to the dreamers of better worlds it pledged an end to wars and national antagonisms. The gap between promise and performance was, of course, to grow wider as the century progressed, to the extent that Leninism in power fell prey to the accusation that it had in fact created the inverse of what it professed. But it was precisely in terms of its own protestations that it was judged and found wanting. It was finally rejected because not only could it not realise the aspirations it had itself promoted, it could no longer maintain, even to itself, that it was making progress towards their fulfilment.

A central contention of this book is that Leninism, in its origins and content, is best understood as a reaction to world war. The capitalist economic and political civilization that had produced this access of carnage, had, in Lenin's eyes, finally and irrevocably forfeited its right to exist. All those who, with whatever reservations or caveats, supported their country's participation in the war, had similarly forfeited their right to be counted progressive, still less socialist. These were Lenin's instant and absolutist judgements at the outbreak of the First World War. They were the foundational propositions from which Leninism as an integrated critique of contemporary capitalism, and as a conviction that the world revolution for socialism was imminent and necessary, was to form itself rapidly in the years 1914–17. It was the war that led Lenin to undertake an analysis of the economic roots of national antagonism and the growth of militarism. The conclusions of this analysis, presented in his book of 1916, *Imperialism, the Highest Stage of Capitalism*, were to constitute the unchanging world view of Leninism for the rest of its career. Capitalism, Lenin concluded, had become monopolistic and parasitic. It could survive only through the ruthless exploitation of its colonial empires. Given the finite territory of the world, and the infinite desires of capitalist regimes to expand their spheres of foreign exploitation, they were, necessarily, drawn into conflict. In the epoch of imperialism, Lenin concluded, capitalism became militarist and expansionist, externally exploitative and internally oppressive. Above all, militarism and war were intrinsic to its survival – they were its most essential systemic features. His analysis of the bourgeois state and politics was similarly premised upon extraordinary wartime conditions. Suppression of civil rights; draconian legislation limiting workers' rights; the invasion of the capitalist state into the management and direction of the economy and society; censorship and enforced unanimity in the face of foreign threat – all these were presented in Leninism as being typical and characteristic of contemporary capitalism in general. It was, oddly enough, precisely the analysis of the threatening totalitarianism of the imperialist state that prompted Lenin, in 1917, to urge the destruction of the nation state, for the reason that it had finally demonstrated itself to be radically at odds with the goals of securing peace or freedom in the world.

Out of the experience of the war Lenin was led to formulate a radical critique of bourgeois politics. The war confirmed and reinforced all his Marxist prejudices about representative or parliamentary democracy. If such a political system could result in barbarism and fratricidal slaughter, then so much the worse for representative democracy. It too had, by this fact, declared its bankruptcy. Lenin now turned to impeccably Marxist arguments that parliamentary or representative democracy was based upon a fundamental illusion. The nature of that illusion was the sedulous belief, nurtured by all bourgeois ideologists that it was both possible and desirable to distil generally acceptable constitutional arrangements peacefully to negotiate the rival claims of different groups within modern society. Politics, in this 'bourgeois' sense, rested on the comfortable and system-sustaining pretence that, given goodwill and proper institutions, a common interest could be accommodated and negotiated. This was the politics of integration and conciliation trumpeted by all major European ideologies, left, right or centre. Each laid claim to represent the real interests of the people as a whole; each maintained that it transcended group, class or regional differences.

Leninism, from the outset, screamed defiance at the very notion of the 'common good' or 'national community'. Its first word was anathema to all those who pursued such chimaeras. They were either the conscious accomplices of the warmongers – the propertied and the powerful – or their ignorant dupes. The basic and fundamental lessons of Marxism had, Lenin concluded, first been quietly forgotten, then overtly betrayed by the socialists of Europe. They had forgotten Marx's methodology that gave primacy to the economic interests that divide classes within society, setting them in hostile opposition one to another. Between owners of the means of production and the non-owners who live by selling their wage labour, there could be no lasting peace. On the contrary, as capitalism moved into its final and moribund phase, the irreconcilability of their opposing interests must become ever more pronounced. The claims made, one on the other, are, according to Leninism, non-negotiable. The capitalist cannot volunteer to give up exploiting his workers any more than the workers can give up their fight to end their exploitation. By its very nature, this clash of interests could not be negotiated away – it was a fundamental confrontation about which class should dispose of wealth, status and authority within society, and it was an absurdity (in Marxist terms) to imagine that this could be conciliated according to the polite and gentlemanly etiquette of parliamentary debating chambers. The logic of Marxism and the lessons of history concurred, according to Leninism, that such fateful issues, bearing on contests between classes about the distribution of wealth and power within society, were resolvable only by force. In this wartime necrosis of a dying capitalist civilisation, it was therefore even more despicable that Marx's erstwhile disciples had not only forgotten this basic message but had positively identified themselves with their 'own' bourgeois masters. In the hour of gravest peril for the imperialist state and the possessing classes, the 'socialist' leaders of Europe had thrown in the towel. Instead of doing their duty by honouring the pledges they had freely made to the Socialist International, to do all in their power to prevent the outbreak of war and, in the event of hostilities commencing, to take advantage of the dislocations it would bring in order to effect a socialist revolution, the leaders of the mighty socialist parties of Europe had in fact made common cause with their 'national' governments. They were acting as recruiting sergeants for a fratricidal war of worker against worker in defence of capitalist profits and colonial ambitions. Lenin immediately declared the old socialism of the Second or Socialist International to be dead and discredited. Its leaders had become renegades to Marxism and traitors to the working class. His conclusions were blunt and dogmatic: socialism would have to be redefined, Marxism purified, the traitors purged, and a new revolutionary International created.

This was the wartime moment of differentiation when Leninism began to be consciously formulated as a distinctive ideology, separate from and antagonistic to not only all bourgeois ideological currents, but also to all other variants of socialism: the year 1914 was the moment of birth of Leninism as a generalized ideological statement.

For the first time in his career Lenin became convinced that he had a unique responsibility to restate the Marxist imperative for revolution on a global scale, and to reformulate it in the economic and political conditions of the modern world. He embarked for the first time upon themes that no longer had Russia as their central point of reference but were intended to be of general European, and indeed global, significance. Up to this point Lenin had never presumed or attempted to write about international political economy, the history of socialism in Europe, or the character of the imperialist state and how to construct and implement a Marxist alternative to it. Indeed, up to this point, Lenin had, actually written almost nothing on the nature of socialism or the conditions necessary for its realisation. From now on he was to write about little else. Within three years of the start of the First World War he had, in most essentials, defined the economic, historical and political world view that was to characterise subsequent Leninism. As an ideology, Leninism is therefore unique in that it was not the synthesised product of large numbers of thinkers spread over a prolonged historical period. It was, on the contrary, the product of one man's mind in an extraordinarily compressed period of time. For these reasons, no doubt, it gained in clarity and cohesiveness but, by these same tokens, it was narrow in compass and frozen in time-frame.

Leninism, as we have seen, was directly and expressly confrontational in its style. It set out to polarise, not to conciliate. Its object was precisely to assault the shared discourse of European politics. It was an outsider and separatist ideology that prided itself not only on breaking with the presuppositions and grammar of European politics, but also on challenging increasingly the Eurocentredness of its political world. The oppressed and exploited colonial and 'backward' regions of the world (comprising the overwhelming majority of humanity) were not doomed to be eternally peripheral – the objects of the politics of the 'advanced' countries rather than the subjects of their own. They were given a prominent, indeed crucial, role in the modern historical process. The Leninist theory of imperialism, and the correlative significance attached to the global anti-imperialist struggle running step-by-step with the struggle for socialism, gave a key strategic role to the development of movements for national liberation. A large part of the attraction and success of Leninism in the twentieth century sprang from its redefinition of the locus in which contemporary politics was to be played out. To the emergent national bourgeoisie of the colonies and semi-colonies it gave an historical explanation of their humiliating subjection to foreign capital and imperial power, and to their exploited workers and peasants it gave an account of the rationale for their exploitation. To both groups it gave the assurance that their struggle for dignity and independence was part of the larger global struggle of progressive mankind. This was arguably its most potent and lasting source of appeal which, in various guises, continues to be influential, and is likely to remain so for as long as the oppressive conditions upon which it reflected remain substantially unchanged.

We have, to this point, passed over the significance of philosophy in the schema of Leninism, but the reader will see that, unlike most texts on the subject, the present book devotes a whole chapter to its philosophy. A brief explanation is in order. Most ideologies, are, as we have noted, either agnostic or eclectic in matters of philosophy. One and the same ideology will, without apparent embarrassment, switch easily from presuppositions borrowed from one philosophical school to those of another in support of its strategic or tactical injunctions. Leninism is the only major political ideology to insist upon a compulsory philosophical standpoint for its adherents – dialectical materialism. This philosophy, it asserts, is the only philosophy compatible with the progressive and transformative aspirations of the oppressed and exploited. It has this status for two principal reasons. In the first place it is a philosophy that consistently maintains that all phenomena of the natural and social worlds are knowable and that they conform, in their evolution and development, to knowable laws. In the second place, it is a philosophy that recognises, as constitutive of each phenomenon, its contextual interrelationship with other phenomena in a process of constant change. Dialectical materialism, it is asserted, is the only philosophy capable of embracing this complex interdependence and permanent flux of things.

The reader might well, at this point, be inclined to believe that the pursuit of such high-level abstractions, is remote from, and largely irrelevant to, the messy business of practical politics. Yet if we are to try to explain the extraordinary self-confidence and certainty in political action that characterized Leninism and its adherents, we really do have to make the effort to understand what I characterize here as its 'philosophy of certainty'. Part at least of the arrogant self-assurance of its leaders (as well as the willing compliance of more humble followers) stemmed from the conviction that Leninism alone had privileged access to a method and a body of knowledge that was more scientific, more rigorous and more exact than any competitor scheme of thought. There was, they believed, nothing that is or was that was incapable of being embraced and explained by its precepts. It was the innermost bastion of its defences, proof against the assaults of all bourgeois and idealist philosophical or ideological assault, not least because, from within its own structure of thought, it could satisfactorily explain the 'real' roots of their critiques. The compulsory philosophical basis was the cement of a separatist political movement committed to the destruction of bourgeois civilisation. It helped to preserve its purity and militancy, gave it illimitable horizons for action, and the comforting assurance that such action was scientifically based.

The rediscovery, by Lenin, of the Hegelian roots of Marx's dialectical structure of thought was highly innovative and, at its time, unique. It was also central to the formative and crucial claim of Leninism to represent the *only* authentic interpretation of Marxism. It was foundational to the antagonism of Leninism to all other variants of Marxism or socialism. It was, chronologically and notionally, the moment of its emergence as a distinctive ideology of the modern world. Never before had Lenin presumed to teach the great luminaries of European socialism anything about Marx's methodology. Still less had he had the effrontery to tell them that they had profoundly traduced and emasculated it. From August 1914 onwards, however, he was to make this the philosophical bedrock of his emergent ideology.

Dialectical materialism was also, as we shall see, a central feature of the power-structure of the movement. Its assertions that science, by its nature, enjoined only one resolution to any problem or situation, demanded (or was used to reinforce) the introduction of decision-making processes that would unanimously and unambiguously issue in a single General Line. Philosophy was, in this guise, central to authorizing and legitimating the discourse of Leninist leaders and, for this reason, was jealously guarded by them as their exclusive preserve.

The intention of this introduction has been to outline the themes that will be elaborated in the chapters that follow and to give some feeling for the seductive complexity of Leninism as an integrated body of thought. Far from intending to vindicate or recommend, this concentration on internal complexity is offered as a more satisfactory and convincing account of the sources of its appeal and its durability by comparison with those interpretations discussed above. It may also disclose the deeper pathos and tragedy of its subsequent career that was manifest in the increasingly evident disparity between its limitless promises and its meagre, and often barbarous, performance.

1

Lenin before Leninism

The Young Lenin – Jacobin or Marxist?

There is, in many Western accounts, an over-determined description of the genesis of Leninism that distorts the historical record, ignores the bulk of Lenin's early writings or trivializes their content. In these conventional and undemanding interpretations, Leninism is not much concerned with theory[1] but is distinctive because of its 'modern' grasp of the persuasive power of propaganda and the manipulative potential of front organisations to mobilise the masses. Its 'origins' are therefore discerned in Lenin's writings in 1902, on organisational matters which, it is argued, were themselves largely influenced more by the indigenous Russian conspiratorial tradition than by the constraints of Marxism.

The tale that has repeatedly been told runs as follows:[2] at the age of seventeen the young Lenin suffered a trauma from which he never really recovered – his elder brother, Alexander, was hanged for his part in a conspiracy to assassinate the tsar. The young Lenin then swore an oath to avenge his brother's death by taking up the cause to which his brother had been a martyr. Psychologically, we are told, this was the birth of Leninism.[3] It is sufficient explanation for the remorseless resolve and almost superhuman dedication that commentators are agreed was basic to the man and his doctrine. It was indeed shortly after this shattering event that Lenin, no sooner admitted to Kazan University than expelled, began to frequent circles of revolutionaries in Samara to verse himself in the doctrines to which his brother had dedicated himself. Here, it is said, he learned at first hand from the veterans of the struggle about their goals, strategy and organisational principles. He was, according to this dominant account, imprinted with the traditions of the Russian revolutionary movement, and bound to it by the blood-tie of his brother's martyrdom. He learned, in particular,

15

to value the role of organisation, the need for clear structures of command and accountability, the importance of secrecy, and of professionalism in conspiratorial work. Very early, he recognised that without a tightly-structured conspiratorial organisation, the revolutionary movement in Russia would come to nothing. From the outset, then, nascent Leninism clearly showed its distinctive marks – it was preoccupied with questions of organisation, mobilisation and manipulation. Out of these fixations would spring Lenin's major work on organisational matters, *What Is to Be Done?* (written in 1902), and his frenzied efforts to get its proposals implemented at the Second Congress of the Russian Social Democratic Party in 1903. It was this Congress that saw the fatal emergence of Bolshevism in confrontation with Menshevism. Bolshevism was, at the time and subsequently, identified with Leninism. The two became synonymous and both were seen to have their roots in the narrow, tough-minded traditions of the Russian revolutionary movement. The role of the masses, their spontaneous movement for freedom and socialism was discounted, their place in the historical process being largely supplanted by that of the disciplined, dedicated elite of professional revolutionaries.

The narrative about the origins of Leninism (or Bolshevism), and its increasing remoteness from what is presented as 'orthodox Marxism', is generally complemented and reinforced by references to Lenin's Jacobinism. Jacobinism itself is frequently, in these accounts, left vague and ill-defined. In general, though, there would probably be some agreement that, in the Russian context, it amounted to the claim that a self-selected elite, by dint of their knowledge, dedication and selflessness, had a surer grasp of the needs of the ordinary people than the people themselves could possess. They felt justified therefore in anticipating the real (but at the time unrecognised) will of the masses, and in acting resolutely on the people's behalf. The prospects for revolution did not therefore depend upon the will of the majority. The Jacobins argued that, given the state's control of education, the church and the army, it was illusory to expect widespread revolutionary consciousness *before* the revolution. The path to secure the support of the people lay through the prior seizure of state power: not through a majority to state power, but through state power to a majority – that was the general political line of Jacobinism. Jacobinism has, in this sense, connotations of the small but tightly-organised band of co-believers forcing the pace of history and refusing to accept such limitations to political strategy as the level of industrial development, class formation, culture and consciousness. It is often presented as being synonymous with voluntarism – the will of a dedicated elite triumphing over such 'objective' restraints. In its Russian variant it is generally associated with those socialists (such as Bakunin, Nechaev, Zaichnevsky and Tkachev) who, despite all Marx's counsel to the contrary, maintained that Russia's industrial and social backwardness was a positive advantage, since the peasants and urban workers had not been corrupted by bourgeois culture.[4] The activating minority of organised revolutionaries therefore had the obligation to lead Russia directly and immediately into socialism without waiting for the so-called 'material preconditions' to mature. Now Lenin had, the tale continues, as a young man sat at the feet of the remaining veterans of this tradition in discussion circles in Samara and Kazan. Many of them were Narodovoltsy, legendary remnants of the once powerful Narodnaya Volya (People's Will) organisation, bound by ruthless discipline and skilled in conspiratorial technique. They were supposed, through the force of their intrepid example, to rouse the masses to action. They were the self-styled advance guard of the revolution, its elite force who succeeded, on 1 March 1881, in assassinating Tsar Alexander II. When the regicide group in which Lenin's brother was a principal leader chose the same date six years later to make their abortive attempt on the life of Alexander III, they identified themselves consciously with the tradition of the frankly Jacobin Narodnaya Volya.

A similar impatient (or voluntarist) disposition is, it is maintained, evident in Lenin's first published writings. In 1894 in 'What the Friends of the People Are' he allegedly dismisses the necessity of Russia undergoing a capitalist phase and was already urging communist revolution.[5] He reverts, according to a chorus of commentators, to this same Jacobin voluntarism in accepting in 1905 Trotsky's theory of permanent or uninterrupted revolution. And in October 1917 he finally consummates his early affair with Jacobinism by masterminding a *coup d'état* that declares the socialist revolution in the most backward country in Europe. In this account, Jacobinism, not Marxism, is the soul of Leninism.

It is clear that we cannot beg the question of the historical origins of Leninism because, as we have seen above, interpretations of its content have been tied closely to interpretations of when and how it came into existence: a case of find the seed to tell the plant. In the alternative narrative set out in the remainder of this chapter, I maintain that the lineage of Leninism lies firmly within the Russian and European Marxist traditions,[6] and that Leninism, as a distinctive ideology, did not exist until 1914. To that point Lenin was more apologetic than proud of the peculiarities forced upon the theory and practice of Russian Marxism by the backwardness of its economic and political milieux. He was almost exclusively concerned with things Russian, and the thought had never occurred to him that he had anything to teach the incomparably more advanced, cultured and organised socialist movements of the West. On the contrary, up to that time he came to them as pupil and penitent. This, of course, is not to say that what was written, theorised and practised before 1914 had no impact upon subsequent Leninism; that would be absurd. Preoccupation with organisational questions has, however, led most commentaries almost to ignore the significance of Lenin's exhaustive writings on the contemporary development of capitalism in Russia that overwhelmingly absorbed his energies and which arguably constitute his single most important contribution to Marxist theory. It was precisely these concerns that established him, at the early age of 24, as the principal spokesman of the most prominent group of Russian Marxists in St Petersburg, in their controversies with populist opponents.

Lenin first became interested, then involved in revolutionary politics, in the year following his brother's death. The trauma of Alexander's execution may well have had a profound psychological effect on Lenin's whole career but we shall never be able to assess it, not only because the impact of such personal tragedies is inherently difficult to gauge, but also because Lenin himself was extraordinarily reticent about the matter. In the whole course of his subsequent career, and in all his voluminous writings and letters, there is only one brief reference to his brother's death. It was perhaps a pain too profound to articulate and we can only speculate on the way it influenced him. We do know, however, from the sort of material he was reading, the people with whom he was associating, and the views he expressed at this time, that from the age of eighteen onwards, the young Lenin was far from being a typical or orthodox Russian Jacobin. Certainly, he attended circles frequented by notorious Russian Jacobins, but these circles were never homogeneous in their ideological orientations. There were, moreover, no other circles available for a would-be revolutionary to attend. Within them could be found moderate populists who believed that only by patient attention to improving the living standards, culture and expectations of the peasantry could the future of socialism be secured. They also contained thoroughgoing Jacobins who maintained that to wait for this transformation would be cowardly and counter-productive. What was needed, they argued, was a cohesive organisation of dedicated men who would lead a coup, seize state power, and utilise it to inaugurate the socialist transformation of Russia.

Theoretical Issues – The Development of Capitalism

Debates within revolutionary circles about organisational and strategic matters were complemented by more theoretical disputes about the likely path of Russia's future economic development. This was the debate over the so-called 'Fates of capitalism in Russia'.[7] Would Russia have to undergo a prolonged (and doubtless painful) period of capitalism before the transition to socialism was viable? Would the country have to retrace the historical path of West European development, as the doctrine of Marx seemed to imply? The 'exceptionalists', or Russian populists, generally believed that Russia was not, and ought not to be, a slave to Western practices. Russia's laws of development were not necessarily the same as those of the West. They pointed in particular to the survival, uniquely in Russia, of ancient patterns of land tenure and distribution that vested the ownership of the land not in individuals but in the community. It was the local peasant community (in Russian the *mir* or *obshchina*) that allocated land to each household and that carried out periodic redistributions so that allotments broadly corresponded to the size of the household. The peasant commune expressed, for the populists, the instinctive commitment to social justice and the natural socialism of the Russian people. It could and should be used as a springboard into socialism. Indeed for many it was a signal of Russia's great historical destiny – to show the rest of the world the road to socialism. It was, so they argued, the commune that had saved the Russian people from the dreadful fate of small farmers elsewhere in Europe – dispossessed from their land by enclosures and the march of large-scale mechanised agriculture they had been forced into poverty, exploitation and wage-slavery in the great industrial cities. To repeat these disasters in Russia was, they maintained, not only morally insupportable but also, happily, impossible in practice.

The impossibility of Russian capitalism being able to flourish stemmed, according to the populists, from a number of natural disadvantages. Russia did not have concentrated centres of population closely connected by good rail, road, canal or sea communications. The population was sparse, widely scattered and without easy lines of communication. Raw materials were similarly scattered and difficult of access, remote not only from markets in Russia but, importantly, from foreign markets. The cost of creating good communications linking raw materials to manufacturing centres, and both of these to domestic and foreign markets, would put such a heavy premium on Russian-produced industrial goods as to make them uncompetitive on the market. Similar considerations applied to the cost of labour. The Russian climate was notoriously severe and inhospitable. Compared to the more temperate countries of Western Europe, workers in Russia would need more expensive clothing, housing, fuel and food simply in order to keep them in condition as labouring beings. This, in turn, would add an extra premium to the goods they produced. The Russian Socialists, in short, concluded that capitalism was ethically undesirable, socially divisive and practically impossible to realise in Russia. Its very existence owed more to government subsidies to establish strategically important sectors of the economy than it did to the natural demands of the internal market. It was, they concluded, a hothouse plant that was fated to expire as soon as the artificial conditions that sustained it were done away with. Authentically Russian socialism would build upon Russia's own institutions, practices and prejudices. It would be highly decentralised (the federation of free communes), suspicious of, if not positively hostile towards, a centralised state, and based upon the communitarian practices and social homogeneity of the peasantry and the artisans.

The tough end of the debate within Russian revolutionary circles in the late 1880s was concerned with the questions of the development of capitalism in Russia: how far had it spread, and was it increasing? Had it penetrated the countryside or was it confined to the towns? At a more technical level there was the argument about the possibility of capitalism being able to reproduce itself or, put more simply, guarantee its own continuity. One of the basic questions here was whether capitalism presumes an already existing and extensive market for the goods it produces, or does it create such a market in the course of its own development? These questions, we know, were hotly debated in the revolutionary circles that Lenin was attending between the ages of eighteen and twenty-four. We also know that from the outset Lenin displayed a strong interest in Marx. At the age of eighteen he had already read volume one of *Capital* and thereafter he was avidly interested in Marxist literature of all sorts. We also know that from his early twenties, Lenin began to establish a local reputation as a persistent and well-informed critic of almost all varieties of Russian populism; Jacobinism included. He had already embarked upon a major project that was to take him until the turn of the century to complete – a thorough study, from a Marxist perspective, of the degree of capitalist production relations and market relations in Russia – particularly in the countryside. By 1893, when he decided to leave Samara for St Petersburg, Lenin had already completed a comprehensive and detailed critique of the economic and social ideas of the Russian Socialists (or populists). The first part of this work was produced in the following year, as the very first published response by the underground Marxists in Russia to populist arguments.[8]

Lenin's principal theoretical concern in these early years was to complete the economic and social analysis of Russia that he had already begun in Samara in 1892–3. He saw the completion of this mammoth task with the publication in 1899 of *The Development of Capitalism in Russia*.[9] In this, incomparably the most important book of his early period and arguably his single most original contribution to Marxist theory, he set out to give a complex account of the stages of the evolution of capitalism, and attempted to place particular regions and trades along this progression.[10] He agreed with George Plekhanov that a crucial impetus had been given to the evolution of capitalism in Russia by the emancipation of the serfs in 1861. Under the terms of the Act of Emancipation, legal title to the land customarily held by the peasant communes had been vested formally in them. The legal obligation of serfs to perform labour service for their local landlords was done away with, but, in recompense, each commune now had to pay what were termed 'redemption monies' to the state. This meant that each commune had to impose a cash levy on each of its peasant households. Abruptly the peasants had to adjust to the very considerable problems of a cash economy. Hitherto they had, very largely, produced only for their own subsistence. They had only been involved in marketing their agricultural produce, or artisan handicrafts, on a relatively modest scale – in order to purchase the goods they could not produce themselves or obtain through barter. Now, however, they had to obtain cash to meet their share of the communal redemption payments. In order to do so they either had to market their produce, or sell their labour power.

There were, inevitably, many peasants who could not meet their redemption payment obligations to their commune. They fell into the clutches of the wealthier peasants who became money-lenders, or usurers, who loaned cash at high rates of interest against the promise of the future production of the poor peasants. Gaining knowledge of increasingly distant markets, having the resources to provide transportation, and to bridge the gap between time of harvest to time of sale, the peasant usurers rapidly became middle-men or merchants. They bought up the small surpluses of the nominally independent peasant farmers and put them together into marketable lots. Naturally, they exacted their profit, and the more dependent the small peasants became, the more the merchants increased their margins and, therewith, the dependence and indebtedness of their clients.

When, as rapidly became the case for a section of the peasantry, the likely future yield from their plots was insufficient surety for their mounting burden of debt, they were obliged to mortgage the only remaining thing of value they possessed – their own labour power. From lenders of money, the merchants now became hirers of labour. They established factories and workshops for the processing of wood, agricultural produce, leather, wool, minerals and so on. This was the second phase of what was termed 'the primitive accumulation of capital'. Merchant capital became manufacturing capital, still based on hand techniques, but with an increasingly sophisticated division of labour. From this it was but a small step to the purchase of labour-saving equipment and machinery and the establishment of large-scale mechanised industrial plants. Manufacturing capital now became full blown industrial capitalism.

Throughout this complex and variegated process, which proceeded very unevenly in different trades and different regions of the country, certain general characteristics increasingly asserted themselves. The scale of the market grew constantly – as much as a result of the impoverishment of the masses as of the enrichment of the few. What the masses of independent peasants and artisans had hitherto produced on their own plots and in their own workshops, they now had to purchase on the market. The fact that as individuals they were able to consume less than they had previously enjoyed was of no moment as far as capitalism was concerned, so long as the total value of what they were obliged to purchase in the market continued to rise. The growth of the market, Lenin concluded, far from suffering from mass impoverishment, in fact depended upon it.

What Lenin sought to demonstrate, in his theoretical analysis of Russian society, was that the peasantry was being more and more split up into a rural proletariat of landless labourers obliged to sell their labour power, and a rural bourgeoisie at different stages of consolidating its capital. The rural proletariat was, in his political strategy, a crucially important group. Unless the urban industrial workers managed to secure its support, the prospects for the democratic revolution would be bleak indeed. Since, however, they shared the same objective interests as wage labourers, and since they had common grievances against capitalist exploitation, there was every prospect that a working alliance could be formed. Within this alliance it was the urban industrial workers who, though numerically smaller, would form the leading core. They were drawn together into huge plants; their lines of communication were much better developed; they were mobile; and they could compare experience one with another and begin to generalise about their condition. They had long emancipated themselves from personal bondage to a particular landlord or usurer, and had escaped the authority of village elders and the Church. They were better educated and had begun to feel the potential strength of their concentrated numbers. They were, finally, concentrated in the most strategically vital towns and cities, particularly the twin capitals, Moscow and St Petersburg. For all these reasons the urban proletariat was 'the sole and natural representative of Russia's entire working and exploited population' (Lenin, 1960–70, vol. 1, p. 299). They, alone of the great mass of scattered wage workers in Russia, had the potential for a properly class existence. The potential for cohesive national organisation existed in a way that it did not and could not among the rural wage workers.

Bridges to the Workers – Politics via Economics

When Lenin arrived in St Petersburg at the end of August 1893, the Marxists of the capital had no formal organization and few contacts with industrial workers. The principal grouping (which Lenin immediately joined) was based on the Technological Institute and it took the form of a discussion circle of students and intellectuals who met from time to time to discuss theoretical matters; its numbers were tiny, its resources few and its contacts with other Marxist groups in Russia very restricted. In the winter of 1893 the St Petersburg group embarked upon its first concerted effort to build bridges to the working class. They recognised that, as long as social democracy was restricted to a student and intellectual milieu, it would remain isolated and ineffectual. The tactic they now hit upon was to take the study circles and Marxist discussion groups out of the Polytechnic and into the workers' quarters. Lenin was given the important Nevsky Gate area of the city and he began to organise worker groups with the intention of inducting them thoroughly into the whole corpus of Marx's writings on economics, history and politics. The objective was to train the most active and intelligent workers so that they would be able to understand the relationship between the economic position and political postures of all classes and groups in Russian society. Those worker propagandists would then, according to the plan, set up their own circles and train new recruits who would, in their turn, do likewise, and so on in geometric progression until the whole working class was conscious and organized. It was what we might term a chain-letter strategy for the generation of socialist consciousness.

In practice, the youthful missionaries of Marxism met with a mixed and often bemused response, even from the most educated and active workers. Some (like Lenin's pupil Babushkin) were enthusiastic converts and aided their teachers directly by gathering detailed information on workers' grievances and establishing contact with the major industrial plants in St Petersburg. Others felt a certain resentment that the 'students' could, as had happened in the past, suddenly appear with promises of support, only to vanish when conflicts broke out (or when vacations took them off to their holiday homes). Others still looked on the circles as a means of acquiring literacy and culture that might allow them to escape from the severities and insecurity of working-class life. And so it was that, when strikes and disturbances occurred in late 1894 at the huge Semyannikov works in the Nevsky district, most of Lenin's students stood almost ostentatiously aloof from what they saw as the primitive reactions of the untutored masses. By early 1895 Lenin was already conscious of the ambiguous role that workers' study circles were playing. They were in danger of creating a kind of worker elite that displayed an overt disdain for the anarchic and combative actions of their fellow workers.

By the spring of 1895 there was already considerable discussion within the central Marxist group about whether to go over to a quite new tactic that would address the immediate and keenly felt economic grievances of the mass of the workers. Lenin was for the new tactic and found a welcome ally in Iulii Martov (who, after 1903, became the leading figure in the Menshevik opposition to Lenin). Martov had just arrived in St Petersburg, having been active as an organiser and propagandist in the much more developed movement among the Jewish workers on the Western borders of the empire. Martov had brought with him a programme that he had helped to write, entitled *On Agitation*. Its basic message was that the workers would come to socialism not from book-learning and theoretical training, but from reflecting on the experiences of the battles they would be obliged to fight to improve their miserable economic conditions. The struggles for better conditions, improved pay and security, relief from the brutal treatment and arbitrary fines typical of many industrial establishments, would teach the workers the importance of solidarity and prior organisation. The economic struggle would necessitate the establishment and administration of strike funds. Co-ordination between shops within a plant and other plants within the locality had to be secured. Grievances would have to be articulated clearly and, wherever possible, printed and circulated. Spokespersons who enjoyed the full confidence of the workers, would have to be nominated. All this would provide a training ground in which the most dedicated worker activists would quickly learn how to organise and mobilise their fellows (aided, of course, by the social democrats).

According to the new strategy, politics would come via economics. The workers could not fail to see that the forces of the law and of the state were deployed to protect the owners' interests and profits. From their own immediate experiences the workers would learn that only through their own activism and organisation, and only by constantly broadening and deepening the struggle, could they obtain any lasting improvements.[11] Industrial action in pursuit of immediate claims, no matter how petty and localized, would itself create a primitive organisational structure. The workers, at first, might well fail in their object for want of solidarity within the plant, or through management intimidation, or via the importing of strikebreakers. The workers would then recognise the necessity for more elaborate preparation and organisation. Strike funds would be established, themselves requiring systems for collection of dues and supervision of the funds; co-ordination with other plants would be seen to be necessary, so delegate meetings would have to be convened. Swiftly the workers would realise that strikes in individual plants and works could be easily picked off (or ridden out) by employers' trade associations pledged to provide mutual assistance in the event of strikes. The workers would then be obliged to organise more general strikes, embracing whole cities or whole branches of trade. This, in turn, required a far more elaborate organisational basis.

Finally, the workers' movement, from the experience of common struggle, would recognise that, regardless of trade, speciality, or regional affiliation, the workers' conditions were everywhere basically the same. Long hours, low pay and lack of rights was the universal lot. At this point they would come forward with demands that were generalised: demands that united all wage labourers. Such were the demands voiced by the European workers in their May Day demonstrations calling for the legal limitation of the working day. News of these demonstrations and the co-ordinating power of the legendary 'International' (the Second, or Socialist International established in 1889) began to circulate widely in flysheets and pamphlets published by the social democrats and copied by workers' groups. This was, in Lenin's view, a crucial point of transition for now the spontaneous workers' movement had, perhaps without realising it, crossed the Rubicon into open political struggle with the government.

It had, of course, always been a watchword of the Russian social democrats that 'Every class struggle is a political struggle'; Marx had said so, and Plekhanov had taken the quotation as the epigraph of his seminal *Socialism and the Political Struggle* – the very first attempt to translate Marxism to Russian conditions.[12] It is, however, frequently the case that the more celebrated a catch-phrase, the more obscure its meaning. For Lenin, the events of 1895–6 revealed both the theoretical and practical truth of this foundation precept with brilliant clarity. The theoretical line of *On Agitation* had prompted Lenin to reflect on the phasal growth of class, consciousness and organisation. Their development was, he asserted, a function of the breadth and depth of working-class activity. Where that activity was small-scale (restricted to a particular plant or factory) and in pursuit of fleeting and limited demands (restitution of holidays or suspension of fines), there the organisation generated would be extemporised and evanescent. There too, the level of consciousness required of the workers and generated by the struggle would be primitive. At the other end of the progression, demands for an eight-hour day, or for minimum rates of pay, by the nature of their generality could not be addressed to particular employees or to associated confederations of employers – they could be granted and implemented only by the state. Without statutory guarantees and enforcement, without a general nationwide system of sanctions against defaulters, such national *class* demands could not be realised. Generalised demands, on behalf of *all* wage workers were, by this token, properly class demands and they, by their nature, were *political* demands that had to be addressed directly to the state.

There was a further crucial extrapolation to be made from this analysis and it was this: agitation, strikes, demonstrations and so on, in pursuit of such generalised class demands, would have to be conducted on a national basis to have any hope of success. The scale of activity, in a word, had to be commensurate with the objective. It followed, therefore, that the organisational structure co-ordinating and leading the struggle, would, equally, have to be national in extension. Such an organisation would have to stimulate and articulate the workers' consciousness of these generalised objectives and, moreover, represent them in an authoritative manner to the government. At this point the regional and trade organisations of the working class would have to be transcended in a political party of labour. In the sphere of organisation too, therefore, when the demands, activity and consciousness of the workers broadened to the general national level an entirely new organisational structure would be required to organise and direct the work – and the formation of a workers' political party became imperative.

What Lenin elaborated at this time was a phasal account of the development of the workers' class activity, consciousness and organisation, expanding from the particular and local to the general and national. It was an evolution directly comparable to the natural history of capitalism, and he transported many of the terms of art and imagery used to describe the latter into his accounts of the former process. The antiquated methods of small workshops (*kustarnichestvo*) with restricted markets or spheres of activity and ill-elaborated division of labour, was associated with the activities of the workshop strike committees. By contrast, the sophisticated technology and complex division of labour of the modern industrial factory required a national and international market or sphere of activity, and this was the simile Lenin used repeatedly to describe the political party. Through it all there ran the familiar Marxist teleology of the ascent from the particular to the general, from the local to the universal.

On a practical level, the huge strikes in the textile and metal-working industries that shook St Petersburg (and other industrial regions) in late 1895, June 1896 and January 1897 seemed, to Lenin, to offer a brilliant vindication of the progression he had sketched, and which had been anticipated in the *On Agitation* programme.[13] The strikes *did* become more general, not only in their geographical spread, but also in the demands they voiced and the organisation they threw up. Beginning in late 1895 with the relatively minor economic demands of particular groups of spinners or weavers, the strikers were, by mid-1896 and early 1897, demanding legal enactment of the ten-hour day and, for the first time in Russian history, forced the regime to capitulate to their demands. The broadening and deepening of the struggle really had, in Lenin's estimation, transformed the workers' consciousness with astounding rapidity. Politics had indeed come via economics, but the process had not been consummated. There still was no national political party to articulate the interests of all the wage-workers in Russia. And without a permanent political organisation with national extension, the workers could not ascend to a properly class existence – they would lack the means and the expertise to fight the political struggle which was, as we have seen, coextensive with the class struggle properly so called.

Building a Party of the New Type – *What Is to Be Done?*

It was, paradoxically, the very success of the strike movement in these years that stymied the development of a national political party. Within a month of the beginning of the strikes in November 1895, the entire leadership group of the St Petersburg Union of Struggle for the Emancipation of the Working Class was arrested and subsequently sent into exile in Siberia. Not until January 1900 did Lenin's term of exile end. In the meantime, the first congress of the Russian Social Democratic Labour Party (RSDLP) had, in 1898, convened in Minsk.[14] It was in almost every respect a false start, since almost all the delegates were arrested shortly after the congress ended. The leadership was once again depleted and dispersed into Siberian exile. Links with the industrial working class became sporadic and unco-ordinated. The clear danger now was that the momentum generated by the great strikes of 1896 and 1897 would be dissipated for want of guidance and leadership. At the very moment when the workers, particularly of St Petersburg, had been radicalised, at the very time when their own manifestos called for radical democratic change and the attainment of political liberties,[15] the role of the Marxists had been reduced to a cipher.

The conclusion that Lenin came to, as early as 1897, was that the social democrats, if they were to have any hope of leading the democratic struggle against the autocracy, imperatively had to tighten their organisational structures. The government, alarmed by the success of the workers' movement in these years, had responded by increasing surveillance, deploying more *agents provocateurs*, and had demonstrated its ability to round up socialists and worker militants whenever it cared to. It had targeted the social democrats and the workers' movement for the good reason that these were the only effective forces challenging its authority. In order to meet the dual challenge of confronting an increasingly sophisticated and oppressive government, and of creating and leading a movement that would unite all democratic forces, the Russian social democrats, operating in conditions of danger and illegality, had no option but to become skilled in the arts of underground organisation. 'Without a strengthening and development of revolutionary discipline, organisation and underground activity, struggle against the government is impossible. And underground activity demands, above all, that groups and individuals specialise in different aspects of work and that the job of co-ordination be assigned to the central group . . . with as few members as possible.'[16] The mass arrests of 1898 simply confirmed Lenin's judgements that the organisational carelessness and amateurism of Russian social democrats, unless rapidly remedied, would continue to make a mockery of the grandiose tasks they had set themselves. To create a cohesive national party able to lead not only the workers but all oppositional groupings in Russian society in the battle for democracy, required expertise, division of labour (and therefore an authoritative co-ordinating centre), and training in conspiratorial techniques. All these ideas, already elaborated in 1897, were to remain constants of Lenin's position up to the overthrow of tsarism in February 1917. They were, of course, to be given expanded formulation in his notorious pamphlet of 1902, *What Is to Be Done?*

By the time *What Is to Be Done?* was published, the internal dissolution of the Russian Marxists, at both organisational and ideological levels, had, in the view of the 'old' leadership (Lenin and Martov now in league with Plekhanov and Akselrod), became even more pronounced. The 'veteran' leaders within Russia had, as we have seen, been arrested wholesale in 1895 and 1898. They had been replaced by a 'young' leadership that was decidedly less radical and less versed in the orthodoxy of Russian Marxism. The conclusion they came to was that engagement in open political activity had been premature and unwise: it had, naturally, attracted the full force of government repression.

On the whole, the new leadership disparaged the overtly political struggle with autocracy. Why, they asked, should the workers pull chestnuts from the fire for the bourgeoisie? 'Let the bourgeois fight for the democratic revolution, our battle is with the employers for better conditions of labour' – this, according to Lenin, expressed the revisionist myopia of the so-called 'young leadership' associated with the journal *Rabochaya Mysl* (Workers' Thought) and the programmatic statement Credo.[17] The consequences of renouncing a proper social-democratic politics had, in Lenin's view, been disastrous. For want of political direction, the workers' movement had capitulated to bourgeois leadership of the democratic revolution, and was in danger of sacrificing its organisational and ideological autonomy. Those sections of the workers who still held firm to the centrality of the political struggle and the leading role of workers within it, were left without any cohesive organisation; worse, the amateurish attempts at co-ordination led to arrests and deportations. The point had been reached where the workers were losing faith in the socialists and hesitated to commit themselves to the revolutionary cause precisely because the social democrats were so slapdash, 'The intellectuals, they say, are much too careless and cause police raids.'[18] Unless and until the political strivings of the workers to overthrow the autocracy were more expertly directed and co-ordinated, there could be no hope of a revival of social democracy.

The crisis of Russian social democracy, Lenin repeatedly insisted in the period 1900–3, was *not* that the class had failed the party but, on the contrary, that the party had failed the class. It had dissolved itself into a multitude of squabbling fragments, none of which had the resources, will, theoretical training or organisational expertise to reconstitute a leading centre capable of co-ordinating and directing the all-Russia workers struggle. The crisis of social democracy in Russia, Lenin emphatically maintained, was '*the lag of the leaders . . .* behind *the spontaneous upsurge of the masses*'.[19] It was not the spontaneity of the masses he condemned, but the organisational and theoretical shortcomings of the 'leadership' to channel and direct it. Far from diminishing the scale and scope of the 'spontaneous movement', the organisation of a properly-structured party would give the movement confidence and bolster the morale of its participants. 'Active participation of the widest masses will not,' Lenin asserted, 'diminish because a "dozen" professional revolutionaries centralise the secret functions connected with this work; on the contrary it will *increase* tenfold.'[20]

We should be clear that what Lenin, Martov and Plekhanov were engaged in, in the period 1900–3, was an overt power struggle. They were attempting to reconstitute the RSDLP under *their* leadership, and its ideological direction would be dictated by an all-Russian newspaper under *their* direction. To confirm the personal, ideological and organisational authority of the veteran and 'orthodox' leadership over the 'youngsters' and revisionists, a Second Congress of the RSDLP would have to be convened, for which intensive preparations would be necessary. This was the context of Lenin's feverish activity, and of all his writings, in the period following his release from exile in 1900 to the convocation of the Party's Second Congress in Brussels, then London, in 1903. First he travelled through Russia setting up his network of collaborators and contacts. He then went abroad to liaise with Plekhanov's group about the publication of a new Party journal. The first issue of *Iskra* (The Spark), edited by Lenin, appeared in December 1900.

The very production and distribution of a national newspaper in conditions of illegality, would, Lenin argued, necessitate the creation of a cohesive, disciplined and efficient organisation. Agents would be required in every locality, both to report on events and to create a clandestine distribution network to the workers in local plants and industries. They would be the party's links with grass roots support, and they would communicate with regional agents of the party who, in their turn, were to be responsible to the editorial board of the newspaper. The editorial board itself would comprise proven veterans of the movement, well-versed in theory and so able to generalise from the particular and to anticipate the next phase of the struggle. In Lenin's view, therefore, the creation of a national newspaper would itself entail the development of a party organisation (or at least the 'skeleton' of such an organisation) with a clearly defined functional division of labour, and vertical patterns of accountability.

Only those who had a direct and continuing functional role within the organisation were to be recognised as members of the party. There were, however, differing levels of induction and scales of responsibility within the organisation. Agents at the local level, concerned, perhaps, exclusively with the distribution of the newspaper or the production of local reports, would not be so burdened as to prevent them from pursuing their normal employment. They would, none the less, require some training in the skills and techniques of working in a clandestine and underground organisation; otherwise they would rapidly compromise others within the network and expose their client worker groups to unnecessary harassment by the authorities. For the workers to trust the party's agents it was, therefore, imperative that they be trained in conspiratorial techniques so as to minimise the risks of reprisal. At higher levels of the organisation, where agents had to be spirited from one safe house to another over extensive regions of the country, it was evidently impossible for personnel to be in normal, settled employment. Such people would have to be professionals in the dual sense that they were reliant upon the Party for their livelihoods, as well as being thoroughly trained and proficient in the whole range of skills and techniques of operating in the underground. These men would, in Russian conditions, have to be skilled, full-time 'professionals'.

The 'party of a new type' could not, for reasons of security, be open and democratic. If it adopted the practices of West European political parties it would rapidly be infiltrated by agents of the tsar, and smashed. It had, of necessity, Lenin argued, to be organised in a professional and clandestine way, and the basis of its organisation would be the party newspaper. This would be, as Lenin put it, 'not only a collective propagandist and a collective agitator, it is also a collective organiser'.[21]

We should be quite clear that *What Is to Be Done?* was designed explicitly as a summary of the political line of the *Iskra* board of editors that was, equally obviously, attempting to establish its claim to be recognized as the leading centre in the reconstruction of the party. It was intended, and widely used, as their joint manifesto for the (Second) Congress of the RSDLP that convened in 1903. It is the most misinterpreted text in the whole corpus of Lenin's writings, exciting more ill-informed commentary than practically anything else he wrote. It is, indeed, often projected as *the* cardinal text of Leninism as an ideology of Jacobin manipulation. Here, it is almost universally asserted, is the origin and real spirit of Bolshevism. It comes as something of a surprise, therefore, to discover that by far the greatest part of the pamphlet is concerned with a blunt restatement of the well-worn (but lately forgotten) orthodoxies of Russian Marxism that harked back to, and directly invoked, Plekhanov's formulations of the 1880s. Lenin, on behalf of the veteran leaders, took it upon himself to berate the varied and often obscure groups that disputed the centrality of the political struggle against the autocracy, and either rejected the notion that the workers' party should lead it, or maintained that it was premature to begin it. Like all polemicists engaged in a power struggle to establish themselves as the leading group, Lenin and his colleagues were, no doubt, highly selective in their use of evidence and prone to exaggerate the derelictions of their opponents. *What Is to Be Done?* was, unambiguously, a key part of this polemical assault.

Lenin and Marx on Socialist Consciousness

In the course of his polemics with these groups, Lenin, in a famous passage, asserted that, left to their own devices, the working class was incapable of developing properly socialist consciousness or of

articulating a coherent ideology of its own. 'Thus, socialist consciousness is something introduced into the proletarian class struggle from
without [*von Aussen Hineingetregenes*] and not something that arose
within it spontaneously [*urwüchsig*].'[22] These words were to generate an
intense and continuing debate over whether Lenin was here declaring
his lack of faith in the proletariat and resorting to a voluntarist politics
in which the disciplined group of party members imposes its will on a
recalcitrant historical process.

We should recall that these allegations were only made *after* the
Second Congress of the RSDLP in 1903 by those who, by then, had
been snubbed by Plekhanov and Lenin, and marginalised in the party's
power structure. Not one of the 'orthodox' Marxist leadership of the
RSDLP, and none of the editors of its journal *Iskra*, raised *any*
substantial reservations about *What Is to Be Done?* when it was first
published. Indeed *all* of the principal themes of this lengthy pamphlet
had already been rehearsed in Lenin's carefully scrutinised lead articles
for that journal, which, again, elicited no adverse comment from the
principal theoreticians of the party. In his lead article for the first issue
of *Iskra* which, by convention, has to be considered the programmatic
statement of the entire *Iskra* board, Lenin insisted that 'Isolated from
Social-Democracy, the working class movement becomes petty and
inevitably becomes bourgeois.'[23] It does so because, as Lenin later
explained in *What Is to Be Done?* the bourgeoisie has enormous
ideological advantages – its ideology is older and more pervasive, it is
more developed and 'has at its disposal *immeasurably* more means of
dissemination.'[24]

Lenin was, as Kolakowski concedes, 'merely stating a truism that
socialist ideology was the product of the radical intelligentsia since,
clearly, no workman could have written *Capital* or the *Anti-Dühring*, or
even *What Is to Be Done?*'.[25] More to the point, commentators almost
invariably ignore the fact that the offending words cited above were
directly and explicitly quoted from the 'pope' of European socialism,
Karl Kautsky. Kautsky had, indeed, been even more forthright: 'The
vehicle of science,' he declared, 'is not the proletariat but the *bourgeois
intelligentsia*'.[26] Plekhanov too had frequently voiced similar sentiments.[27]

We might well lament the patronising and arrogant tone of these
views, but we would be wrong to attribute them especially to Lenin.
They were part of the stuff of contemporary European and Russian
Marxism and are, arguably, intrinsic to Marx's own politics. Marx
himself had, after all, carried on an unrelenting battle with *every* native

proletarian theorist of socialism. He had rounded upon the naïvety and eclecticism of such men as Weitling and Proudhon. His stewardship of the post of secretary to the General Council of the Working Men's International Association (or First International) had, he wearily declared, been nothing but 'a *continual struggle* against the sects and amateur experiments which attempted to assert themselves within the International itself against the genuine movement of the working class'.[28] Later in this same letter, Marx declares that the working class 'will remain a plaything' in the hands of the ruling classes unless it is 'trained by continual agitation . . . to undertake a decisive campaign against the collective power, i.e. the political power of the ruling classes'.[29] It would be difficult to make sense of Marx's own life's work, his extraordinary commitment to the construction of a cohesive proletarian ideology, if we are to believe that he thought it would, in any case, be produced spontaneously by the workers themselves. The whole history of the British working class was testimony enough (to him and later to Lenin) to the fact that the spontaneous labour movement, unassisted by social democratic theory and organisation, fell easy prey to bourgeois political manipulation. And this applied, let us remember, to incomparably the largest, most concentrated and mature, the best organised and the most free working class in the world. The enigma of England, as Marx observed, was that it not only had a bourgeois aristocracy and a bourgeois bourgeoisie, it even had a bourgeois proletariat. It demonstrated the point that the working class does not naturally or spontaneously create either socialism or an independent political party.

The privileged role allotted to the socialist intelligentsia in organising and articulating the grievances of the proletariat and leading their political struggle, far from being a Leninist deviation from Marxism, is central to the arrogance of Marxism as a whole. Marx (and all subsequent Marxists) had to assert that he had a more profound awareness of the long-term interests and objectives of the proletariat than any proletarian, or group of proletarians could themselves possess. Early in his career, Marx was clear that, in matters to do with appraising the goals of the proletarian movement, there was no point at all in consulting the workers themselves:

> The question is not what this or that proletarian, or even the whole of the proletariat at the moment *considers* as its aim. The question is *what the proletariat is*, and what, consequent on that *being*, it will be compelled to do. Its aim and historical action is irrevocably and

obviously demonstrated in its own life situation as well as in the whole organisation of bourgeois society today.[30]

In *The Manifesto of the Communist Party* he is equally clear that it is 'a portion of the bourgeois ideologists, who have raised themselves to the level of comprehending theoretically the historical movement as a whole' that 'supply the proletariat with fresh elements of enlightenment and progress'.[31] These, evidently, are the leaders of the Communist Party who 'have over the great mass of the proletariat the advantage of clearly understanding the line of march, the conditions, and the ultimate general results of the proletarian movement'.[32] These individuals uniquely escape the general rule of Marx's own determinist sociology of knowledge, in terms of which, 'It is not the consciousness of men that determines their social being, but, on the contrary, their social being that determines their consciousness.'[33] The leaders of the Communist Party not only manage to escape the constraints of their own bourgeois social being, they even manage to express the true consciousness of the proletariat far better than those whose social being is proletarian. Indeed, it would seem that without their guidance and leadership the proletariat would (as it had in England) forever wallow in false consciousness and be the 'plaything' of the political designs of the possessing classes. Lenin counselled his followers to:

Call to mind the Communist Manifesto of Marx and Engels, which speaks of the *transformation* of the proletariat *into a class* in keeping with the growth not only of its unity, but also of its political *consciousness*. Remember the example of such countries as England, where the class struggle of the proletariat has been going on everywhere and at all times, in spite of which the proletariat has remained disunited, its elected representatives have been bought up by the bourgeoisie, its class-consciousness has been corrupted by the ideologies of capital, its strength has been dissipated through the desertion of the masses of the workers by the labour aristocracy.[34]

The curious tactic of using the 'democratic' and 'workerphile' Marx as dramatic foil to the elitist, manipulative Lenin has become almost a reflex with Western commentators on Leninism. The tactic is unconvincing, because it is far from clear that in denouncing those who believed that socialism was a natural and spontaneous outgrowth of the labour movement Lenin was at all out of accord with the spirit and actions of Marx. What is indisputable is that if we are to condemn him then we must also arraign Karl Kautsky for failing to comprehend or interpret Marxism – and that is either arrogant in the extreme, or plain daft.

The purpose of Lenin's *What Is to Be Done?* (as is entirely evident from the balance of the text) was primarily to make a *political* rather than an organisational point. The political message was this: Russian social democracy, according to all its authoritative texts, programmes and leaders, has set itself the task of leading the workers as the foremost champions of the democratic revolution against the tsar. The moment for it to assume the leadership came in 1900–1 when workers and students increased significantly their spontaneous assaults on the autocracy. The centre of gravity of the movement had, therefore, to shift from largely localised economic struggle to a general cross class, all-Russian battle for political transformation. It would therefore have to take on (as the main text of *What Is to Be Done?* in fact does) all those who had infiltrated the movement and who denied the appropriateness of this account of the politics of social democracy. Accepting the specification of the political goals of the movement was, for Lenin, tantamount to accepting its organisational entailments of centralisation, secrecy and professionalism: 'The only serious organisational principle for the active workers of our movement should be the strictest secrecy, the strictest selection of members, and the training of professional revolutionaries.'[35]

It was only after the Second Congress of the Russian Social Democratic Labour Party that fitful attempts were made to castigate the 'unMarxist' propositions of Lenin's *What Is to Be Done?* By this time, we should recall, the party had once more been riven with bitter political dispute and acrimonious personal confrontation. Lenin and Plekhanov had insisted upon the need to reduce the editorial board of *Iskra* from six to three (Lenin, Plekhanov and Martov) wounding the pride of the veteran exiles (Zasulich, Deich and Akselrod) who had honorifically swelled its numbers but contributed next to nothing to its production. The veterans won Martov to their cause and rallied to his 'soft' or 'loose' definition of a party member against the 'hard' or 'narrow' specifications of Lenin and Plekhanov. In this bitter debate over Article 1 of the party rules, political and personal wounds, which seemed out of proportion to the substantive issues involved, were again exposed.

Both Lenin and Plekhanov insisted that a revolutionary political party, fighting in conditions of illegality, had to be a party of committed activists prepared to 'support the party both materially and by participation in one of the party's organisations'. Martov's formulation extended membership to anyone 'who gives the party his regular personal cooperation, under the direction of one of the party organisations.' It was, allegedly, this dispute about the desirability of a narrow or broad party that fatefully split the Russian social democrats into Bolsheviks (majority men) and Mensheviks (minority men) in 1903. In fact, the difference between the two rival formulations was shown to be of marginal significance since, within three years, the Menshevik-dominated 1906 Unity Conference of the RSDLP accepted Lenin's formulation of clause 1 of the party rules. The alleged grave departures from Marxism it embodied had, it seems, already been forgotten by Lenin's erstwhile critics.

Paradoxically, by this time, Lenin himself had moved on to embrace a more fluid, open and democratic conception of party procedures and style of work that he characterised for the first time in 1906 as 'democratic centralism'. It was, explicitly, a response to the greatly changed political situation in Russia in which the tsar's power had effectively been drained by a near nationwide general strike, and he had been forced to concede the convocation of an elected representative assembly.

2

The Revolution of 1905

Tsar and Duma

On 22 January, 1905, a priest, Father George Gapon, led a great mass of peaceful petitioners to the square in front of the tsar's Winter Palace in St Petersburg to implore the tsar to relieve their miserable conditions. Their grievances were diverse, but the petition they carried reflected the increasingly assertive demands of industrial workers who had recently paralysed the capital with mass strikes:

> Sire! We workers, our children and wives, the helpless old people who are our parents, we have come to you, Sire, to seek justice and protection. We are in great poverty, we are oppressed and weighed down with labours beyond our strength; we are insulted, we are not recognised as human beings, we are treated like slaves . . . Despotism and arbitrary rule are strangling us, and we are suffocating. Sire, our strength is at an end! The limit of our patience has been reached; the terrible moment has come for us when it is better to die than to continue suffering intolerable torment.[1]

And die they did that fateful Sunday, more than a hundred dead and 300 wounded by fusillades from the guards regiments. The outrage shocked the whole world and galvanised Russia into a strike wave that, by mid-October, had become nearly universal. All the railways closed down, general strikes of industrial workers, professional unions and liberal professions all demanded democracy and a constitution. Simultaneously, first in St Petersburg and then in other major industrial centres, the workers established soviets (or councils) of deputies from all the major plants, to co-ordinate the general strike and to press for the immediate convocation of a Constituent Assembly on the basis of universal, equal and direct suffrage. On 30 October the tsar

38

capitulated and issued a Manifesto promising the convocation of a representative assembly, freedom of speech, conscience, assembly and association, constitutional government for Russia. Shortly thereafter he promised amnesty to those who had been arrested during the continuous demonstrations and strikes since January.

The right-wing moderates (now calling themselves Octobrists to signify their acceptance of the tsar's Manifesto) were jubilant at having at last attained what the tsar had consistently dismissed as a 'senseless dream'. The liberals formed the Constitutional Democratic Party (or Kadet Party) which was, in general, committed to making use of the proposed Duma to extend democracy and governmental account-ability. The workers, exhausted by months of strikes and privations, heeded the call of their Soviets and returned to work. With this, the steam went out of the revolutionary movement. The tsar was able to regroup his forces and begin the fight back against the forces that had humiliated him. Pogroms against the Jews were unleashed, with the evident connivance of the highest authorities, and after the calling of a general strike in St Petersburg in January, which saw the erection of workers' barricades and fierce street fighting, the regime moved in earnest to liquidate the revolutionaries. Summary executions and wholesale deportation into exile were unleashed to terrorise and cow the opposition.

By the end of 1905 the tsar's forces were once again in control of the country and his administration pursued a consistent course of limiting and attenuating the impact upon the tsar's autocratic powers that were entailed by his own October Manifesto. The Manifesto had promised a broad franchise that would become universal. When the electoral law was published, however, the large landowners and urban property holders were disproportionately advantaged. Freedom of assembly, promised in the Manifesto, was now governed (and largely negated) by the rider that the police would have to judge whether its exercise was compatible with public order. Freedom of the press was, similarly, hedged with restrictions that were so broad and vague that they could be used to prohibit all but the mildest criticism.

When the first Duma convened in May 1906 it proved, despite all the manipulation and intimidation of the regime, to be a body bent on radical reform and constitutional change. It stridently gave voice to all the demands of 1905 – universal, direct and equal suffrage, a government administration responsible not to the tsar but to the elected Duma, and wide-ranging agrarian reform that would cede Crown lands and those of the large estates to the peasants. For two months the tsar (with ill-concealed contempt) allowed the Duma debates to continue, while preparing the ground for a counter-attack. In July, the Duma was summarily dismissed, and the call of its outraged deputies for a campaign of passive resistance and civil disobedience to the regime fell on deaf ears. With the dynamic and intelligent Stolypin as first minister the regime initiated a long-term strategy to mollify the peasants (particularly the more industrious and ambitious individuals) by giving them the right to leave their commune if they so chose and to claim, as their personal property, all the land they farmed at that time. Allotments of free land were made available in Siberia, and state and Crown land transferred to the Peasants' Bank. In this way, it was hoped that peasant land-hunger would be met and a mass base would be built for the regime of loyal, prosperous and independent farmers. The regime staked its future on the presumption that a satiated and prosperous peasantry would prove an effective conservative foil to the radical turbulence of urban workers and the intelligentsia. To a large extent the gamble paid off, because the years 1906–14 brought consistent economic expansion, an increase in real wages and, consequently, a degree of stability.

The government's conciliatory response to the economic grievances of the peasantry was, however, complemented by a carefully prepared onslaught against the pretensions of the democrats and the revolutionaries. Police intimidation of the Kadet Party accelerated with the approach of elections for the second Duma. Suspected revolutionaries were rounded up, sentenced by summary court martial and executed or sent into exile. When the elections took place it became clear that all the authorities had succeeded in doing was to polarise political opinion, with the result that both the extreme right and the extreme left profited at the expense of the moderates (the Kadets). The tsar was, once again, faced with an unruly, unmanageable Duma. Radical socialists (Socialist Revolutionaries and Social Democrats) with the frequent support of the peasant *Trudoviki* (or Labour) group, formed the largest, most cohesive and most militant grouping that was more concerned with inflammatory popular appeals than with concrete legislative proposals.

After less than three and a half months of political tumult the tsar dissolved the Duma (16 June 1907) and, on the same day, unilaterally promulgated a new electoral law so as to weight votes even more decisively in favour of the big landowners. The tsar's fleeting experiment with democracy and constitutional government was clearly at an end. In abruptly changing the electoral law he openly flouted the

Fundamental Law he himself had promulgated. In summarily dismissing two successive Dumas he had demonstrated his contempt for the democratic process and its results. He had, in any case, steadfastly refused to contemplate even the prospect that government finances, or his cabinet of ministers, should be supervised by an elected assembly, no matter how narrow its basis of representation. It was the tsar himself (prompted by his ever more paranoid and unstable tsarina) who unambiguously rejected the option of modernising the monarchy and establishing a stable constitutional regime. By his actions in 1906 and 1907 he appeared to confirm the analysis of the revolutionaries, that the almost universal aspiration for civil freedoms and democracy, so loudly voiced in 1905, could be realised only by revolutionary action. The tsar, they cogently argued, would not be moved by public opinion, mass demonstrations or the result of democratic elections; force alone would move him. What is beyond doubt is that his actions demoralised the moderate Constitutional Democrats and, to a large extent, discredited their programme.

For a Permanent Revolution?

It was during these turbulent years which, came to be known anachronistically as the great rehearsal for the Revolution of 1917, that clear policy differences began to emerge between the rival socialist groupings. The Mensheviks, were, in the first half of 1905, second to none in the radicalness of their proposals. Better placed than the Bolsheviks to influence the workers and their Soviets, they urged them on to mass political strikes which, they anticipated, would lead to final revolutionary overthrow. The Mensheviks even gave space, in their journals, to the outpourings of Parvus and Trotsky, who advocated the constant escalation of worker and party demands up to and including the realisation of a workers' government that would pursue frankly socialist policies. Why, they asked, should it be the workers who were called upon to make all the sacrifices while the bourgeoisie gained all the advantages? It was, they argued persuasively, the mounting general strikes of workers in all the principal industrial areas of Russia that had provided the spur for all other sectors of society to press for radical change. It was the workers and their families that had suffered the greatest economic losses, and it was they who had put not only their livelihood but their lives on the line by leading the illegal mass demonstrations that eventually forced the tsar to capitulate. Why, then, should they abide by the self-denying ordinance of the social democrats that socialism would have to be preceded by a more or less prolonged period of bourgeois democratic rule? The dynamics of the Russian revolution were such, they contended, that the abstract theoretical constraints of party orthodoxy would be swept aside by the accelerating radicalism that the revolutionary situation itself created. It was, they argued, psychologically implausible and strategically naïve for the party to lead its troops into battle under the watchwords 'Fight hard but do not win'.[2]

What Parvus and Trotsky were propounding was a fundamental departure from the old orthodoxy of Russian social democracy that specified a two-stage revolutionary process. The first stage would sweep away the autocracy and destroy its feudal economic and social bases of support. This would, in turn, greatly promote the growth of capitalist economic relations in town and country, with the result that the class of wage workers (the chosen constituency of the social democrats) would expand greatly. As capital consolidated itself, as the technological basis of industry was transformed, and its productivity consequently augmented, the material (or 'objective') basis for an advance towards socialism would be created. There could be no possibility of realising the goal of socialism 'from each according to his ability, to each according to his need', without the prior development of a capital-intensive and highly productive industrial base. It was, in short, the business of the bourgeois-democratic revolution to modernise Russian industry, spread capitalist relations throughout Russia, and create a majoritarian working class. Only when that had occurred, the Mensheviks argued, was it possible or desirable to put the socialist revolution on the agenda. It followed that the leadership of post-tsarist Russia could only go to the bourgeoisie.

Lenin, for his part, occupied an uneasy and complex position between these two extremes. He was neither for a workers' government with socialist objectives, nor for bourgeois leadership of the anti-autocratic revolution. Nothing but the most absurd and reactionary consequences, 'both in the economic and political sense' he declared, would issue from any premature attempt to overstep the limitations imposed by the ill-developed state of Russian industry.[3] He was therefore flatly opposed to the Parvus/Trotsky line of permanent revolution. The Russian revolution, he insisted, would not and should not proceed without interruption from its democratic to its socialist phase. He none the less agreed with them that, in the peculiar circumstances of Russia, the democratic revolution could only be brought to a successful conclusion under the leadership of the industrial workers (or proletariat). Unlike the permanent revolutionists, however, he contended that this outcome could not be realised as long as the workers relied solely upon their own strength. They were unquestionably the most active, most politically conscious and best organised section of the revolutionary forces, but their numbers were relatively small and they were concentrated in comparatively few major centres. They would remain strategically vulnerable to Russia's vast agrarian hinterland unless the revolutionary movement (under worker leadership) mobilised the peasantry. The idea of the urban industrial workers becoming the vanguard and spokesman 'of all working and exploited people' was, as we have seen, a principal conclusion of Lenin's economic and social analyses dating back to his first published work in 1894. It was, indeed, one of the constant strategic themes in Lenin's writings that was to resurface in 1917 and, with renewed insistence, in the period from March 1921 until his death in 1924 – without peasant support, not a single important revolutionary advance could be made secure.

With the Bourgeoisie or with the Peasants?

The social and economic presuppositions that informed this strategy were not nearly as unorthodox (in Marxist terms) as commentators generally allege. Lenin banked upon the development of capitalism splitting the peasant (feudal) social estate increasingly into its modern class components of rural proletariat and rural bourgeoisie. As capitalism in agriculture advanced it would inexorably create (as a necessary condition of its own existence) an ever larger pool of landless wage workers. The poor peasantry was, in short, everywhere being converted into a rural proletariat more ruthlessly exploited by capital than even the urban industrial workers.

The question of land was, in Lenin's view, of far greater significance in the anti-tsarist struggle of 1905 than constitutional projecteering or wrangling over the exact specifications of civil rights.[4] It was the pivotal question around which all the others revolved. The peasants wanted *all* the land. Their Duma representatives, the *Trudoviki*, were insistent that only the tillers could lay claim to the land and its produce. They wanted all the lands of church, state and landowning nobility to be handed over and divided up. The simplest stratagem to accomplish this goal, was, in Lenin's view, for the revolution to proclaim the nationalization of all land, leaving the peasants to decide its actual allocation. The nationalization of the land became, therefore, the central plank in Lenin's 1905 programme. Its implementation would simultaneously accelerate capitalist accumulation in agriculture and eliminate the landed nobility as the social and political prop to tsarism.

It may appear paradoxical that nationalisation appears here as part of the programme for the democratic revolution, which Lenin insisted ought not to pursue socialist goals. In fact, to orthodox Marxists, the nationalisation of land was part of the so-called 'minimum programme', that is, those economic and political demands whose implementation was compatible with the maintenance of capitalist economic relations. In the case of the nationalisation of land they could point to Marx himself. In *Capital*, Marx had shown how private ownership of land was one of the large impediments to the growth of capitalism in agriculture. Purchase of the land absorbed a huge proportion of agrarian capital that could have found more profitable use financing purchase of advanced equipment, improving livestock, or the processing and marketing of produce. Advocacy of nationalisation of land was, therefore, far from being inconsistent with the democratic (or anti-feudal) first stage of the revolution. It was, on the contrary, a 'bourgeois measure'[5], which, by 'transferring rent to the state',[6] would accelerate the development of capitalism in agriculture.

In tactical terms, therefore, the only stable alliance that would press the democratic revolution through to its successful completion was between the workers and the peasantry (particularly the poor peasants). The Russian bourgeoisie was (as the programme of the RSDLP told its members) weak and cowardly.[7] It was tied to the nobility by all sorts of family, cultural and social ties. More to the point, it would feel its own interests threatened by any invasion into the sacred rights of property that the peasants' radical demand for *all* the land clearly entailed. According to Lenin's prognosis, therefore, the bourgeoisie would concentrate wholly on legal and constitutional reform to increase their own political influence. They were, however, too weak to withstand the growing militancy of both peasants and workers and so, at the moment when the regime was most weakened by the revolutionary upsurge, they would compromise with the autocracy to wrest from it maximum advantage to themselves. They would then renege on all their easily given pledges for manhood, equal suffrage, and radical land reform. Classes, he insisted, would act according to rational calculation of their basic economic interests, rather than according to rhetorical ideological flourishes and paper commitments.

The vulnerability of the bourgeoisie would oblige them to make common cause with other property holders – and with the armed power of the existing state – the moment the revolution threatened their own economic stability. That, Lenin reminded his followers, had been the whole burden of Marx's analysis of the failed European democratic revolutions of 1848 – the bourgeoisie betrayed democracy and sold out to the reaction the moment its purse-strings were threatened. It was, he maintained, hardly to be imagined that the much smaller, more exposed and politically less developed Russian bourgeoisie would, or could, act differently.

Lenin's analysis of class forces and political alignments in the revolutionary period 1905–6 was dogmatic and doctrinaire – it was convoluted and over-theorized. It was small wonder, then, that he and his followers had little impact upon the course of events. The bourgeoisie was, as we have seen, an unreliable partner for the proletariat because they had an interest in seeing to it that the democratic revolution was not fought through to its radical conclusion. Its whole class position obliged it to play the people off against the tsar and the tsar against the people.[8] The tactics of social democracy ought therefore, in Lenin's view, to be directed at exposing bourgeois vacillations and double-dealing, obliging them at an early stage of the revolution to align themselves with the autocracy and the big landowners. Otherwise they would posture as the leaders of the revolution and win popular confidence, only to leave the people defenceless and leaderless when the moment of betrayal arrived. The social democrats ought therefore to promote worker leadership of the democratic revolution, but in alliance with the poor peasantry.

In order to secure peasant allegiance and, simultaneously, to force the bourgeois liberals to show their hand, the party must aggressively canvass the nationalization of all land. Above all Lenin was insistent that nothing worthwhile could be accomplished by wringing concessions from the tsar. It was not a question of obliging the autocracy to reform itself by donning a pseudo-constitutional garb. It was, rather, a question of overthrowing the whole social and economic edifice upon which tsarism was grounded. The revolution could only consummate itself as a 'revolutionary-democratic dictatorship of the proletariat and the poor peasantry'. Under such ponderous watchwords, Lenin summoned his followers to the fray.

Revolutions, Lenin insisted, do not negotiate, they do not humbly petition cap in hand; they demand and they fight. A revolution, he reminded the party, was precisely that time in the life of nations and classes when, in Marx's words, the arm of criticism was replaced by the criticism of arms. They occur precisely because the limits of negotiation have been reached; that is when the basic antagonism between social groups has become clearly apparent. *A la guerre comme à la guerre*. The civil war that was unfolding in Russia, which all sections of the RSDLP supported (at least until late 1905), was not a matter for dilettantes and the faint-hearted. It demanded expertise and audacity. Its leaders must be versed in military tactics (so Lenin spent the early months of 1905 digesting von Clausewitz and Engels on military strategy). Its activists needed to be trained in the use of arms, the building of barricades and the tactics of urban guerilla fighting. It was, he maintained, thoroughly irresponsible for leaders like the Mensheviks, to call the people to armed insurrection while rejecting the necessity of providing them with arms, training or military expertise.

It was not until the last weeks of December 1905 and the early months of 1906 that the nascent differences between the Bolsheviks and the Mensheviks hardened into fundamentally different appraisals of the revolution and the role of the working class. Following the arrest of the entire St Petersburg Soviet on 16 December, the Moscow Soviet joined by the Mensheviks, Socialist Revolutionaries and the Bolsheviks, issued a call for a general strike and a rising of the workers against the regime. It was, however, the Bolsheviks who provided the leadership and most of the fighting detachments for the insurrection that followed. Street fighting continued for two weeks and was only put down by government forces in the final days of 1905. It was in the aftermath of this failed attempt at resort to arms that the apparent unity that the RSDLP had displayed during the revolutionary upheavals disintegrated rapidly.

Plekhanov had from the outset condemned the Moscow rising as a putschist adventure, the effect of which would be to alienate the support of middle-class radicals and drive them into the reactionary camp. Akselrod, Plekhanov's long-time companion in exile, added his voice of moderation, counselling the party to co-operate with the liberals and the Kadets, and to make use of all the legal channels available to carry its propaganda to the people: 'I will venture to say that even the most wretched caricature of a parliamentary system offers immense advantages compared with the useless means that have so far been at our disposal.'[9] Within months, the majority of the Mensheviks came round to similar views. The new consensus among them had it that the heroic, militant period of the revolution was over. Any further political mass strikes or insurrectionary activity would be counter-productive – it would force the bourgeoisie 'to recoil'. Given the fact that the workers were exhausted and their soviets suppressed, there was now no other force, apart from the liberal Kadets, capable of leading the democratic struggle and emerging as the governing party. The task of social democracy, in these circumstances, was to support the Kadets in their struggle against the tsar while, simultaneously, using the Duma as a vehicle for socialist propaganda. For the time being, therefore, the party could play no other role than that of left opposition preparing the people for the relatively distant socialist phase of the revolution when, finally, the question of forming an administration that included socialists, might appear upon the agenda.

Since the tasks of the socialists were, in this Menshevik formulation, modest, and since their underground organisations had been decimated by the regime, the RSDLP should concentrate its remaining resources on developing to the utmost legal means of rebuilding their strength 'in the trade unions, co-operatives, workers' educational institutions and clubs . . . still tolerated by the government'.[10] According to Fyodr Dan:

> We must make every possible use of the available means of fighting to maintain, consolidate and extend our legal positions, from the courts to the press, congresses, organs of self-government, and the *Duma*, together with a broadly based programme of agitation directed at the working masses.[11]

All this was anathema to Lenin. At the first setback, the Mensheviks displayed their spinelessness and their unprincipled contempt for the most basic precept of the party's general political strategy. The principle that the proletariat should lead (or, in Plekhanov's earlier formulations, exercise 'hegemony' over) the democratic revolution was a corollary of its repeated insistence that the Russian bourgeois was weak in numbers and politically immature. It was enshrined in the texts that defined the orthodoxy of Russian Marxism and it was defence of this principle (against the revisionists and 'economists') that had inspired the foundation of *Iskra*. Now the Mensheviks 'quietly abandoned this once cherished doctrine. Trotsky described "hegemony" as "hypocrisy" and Plekhanov as "absurd"'.[12] In the space of one year they had moved from flirting with permanent revolution to embracing the thoroughly revisionist proposition that only the bourgeoisie could lead the anti-autocratic struggle. Abruptly, the Mensheviks (led by Plekhanov) were keen to attribute to the Russian

bourgeoisie a resolve, strength, political steadfastness and sophistication that the whole of their earlier analysis had expressly denied. From
that time Lenin consistently dubbed them 'liquidationists'. They were,
he maintained, bent upon the liquidation, not only of the theoretical
bases of the RSDLP, but also of its underground political structure.

Lenin, for his part, stuck firmly to the precepts of the old orthodoxy.
The historical record penned by Marx concurred with his own
economic and social analyses – the bourgeoisie *would* betray. They
had no objective interest in the overthrow of tsarism. They had neither
the political will nor the organisational basis to constitute a serious
oppositional force. Subsequent events confirmed him in his prognosis.
The peremptory dissolution of the first Duma (this long-awaited
embodiment of the liberal dream) was, admittedly, condemned by the
Kadet deputies, who called for popular resistance. But their impact was
nugatory. The response in the country at large was pathetically small,
given the enormity of the tsar's breach of faith and the depth of the
hopes that had been invested in Russia's very first experiment in
democracy. The Kadets were exposed – they were seen to be powerless
and the experience chastened them, just as the failure of the Moscow
rising had cooled the ardour of the Mensheviks. When push came to
shove they blustered a little, but capitulated. And so it was with every
subsequent erosion of the tsar's promises of October 1905, each
narrowing of the franchise and suspension of civil rights, each
suspension of the Duma and arrest or exile of deputies; in the face of
every provocation the Kadets called for patience and restraint.

The general judgements that Lenin, in 1905–6, by courting the
peasants, opportunistically forsook Marxism; by rejecting the leading
role of the bourgeoisie, displayed his Jacobin proclivities; and by
interesting himself in military matters, revealed his Blanquist disposition, are trite and glib. He held, on the contrary, to an unswervingly
consistent strategic line. He had an unshakeable, dogmatic conviction
that the correctness of his earlier economic and social analyses of
Russia would be revealed in the searchlight of actual political struggle.
The strength and deficiencies, aspirations and allegiances of all classes
would, he believed, be demonstrated graphically in open political
debate and, particularly, in mass actions. The revolutionary events of
1905–7 simply confirmed him as a deeply doctrinaire politician, more
inclined by far to press events and actors into a preconceived scenario
than to alter the story-line with each major shift of the political scene.
It should not, of course, be thought that to claim theoretical
consistency in any way connotes approval or sympathy. On the

contrary, the critical stance implicit in this book is that we are better served by politicians less implacable, more eclectic and, above all, more tolerant. In short, if Lenin had been as opportunistic a trimmer, and as careless about doctrine as many commentaries make him out to be, his impact upon the world (and the impact of the ideology he created) would have been far more benign.

By December 1907 Lenin was once again driven into exile, and there ensued almost nine and a half years of European wanderings until his final return to Russia in April 1917. The years from 1908 to 1912 were particularly bleak. After that the labour movement within Russia began to revive considerably. The party organisations within Russia had been smashed, and hundreds of revolutionaries had been imprisoned or exiled. Finance was a constant worry and, worst of all, within his own small faction of Bolsheviks, his political and intellectual authority was severely challenged by Bogdanov and Lunacharsky. Politically they maintained an ultra-left line of recalling all the Bolshevik deputies from the emasculated Duma. Lenin had to fight simultaneously against the Menshevik moderates (Liquidators) and the maximalists in his own party (the recallists or *Otzovists*). On the philosophical front, he felt impelled to combat what he perceived to be Bogdanov's lapse into eclecticism and idealism. He reluctantly embarked upon a lengthy (and somewhat turgid) riposte: *Materialism and Empirio-Criticism* (discussed further in Chapter 9). This was a period of schism that culminated at the Prague Conference of the RSDLP in January 1912 in the formal separation of the Bolsheviks from the Mensheviks. It was a period of political dissolution, both within Russia and in the emigré movement, in which Lenin's political thought merely marked time.

Conclusion

I have argued that Lenin was, in his pre-1914 writings, a coherent and thoroughgoing Marxist. The aberrations commentators claim to find are, too often, plucked out of context or ignore the ambiguities (and dangers) in Marx's own writings. Throughout these years Lenin considered himself to be no more than a faithful disciple of Marx and of Marxism as interpreted by the father of Russian Marxism – Plekhanov. He made no attempt to generalise from the Russian experience or to pretend that any of his theoretical or organisational reflections had a universal relevance. The idea that he was propounding a new ideology; a novel mental map of the contemporary world just did not occur to him. He had written barely a word about the international situation apart from the impact it had upon domestic Russian politics. He had, no doubt, a claim to recognition as the single most prominent leader of Russian social democracy but that was, after all, small beer. He himself recognised frequently that the movement in Russia was only but a side-show to the main performance whose theatre was in Western Europe, and especially in Germany. The themes he had written about – the two-stage revolution, the leading role of the proletariat in the democratic revolution, the development of capitalism out of feudalism, the political capacity of the poor peasantry, and the principles of building a socialist party in conditions of illegality – all these had resonances only for Russia and perhaps some other peripheral backwaters of the class struggle. It is therefore unsurprising that at no time during this period did Lenin suggest any of his writings had any applicability outside Russia.

Until 1914 Lenin was the little-known leader of one part of a hopelessly schismatic Marxist party in every respect at the extremities of European socialism. His writings were virtually unknown, for the sufficient reasons that they were almost wholly parochial, issued in small editions and untranslated, or else they were concerned with matters (such as philosophy and dialectics) that were felt by the practical leaders of mass political parties to be largely irrelevant. The thought that he might, prior to this time, have had anything of general relevance to contribute to a redefinition of socialism or Marxism, had not only not occurred to him but would also have been treated with amazement and derision in Europe as a whole. If he did appear odd to his fellow European socialists it was not because of his Jacobin or Russian background, but rather because, to their frequent embarrass-ment, he took Marxist doctrinal purity so seriously.

The leaders of European socialist parties had other things to occupy their time. They had to attend to their parliamentary work, cultivate their constituencies, liaise with trade union bodies, raise funds, contribute to the party press, attend local and regional conferences and congresses, and so on. They had little time, and generally little inclination, to go dipping into the works of Marx and Engels, or digest statistical or economic analyses of contemporary capitalism. Years of experience of working in democratic national organisations, with all their diverse groupings and expectations, had taught them the necessity of compromise and accommodation. Lenin, up to October 1917, had virtually no experience of this sort. He was, throughout this period, a theoretician and a writer with no popular constituency to answer to, and almost no direct experience of democratic mass movements. His commitment to the politics of confrontation and class war ran flatly counter to the overwhelmingly moderate politics of accommodation that typified West European social democratic parties. He was regarded as something of an anachronism.

The economic and political conditions of his Russian background had frozen him in a kind of fundamentalism that was felt to be hopelessly out of tune with contemporary reality. Constitutionalism, manhood suffrage, the rapid growth of socialist parties and trade unions, improvements in education, welfare provision, and standards of living, had created in Western Europe new possibilities of peaceful advance through democratic means. Socialists had, consequently, to adapt their theory and their practice to meet these new conditions, and the measure of their success was the seemingly remorseless growth of the socialist vote. All of this had passed Lenin by. Until 1917 he made no real impact upon the general disposition of European socialism. His was the voice of an outmoded doctrinaire. His Marxism was bookish and academic and, precisely *because* it derived from a thorough reading of the classic texts, it harked back to times and themes that had been largely forgotten by European socialists.

3

The Disintegration of Social Democracy and the Genesis of Leninism

On 4 August 1914 the socialist parties of Germany and France, in Parliament solemnly assembled, voted war credits to their governments and pledged support to their governments for the duration of the war that was already upon them. Throughout Europe there was grim foreboding that things would never again be the same, but for Lenin the events of 4 August were a cataclysm that turned his world upside down. It was out of this trauma that Leninism, as an integrated ideology of global revolution, was rapidly to emerge. Within three years he had outlined a global economic analysis, a historiography, philosophy and politics, woven into a cohesive and militant ideology. It was expressly presented not merely as an alternative to all existing ideologies, bourgeois and socialist, but as the ideology of a new world and a new time that would sweep them all away. It was, if anything, more bitter in its denunciation of rival socialist and Marxist schemes of thought than it was of liberalism or conservatism. Such sensitivity tells us a good deal about its origins, because it was out of a profound sense of betrayal by erstwhile comrades that Leninism was born. What began as denunciation expanded, as we shall see, into comprehensive critique, and an equally comprehensive alternative account of the present situation and future tasks of socialism. Leninism was, from its origins to its eventual demise, an argument about the soul of socialism largely conducted against opponents (traitors, Lenin called them) within the socialist tradition. In order to locate it as an ideology we must therefore explore in some detail the trends in international social democracy that were found to be so pernicious.

The International and the War

Lenin was, at first, so stupefied by the news of the votes for war credits that he preferred to credit the bourgeois press with black propaganda attempting to destabilise and unhinge the working class of Europe. It simply had not occurred to Lenin, even as a worst case scenario, that the leaders he had revered all his adult life could play so false. They had, at one stroke, killed off the Socialist International – the sole depository, in Lenin's view, of the genuine loyalties of the working class. Worse, they had thrown the moral and organisational power of social democracy behind their capitalist and militarist governments. Their apostasy could not have been more complete. The gap between their professions and their actions could not have been wider. Nor could they take refuge in the contention that they had to make an instant response to a quite unforseen situation. On the contrary, the whole history of the Second International displayed an almost obsessive concern with questions of war and militarism. Both within the national parties and in the congresses of the International, there had been incessant debate that had finally been resolved at the Stuttgart Congress of 1907. Here, according to Lenin, the International and all its national parties finally committed itself to a common, agreed, and therefore obligatory, strategy with regard to war. A great deal was to hang on the interpretation of the Stuttgart Resolution and it is as well that we should have at least the last two paragraphs of this lengthy statement verbatim:

If the outbreak of war threatens, it is the duty of the workers and their parliamentary representatives in the countries involved, with the aid of the International Bureau, to exert all their efforts to prevent the war by means of co-ordinated action. They shall use the means which appear the most appropriate to them, and which will necessarily vary according to the sharpness of the class struggle and the general political situation.

If war should nevertheless break out, they have the duty to work for its speedy termination, and to exploit with all their might the economic and political crisis created by the war to arouse the population and to hasten the overthrow of capitalist rule.[1]

The original resolution, formulated and proposed by the German moderate leader August Bebel, had not included the final clause; it had ended with the phrase 'to work for its speedy termination'. The radical sting in the amended resolution had been drafted by Martov and Lenin from the Russian party and Rosa Luxemburg from the Polish party. The ferocity of Lenin's response to the events of 4 August 1914 stemmed, in part at least, from a sense of personal betrayal that the strategy of the International, that he had helped to formulate on this crucial issue, had been so gratuitously ignored. Had he been more honest with himself he might perhaps have recognised that the huge faith he had reposed in the International, and particularly its leading cohort – the German Social Democratic Party or SPD – had been a product of his own self-delusion that flew in the face of a mass of contradictory evidence he was well aware of but preferred to ignore.

Lenin knew full well that the Stuttgart Resolution, which was the basis of the International's policy on war (being reaffirmed at Basle in 1912), was itself a complex compromise that reflected the complexity and irreconcilability of opposing forces both within individual national parties and within the International as a whole. He knew that Bebel, in close alliance with the executive of the German trades unions, had used every procedural ploy, and the most varied and incompatible arguments, to resist all the pressures from his own left wing and from the French and British, to radicalise the stance of the International on the question of war. He was, in particular, insistent (and the German unions were even more adamant) that he would not commit the SPD to any specific anti-war activity that might threaten 'the normal life of the Party'. It was all very well for the French, British, Poles, Belgians or Russians to make declamatory gestures in favour of anti-militarist propaganda within the army and the reservists, and call for political general strikes to paralyse the economy in the event of war, but their rhetoric was empty and irresponsible. They knew that their parties did not dispose of the power to implement such extreme measures, yet they were trying to force it upon the one party that did. There was, Bebel had argued, too much at stake to be carried away by 'the socialism of the phrase'.

German Social Democracy: Minimum and Maximum Programmes

The SPD was, undoubtedly, the model party of the International. It had gone from strength to strength to emerge as the largest and incomparably the best organised political party in Europe. Despite everything the imperial government had thrown at it – the slanders and harassment, and the imposition of anti-socialist legislation that made even propaganda for socialism a criminal offence. In spite of, or perhaps because of, the closure of its papers and imprisonment of its leaders, the SPD had consistently expanded its support. At the beginning of the imposition of the anti-socialist laws in 1878 the party had counted perhaps a few hundred thousand supporters (the elections of 1881 gave it 312000 votes). By 1890, when the laws were finally repealed, the party won 20 per cent of the national vote in the Reichstag elections, securing 1 427 000 votes.[2] By 1903 its share of the vote had risen to a third of the total, standing at more than three million, and by 1912 this had swollen to four and a quarter million votes. At the time of the outbreak of war it had more than a million members and it employed more than three and a half thousand full-time officials.[3] This was the great engine driving the International, the prime mover that provided the inspiration to so many others – particularly the Russians and East Europeans. Behind this impressive, seemingly irresistible advance, there lay an increasingly sophisticated and centralised administrative apparatus, and a comprehensive web of national, regional and local newspapers. By the early 1890s the SPD was running 19 daily newspapers and 42 weeklies; by 1914 it had 90 dailies.

One and three quarter million affiliated trades unionists constituted far more than the party's industrial base – it provided a case study of the values and institutions of a co-operative alternative to capitalist individualism. The trade unions and the party developed extensive social security schemes for their members. In return for their weekly contributions, the workers assured themselves against ill-health, infirmity and unemployment. There were maternity benefits and funeral schemes that gave substance to the boast that the party looked after its members from the cradle to the grave (or, as one wag put it, from womb to tomb). Social democratic clubs and associations of all types flourished, catering to the recreational, sporting and cultural needs of the workers. For decades the party laboured to create a 'state within the state'. Its activists dreamed of a self-sufficient and autonomous world where the workers would fit themselves for the socialist future by learning not only its values but also by gaining the confidence, and practical and administrative skills, necessary to manage their own affairs. Its watchword was the militantly separatist slogan *diesen system keinen Mann keinen groschen* – 'not a man, not a penny for this system'. In the light of official contempt and legislative harassment this was, no doubt, an admirable idea, but it brought its own restraints and limitations.

The SPD became, in effect, trapped in a paradoxical dialectic of success. Its Marxist orthodoxy and political rhetoric committed it to revolutionary overthrow of the existing system, while the spectacular success of its electoral strategy and organisational consolidation presumed patient and peaceful advance. It came to have a large stake in the preservation of social peace. As it grew in the breadth of its appeal and the strength of its resources, so it became more cautious. It was, above all, anxious to give the government (which remained responsible not to the elected Reichstag but directly to the king/ emperor) no pretext for using the power of the state to suppress the party and the workers' movement. The party funds (by 1914 it had capital assets in excess of 20 million marks), its press, its affiliated trades unions and their social assurance funds were all regarded as key indices of socialist advance that it was impermissible to squander in quixotic insurrectionary gestures. Not until the great majority of the population had been won for socialism – when (presumably) at the same time, capitalism demonstrated its incapacity to renew and develop itself – only then would the moment of the great transition be finally signalled.

Minimum and Maximum Programmes

In the long meanwhile of the preparatory period the party, the party's cadres and its followers were to be guided by the watchwords *organisieren, propagandieren, studieren.* In strategic terms the goals of the party would, similarly, have to be restricted to moderate claims that did not go beyond the bounds of bourgeois democracy. The preparatory period was, after all, that period in which (a) the majority were not yet conscious advocates of socialism; and (b) capitalism had not exhausted its capacity to expand and innovate. It followed, therefore, that it would be premature and irresponsible to press properly socialist demands; that is, demands that threatened the very bases of private property and individual appropriation. It might, in this period, press for better terms for the sale of labour (minimum pay rates, holiday and sickness entitlement, protection of minors, and so on), but it should not urge the end of the whole system of the buying and selling of labour. We are at this point led to the highly important distinction (insisted upon by many of the member parties of the Second (or Socialist) International) between minimum and maximum programmes.

Minimum programme demands were those of the preparatory period when the conditions for socialist advance had not yet matured. The extension of democratic and civil and political rights featured prominently in all socialist programmes at this time. Throughout the latter part of the nineteenth century, the socialist parties were alone in calling for the suffrage to be made universal, that is, to include both men and women. They called for proportional representation; extensive use of the referendum; the right of electors to recall their representatives; and the direct election of all public officials. Substitution of the standing army by a people's militia was the most radical of the democratic reforms of the minimum programme. On the economic front the minimum programme pressed for the improvement of conditions for young workers and women, greater dignity and security for all workers, to be attained through an extension of the social security system and the implementation of the eight-hour day. A graduated income tax was called for, to ensure that the financing of state provision of educational and welfare services would be met by those best able to pay. The most radical of the economic demands was that land should be nationalised and made available for rent. None of these measures, it was argued, threatened the capacity of capitalism to reproduce itself, but they would, none the less, provide the necessary conditions for the further growth of the socialist and labour movements.

The maximum programme, by contrast, embodied the full-blown socialist aspirations of the party to transfer the 'land, mines, raw materials, machines, and transportation' to social or state ownership.[4] This would require the conquest of political power by the working class which would exercise a transitional 'dictatorship of the proletariat'. Commodity production and exchange via the market would eventually disappear and, with that, labour would no longer be bought and sold. Finally, with the disappearance of classes, the state would lose its function as an agency of class domination and would wither away. This was, of course, the progression towards socialism that Marx and Engels had sketched in *The Manifesto of the Communist Party*.[5] The theoretical preamble to the party programme justified this radical stance by appealing to the same Marxist orthodoxy which consistently maintained that, under capitalism, no lasting or meaningful improvements to the workers' conditions of life could be secured. Escalating crises, induced by the falling rate of profit and the disparity between production and consumption, would erode the temporary gains secured in periods of boom. Insecurity, unemployment and increasingly severe exploitation would, in their turn, fuel an ever more bitter class struggle between bourgeoisie and proletariat.

It was the 1891 Erfurt Programme of the SPD (drafted by Karl Kautsky) that enshrined the division between minimum and maximum, democratic and socialist, present and future aims of the party. It seemed, at the time, to be a neat and appealing resolution of the problems of party strategy, but it fairly soon became clear that it only succeeded in reformulating the basic divide between a revolutionary and a reformist tactic. There was, from the outset, a question mark about the party's good faith in pursuing the minimum programme at all. If theory maintained, and historical experience demonstrated, that no meaningful and lasting improvements of the workers' lot could be wrung from capitalism, was it not hypocritical to campaign for such improvements and to make them the centre of electoral propaganda? Was the party here engaging in a rather cynical exercise of arousing expectations that it knew could not be fulfilled? The morally insupportable logic of the party's position, as Eduard Bernstein later pointed out, was that the realisation of socialism was premised upon the party setting itself against all improvements in working and living conditions.[6] In principle it had to assent to the formula: better worse but better. It followed, after all, that the more successful the party and the labour movement became in securing the goals of the minimum programme, the more the imperative to revolution would diminish.

This strategy of patient electoral advance and organisational consolidation had, it was widely contended, received the seal of approval of the great Friedrich Engels himself. In his last testamentary bequest,[7] the co-founder of Marxism had conceded that the age of old-style revolutions, street fighting and barricades was now over. Advances in communications (particularly the railways), in urban architecture, and above all in the firepower available to professional armies, had immeasurably increased the power of the state and disadvantaged the insurrectionists: 'Let us have no illusions about it: a real victory of an insurrection over the military in street fighting, a victory as between two armies, is one of the rarest exceptions.'[8] The ballot box had, in Engel's view, long eclipsed the bullet as the most promising means of socialist advance and, in this respect, the German workers had blazed a path for all to follow: 'they have used the franchise in a way which has paid them a thousandfold and has served as a model to the workers of all countries'.[9] Their two million voters (in 1895) 'form the most numerous, most compact mass, the decisive "shock force" of the international proletarian army'. Intimidation and proscription by the government could not halt its steady advance. The only thing that threatened its future pre-eminence was that it should rise to government provocation and engage in mounting skirmishes leading to 'a clash on a big scale with the military'. That was precisely what had happened in Paris in 1871, with the result that the movement had been thrown back many years. The party's principal duty was, therefore, 'To keep this growth going without interruption . . . to keep it intact until the decisive day, that is our main task'.[10] It was ironic, he concluded, that 'We the "revolutionists", the "overthrowers" – we are thriving far better on legal methods than on illegal methods and overthrow'.[11] Even more ironic (for Lenin at least) was that the very man Engels appointed as his literary executor, the man who first published Engels' 'Testament', was none other than the arch apostate Eduard Bernstein.

Bernstein's Revisionism

By the turn of the century Bernstein had produced a comprehensive and devastating critique of the fundamentals of Marxism as a contemporary theory of class war and revolution that scandalised the orthodox establishment of European Marxism. Rebuffed and solemnly condemned by his own and other parties, the revisionism he gave voice to refused to go away. On the contrary, it flourished as an international phenomenon precisely because it seemed so much more in accord with the realities of the contemporary world and the actual practice of European Socialist parties.

Bernstein's general position needs to be understood, for the good reason that it expressed, according to Lenin, all that was rotten in European socialism. Revisionism, in Lenin's view, forsook all that was specific and essential to Marxism: it rejected everything that was unacceptable to the radical bourgeoisie. It made of Marxism an anodyne creed that preached integration rather than class war, and incremental change via existing institutions rather than revolution issuing in the class dictatorship of the proletariat. Leninism was, as we shall see, a restatement of the militant separatism of Marxism. It was a declaration of war against all the faint-hearted who had no stomach for its fiery spirits. Its vehemence of tone and language is closely akin to that of religious fundamentalism, it speaks of apostasy and breach of faith and knows no gradation or intermediate position between the kingdom of the elect and the realm of the damned. Those who are not with us are against us. Within this Manichaean scheme of things one feels that Bernstein lurks as the constant Antichrist to Lenin's Luther.

According to Kautsky, the most revered of all the theorists of the SPD, Bernstein's book *Evolutionary Socialism* was 'The first sensational piece of writing produced in the literature of German Social Democracy'.[12] It was sensational because it confronted directly the mythology and the everyday rhetoric of the party. The justifying rationale of all the party's work was that it was preparing itself, and the German workers, for the coming revolution. Participation in electoral campaigns was therefore presented as an effective barometer of revolutionary preparedness – a gauge of public support for the overthrow of capitalism, no more than an effective means of avoiding premature risings. Similarly participation in Parliament, according to the old Marxist orthodoxy, was not intended as a means of transforming the existing power structure, but rather as a legally protected vehicle of revolutionary propaganda. As Bebel had put it, social democrats were in Parliament not to attempt the impossible task of convincing their class opponents inside Parliament, but 'to speak through the windows to the land outside'.

For Bernstein, the rhetorical revolutionism of the SPD was both irresponsible and hypocritical. Irresponsible because the practicalities of the present were never confronted. Policies were never explored in concrete and difficult detail, on the grounds that all would be transformed by the revolution. The revolution had become a sort of magical invocation – 'a good fairy that would make all personal problems and social ills disappear; a fable for children, one sees what sort of political children the force frenzy can make out of otherwise well-informed people'.[13] It was hypocritical because nowhere and at no time did the party engage in even seriously thinking through what a revolution in Germany might involve, still less was it taking any steps to prepare its own cadres for armed confrontation with the authorities. It was time, Bernstein concluded, for social democracy to outgrow its childish beliefs and to confront the complexities of a world that had greatly changed since Marx's day.

The categorical that revolution was necessary and inevitable – what Bernstein referred to as the 'theory of catastrophe' – derived from a number of propositions that were, in Bernstein's view, philosophically questionable or empirically refutable:

(i)   Marx had inherited from Hegel an analytical mode of reasoning which held that development emanated from the clash of opposites. Marx's own method therefore predetermined his conclusions. 'The whole monumental work of Marx,' according to Bernstein, 'aims at being a scientific enquiry and also at proving a theory laid down long before its drafting.'[14] It was time to drop the pseudo-scientific dialectic and, in its place, insert a properly humanist morality – 'Kant not cant'.

(ii)   Marx's economic analysis found that capitalism inevitably produced crises of overproduction and underconsumption that would, eventually, lead to general economic breakdown. In fact, according to Bernstein, modern capitalism had developed regulatory countervailing mechanisms to stabilise its further development.

(iii)   Marx's social analysis was, similarly, flawed or outdated. The concentration of wealth in fewer and fewer hands, with its accompanying growth of impoverishment among the masses, had not, according to Bernstein, occurred. The middle class was not disappearing, nor was the working class becoming increasingly pauperised. Both between and within the different classes the modern economy had created a continuous and complex range of gradations. Society was not, in short, splitting up into two increasingly hostile camps of magnates of capital on the one hand and a homogeneous mass of pauperised workers on the other: 'Far from society being simplified as to its divisions compared with earlier times, it has become graduated and differentiated both in respect of incomes and of business activities.'[15]

There were more technical arguments that Bernstein also deployed, having to do with the labour theory of value (the holy of holies of Marx's economic analysis, which Bernstein complained, was a 'key that refuses service over and above a certain point')[16] and the crucial finding that the rate of profit under capitalism tended to decline: neither, in Bernstein's view, would stand up to critical scrutiny or to empirical evidence. The whole set of arguments upon which the Marxist theory of revolution had been constructed was shown to be in error.

Bernstein's devastating critique of the presuppositions and conclusions of the strategy of catastrophe was complemented by his positive proposals for the reorientation of social democratic politics. The movement must, he argued, 'stand unreservedly on the theory of democracy'.[17] By this he meant, among other things, that democracy had to be conceived not at all in the instrumental sense as a convenient means of spreading revolutionary propaganda, but as an end in itself.

The principle of democracy and of parliamentary government was, he asserted, that of rational debate between alternative programmes. It was a process that was, or ought to be, informed and careful about the likely consequences of acting in certain ways. It was therefore greatly to be preferred to the irrationality of violent revolutionary activity: 'In legislation, intellect dominates over emotion in quiet times; during a revolution emotion dominates over intellect . . . legislation works as a systematic force, revolution as an elemental force.'[18] Above all careful legislation was the only credible path to attain the type of society that socialism aspired to.

A harmonious, highly productive society in which the dignity of each was assured by respect and tolerance for all – such a society, Bernstein insisted, could never be realised by means of civil war. A prolonged and bitter civil war (for that was the real meaning of revolutionary phraseology) would brutalise a generation, leave a legacy of bitterness, and would produce huge material and human destruction. The very conditions that were least suited to the implementation of socialism would be promoted, while the material and moral values proper to socialism would increasingly be discounted.

Modern socialism, Bernstein concluded, had to take its stand on the reality of a complex, highly differentiated society that reflected the complex differentiation of the economic base of society. If socialism was to be implemented successfully, then it had to be welcomed not only by the blue-collar labourers but also by the crucially important technical, scientific and managerial specialists. These men (and they were, at this time, almost wholly men), the engineers, surveyors, chemists, toolmakers, foremen, bookkeepers and plant managers; the men who were in the process of creating the second industrial revolution associated with electricity and the internal combustion engine – were all vital to the flourishing of the modern economy. They would be even more important to the building of socialism than they were to the maintenance of capitalism. They were men of reason and science, ill-disposed to romantic vagueness or calls to revolutionary action. They were, increasingly, men of substance whose scarce skills commanded high wages and security of employment. They had a good deal more than their chains to lose. To such people the call to revolution would fall on deaf ears. Without them, Bernstein insisted, the mass of the unskilled workers simply does not dispose of the knowledge and training to run the modern economy. It was time, he insisted, to stop the irresponsible game of attributing to the 'proletariat' by way of fiction, skills and knowledge that they patently did not dispose of and which lack of leisure, education and security prevented them from acquiring.[19]

Bernstein's book was one of the few in the socialist literature of continental Europe ever to broach the issue of the problems of the transition from capitalism to socialism. The fanciful talk of romantics (such as Parvus) of bringing the whole economy under social control so that within 'half a year the power of government, and the capitalist society would belong to history', or Jules Guesde's assertion that economic transformation could be accomplished in 'a matter of months, nay, perhaps of weeks',[20] were symptomatic of Utopian arrogance or ignorance. Only by patient incremental advance could the proletariat, its party, and its skilled and educated allies, develop that 'abundance of judgement, practical knowledge [and] talent for administration'[21] that the business of socialising the economy demanded. This conclusion was, clearly, deeply influenced by the English Fabians. Though much maligned, the Fabians had been the only socialist group to examine in detail the administrative and financial complexities of bringing specific industries and utilities under state or municipal control.

Bernstein's conclusions were, then, purposively directed against the militant class-war revolutionary Marxists; all the evidence was against them. Classes were not tending to polarise, the working class was not becoming increasingly poor and homogeneous, and the middle classes were not disappearing. Capitalism had not exhausted its capacity for further development and innovation; on the contrary, it stood at the threshold of a second industrial revolution. The economy, and society, became increasingly complex and differentiated embracing widely differing groups with different abilities, skills, life patterns and expectations. Socialism ought to harness and cultivate such differences rather than enforce a homogeneous culture. Above all, the socialisation of industry would be an incremental, rational and peaceful process, initiated and controlled by parliamentary legislation. Commodity exchange would continue for the foreseeable future, as would the state and conventional politics. It would be foolish for the state immediately to grant a universal 'right to work', and still more noxious for it to undertake the direction of all labour.

There was, in short, to be no single act of redemption, no day of jubilee upon which all the wrongs of the past were righted, institutions transformed, and man made anew. Socialism had to deal with the concrete realities of the existing world. It had therefore to develop to the limits of their potential all those institutions (the state, trades unions, co-operatives, municipalities) in order to make a more dignified and secure life for all.[22] As with institutions, so too with practices and values. Socialism, in Bernstein's account, came not to destroy, but to complete liberalism – to press it to the limits of its liberatory possibilities: 'There is, actually, no really liberal thought which does not belong to the elements of the ideas of socialism.'[23] The task of socialism was, he argued, that of 'organising liberalism'[24] and deepening and broadening its goal of freedom for the individual by finally putting an end to economic compulsion. Nowhere was this more true than with respect to the theory and practice of democracy which unequivocally had to become 'not only the means but the substance of socialism'.[25]

The basic theme of Bernstein's revisionism was that socialism could only prosper as a theory and a practice of common, active citizenship. It had to be integrationist rather than separatist. It built upon what already existed rather than a nebulous and unknowable future. It was rational, pacific and developmental, rather than elemental, violent and abrupt. It was, to put it shortly, the ideology of an insider rather than that of an outsider. Bernstein set out in comprehensive form his critique of the method, strategy and goals of unreconstructed Marxism. Socialism, he maintained, could only develop and renew itself through constant criticism and revision of its own doctrines, Marxism included: 'The duty of the disciples consists in doing this and not in everlastingly repeating the words of their masters.'[26]

Having rejected dialectics, and challenged the capacity of Marxist economic determinism to predict the future, it followed, for Bernstein, that there could be no single goal of socialism that gave meaning to present struggles. Those who, like Rosa Luxemburg, maintained that the battle for reforms in the here and now was only significant to the extent that it promoted the coming of the future revolution[27] were, he argued, still blinded by 'dialectical fireworks' and a naïve belief that history was propelled by an immanent purpose. The revolutionaries were, in his view, all teleologists of this sort, believing in the historical mission of the proletariat as the class that was to destroy capitalism, and appraising its development wholly in terms of the growth of revolutionary consciousness. The other side of this coin was their lofty deprecation of the day-to-day needs of ordinary workers, and their patronising attitude to the trades unions the workers themselves had built to protect their interests. It was high time, in Bernstein's account, for the party to devote itself to the immediate, proximate demands of the working class. It was time to stop the arrogant game of counting the class as important only to the extent that it agreed to be inserted into the revolutionaries' historical teleology. Against all this romantic preoccupation with goals and ends, Bernstein repeatedly affirmed a humane scepticism: 'Unable to believe in finalities at all, I cannot believe in a final aim of socialism. But I believe strongly in the socialist movement, in the march forward of the working classes'. . .[28] 'To me that which is generally called the ultimate aim of socialism is nothing, but the movement is everything.'[29] 'Whether it sets out for itself an ideal ultimate aim is of secondary importance if it pursues with energy its proximate aims.'[30] There was a consistent logic running through Bernstein's work, but we cannot avoid the conclusion that, by expressing himself in crisp epigrams of this sort he was being needlessly provocative.

For Marxists such as Lenin it was precisely the disparagement of the idea of a final goal of socialism that was the diagnostic mark of all the traitors to Marxism. Leninism was, as we shall see, expressly formulated to reinstate the dialectic as the methodological foundation of Marxism, and to insist that without a substantive goal – specifying socialism as a unique set of values and institutions – socialism would inevitably become trivial and bourgeois. In the chapters that follow we shall see that Leninism was a self-conscious engagement with all those theorists and practitioners of socialism who tried to make of it an ideology of accommodation to liberal-democratic, or any other species of capitalism. Of all such accommodationists, Bernstein was, for Lenin, the perfect archetype. His revisionism was the demonstration of how Marxism had become debased and emasculated from the moment a single element of its integral structure was removed or 'improved' upon.

There was little that Bernstein said that had not been stated earlier by the English Fabians (with whom Bernstein was in close contact during his extended stay in England from 1888 to 1901). So comprehensive was this influence that Kautsky sadly concluded, in a letter to his friend, 'You have decided to be an English man . . . become an Englishman.'[31] Bernstein's position within the German movement was, however, bound to cause a furore. He was, to the embarrassment of the orthodox, Engels' literary executor. He was also on the editorial board of the principal theoretical organ of the SPD, the *Neue Zeit*. The manner in which Bernstein expressed himself also played its part in contributing to the scandal. His critique was comprehensive, confrontational and, it must be said, even patronising. The ill-elaborated and utopian projects of the left (Parvus, Guesde and Rosa Luxemburg in particular) were ruthlessly exposed, but no less was the centre spared for its lack of critical rigour and its failure to think through the disastrous implications of its revolutionary mythology. He was too prominent within the movement, his critique was too fundamental and, above all, too public for his opponents to ignore.

Lenin had, in Siberian exile, lambasted the first appearance of revisionism in Russia in the highly successful newspaper *Rabochaya Mysl* (Worker's Thought). In 1899 this journal published a 'Separate Supplement' to its issue No. 7 that contained an article by Bernstein and glowing tributes from the editors.[32] Their ideas, Lenin concluded, were 'simply a copy of Bernstein's "fashionable book"'[33] which represented, in every sense, 'A Retrograde Trend in Russian Social Democracy'.[34] Thereafter Lenin wrote little that was overtly directed against Bernstein or revisionism in the German movement, leaving that task to Kautsky, Plekhanov and Luxemburg (although he continued to inveigh against the slightest economism or revisionism within the Russian movement). Lenin took solace from the fact that the 1899 SPD Hanover Congress resolutely affirmed the continued relevance of the Erfurt Programme and rejected 'any attempt to alter or obscure . . . the party's antagonistic attitude towards the existing state and social order and towards the bourgeois parties'.[35] He was further heartened to note that, at this Congress, Bernstein himself 'despite his errors, despite his obvious striving to retrogress both theoretically and politically, still has sufficient intelligence and sufficient conscientiousness *not to propose changes* in the programme of German Social-Democracy . . . he declared his acceptance of Bebel's resolution, a resolution that announced solemnly to the world that German Social-Democracy would stand by its old programme and its old tactics'.[36]

In the years that followed the publication of Bernstein's book there were repeated formal denunciations of its strategy of accommodation and gradual, peaceful reform. The big guns of the International, Kautsky, Plekhanov and Rosa Luxemburg, fired their heavy salvos across his bows, and the Dresden Congress of the SPD in 1903 was even more emphatic than the previous congress in rejecting 'revisionist efforts . . . to supplant the policy of a conquest of power by overcoming our enemies with a policy of accommodation to the existing order'.[37] All, it seemed, was in good order, the revisionists had been put to rout and the revolutionary orthodoxy reaffirmed The man who Lenin (already in 1900) referred to as 'the ex-Marxist, or, more precisely, the "ex-socialist"',[38] had been firmly put in his place.

The Mass Strike – Attrition or Revolution?

Though ritually condemned for his views, Bernstein's influence was far from extinguished. This 'ex-Marxist' and 'ex-socialist', far from being expelled from the Party, continued to enjoy cordial relations with its leadership. The increasingly powerful trades unions were far more sympathetic to his views than they were to those of the more radical and orthodox Karl Kautsky. In the south of Germany, and in most regions outside the large industrial conurbations, it was his general strategy that recommended itself to party officials keen to capture the votes of artisans, schoolteachers, functionaries and peasants. The effective preponderance of his more moderate stance was revealed in the aftermath of the Russian revolution of 1905. The left, emboldened by the Russian experience and the rhetoric of Rosa Luxemburg, urged the adoption of the political mass strike as the most effective weapon available to the party to force concessions from the government. At the Jena Congress of the SPD in September 1905, the left won a momentary victory. Bebel's cautiously worded resolution acknowledged that the political mass strike might be employed as a defensive tactic to defend rights and institutions under threat. Already, however, the counter-attack was under way. The unions, jealous of their prerogatives in industrial matters, and contemptuous of the left-wing intellectuals who knew nothing about the practicalities of trade union organisation, rejected the idea of the political mass strike in the most uncompromising terms. They carried their battle into the highest ranks of the Party and, at the Mannheim Congress the following year, the unions successfully resisted the attempts (led by Kautsky) to subordinate them to the general line of the party. They demanded and got parity with the party. They further insisted that, in all matters (including discussion of the mass strike) concerned with industrial action, the unions and the party had to arrive at a mutually agreeable strategy. It was abundantly clear that the moderate union leadership had not only prevailed over the left, they had also fundamentally altered the power structure of the SPD and given notice to the party that, in the future, it had to rein in its revolutionary firebrands.

In the International the tale was much the same. The vehemence of the German party in defence of orthodox Marxism was matched only by the depth of its opposition to any proposals that might commit it to any specific form of action against the existing status quo. Thus Bernstein and his doctrine were denounced vigorously at the 1904 Congress of the International in Amsterdam in a motion that was word-for-word the same as the SPD's Dresden resolution condemning revisionism. On the other hand, from the first (Paris) Congress of the International in 1889 to the last (Basle) in 1912, the German party bitterly resisted all attempts by the French and English to commit all parties of the International to the general strike as the most effective means of furthering the goals of socialism. In the early congresses, the idea of a simultaneous cessation of work on May Day was widely cherished as a practical demonstration of the international solidarity of labour. The workers of the world, united under the slogan of the eight hour working day, had indeed been the original inspiration for the creation of the International. From the outset, the German party resisted both the general proposition that the International should promulgate obligatory tactics for all of its sections, as well as the more particular logic of the general strike itself.

In rejecting the utility of the general strike the Germans stood on firm doctrinal grounds. Both Marx and Engels had asserted the primacy of the political struggle over the economic. Trades unions, in their estimation, were essentially defensive organizations whose limited goals stopped well short of overthrowing capitalism and erecting a wholly new social order. It became part of Marxist orthodoxy to argue that long before the exacting pre-conditions for a successful general strike could be realised, the electoral and political ascendancy of social democracy would render it redundant.

The general strike was, in any case, a slogan/policy associated with the bitter antagonists of the Marxists within the labour movement – the syndicalists. To accept the utility of the general strike was, therefore, to give comfort to those who argued that the terrain of struggle for socialism ought to be located wholly within the industrial and productive base of society. The syndicalists, for their part, vehemently rejected conventional politics, parties and parliamentary activity – that way, they insisted, led to the deradicalisation of the working class, its tutelage to a bureaucratic and stifling bureaucracy, and the dominance of 'bourgeois' intellectuals. In an escalating series of mass strikes, culminating in a general strike, the workers would, by contrast, be trained in militant self-reliance, they would learn from every defeat and build on every success. The syndicalists took the class war entirely seriously and maintained that its only pure expression was in the direct industrial confrontation of workers with bosses and, eventually, with the state.[39] These ideas had wide appeal in France (where the syndicalists dominated the labour movement from the 1890s to 1914) and were very strong too in Spain and Italy.

For Marxists, the policy of the general strike was associated with the infancy of the labour movement. In their view the general strike, to quote Marx, was general nonsense. It was an industrial rehash of the spontaneous peasant rising that disparaged permanent and disciplined organisation in favour of violent confrontation. It was tarred with the anarchist brush and threatened to deliver the movement into the hands of irresponsible fugitive rabble rousers like Levin, portrayed in Emile Zola's *Germinal*. The tactic would not only lead to the eventual demoralisation of the workers; its uncontrollable excesses would also inevitably strengthen the hand of those who wanted the full force of the state to be directed against the threatening workers' movement. Europe in the 1890s was the scene of numerous anarchist outrages. Bombings, assassinations and industrial sabotage had prompted intergovernmental action which, the SPD plausibly argued, could well be given a much broader purview.

It was left to the immaculate Kautsky to deliver the final Marxist judgement on the mass strike.[40] It was, Kautsky maintained, a tactic appropriate to the phase of the final collapse of capitalism, to a time when the proletariat was fully organised and conscious. That time was not now. For the moment, the reactionaries were still firmly in control and, in this situation, a strategy of attrition rather than a strategy of overthrow was the appropriate one. Kautsky invoked the authority of Quintus Maximus Fabius known as Cunctator (the Delayer) and the wisdom of his strategy of refusing to give battle to his superior foe until he had worn down his enemy's morale and commensurately increased the effectiveness and battle-readiness of his own troops. (It was, paradoxically, precisely this cautious strategy that commended itself to the British middle-class socialists who adopted the Cunctator's name as their own and called themselves Fabians.) German social democracy, according to Kautsky, 'From its beginnings . . . accepted the strategy of attrition and developed it to the full.'[41] The failure of the Paris Commune of 1871 confirmed the hopelessness of the strategy of overthrow, and Engels' own political testament reinforced the message. The closer the moment came for frontal assault on the existing system, the more important it became to maintain discipline, to conserve one's forces for the chosen time and place:

It is precisely because we are convinced that we are facing great and serious struggles and close to the point at which the strategy of attrition must go over to the strategy of overthrow that it is all the more necessary for us not to allow ourselves to be carried away by impatience into premature actions and fire our last rounds in the opening skirmish.[42]

An increasingly familiar pattern of 'French' revolutionary enthusiasm versus 'German' organised restraint, characterised the later debates in the International with regard to the use of the general strike as an antidote to the threat of international war. The French, led by the anti-militarist firebrand Gustav Hervé, took up the cause that had earlier been voiced by the Dutchman Domela Nieuwenhuis. Back in 1891, Nieuwenhuis had put the simple proposition that 'The socialists of all lands will reply to a proposal of war with an appeal to the people to proclaim a general strike.'[43] The same simple, direct appeal was made by Hervé at the Stuttgart Congress 'General strike against war . . . No matter which government is the aggressor we refuse to give one drop of our blood . . . we will fight only in one cause, to instal a collectivist order.'[44]

The response of orthodox Marxists to this short, seductive message remained basically the same throughout the career of the International. At the theoretical level the romantic voluntarism of the general strikers was countered by the weighty generalisations of the determinist view of history: capitalism, of its nature, was divisive and competitive; the aggressive pursuit of scarce resources brought individuals, and later whole countries, into permanent conflict. Only by ending the exploitation of man by man, country by country, and instituting a co-operative internal and international regime in which equity and social justice prevailed, was it possible to end war. An essential precondition for popular hegemony was the elimination of standing armies and their replacement by people's armies or militias. Unlike a professional officer corps, ordinary people had no interest in prosecuting foreign wars against their neighbours or in distant lands. They would limit themselves to purely defensive action – to preserve the integrity of their lands and homes. Such a defensive war was, it was generally argued, just, and deserving of support.

On a more practical level, it could be argued persuasively against the general strikers, that the paradox of their situation was that those countries in which the movement was best organized and the proletariat most conscious, would, through the very success of their general strike, leave themselves prey to their more backward and barbaric neighbours. It was not hard to discern, lurking behind this logic, the long-standing German fear of the Russians. In the interests of political correctness it had fallen to the Russian spokesman of the

'German theory' to make this point. The general strike, Plekhanov declared, would 'deliver Western Europe as prey to the Russian cossacks'.[45] (When war in fact broke out in 1914, Plekhanov became a fervent patriot, declaring that only age and sickness prevented him joining the army and deprived him of the pleasure of bayoneting his erstwhile German comrades.[46])

While the Germans rejected Hervé's 'socialism of the phrase' he, for his part, poured scorn on their incapacity to transform theory into practice. 'You are nothing but an admirable dues-collecting machine. You have no conception of revolution. You can penetrate very deeply into the mists of thought, but faced by the government, you recoil . . . You are afraid of prison.'[47] It was much the same taunt that his fellow countryman, Jean Jaurès, had earlier directed against the SPD Its paradoxical situation was that the greater its electoral success and the more extensive its union organization, the more moderate and pusillanimous the party became: 'Behind the inflexibility of the theoretical formulas which your excellent comrade Kautsky will supply you to the end of his days, you have concealed from your proletariat, from the international proletariat, your inability to act.'[48]

What is, in retrospect, surprising about these debates is that Lenin sided consistently with his German Marxist mentors against 'the theoretically absurd and nonsensical way in which Hervé himself presents the issue'.[49] He warmly endorsed Clara Zetkin's critique of 'the banal anti-militarist sport of the French semi-anarchists of the Hervé type'.[50] Echoing Kautsky, Lenin dismissed Hervé's plan for a general strike and an insurrection in the event of war as mere 'heroic folly'.[51]

Part of Lenin's case against the extreme anti-militarists was their lack of discrimination and nuance. Theirs was a blanket rejection of *all* wars and a call to the workers of *all* countries to strike and revolt. It might be true, Lenin elucidated, that 'working men have no country . . . But it does not follow from this that Hervé and his followers are right in asserting that it is of no concern to the proletariat in what country it lives – in monarchical Germany, republican France or despotic Turkey'.[52] Lenin himself would live to regret this formulation. It left a door half open through which, in August 1914, virtually all the socialists of Europe were to pour in an undignified rush.

The reverse side of the universal protestations about international proletarian solidarity was the equally widespread but contradictory insistence that love of country, indeed a moderate patriotism, was not at all incompatible with being a socialist. The French socialists certainly wore their revolutionary heritage with pride. By the late nineteenth century, they were even prepared to fight alongside radicals and liberals to defend the democratic republic against mounting clerical and nationalist attempts to discredit it. They battled in defence of the victimised Jewish army officer Dreyfus, and were even prepared to tolerate one of their number – Millerand – entering a bourgeois government. Even Kautsky was prepared to acknowledge that, in extraordinary circumstances, and with the approval of the party, socialists might actively support, or even enter, bourgeois governments. In the case of Germany, for instance, a broad coalition of all left and radical forces could be an appropriate response to an invasion by reactionary Russia. This was no more than a restatement of the SPD line that the workers of Germany were far from indifferent to the integrity of their own native land.[53]

The history of the Second International was a history of persistent and unresolved tensions. These tensions could be expressed in a variety of ways. There was, in the first place, the continuum between revisionism or reformism on the one hand, and revolution on the other. This itself was not as clear-cut as it seemed, since, on closer inspection, it spanned a very large range of positions, from the advocates of permanent revolution at one extreme, to the careful moderation of the British Fabians at the other. Between them were positions that ranged from the advocates of the extra-parliamentary political mass strike (represented most cogently by Rosa Luxemburg), to those who believed in the combination of legal and illegal methods (such as Lenin), to those who (like the centre of the SPD) were suspicious of any form of action that was not under the immediate control of the party and conducted within the narrow bounds of legal and constitutional propriety. As far as this basic issue in international socialism was concerned, Lenin was far from being an extremist. He occupied a comparatively moderate left-of-centre position that differed little from the stance of his mentor Karl Kautsky.

The National Question and Socialist Patriotism

It was, in many ways, a similar tale with respect to the national question and the related issue of anti-militarism. The enragés on the left (such as Nieuwenhuis and Hervé) were contemptuous of any claim on their loyalty by nation or country. The great majority of socialists felt, however, that moderate patriotism was quite compatible with internationalism. There was, indeed, a general awareness that socialism, if it was to emerge as a powerful movement, had to dress itself in national colours. The rhetoric, style and mind-set of German socialism was as far distinct from French socialism as it, in turn, was from that of the British. Jean Jaurès frequently proclaimed the identity of French socialism with the French revolutionary tradition, while the German leader Bebel adjudged the absence of patriotism in any man or movement to be a 'monstrosity'.[54] From this it was but a short step to argue that socialists had an interest, alongside all their fellow countrymen, in defending the national soil. Wars of national defence were therefore considered to be just wars. Engels himself had been unambiguous 'If Russia should attack Germany, then we are as much concerned as those who rule Germany and we will resist.'[55] In this Engels exactly anticipated the tone that informed the momentous declaration of the SPD Reichstag deputies in unconditionally approving war credits on 4 August 1914:

> For our people and its peaceful development, much if not everything is at stake, in the event of the victory of Russian despotism, which has stained itself with the blood of the best of its own people. Our task is to ward off this danger, to safeguard the civilization (*Kultur*) and the independence of our own country. And here we make good what we have always emphatically affirmed: we do not leave the Fatherland in the lurch in the hour of danger.[56]

The large problem that was ignored was, of course, that 'despotic' Russia was tied by treaty to republican democratic France. In this situation, could Germany be justified in directing a pre-emptive strike against France or its neighbours? Even though, in the course of the Reichstag debate on war credits, it was revealed that German troops had already crossed into Belgium, the SPD deputies decided to stick to their pre-prepared resolution.

The question of when a war was offensive or defensive was further aggravated by the obvious fact that, in times of acute international tension – times when socialists, along with all other groups, had to make swift decisions – at these very times the trump cards were all held by the government. They could stage provocations in order to justify retaliation, they could withhold crucial information about military matters, they could muzzle and misinform the media, they could and did prepare draconian measures to deal with any opposition to national mobilization. Both the French and the German socialist party leaders were well aware that their governments had carefully prepared a comprehensive onslaught against them in the event of any concerted party opposition in time of war. Lists of national, regional and local officials, of the men who were to be arrested, had been prepared. Party, and, if necessary, trades union funds were to be impounded. The whole movement was to be subjected to a military state of seige. To vote against war credits was, therefore, to invite the destruction of the parties by the state. The leaders were, in 1914, 'torn between their loyalty to principle and their loyalty to the party as the institutional embodiment of proletarian solidarity. To grasp the magnitude of the decision to go into open opposition, we must understand that the party was almost life itself to these individuals. The party had given them that psychological security, that ethical satisfaction, which they had not found in society as a whole'.[57]

It was, finally, easy for each of the contesting governments to portray itself as the injured party and to inflame patriotic sentiment with the rallying call of the Fatherland (or *la patrie*) in danger. The social democrats, though forlornly attempting to counteract the elemental waves of popular jingoism, were, finally, forced to recognise that to continue their opposition to preparation for war threatened to alienate them from their mass base and even their own party members and activists. Schorske neatly summarises the situation of the SPD at the beginning of August 1914: 'The fear of the severity of the law of siege might have been enough to determine the vote for war credits. But to this factor, two others, quite as real were added: the fear of defeat, especially at the hands of the Russians, and that of the loss of working-class support.'[58] As one SPD Reichstag deputy put it at the time: 'The Party could not act otherwise. It would rouse a storm of indignation among men at the front and people at home against the Social Democrat Party if it did. The Socialist organization would be swept clean away by popular resentment.'[59]

There was, in conclusion, a widely-shared conviction that, in the approaching and sadly unavoidable excesses of international war, one voice of sanity, calling for reconciliation and a negotiated and honourable peace, needed to be preserved. It is, in retrospect, easy to see how seductive these arguments were for the socialist deputies who, on 4 August 1914, had to decide whether or not to vote war credits for their governments. The German party, disciplined and united as ever, voted unanimously in favour, and the French followed suit. Only the Russian and Serbian parties declined to vote war credits, though the socialist opposition in Britain was, in many ways, firmer and more extensive. The two great bastions of socialism in Europe, the SFIO (Section Française de L'Internationale Ouvrière) and the SPD abruptly found themselves deeply involved in their own countries' war efforts. In France, the anti-militarist apostle Gustav Hervé overnight became a fervent patriot, the Marxist leader Jules Guesde joined the war cabinet, and in Germany the SPD and the unions collaborated to ensure the strictest worker discipline and to endorse the policy of civil peace (or *Burgfrieden*) 'which gave the government "a dictatorial right to decide all military, political and economic questions"'.[60] The International was dead, its promises were not only forgotten, many of its leaders in fact exulted in the sense of relief that, at last, they had come in from the cold into the warm embrace of their national communities.

Lenin's Reaction to the Outbreak of War

Lenin was, in that fateful summer of 1914, an isolated and thoroughly marginal character. He was living in Novy Targ in Austrian Galicia and, with the war just a few days old, had been arrested by the local police on suspicion of being a Russian spy. It was, paradoxically, only the intervention of prominent Austrian social democrats (all supporters of their country's war effort) that fairly swiftly secured his release. They assured the Austrian government that, far from being a spy, Lenin was resolutely hostile to the Russian government and could be more useful outside prison than inside. With his wife Nadezhda Krupskaya and his mother-in-law, Lenin took train for Switzerland, arriving in Berne on 23 August. As usual, the two women brought order and whatever comfort they could to the life of the itinerant revolutionary. Krupskaya organised the books and papers, dealt with correspondence, and kept comrades at bay while Lenin was working. Her mother saw to the shopping, cooking and cleaning. The more turbulent the times and the more at odds he felt himself to be with the so-called realities of the world, the more Lenin cherished the ordered discipline of his daily routine and the smooth functioning of his household. By this time, Lenin had already formulated his views on the nature of the war and the strategy of revolutionary social democrats in this wholly changed environment. On the day following his arrival in Berne he presented his conclusions to a hastily convened conference of Bolsheviks. His theses were uncompromisingly radical and so far out of joint with the all-pervading mood of patriotic jingoism that even his own comrades in arms doubted his grip on reality. Here, however, were the terse and dogmatic formulations that he consistently maintained throughout the hostilities. They constituted the first statement of Leninism as an international revolutionary alternative to all competing ideologies – particularly to the socialism of the Second International which, in Lenin's analysis, was already disgraced and dead.

The conduct of the leaders of the German Social Democratic Party was, he asserted 'a sheer betrayal of socialism' and the same applied to the leaders of the French and Belgian socialist parties. This general betrayal 'signified the ideological and political bankruptcy of the International'.[61] It had been presaged by the growth within it of 'bourgeois reformism', class collaborationism, and unquestioning acceptance of the parliamentary and legal road to socialism. A merciless struggle had to be conducted against those leaders 'of all countries without exception' who had strayed into patriotism so that a new and genuinely revolutionary International might be created.[62]

Since the war was 'a bourgeois, imperialist and dynastic war' for the division of world markets and 'to loot foreign countries'[63] the workers could have no interest in it – they were being brought to a fratricidal slaughter simply for the benefit of capitalist profit. The task of revolutionary social democracy was therefore, to engage in:

all-embracing propaganda, involving the army and the theatre of hostilities as well, for the socialist revolution and the need to use weapons, not against their brothers, the wage slaves in other countries, but against the reactionary and bourgeois governments and parties of all countries.[64]

In the case of Russia 'the defeat of the tsarist monarchy and its army . . . would be the lesser evil by far',[65] and adherence to revolutionary defeatism was to be the acid test of a genuine socialist.

The axiom that underlay this whole strategy, one that flew in the face of all the available evidence, was that the working masses still retained a revolutionary consciousness 'and are in most cases hostile to opportunism and chauvinism'.[66] It was to this almost wholly imaginary constituency that Lenin addressed himself, with negligible results, in the three years that preceded the Russian Revolution of February 1917. He attempted feverishly to co-ordinate and radicalise the scattered groupings of anti-war revolutionaries at the Zimerwald and Kienthal Conferences of 1915 and 1916, but his efforts bore little fruit. In the extremity of his views he remained almost isolated among the extremist groups of the European left. Only the Russian Revolutions of 1917 transformed Lenin's situation. From occupying a position of insignificant marginality Lenin was abruptly precipitated to centre stage of Russian and European politics. In the meantime he had, as we shall see, constructed a comprehensive alternative to all species of bourgeois and socialist ideologies.

Lenin's reaction to the war (out of which his rounded ideology would emerge), far from being opportunist, was a doctrinaire restatement of the fundaments of Marxism – loyalty to the international class struggle of the workers in the battle for socialism was the only proper course available to Marxists. If this meant going against the tide of public opinion, proclaiming the excommunication of virtually all the established socialist leaders of Europe, and even scandalising his own party members; then so be it. Leninism came into the world as a boisterous foundling, screaming defiance at a circle of hostile faces.

Lenin swiftly recognised, however, that for his critique to be effective he would have to progress beyond impotent denunciation of his adversaries, and construct a plausible explanation of their treachery that was bedded in the changed economic and social milieux of the time. He began a critical reappraisal of the whole history of the Second International.

There was an even more basic task that had to be undertaken. It must, Lenin instinctively felt, be the case that the great betrayal of Marxism by the very guardians of its doctrine, had proceeded from a fundamental miscomprehension (or wilful denial) of Marx's methodology. It was the dubious virtue of Bernstein's position that he had at least been open in attacking the dialectic as metaphysical nonsense. The other leaders of the International were, Lenin came to believe, more culpable, because they had been more dissimulating. They did not openly confront Marx's method, they simply ignored the troublesome constraints of dialectical thinking. Revisionism had, in its insidious way, sapped the revolutionary soul of Marxism which was, Lenin now believed, enclosed in its dialectical structure of thought. His very first priority, in the first turbulent months of the war, was therefore to reconstruct the methodological origins of Marxism in Hegel's dialectic. He was sure that, devoid of proper theory, no effective revolutionary action could be mounted. His reaction to the war demonstrated, above all, a deeply doctrinaire and scholastic disposition to the world. In the midst of unparalleled tumult he shut himself away in Berne public library with Hegel's *Logic*. He was establishing the methodological basis of his new ideological position, whose profound implications will be explored later in Chapter 9.

He realised too that he would have to provide a similarly plausible economic analysis of the causes and nature of the current war. Out of this would grow the conviction that the war was a necessary product of the contradictions of a dying capitalist civilisation – it was, therefore, the long-awaited signal for the transition to socialism on a global plane. Here, in brief, were the essential elements of the new ideology. Unambiguously, it was the war that led Lenin to Leninism.

4

Revolution in Russia

Dissatisfaction with the tsarist regime and its conduct of the war had, by late 1916, affected every section of Russian society. The scandalous goings on of Rasputin and the political meddling of the tsarina, the weakness of Tsar Nicholas and his evident distaste for efficient and competent ministers, had led to profound disenchantment and despair even within the inner circles of the court and high nobility. As the situation at the front worsened, so Nicholas's position as Commander-in-Chief became increasingly compromised. Simultaneously, in late 1916 and early 1917, food and fuel supplies to the major towns fell to crisis levels. Bread queues grew, dissatisfaction spilled over into disorder, and Nicholas responded, as ever, with repression. The worker representatives to the War Industries Committee were arrested in mid-February, but this time the workers of Petrograd would not be cowed. Disturbances at the massive Putilov works resulted in the entire workforce of 30 000 men being locked out on 8 March. By the following day, some 200 000 workers had gone on strike, and by 10 March the strike had become a general strike paralysing the industrial life of the capital. The tsar's orders to suppress the disorders proved impossible to implement and, within two more days, almost the whole of the Petrograd garrison had gone over to the side of the workers. On 12 February 1917 the fate of the Romanov dynasty was effectively sealed. The workers, recapitulating the events of 1905, established their soviets, and a Provisional Executive Committee of Workers' Deputies. Soon they were complemented by soviets of soldiers' deputies.

In the bloodless revolution that toppled the tsar it was the industrial workers of Petrograd who led the way. With stunning rapidity, and with no effective opposition, they put paid to 300 years of autocratic power. Effective power in the capital was now in their hands, but they were reluctant to use it. True to the self-denying ordinance of the socialism they espoused, they begged the middle-class leaders of the

Duma to take the cup from their lips. Only after some hesitation and reluctance did the provisional Committee of the Duma assume the title 'Provisional Government', but its powers were, from first to last, more apparent than real.

The tsar had ordered the dissolution of the Duma but, in a unique moment of defiance, the Duma countermanded the ukase and voted the establishment of a Provisional Committee vested with its full authority. It did not immediately present itself as a counter-government, preferring to see its role as that of a broker between the monarchy and the threatening radicalism of the turbulent mass. Its instinct was indeed to preserve the solidity of a royal head of state on the model of the British constitutional monarchy. Only the refusal of Grand Duke Mikhail to assume the crown abdicated by Nicholas, forced the hesitant Duma committee to centre stage. The Provisional Government was dominated by the liberal Constitutional Democrat (or Kadet) Party with Prince Lvov as prime minister, Guchkov as war minister, Miliukov at foreign affairs and Kerensky as the sole socialist member of the cabinet.

Though the soviet leaders (the Mensheviks Chkeidze and Tseretelli, and the Socialist Revolutionary Chernov, were the most important and best known) refused to govern, they insisted upon their right to control the activities of the government in the interests of 'revolutionary democracy' and the 'toiling masses'. They pressed, in particular, for the establishment of regimental committees and soldiers' soviets to democratise the army and free the soldiers from the tutelage of their officers. They insisted, moreover, that 'the troops that have taken part in the revolutionary movement shall not be disarmed or removed from Petrograd'; they were to be permanently present 'to protect the achievements of the revolution'.[1] It was small wonder, therefore, that the loyalty of the crucial Petrograd garrison was overwhelmingly to the soviet rather than to the 'bourgeois' Provisional Government. From the outset, the government was made aware of the narrow limits of its own power.

Until Lenin's return to Russia in April 1917 there was a broad socialist consensus that the revolution in Russia should not go beyond its bourgeois-democratic limits. The tsar's abdication on 15 March and the proclamation, on the same day, that a Provisional Government had been established, appeared to most socialists to signal the beginning of a more or less prolonged period of bourgeois dominance of Russian politics. The new government had pledged itself to democracy and the summoning of a Constituent Assembly that would, at last, settle authoritatively the constitutional future of Russia. It promised to create a government of national unity that would command popular sympathy and galvanise the war effort that had been so lamentably organised by the tsarist administration. Russia, after so many centuries of arbitrary rule, was at last free. Russia could restore its pride as a democracy fighting alongside the other great European democracies, Britain and France, against the expansionist ambitions of the German Imperial regime.

In such changed circumstances, almost all socialists in Russia agreed, a defensive war was wholly justified. The tasks in hand were therefore to restore order, restrain the sometimes excessive demands of the workers, and to create a genuine people's army that would break German militarism and so prepare the ground for an eventual socialist transition in Europe – after that, of course, the prospects for socialism in Russia might well be transformed. Even the Bolsheviks broadly supported this general line. The Party newspaper *Pravda*, under Stalin and Kamenev, expressed guarded support for the Provisional Government while warning constantly of the dangers of the counter-revolution. On the war, it was no less conformist in maintaining that, for as long as German aggression continued, the Russians must answer 'bullet for bullet and shell for shell'.[2] Above all, the leaders of the all-important Soviet organisations were unambiguous that, given the wartime situation of acute national crisis, the only government that could secure broad-based unity had to be based upon the middle-class Duma majority.

Lenin's April Theses

In April 1917 Lenin returned to Russia in the famous 'sealed train' that had been made available by the German authorities. Descending from the train at the Finland Station in Petrograd he believed that he would be arrested but was, instead, met by a large reception committee from the soviet that had been sent to greet him. He fidgeted and stared blankly around the splendid Imperial reception room of the station during Chkeidze's brief speech of welcome which exhorted him to preserve the unity of the socialist forces and to pursue a moderate and responsible line. Sukhanov, the most perceptive witness to these events, was struck by the incongruity of the occasion. It was, he said, as if all that was going on – the dignitaries in sombre dress, triumphal arches, banners, floral tributes, and the uniformed band and guard of honour – had nothing whatever to do with Lenin. He inhabited a different world, in which these people, their sentiments and opinions, and all that went with them, had no part.

Ignoring Chkeidze, he turned to the crowd on the platform, hailing them as the Russian vanguard of the international civil war for socialism. The war of plunder that had consumed the world would shortly be transformed. Germany was seething, European and world capitalism was teetering, but the momentum had to be sustained. It was the signal honour of the Russian workers to have inaugurated the world-wide socialist revolution; it was now their duty to continue it. Chkeidze's pleas for socialist solidarity and moderation had fallen on deaf ears. Lenin had made no attempt whatever to respond to his welcoming speech. His response 'entirely failed to echo the "context" of the Russian revolution as accepted by everyone, without distinction, of its witnesses and participants'.[3]

Lenin then strode past the dumbfound welcoming party to the square outside that was besieged by a huge throng of people demanding that he should speak. First, he tried standing on the bonnet of a car, then he was lifted on to an armoured car in the square – a mounted searchlight dramatising the man and the moment. His message was again blunt and categorical – the war was a war of imperialist pirates in which the working class could have no interest, the peoples of Europe must turn their arms against their own exploiters and follow the way of the Russian workers who had prepared the way for a new epoch – the epoch of the world-wide socialist revolution. At every crossroads en route to Bolshevik headquarters Lenin repeated his message. Finally, in a two hour speech, he elaborated his position to his Bolshevik colleagues which he then condensed into a cryptic ten-point programme, 'The Tasks of the Proletariat in the Present Revolution' – his celebrated *April Theses*.[4] This was the crucial moment of the public emergence of Leninism as an ideology.

Lenin presented the general analysis and the concrete programme that he was unswervingly to follow right up to the October Revolution. He made not the slightest concession to the popular mood, to the scandalised leaders of other political parties, or even to the hostility and stunned disbelief of almost all of his own comrades. Within his own party, barely one prominent leader supported him, and *Pravda* (to whose editorial board Lenin had already been appointed) took the extraordinary step of disassociating the party, and the editorial board as a whole, from Lenin's *April Theses* which, it pointedly informed its readers, were being published as the *personal* views of comrade Lenin. It went on to insist that his general analyses were unacceptable since he 'proceeds from the assumption that the bourgeois democratic revolution is finished and counts on the immediate conversion of that revolution into a Socialist revolution'.[5]

It was perhaps hardly surprising that not a single prominent leader of either the Mensheviks or the Bolsheviks could follow, still less sympathise with, Lenin's uniquely radical position. They had not been privy to his intellectual evolution over the previous three years, or if they had, they had not understood its implications for political practice. The reader may well be in an analogous position, since the theoretical framework that informed Lenin's view has not yet been adequately outlined in this book (see Chapter 5). It was, however, directly and explicitly on the basis of this theoretical analysis that Lenin set out his programme from the moment that he arrived back in Russia.

Imperialism and the War

Everyone who had a mind to enquire knew, of course, that Lenin was vehemently against the war, but so too were the majority of the soviet leaders, who proudly professed themselves to be adherents of the Zimmerwald manifesto that called for a negotiated peace on the basis of no annexations, no indemnities, and the rights of all nations to self-determination. To Lenin this position was sentimental and inconsistent. It utterly failed to understand the nature of contemporary imperialism and could, therefore, provide no solutions to its contradictions.

We need, at this point, to compress in summary form some of the exposition that comes later in the book, in order to comprehend the logic of Lenin's argument. Imperialism signified to Lenin all these things: monopoly and technological retrogression; militarism and the production of means of destruction; internal and external oppression; the growth of a gigantic and parasitic state at the expense of individual and group autonomy; and, finally, the universalisation of its contradictions by subjecting the whole world to its sway. It was the terminal, degenerate form of capitalism as a mode of production and as an historical epoch that had, in the global war it had fomented, finally declared its own bankruptcy. Lenin had, from this analysis, already arrived at the propositions that were foundational to his revolutionary strategy in 1917:

(i)   There could be no way out of the war without the overthrow of capitalism: 'Outside of socialism there is *no* deliverance of humanity from wars, from hunger, from the destruction of still more millions and millions of human beings.'[6] History had entered the epoch of the international revolution for socialism.

(ii)   Overthrowing capitalism could only be achieved through overthrowing the state form to which it was bound intrinsically. 'It is *impossible* to slip out of the imperialist war and achieve a democratic non-coercive peace without overthrowing the power of capital and transferring state power to *another* class, the proletariat.'[7] It had fallen to Russia to create the popular agencies – the soviets – through which this transcendence could be accomplished.

(iii)   Capitalism itself, in its state monopoly form, had created the organisational structures through which the socialised management of the economy could be organised and democratised – the trusts, cartels and big banks.

It followed from the first of these propositions that all those calling for an 'honourable' or negotiated peaceful settlement to the war (the position of most of the leaders of the soviets) were just as much in error as those who believed that an epoch of peace could be secured through the triumph of the Alliance (the position of the Provisional Government). Both positions had to be rejected because both failed to comprehend how war, militarism, monopoly capitalism and the state were intrinsically linked. Lenin conceded in the April Theses that this was the central educative and propaganda task: 'to explain the inseparable connection between capital and the imperialist war, and to prove that without overthrowing capital *it is impossible* to end the war by a truly democratic peace'.[8] In practical terms, this meant that the Bolsheviks must adopt slogans openly denouncing the Provisional Government which, from first to last, endorsed the Allied war aims enthusiastically and prided itself on being an administration backed by popular enthusiasm that could, therefore, more energetically pursue these aims: 'No support for the Provisional Government: the utter falsity of all its promises should be made clear.'[9] The stance of the moderate socialists, the internationalist Mensheviks who dominated the soviets at this time was, equally, to be roundly condemned: 'not the slightest concession to "revolutionary defencism" is permissible'.[10]

Power to the Soviets – the Commune State

The second proposition led directly to 'the necessity of transferring the entire state power to the Soviets of Workers' Deputies . . . Not a parliamentary republic . . . but a republic of Soviets of Workers', Agricultural Labourers' and Peasants' Deputies throughout the country from top to bottom';[11] 'I write, announce and elaborately explain: "The Soviets of Workers' Deputies are the *only possible* form of revolutionary government".'[12] Already, Lenin was clear that the Soviets corresponded to '*our* demand for a "commune" state i.e., a state of which the Paris Commune was the prototype'.[13] In the April Theses he gives an abstract of Marx's account (in *The Civil War in France*) of the programme of the Commune:

Abolition of the police, the army and the bureaucracy . . . The salaries of all officials, all of whom are elective and displaceable at any time, not to exceed the average wage of a competent worker.[14]

Lenin's idea of a 'commune state' was, undoubtedly, the most stupendously radical feature of his whole programme. Behind it lay his theorised conviction that the nation state, whose apotheosis was the tyrannical and militarised state capitalist trust, had, finally, outlived its historical role.

Lenin's third proposition is not developed at any length in the *April Theses*, but it certainly lies behind his demand for 'The immediate amalgamation of all banks in the country into a single national bank and the institution of control over it by the Soviet of Workers' Deputies'.[15] According to Lenin's earlier analysis of monopoly or finance capital, the role of the banks as the very nerve centres of the accumulation and circulation of capital had become paramount. They had, in his view, largely displaced stock exchanges as the sites in which the fundamental decisions with regard to allocation of investments and restructuring of industry were taken. The big banks therefore provided a ready-made mechanism for directing, and holding accountable, the productive and distributive networks of the economy. Here was, *par excellence*, the organisational structure, created by monopoly capitalism itself, through which the socialisation of the economy could be greatly facilitated. The only other economic measure he insisted upon was the 'Confiscation of all landed estates. Nationalisation of *all* lands in the country, the land to be disposed of by local Soviets of Agricultural Labourers' and Peasants' Deputies.'[16] This was no more than a terse restatement of Lenin's agrarian programme of 1905. Ownership of the land remained an unresolved question of the democratic revolution. Under intense pressure the tsarist regime had made quite radical changes to peasant land tenure but the peasants continued to regard with envious eyes the remaining estates of the landowning nobility, the Church and the state.

The Menshevik Critique

It is one thing to reconstruct retrospectively the development of Lenin's thought in the period 1914–17 and the logic that led him to his extreme conclusions, but it is quite another to appreciate the impact they had upon his contemporaries. The immediate reaction of his Bolshevik colleagues was, as we have seen, one of stupefaction, disbelief and unease. Amongst the Mensheviks (and Lenin read his theses to a 'unity' conference of Bolsheviks and Mensheviks the day after his arrival in Petrograd) there was outrage and accusations that 'Lenin has raised the banner of civil war within the democracy'.[17] Bogdanov condemned it as 'the delirium of a madman'[18] – a judgement endorsed by the aggressively patriotic Plekhanov. Steklov, one of the 'unifiers' and a prominent leader of the Soviet, was more hopeful (but more condescending):

> Lenin's speech . . . consists of nothing but abstract constructions that prove the Russian Revolution has passed him by. After Lenin becomes acquainted with the state of affairs in Russia he himself will reject all these constructions of his.[19]

The ministers of the Provisional Government were reassured by the moderate socialists that Lenin's 'lunatic ideas' condemned him to isolation: 'a completely lost man standing outside the movement'. Sukhanov, the most reliable witness of this initial reception of Lenin's ideas, 'agreed in general with this estimate of Lenin's ideas and said that in his present guise he was so unacceptable to everyone that now he was not at all dangerous to our interlocutor, Miliukov'. He too was convinced that, 'after he had escaped from his foreign academic atmosphere . . . he would . . . throw overboard the bulk of his anarchist "ravings".'[20] According to the memoirs of one of her friends, even Lenin's wife, Krupskaya, concluded that 'I am afraid it looks as if Lenin has gone crazy.'[21]

We should be clear that, at the point when Lenin first outlined his programme for a second revolution in Russia, not a single prominent socialist leader agreed with him on any of its substantial points. On the key question of where power was to reside within the state (which, as Lenin repeatedly insisted, was the all-important question of all revolutions) they were almost unanimous that the Provisional Government, the bourgeois-dominated successor to the tsarist Duma, was the proper constitutional form for the bourgeois-democratic phase of the revolution. It was, they maintained, the only constitutional form that would reconcile the bourgeoisie to the revolution and to the cross-class commitment to democracy. As a leading Menshevik and Soviet leader had put it, when addressing the Petrograd Soviet less than two weeks before Lenin's return:

> You understood that a bourgeois revolution is taking place, that it represents a stage of the social revolution . . . The power is in the hands of the bourgeoisie. You transferred this power to the bourgeoisie, but at the same time you have stood guard over the newly gained freedom . . . The Provisional Government must have full executive power in so far as this power strengthens the Revolution, so far as it is overthrowing and breaking down the old order.[22]

Any revolutionary adventurism on the part of the proletariat or its socialist parties would, according to this consensus, alienate the middle classes and the professional unions, split the democratic forces, and prepare the way for a reactionary coup. The working class was, in any case, too small in numbers and too politically and organisationally immature, to assume power by itself. This was, in all essentials, a re-statement of the Menshevik standpoint of late 1905 and 1906.

The Menshevik *Rabochaya Gazeta*, immediately after Lenin's presentation of his '*Theses*', concluded that to ignore the objective constraints of 'the state of the productive forces, the level of mentality of people corresponding to it, etc.' was to render a service to reaction which Lenin assuredly had. The struggle against Lenin was, therefore, the struggle against reaction.[23] Thereafter, through their press and their soviet party spokesmen, most of the Mensheviks denounced the slogan 'All Power to the Soviets' as a counter-revolutionary provocation (not until after the attempted coup by General Kornilov in late August did the left-wing Mensheviks and Socialist Revolutionaries recognise the need for the soviets to claim power for themselves).

The Russian Revolution as Premature

The principal claim of the Menshevik critique of the Bolshevik seizure
of power in Russia in October 1917 was that the conditions specified by
Marx (and generally accepted by Western socialists) for the transition
to socialism had not matured. According to this interpretation, Marx
had laid down clear and exacting specifications to guide his followers
so they would be able to know when the decisive moment for a socialist
revolution had arrived. The most basic of these specifications was that
modes of production have, to a large extent, an autonomous historical
logic.

Different modes of production in history (slavery, feudalism,
capitalism, for example) had very differing ways of extracting surplus
value from their labourers. They were based upon qualitatively
different levels of technological sophistication and had, consequently,
widely differing patterns of division of labour, and different ways of
allocating status, power and wealth within society. None the less, each
mode of production necessarily had to develop a tight internal
consistency between its legal and constitutional practices, its systems
for allocating rewards and status, and its management of the business
of producing and distributing goods. Each mode of production had its
own internal contradictions but – once established and dominant – each
was destined to play out its historical role until all of its progressive
potential had been exhausted. By progressive potential, Marx generally
meant its capacity to augment mankind's productive output. It was
only at the point at which a particular mode of production had finally
exhausted its capacity for further development and felt itself threatened
by new, more efficient and sophisticated systems of producing and
exchanging goods, that the signal was given for the end of its natural
life span. At this point its own internal contradictions would grow more
and more pronounced; they would become irresolvable. Simultaneous
crises would shake not only the systems for producing and exchanging
goods, but also the whole integrated systems through which that society
governed and conceived of itself.

The *locus classicus* for this determinist specification of revolutionary
ripeness was Marx's famous 'Preface to the Critique of Political
Economy'. Here, it would appear, Marx lays down clear conditions for
the transition:

> No social order ever perishes before all the productive forces for
> which there is room in it have developed; and new, higher relations

of production never appear before the material conditions of their existence have matured in the womb of the old society itself.[24]

These were what were known as the 'objective conditions' that had to be satisfied and, on this apparently solid ground, the Mensheviks stood firm against any suggestions that the revolution in Russia could be pressed in a socialist direction. It was, they forcefully argued, quite implausible to maintain that capitalism in Russia had come anywhere near exhausting its potential for further development. The pockets of advanced machine industry within Russia were surrounded on all sides by a vast hinterland in which pre-capitalist economic forms coexisted uneasily with the very early stages of capitalist accumulation. The Mensheviks generally held firm to a specifically Russian framework for their economic and social analyses. They were either unaware of, or unconvinced by, the theory of international finance capitalism whose focus was a global economy of which Russia formed a part, and which insisted upon appraising conditions of revolutionary ripeness at the international level. This was the principal theoretical divide in Russian Marxism in 1917 and it generated, as we have seen, fundamental divergences of political strategies and tactics. Being for or against advancing towards the socialist revolution revolved around the prior question of whether or not one accepted the analysis of international finance capitalism.

The other condition which, according to the Mensheviks, orthodox Marxists were duty-bound to accept, was the level of development of the proletariat itself. Unless the proletariat formed the majority in the country and was conscious of its historical mission to implement socialism, then, once again, it would be irresponsible to talk of an immediate prospect for socialist revolution. These were the equally necessary 'subjective conditions' for revolution that had to do with the numerical size, maturity, organisational cohesiveness and revolutionary awareness of the working class. On each of these criteria (except, perhaps, the last), the Mensheviks maintained, the Russian working class in 1917 had a long long way to go. Numbering perhaps three million out of a total population of approximately 120 million, the working class was, unequivocally, a small minority of the Russian people. Its maturity and organisational coherence had been grievously held back by the autocratic prohibition not only of working class political parties but even of a trade union defensive organization. It was, in these circumstances, impossible to maintain that the Russian working class came anywhere near satisfying Marx's specification that 'the proletarian movement is the self-conscious, independent movement of the immense majority, in the interests of the immense majority'.[25]

For the Mensheviks and the moderate Russian socialists the case was clear – Russia did not fulfil either the objective or the subjective conditions necessary for an advance to socialism. Those who irresponsibly spurred the workers on in this direction they regarded as demagogues and anarchists. Such people fomented the real grievances of workers without bread, peasants without land, and soldiers who wanted peace. But the slogans 'Bread, Peace and Land' had nothing to do with the real programme of socialism. The severities of war, they recognised increasingly, were radicalising all sections of Russian society, and were producing an anarchic revolutionary temperament among parts of the proletariat. But this should not be used as an argument for what could only be a premature and disastrous attempt to overstep the limits of the bourgeois-democratic revolution. Socialists should, on the contrary, bend their efforts to restraining the workers' naïve utopianism. The proletariat and its political parties had to reconcile themselves to the prospect of becoming a responsible opposition for the foreseeable future.

It was not simply the leaders of his own party, those of the Mensheviks, the Socialist Revolutionaries, and the soviets that stood opposed to Lenin, the mass of the workers, and particularly the soldiers did so too. Lenin's denunciation of a war of defence, and his summary dismissal of a peace without annexations and indemnities, smacked to many of treason, not merely to Russia but to the freedoms won by the February Revolution. The treasonous aura surrounding him was fanned by persistent claims that he was a German agent, supported by German money, and adroitly delivered by German train to wreck the Russian war effort. It can, in short, be said that nothing could be further from the truth than the often repeated claims that Lenin's revolutionary programme, as presented in the *April Theses*, was a carefully contrived set of opportunistic propositions designed to flatter the prevailing moods of the Russian populace. On the contrary, in the extremity of his views he was effectively in a minority of one.

The bare outlines of how, from being a minority within his own party in April, to becoming the majority in the principal soviets of Russia by September, can be told fairly simply. The resistance of the party itself crumbled swiftly. Lenin subjected its Petrograd and all-national conferences in mid- and late May to a non-stop barrage of speeches, pamphlets and reports, in which he repeated and expanded tirelessly upon his 'Theses'. He demonstrated, once again, what some acute contemporary commentators had already observed, that Lenin could think and act independently of the party, but that the same was not true in reverse. By the end of April only a few prominent doubters held out (Kamenev, Rykov and Milyutin). Intellectually and psychologically, the party was too much Lenin's creature – it might be capable of surviving for a time without him, but not against him.

Thereafter the party turned its attention to the people as a whole, or rather to the industrial workers of the capitals, who would, Lenin insisted, play a disproportionately important role in the revolution that was unfolding. As in 1905 Petrograd was the centre towards which the eyes of Russia naturally turned.[26] As in 1905, it would be the advanced industrial workers of the capital, the best organised, most literate and mature workers of the whole country, who would prove to be the catalyst of a more generalised class advance. From the outset, Lenin's discourse, and his whole political strategy, was established upon a series of projections or predictions (as indeed are all theories of revolution):

(i)   The central and basic problem of the war could not be resolved by the other political parties.

Accepting as they did the bourgeois-democratic limitations of the revolution, the Mensheviks and Soviet Revolutionaries would be compromised increasingly by the Kadet insistence that the war be fought to a victorious conclusion.

(ii)   The land question, similarly, could not be resolved by any coalition in which the Kadets had an effective say. They would fight for the sanctity of private property and frustrate the peasant drive to take all the land, and they would, as a consequence, have to intervene actively to suppress the agrarian revolution as inappropriate to the bourgeois democratic phase.

(iii) Much the same applied to the national question – for fear of antagonising the Kadets, the 'petty-bourgeois' Mensheviks and Socialist Revolutionaries would, in practice if not in words, be forced to retain the oppressive integrity of the Russian empire. They would be forced to the conclusion that a renegotiation of Russia's boundaries and her Constitution was inappropriate in a wartime crisis that threatened the very existence of the state.

(iv)   The escalating economic crisis that had brought real privation to the army and to the urban population could not, once again, be resolved by insisting upon the sanctity of existing property relations. A rational allocation of national resources could only be achieved through state control over the banks and the formation of state trusts in major sectors of industry. Corruption and profiteering could only be restrained by workers' control in industry; and the regeneration of trade and exchange required the co-operatives to assume a growing role.

According to Lenin's analysis – or rather the prognosis he had already elaborated in April 1917, the objective situation in Russia of ever-increasing military, industrial, agrarian, fiscal, and political collapse and threatening catastrophe, could not be averted by keeping the revolution strictly within the bounds of existing property relations. It was, therefore, futile to attempt to preserve the alliance with the bourgeois political parties.

Neither Capitalism nor Socialism but Something in Between

We should, at this point, note that Lenin repeatedly and emphatically rebutted the allegations that he was urging the immediate introduction of socialism in Russia. The nationalisation of the land, for instance, the centrepiece of his agrarian policy in 1917, as it had been in 1905, was not only in accord with the stated interests of the peasant proprietors, it also conformed to the minimum programme of the RSDLP and to Marx's own insistence that it was a measure that would hasten rather than retard the growth of capitalist commodity relations in the countryside. The demands for a single state bank and the creation of a number of state-dominated Trusts within the principal sectors of the economy were, Lenin argued, measures that were typical of state monopoly capitalism, and the same applied to universal labour service. The plan for workers' control of industry, as Lenin repeated constantly, meant control, but not ownership; 'control' in the sense of having access to the books to prevent profiteering and the plunder of the state. The project for a 'commune state' was, similarly, projected as the most radical extension of democracy and the only way in which the masses could be galvanised to save Russia from ruination.

The immediate goals of the revolution in Russia were, therefore, not socialist: 'No one talks about a "socialist experiment"'[27] . . . 'Under no circumstances can the party of the proletariat set itself the aim of "introducing" socialism in a country of small peasants so long as the overwhelming majority of the population has not come to realise the need for a socialist revolution'[28] . . . 'We cannot be for "introducing" socialism – this would be the height of absurdity. We must preach socialism.'[29]

The regime he had in mind, in its economic, social and political components, was a unique and hybrid formation that had not been anticipated theoretically, but which had, in practice, been prepared by the growth of state monopoly capitalism. Imperialism, in this sense, was itself an intermediate formation. It was at once the apogee of the process of capitalist accumulation, socialisation of labour and monopolisation, and, simultaneously a harbinger of socialism. It was 'in a sense, a transition stage to socialism'.[30] In the trusts and huge banks that were its engines, it created the mechanisms through which the socialisation of the entire economy could be facilitated enormously. The war itself, and the growing need to mobilise the entire economy and workforce, had extended and accelerated these processes greatly in the belligerent countries. In the epoch of trusts, capitalism itself had begun to rectify the anarchic planlessness that typified capitalism in its competitive phase: 'Engels remarked that "when we come to the trust, then planlessness disappears" though there is capitalism. This remark is all the more pertinent today when we have a military state, when we have state monopoly capitalism.'[31] Lenin was in no doubt that:

The objective conditions for a socialist revolution . . . have been ripening with tremendous rapidity as a result of the war . . . The concentration and internationalisation of capital are making gigantic strides; monopoly capitalism is developing into state monopoly capitalism. In a number of countries regulation of production and distribution by society is being introduced by force of circumstance. Some countries are introducing universal labour conscription.[32]

Lenin's proposed 'Amendments to the Doctrinal, Political and other sections of the Party Programme', written at the end of April, make it abundantly clear that he assigned first priority to defining at length the changed nature of contemporary capitalism; to specifying, in short, the 'objective conditions' that prevailed, which therefore defined the limits of political strategy and of the goals it should pursue. This was his most authoritative statement on the foundational question of the whole Party Programme, and from it he concluded that:

Objective conditions make it the urgent task of the day to prepare the proletariat in every way for the conquest of political power in order to carry out the economic and political measures which are the sum and substance of the socialist revolution.[33]

It is clear that Lenin is here talking about capitalism in general, as a global phenomenon, and he was in no doubt that, given its intrinsically international character, this was the only way to characterise it. It was, he asserted 'absurd to restrict oneself to conditions in one country alone, since all capitalist countries are closely bound together', in the war 'this bond has grown immeasurably stronger. All humanity is thrown into a tangled bloody heap from which no nation can extricate itself on its own'.[34] In the developed countries of the West, socialist revolution was unambiguously on the order of the day. In Russia, however, as we have seen, the question was not one of expropriating the capitalists and the transfer of their assets to the state. It was not the expressly socialist commitment to transforming property relations but, rather, the insistence upon state *control* over the banks, trusts and syndicates. This would neither be capitalism nor socialism. It would, as he explained to the First All Russia Congress of Soviets, be 'something in between, something new and unprecedented'.[35] Universal labour conscription directed by the soviets would, once again, '*still not* be socialism, but it will no longer be capitalism'[36] and the same, exactly, applied to control of the banks.[37] All these measures would, none the less, constitute steps *towards* socialism; their implementation would ensure that 'Russia will have one foot in socialism'[38] so that the future transition to a genuinely socialist economy and society would be assured.

What Lenin envisaged for Russia was, then, a curious hybrid of a regime that in its productive base took over many of the characteristic institutions of state capitalism, and anticipated the extension of the co-operative movement to embrace the whole people constituting the distributive mechanism, while subjecting both to the overall control of the Soviets. The democratisation of the whole structure was to be measured in terms of the degree of mass participation in the deliberation and execution of public business via the Soviets, the militia, the agencies of workers' control, and the plethora of *ad hoc* communes that would attend to particular functional or local issues. Given the complex, hybrid nature of the regime he anticipated issuing from the revolution, it is hardly surprising that both Lenin and his allies and opponents were frequently confused about the question of whether socialism was, or was not, on the immediate agenda. (A similar confusion surrounded the question of whether commune-type administration did, or did not, qualify as a state form properly so-called.)

Despite his qualifications and reservations with regard to the revolution immediately 'introducing' socialism to Russia, Lenin was entirely confident that the successful seizure of power by the Soviets and the proclamation of people's power that it would represent, together with the proposed package of economic measures to bring capitalism under popular control, could not fail to have a galvanising effect upon the developed West. He was convinced that Germany and France, in particular, were on the verge of socialist revolution, and that where they led the other countries of Europe would swiftly follow. A world 'drenched in blood',[39] devastated economically, famine-stricken and approaching the collapse of all civilization would, Lenin argued, finally realise that only socialist revolution could save it. 'The time is approaching when the assertion of the founders of scientific socialism . . . that world war would inevitably lead to revolution, is being everywhere proved correct.'[40] Both the objective and the subjective conditions for revolution were being hugely accelerated by the war itself.

To Russia fell the historic responsibility of inaugurating the world revolution. Her proletariat, though comparatively small in numbers, was cohesively organised on a class basis through the Soviet system. They enjoyed, uniquely in Europe, complete freedom of assembly and the press. Above all, they were armed and had been joined by the revolutionary soldiers. 'To whom much is given much is expected.' It fell to the Russian workers and soldiers, in Lenin's view, to begin a new epoch in human history – the epoch of the final emancipation of humanity from moribund capitalism, and the wars and devastation it had wreaked. Theirs was the honour and duty of starting 'a new *phase* that became *objectively* essential with the outbreak of the first imperialist world war, which inaugurated *the era of social revolution*'. Though they themselves could not unambiguously be the bearers of socialism, it was their duty to light the torch that was to consume capitalist civilization. 'The great honour of beginning the revolution has fallen to the Russian proletariat.'[41]

Class and Political Polarisation

As with his analysis of 1905, Lenin was convinced also in 1917 that the unfolding events would demonstrate the correctness of his prognoses. The experience of the revolution, the unprecedently extensive mass participation in politics, would openly reveal the true class polarities of

Russian society – the whole unbridgeable gulf between the interests of the propertied and those of the propertyless. All the parties and groups that attempted to stand in the middle – the moderates and conciliators, the dreamers of social harmony – would be swept away. Just two days after his *April Theses* were published, Lenin wrote in *Pravda*:

> let us rally our ranks for proletarian class work; and larger and larger numbers from among the proletarians, from among the *poorest* peasants will range themselves on our side. For *actual experience* will from day to day shatter the petty-bourgeois illusions of these "Social Democrats" . . . the "Socialist Revolutionaries", the petty bourgeois of an even purer water and so forth . . . The bourgeoisie stands for the undivided power of the bourgeoisie . . . The class-conscious workers stand for the undivided power of the Soviets of Workers', Agricultural Labourers', Peasants', and Soldiers' Deputies – for undivided power made possible not by adventurist acts, but by *clarifying* proletarian minds, by *emancipating* them from the influence of the bourgeoisie . . . This is the *actual*, the *class* alignment of forces that determines our tasks.[42]

The tactics were clear – expose the vacillations and half-heartedness of the petty-bourgeois 'socialist' leaders of the existing Soviets and of the moderate socialist parties; show how they could not pursue a determined policy to end the war because they were tied to the coat tails of the liberal Kadets – the party of the bourgeoisie which was, in turn, subservient to the interests of foreign imperialists; and reveal how the self-denying ordinance of the moderate socialists to limit the revolution to bourgeois-democratic objectives necessarily committed them to opposing any deepening of revolutionary democracy, or any real restraints on capitalist excesses and profiteering. Above all, Lenin staked his future, and that of his party, on his belief that the mass of the workers, soldiers and peasants would repose their faith increasingly in their own Soviets rather than in the 'bourgeois' Provisional Government and its regional and city dumas.

In the months from April to October 1917, these rival conceptions of the class bases, goals and limitations of the revolution, were put to the test of the times and spiralled up and down with dizzying rapidity. Internal and external events, political crises, economic dislocation and the rise and fall of military fortune were grist to the mills of the opposing standpoints. Russia was flooded by an unprecedented deluge of newsprint. A plethora of journals, newspapers, flysheets, manifestos, posters and pamphlets, dissected and analyzed each fresh turn of events, struggling to make them conform to a pattern, to some developmental process. The same could be said of the endless round of meetings, conferences and popular demonstrations in the streets, barracks, factories and soviets. All of Russia, and not just its principal cities (as social historians have demonstrated convincingly), seethed with political controversy. And the more it seethed, the more the Bolsheviks came into the ascendancy. From month to month it seemed as though events, and popular appraisals of them, were confirming Lenin's prognosis.

On the crucial question of war and peace, each month brought further testimony to the Bolsheviks' contention that the Provisional Government was determined to pursue the war to a victorious conclusion. Shortly after Lenin's return there was the scandal of the Miliukov Note, in which the Minister for Foreign Affairs (the most prominent Kadet leader) pledged the government to fight the war to a finish and to honour all its obligations to the allies. The Soviet line for an end to the war on the basis of a just peace without annexations or indemnities was, it seemed clear, gratuitously ignored by the government. Mass street demonstrations revealed, for the first time, that Lenin's slogans 'Down with the War' and 'All Power to the Soviets' were already making inroads.[43] The tide of anti-war sentiment that began to sweep the country (and the army) was, at every point, strongly resisted by the government, even after the Socialist Revolutionary Kerensky became Minister of War in May.

In the middle of June, the government decided to launch a major offensive in Galicia and for three weeks it registered significant successes. By the end of the first week in July, however, the Russian armies were in chaotic retreat. The Mensheviks and Socialist Revolutionaries, who were by this time prominent within the government, inevitably shared the ignominy. Only the Bolsheviks clamoured for an immediate end to the war, impugning all the other parties for their weakness and their subservience to the bourgeois Kadets and their foreign masters. It was not entirely clear what the Bolsheviks' peace policy (if indeed it was such) amounted to, and since they were not the governing party it no doubt suited their interests to keep it somewhat vague. Lenin repeatedly claimed that the Bolsheviks would not make a separate peace with Germany, partly perhaps to give the lie to the persistent rumours that he was a German agent. What he promised was the offer of an ill-defined democratic peace and, in the event that this was turned down, the threat of revolutionary war to be waged by the whole Russian people in arms. This latter prospect was, however, only infrequently broached, since Lenin was confident that the further development of the revolution in Russia would provoke a revolution in Germany. Whatever the vagueness of Bolshevik policy on the war and the unpredictability of the international projections upon which it was based, there is little doubt that in the popular mind they were increasingly credited with being the only radically anti-war party.

A similar tale unfolded with regard to the question of soviet power. The other parties consistently underestimated the depth of popular attachment to the soviets as the embodiment of the people's revolution. They were, in these months, without question the agencies of mass mobilisation and democratisation through which millions, for the first time, felt they not only had a voice but also the power to change things. We should again be clear that this was a movement that was far from being restricted to the capitals or the principal industrial regions. On the contrary, the mushroom growth of soviets or their equivalents (names differed in different parts of Russia) swiftly penetrated almost every village and every last outpost of the army. There is, indeed, a case for arguing that in parts of the countryside and in the smaller towns the soviet movement was at its strongest. Over large areas of Russia the establishment of soviets signified the liquidation of the complex of administrative agencies of the tsarist regime through which the Provisional Government attempted to govern the country. The local and regional dumas, the *zemskii nachalniki*, the police and the land captains were in many areas displaced, put under arrest, or chased out. Virtually all the attempts of the Provisional Government to assert its authority over the local and rural soviets met with fierce, and generally successful, resistance.

In part, this intense assertion of village autonomy was rooted in ancestral distrust of the towns and the interference of government of any hue – particularly when that government attempted (as both the tsarist and the Provisional Government administrations had) to impose a state monopoly on the trading of grain. More to the point, many soviets and rural communes (which enjoyed an enormous resurgence in 1917) feared that their *de facto* appropriation of landlords' fallow lands, forests, pasturage and whole estates, would be reversed by government action. There was here a powerful coincidence of political principle, and local and personal interest, that tied the slogans 'All Power to the Soviets' and 'All Land to the Peasants' closely together. It was, once again, the Bolsheviks alone who had made these slogans their own while all other parties vainly struggled against them.

July Days and Kornilov Revolt

There were, of course, ups and downs in Bolshevik fortunes in these turbulent months before the October Revolution of 1917. The steady growth of the party's influence was checked, and temporarily reversed, by the mass demonstration that nearly became a rising in the early part of July. Armed soldiers and sailors joined Bolshevik-led workers in a confused *émeute* that the Bolshevik leadership had organised, then cancelled, too late to prevent the participants assembling, then allowed to proceed to test the waters. The half-revolt collapsed when it became apparent that not only would the leaders of the Petrograd soviet (Mensheviks and Socialist Revolutionaries) not agree to take the power the demonstrators demanded they should seize from the Provisional Government, the leaders also made it clear that they would defend themselves with force against the insurgents. Among the increasingly radicalised workers and soldiers the mood of resentment grew against the existing leadership of the Soviets – it seemed incomprehensible that their leaders, when offered power on a plate, should appeal to their right to use force if need be against those who insisted upon offering it to them.

The immediate aftermath of the July days saw a concerted campaign by both the Soviet and the government against Lenin and the Bolshevik Party. Warrants were issued for the arrest of the top leaders, who consequently had to flee the city. The press and offices of *Pravda* were wrecked, and official sanction appeared to be given to the widespread allegations in the popular press that Lenin was indeed a German agent.

It now seems that the setback of the July Days was less serious than commentators have been inclined to believe. It did cause Lenin, in late July and early August, to withdraw his slogan 'All Power to the Soviets', leading him to conclude that government oppression and political prescription would now make it impossible for the party to win a majority peacefully. He concluded, therefore, that in these circumstances an armed insurrection was the only way forward.

It was the Kornilov revolt in late August that, more than any single event, accelerated the rise in Bolshevik repute and organisational strength. By like token, its ignominious failure demonstrated how weak the forces of right-wing counter-revolution had become. This was bound to raise questions about the rationale for the Menshevik/ Socialist Revolutionary alliance with the Kadets, and their joint refusal to contemplate radical constitutional or economic measures for fear that moderates would be driven into the camp of the counter-revolution. On 25 August the recently appointed Commander-in-Chief of the Army, General Kornilov, issued a Proclamation in which he took it upon himself, on behalf of all the patriotic forces, to bring order and discipline back to military and political life. He planned to march on Petrograd at the head of the Cossack Savage Division, to quell the 'anarchy' of the Soviets and to save the country from Bolshevism. In the event, the issue hardly came to a fight at all. Socialist agitators, workers and soldiers from Petrograd infiltrated the ranks of Kornilov's soldiers and either won them over, or sapped their resolve, the railwaymen sabotaged his troop movements and telegraph communications. It was, in any case, clear that the attempted coup had been ill-prepared and poorly co-ordinated. In the hour of real danger, however, the Petrograd soviet rescinded its anti-Bolshevik measures and the party responded by galvanising the workers and Red Guards under its influence. Leon Trotsky was appointed leader of the Soviet's Military Revolutionary Committee and he took full advantage of his authority to arm worker detachments – some forty thousand rifles were distributed. It was the Petrograd soviet, with Bolsheviks projecting themselves as its most energetic supporters, that proved to be the mobilising and organising agency of the anti-Kornilov forces.

The Bolsheviks were the beneficiaries of the Kornilov affair. The powerlessness of the Provisional Government was apparent to everyone. Worse, it was widely rumoured (not without some evidence to support it) that Kornilov had acted at least with the knowledge, if not consent, of the man who had appointed him – the prime minister, Kerensky. The other side of the coin was that the affair revealed the centrality of the Soviet as the only sure defender of the gains of the revolution and the only body capable of inspiring and mobilising the people. As the Bolshevik paper *Rabochii Put* expressed it: 'in the days of Kornilov the power had already gone over to the Soviets'.[44] The whole strategy of the moderate socialists in the revolution was called into question not only by their erstwhile supporters who were deserting them, but also by prominent men within their leadership groups. Martov and Dan led the 'internationalist' Mensheviks into a stance that was increasingly hostile to the Provisional Government and the bourgeois parties. They had come round to the view that the period of dual power no longer served the interests of the revolution, and that the Soviets ought to prepare for power. A similar split occurred among the Socialist Revolutionaries. Its left wing assumed positions on the land, the war, and the soviets, that were qualified versions of the Bolshevik programme.

Lenin Prepares the Bolsheviks for Power

By early September it was clear that time was running out for the Provisional Government. The Bolsheviks had secured majorities in the soviets of both Moscow and Petrograd. In the crucial Petrograd soviet, which enjoyed the greatest national esteem, Trotsky had replaced the moderate Menshevik Chkeidze as president. Lenin now made no bones about his intentions to take and hold undivided power – his programmatic statement at this time, *Can the Bolsheviks Retain State Power?*, posed and answered the question in unambiguous terms.

By this time, in any case, the limited power the Provisional Government disposed of was rapidly ebbing away. Many provincial towns and some whole provinces were following the earlier examples of Kronstadt, Tsaritsyn, Baku, Tiflis and Saratov in declaring their soviets to be the sole repositories of governmental power. The transfer of land to locally elected Soviets or committees accelerated, as did the disintegration of the army.

The ineffectiveness of the government and the disarray into which it had fallen was plainly apparent at the State Conference of leaders of regional, functional, soviet and political groups that Kerensky convened in Moscow in mid-September. It was the regime's last attempt to counter-balance the increasing prestige and restiveness of the Soviets, and thereby to relegitimate government power and deter the Bolsheviks from a seizure of power that was being openly canvassed in the party press. The Conference, unhappily, exacerbated rather than alleviated the Government's problems. On no major issue was there a clear government majority and, to make matters worse, the depth of the economic, military and political crises facing the country were very publicly and very frankly exposed. Much the same fate befell the so-called Pre-Parliament, a body established by the government as a kind of anticipator of the Constituent Assembly, elections for which were, at last, set for November. On 25 September the last coalition of the Provisional Government was formed under Kerensky's leadership, comprising four Mensheviks, four Kadets and three Socialist Revolutionaries, with six non-affiliated ministers (including four well-known millionaires).

By this time, Lenin was already trying to convince the Central Committee of his party that the time had at last arrived when the die had to be cast, forces mobilised, key strategic positions secured, and power seized. From day to day his instructions and exhortations grew more urgent and more peremptory. By the end of September he was already tendering his resignation to the Central Committee in protest against its inaction.[45] There could, in his view, be no excuse for further delay. Neither the upcoming convocation of the All-Russia Congress of Soviets, nor the more distant meeting of the Constituent Assembly, could alleviate the pressing problems of the people.[46] The imminent German advance would not wait, nor would the government hesitate to deliver Red Petrograd and Kronstadt to the Germans if that would stymie the advance of the revolution: 'Kerensky and the Anglo-French capitalists *have conspired* to surrender Petrograd to the Germans and thus *stifle* the Russian revolution.'[47]

Lenin returned repeatedly to his theses of 1905: in time of revolution there can be no standing still. Passively following the turn of events, and trusting that the errors and provocations of one's opponents will provide a pretext for an advance (disguised as 'defence of the revolution') was a recipe for disaster. This, Lenin insisted, was the path of the philistine and the petty-bourgeois, the path of one who knows neither Marx nor history. When matters between classes come to the point of decision, it is, he insisted, always to the bold that the victory goes. Marx, he reminded his followers, was unambiguous, and they would succeed only if they heeded his words:

Insurrection is an equation with very differing magnitudes, the value of which may change every day; the forces opposed to you have all the advantage of organisation, discipline and habitual authority . . . unless you bring strong odds against them you are defeated and ruined. Secondly, once you have entered upon the insurrectionary career, act with the greatest determination, and on the offensive. The defensive is the death of every armed rising; it is lost before it measures itself with its enemies. Surprise your antagonists while their forces are scattered, prepare the way for new successes, however small, but prepare daily. Keep up the moral superiority which the first successful rising has given to you; rally in this way those vacillating elements to your side which always look out for the safer side; force your enemies to retreat before they can collect their strength against you; in the words of Danton, the greatest master of revolutionary tactics yet known: *de l'audace, de l'audace, encore de l'audace!*[48]

The conditions that had been absent in the abortive rising of July had, Lenin maintained, now matured: the majority of workers and soldiers of the capitals and elsewhere supported the Bolsheviks. Then there had been no 'country-wide upsurge', now there was; then the political and class opponents of the revolution had been united, now they were vacillating and in a state of disarray.[49] Meanwhile, the party had fallen for the soporifics that Kerensky, in desperation, had resorted to. Against Lenin's advice, they had participated (however fleetingly) in 'the despicable talking shop' of the Democratic Conference.[50] The time for speeches was over; the imperative now was the purposive organisation of the military forces of the revolution in the barracks and the factories. 'History,' Lenin insisted, 'has made the *military* question the fundamental *political* question'.[51] A secret committee of absolutely reliable men must therefore be formed which would act as the headquarters of the insurgency. It must collect precise data on all troops, sailors and Red Guard detachments available to the revolution, and assess the mood of readiness among its proletarian advance guard. It must detail all the key strategic points in Petrograd and draw up precise plans for their capture and reinforcement – the telephone and telegraph exchanges, the railway stations and the bridges linking central Petrograd to the working-class suburbs.

Again and again he attempted to stiffen the resolve of the Central Committee, and tried to meet the varied doubts they expressed. The proletariat, led by the Party, would, he insisted, be able to administer the economy and the country.[52] Capitalism itself had bequeathed them the agencies for nationwide book-keeping and control. They were available immediately; and they could be set in motion at a stroke.[53] The peasants, as ever, had to be led, and they would assuredly follow a proletarian government. The soldiers were solid behind the Bolsheviks and would never march against a government of Peace. The international situation was developing rapidly towards proletarian revolution, needing just one spark from Russia to set all the fissile material in Europe ablaze. He concluded:

> The crisis has matured. The whole future of the Russian revolution is at stake. The honour of the Bolshevik Party is in question. The whole future of the international workers' revolution for socialism is at stake . . . The crisis has matured.[54]

The Vacillations of the Bolshevik Party

The only substantial obstacle in the way of the revolution was, according to Lenin, the irresolution and fear in the Party itself. It is certainly true that the Bolshevik Central Committee was at least as scandalised by Lenin's call for an armed uprising as it had been by his *April Theses*. It took Lenin longer to win them round, and he had to resort to more extreme measures to impose his will than had been the case in April. Two of his most prominent veteran disciples, Zinoviev and Kamenev, broke ranks and, in an unprecedented breach of discipline, denounced the proposed bid for power in the columns of the non-Party press. They were not the only detractors; on the contrary, right up to the eve of the October Revolution even those charged with the military preparations were distinctly pessimistic about its prospects of success. All the pressure, the vehement letters and broadsheets, the demands for removing the 'traitors', and insistent resolutions on the preparation and timing of the revolution came from Lenin. The Central Committee, for its part, tried every stalling device it could construe, it raised fresh objections almost daily, and it failed to respond to Lenin's increasingly frenzied demands for the decision to be taken and the date to be set. It even resolved to destroy his communications and to refuse Lenin leave to return to Petrograd.[55] Its reports on the mood of the workers and fighting capacity of loyal troops were at best ambiguous and, once again, Lenin had to conduct a prolonged and almost solitary campaign to convince them that the time was ripe. Initially, as Trotsky relates, 'all the members of the Central Committee, although for different motives, rejected the proposal'.[56] Once again, as had been the case in April, Lenin had to use all his authority and powers of persuasion to effect a change in the Party's stance and, once again, he demonstrated that their reliance upon him was greater than his upon them. At both of these critical junctures, Lenin had to contend with the dogged resistance of the Party leadership.

Without Lenin there would have been no second 'October' or 'Bolshevik' revolution in 1917. This was, as Trotsky conceded in his *History of the Russian Revolution*, a supreme manifestation of the triumph of one man's will. This was true not merely in the sense that it was Lenin who single-handedly steeled his colleagues to hazard the attempt on power; it was also true in the stronger sense that he had, since April, tirelessly disseminated the ideas that anticipated and helped to form the public attitudes that made the revolution possible. The prospects for a Bolshevik-led advance to socialism that seemed in April to be risibly remote were, by early October, being debated by all shades of political opinion throughout Russia. The momentous nature of this shift in the public mood can hardly be over-emphasised – for the first time in history, millions of people were won over to a programme of such extreme radicalness that the army, police and bureaucracy were to be done away with.

On 10 October, Lenin was at last allowed to address the Central Committee and, despite the gloomy predictions of military support, the majority was browbeaten into accepting Lenin's stance. Six days later, a sort of expanded revolutionary council was convened by the Central Committee, at which there was a more comprehensive and detailed attempt to gauge the strength of the forces supportive of a Bolshevik rising. Once again, the reports were mixed and indecisive. Even among the Petrograd metalworkers (long considered to be the 'avant-garde of the avant-garde' of the working class, and a stronghold of Bolshevik influence) Shlyapnikov was obliged to report that 'a Bolshevik rising is not popular; rumours of this even produce panic'.[57] Zinoviev, in his critical summary of the situation, concluded that 'we have not made technical preparations for an armed insurrection. We do not even have a centre yet. We are going half-consciously to defeat'.[58] The crucial lines of communication – posts, telegraph and railways – were not centres of Bolshevik strength. The garrisons were unreliable, they were firmly for Bolshevik peace proposals, but there appeared to be little will to fight for the success of a Bolshevik revolution. Above all, it seemed clear to Zinoviev that the public mood had calmed considerably since June. But Lenin was adamant that the party could only go forward; it had to act; otherwise it too would be discredited in the eyes of the masses. The proletariat would rise, the peasants would follow, the opposition was demoralized and negligible, victory was assured, the international revolution was at hand.

On 16 October the Bolshevik Central Committee finally committed the party 'to make comprehensive and intensive preparations for an armed uprising'.[59] The resolution still, however, left in abeyance the crucial questions of 'the favourable moment and the appropriate methods of attack'. In the event, the Central Committee decided to mount the seizure of power on the night of 24–5 October, and most of Lenin's immediate strategic projections proved to be accurate. The workers did indeed respond to the call – more ardently than most of the leading Bolsheviks had believed possible. The Red Guard detachments, that had sprung up in a wholly unco-ordinated way within the big factories, were everywhere in the van, more motivated and more reliable than most of the military detachments. In Petrograd the revolution was accomplished with almost ridiculous ease.

The insurrection met virtually no resistance. Almost nobody was prepared to die for a regime that had prevaricated for so long that it had lost the sympathy even of its old supporters. Its ministers were arrested at the Winter Palace. Kerensky ignominiously fled the capital, whose strategic points and communications' centres were, by the morning of 25 October, firmly under Bolshevik control. That evening the delayed inaugural session of the Second All-Russian Congress of Soviets convened in Petrograd. Though legitimizing itself under the cloak of 'All Power to the Soviets', it was clear (and part of Lenin's express intention) that the Bolsheviks had pre-empted and usurped its power. Its will had, as Trotsky put it, 'been *predetermined* by the uprising of the Petrograd workers and soldiers'.[60] The Soviet none the less had a Bolshevik majority, which proceeded to approve Lenin's drafts of the Decrees on Land, and Peace, and the proclamation of Soviet power.

Interpretative and Methodological Problems

The period from April to October 1917 was, clearly, of critical importance in the development of Leninism. If it had not been successful at that point it might well have featured as no more than a large footnote in the history of the twentieth century. To explain its success is, however, extremely problematic – we are back to the competing interpretative styles where, it seems, the most flatly contradictory stances can all flatter themselves that the evidence supports their case. The question, of course, is *how much* of the evidence can be accommodated and how much discreetly ignored.

To some, Lenin's thought and activity in these crucial months amply demonstrates that he was, indeed, a Jacobin or Blanquist. He forged his instrument of mass mobilisation and insurrection, on strictly hierarchical, secretive and centralising principles. He struck decisively at the moment of greatest weakness of his opponents and maximum strength of his own force. And when he seized state power he used it systematically to consolidate his own base and to destroy his opponents. There is no denying the seductive simplicity of this line, but we should take stock of the large volume of evidence that cannot be accommodated by it. What, for instance, are we to make of Lenin's insistent and repeated claims that the whole object of the revolution was not to consolidate and augment the power of the nation state, but to dissolve it into the Soviets and Communes? What are we to make of the equally insistent motif that the revolution aims to do away with standing army, police and bureaucracy, and to deliver their preroga- tives to the armed people? It could, of course, be countered that these were simply demagogic displays designed to mask his true intentions. It is clear, however, that *The State and Revolution*, Lenin's principal text of this period, and the most 'anarchistic' of all his writings, was not written for a mass audience and was not intended for immediate publication (it was left unfinished at the moment of the October Revolution and not published until 1918).

If Lenin was not wholly a Blanquist at this time (though as with Marx, elements of Blanquism were certainly written into his doctrine) neither was he simply an opportunistic power seeker. According to this notation, Lenin seized upon the ill-articulated grievances of the people, gave them voice, and amplified and combined them into a cacophony of protest that swept away Russia's legitimate government. The other side of this coin is the contention that Lenin flattered and stimulated the aspirations of any group he thought might be instrumental to his overweening lust for power – regardless of the consequences for the socialist project. We have only to look at his *April Theses* and the furore with which they were greeted, in his own party as well as the country at large, to realise how deceptive this position is. Lenin had, before he returned to Russia, already formulated his doctrinaire and deeply unpopular position that appeared so out of touch with prevailing views. As Sukhanov accurately noted, his was a voice from outside. No one of consequence, at this point, had propounded his slogans – 'All power to the Soviets', 'down with the provisional government, 'all land to the peasants' and 'freedom to the nationalities', 'down with the imperialist war' and 'an international civil war for socialism'. These slogans were themselves merely shorthand formulations of a deeply theorised analysis that had been gestating for more than two years.

The interpretation that is advanced in this and subsequent chapters is that the strengths, weaknesses and dangers of Leninism arise from its imperious attempt to oblige reality to conform to theory. Its leitmotif, its guiding text, is, in this general sense, Marx's own deeply Promethean and dangerous proposition that 'It is not enough for thought to strive for realisation, reality must itself strive towards thought.'[61] Theory here does not simply reflect what is evident, rather it anticipates and projects; moreover, it inserts itself as the key element in the whole practical business of transforming reality. As Marx insisted, it was precisely through theoretical reasoning that war should be proclaimed on existing conditions which were '*below the level of history, beneath any criticism*'.[62] Lenin burnt with the same rage against all those conditions that had produced a world war of unmitigated brutality and destruction; a civilization that had issued in barbarism. For Marx 'the Germans *thought* what other nations *did*. Germany was their *theoretical consciousness*'.[63] For Lenin, it was a matter of honour that the Russians, in the twentieth century, were destined to break out of the emasculated realm of theory into the domain of practice. And he had no doubt that his whole life's experience fitted him uniquely to be the vehicle of this transformation. The criticism of weapons was, at last, to replace the weapon of criticism. In this situation, of course, prosaic and hitherto neglected matters having to do with mobilization, training and disposition of one's forces, was invested with a special, even decisive, importance. Revolution had to be treated as an art – otherwise it became an idle word game for chatterers and dilettantes.

What impressed Lenin's followers throughout this period was his certainty: he knew beyond any doubt where he was going and where the revolution was going. As was the case with the revolution of 1905, he began with a theorised prognosis of the limits of political and economic policy that each class and political party aspired to, or was prepared to concede. Revolutionary strategy then dictated (as it had in 1905) that these differing limits should, as rapidly and as graphically as possible, be exposed. It was the differences, the antagonisms (or as Lenin put it, the contradictions) that revolutionary politics must reveal. Theory, whose task it was to chronicle the emergence and refinement of class differentiation, here had to be translated into policies and slogans that would polarize society.

It was precisely this capacity, that Lenin undoubtedly had, to relate each moment of the revolutionary process to his overarching class analyses and general strategies, and those, in turn, to more deeply theorized accounts of the nature of the epoch, that most impressed his disciples. Trotsky put it in this way: 'Almost automatically he was translating algebraic formulae into arithmetical realities.'[64] Georg Lukács was similarly certain that what distinguished Lenin from all his contemporaries was his theoretical clarity, his ability to grasp the total process and to render it down 'to establish firm guide-lines for all questions on the daily agenda . . . Lenin alone took this step towards making Marxism, now a quite practical force, concrete. That is why he is in a world historical sense the only theoretician equal to Marx yet produced by the struggle for the liberation of the proletariat'.[65]

From the moment of his return to Russia, Lenin, on the basis of his class analysis, knew that the moderate socialists (the Socialist Revolutionaries and the Mensheviks), so long as they sought to preserve cross-class national unity – that is, to retain the good will of the liberal Kadets – could not satisfy the aspirations of the popular masses: the workers, the soldiers and the peasants. The narrow limits they set to the bourgeois democratic phase of the revolution would condemn them increasingly to the role of acting as the guardians of bourgeois order, bourgeois economics and bourgeois politics. It was *their* static and narrowly theorized conception of the limits of the bourgeois democratic revolution that would condemn them to irrelevance – they would be paralysed politically. They would not be able to bring the war to a speedy conclusion, they would not be able to attend to the question of the land, they would be unable to deal with profiteering and industrial dislocation. Above, all they would have to stand firm against the workers (or the soviets) having the decisive say in the government of the country. All these matters, Lenin predicted, would loom larger and larger in the life of the country and would demand radical resolution. But so long as the moderate socialists were tied to the apron strings of the Kadets and locked in the straitjacket of their democratic revolution, they would be condemned to impotence. Their theoretical parameters compelled them to attempt to anchor the revolution to its February moorings – all that should have been accomplished had been accomplished. If the people wanted more, they were in error and needed guidance and restraint. As one prominent Menshevik later put it:

> The Mensheviks proved unable to harness this revolutionary potential to any practical purpose. They were blinded by their rigid marxist formula of 'bourgeois revolution first, socialist revolution later' and tried to restrain the masses. They preached self-abnegation to them, told them to stand aside until such times as the bourgeoisie had built a solid capitalist system . . . the Mensheviks were paralysed by indecision . . . their fatal self-restricting dogma led them from one mistake to another; from merely supporting the Provisional Government to actually joining it . . . Fedor Dan admitted in 1946 that the Menshevik concept of the bourgeois revolution rested on illusions.[66]

It seemed to many almost uncanny that Lenin's predictions, which had seemed so wild and extravagant in April, were, by September, being realized. The army was disintegrating; it could not or would not continue to fight, yet Russia was further than ever from a peace settlement. Petrograd and Kronstadt were, after the fall of Riga, dreadfully exposed to German attack. The countryside was in turmoil, peasant expropriations proceeded apace. The economy was collapsing under inflation and acute supply problems. The political structure of the country was chaotic. The Democratic Conference gave way to the Pre-Parliament amid a welter of words, little agreement, and no decisive action. Great areas of the country were, in any case, effectively outside government control – their Soviets had proclaimed their independence. Power was ebbing away from a government that was bereft of initiative and leadership. It almost seemed as if providence was helping Lenin in the triumph of his programme, but what this understates is the extent to which Lenin constructed his own fortune.

In making his projections for the future, Lenin would have been too modest to write into his calculations his own contribution to the unfolding plot. He preferred to see himself as only the vehicle for irresistible historical forces. And yet, as we have seen, his personal interventions at the crucial points, in April and October, decisively affected the course of the revolution. By 'decisively' we mean that without the presence of Lenin, the power and persuasiveness of his ideas, his enormous personal authority, and, above all, his steely certitude, there would have been no second or socialist revolution in Russia in 1917. That he did not make the October Revolution single-handed goes without saying. When the moment came, the success of the revolution did indeed depend upon the initiative and audacity of Red Guard detachment leaders[67] and the organisational genius of Trotsky, who was largely responsible for the co-ordination of forces and detailed strategy of the insurrection. Yet still the Marxist Trotsky, in his own history of the revolution, concluded that each and every participant in these events, himself included, could with impunity have been replaced by another – with the sole exception of Lenin. Without him, Trotsky insists, there would have been no revolution. This admission, which it is difficult indeed to refute, puts the fervent and complex theoretical disputes between Bolsheviks and Mensheviks into perspective. In the last analysis, no amount of Marxist debate about the levels of productive forces, consciousness or international ripeness could settle the issue of whether Russia would or would not go beyond the bounds of the bourgeois democratic revolution. It was, in fact, settled by the 'accidental' presence of one man with an unshakeable belief that one civilisation was foundering and that imperatively another had to be born.

This is to say no more than that Marxism never was a 'science of revolution' and the search for definitive guidance with regard to the 'objective' limits of action, particularly and especially in periods of revolutionary trauma, was doomed to failure. It was precisely at such times, as Engels freely admitted, that detailed and accurate data about changing patterns of ownership relations and class differentiation were least likely to be available. There was, in short, necessarily a considerable temporal lag between the occurrence of major changes in the economic base, and revolutionaries' access to data on the depth and extensiveness of such changes. In the meantime, of course, they had to act, and either had to resort to treating 'this, the most decisive factor, as constant', or else they would be obliged to extrapolate from the 'patently manifest events themselves' and conjecture causes from the appearance of symptoms. Engels went on:

It is self-evident that this unavoidable neglect of contemporaneous changes in the economic situation, the very basis of all the processes to be examined, must be a source of error. But all the conditions of a comprehensive presentation of current history unavoidably include sources of error – which, however, keeps nobody from writing current history.

When Marx undertook this work [*The Class Struggles in France*], the source of error mentioned was even more unavoidable. It was simply impossible during the period of the Revolution of 1848–49 to follow up the economic transformations taking place at the same time or even to keep them in view.[68]

Engels makes light of this fatal methodological flaw lying at the heart of the Marxist theory of revolution. His flippant disclaimer that this unavoidable source of error in 'the very basis of all the processes to be examined kept nobody from writing current history' is irresponsibly evasive. It was so because what the ideology of Marxism exhorted masses of people to do was to lay their lives on the line in a civil war, out of which, they were promised, their present powerlessness and poverty would be swiftly redeemed. There was a world of difference between the scale of commitment and enduring consequences involved in writing history on the one hand, and making it on the other.

Precisely the same strictures can be levelled against Lenin's theory of imperialism (the economic constant of his whole analysis), and his derivative theory of the state. As a structure of ideas, they had an impressive coherence that has largely been ignored by critics. Lenin was not, however, an academic. According to his own yardstick, he was to be appraised not for the internal consistency and coherence of his ideas, but for the accuracy with which they mirrored contemporary reality.

The whole fate of Lenin's project for socialism evidently rested upon the adequacy of the international economic analysis upon which it was based. Would capitalism be able to redeem the economic chaos and deprivation into which Europe was falling increasingly? Could it effect the transition to a peacetime economy and stabilize itself successfully? Would successful revolutions in the peripheral countries of world capitalism have fatal repercussions on the metropolitan countries? Finally, would successful socialist revolution in the metropolitan countries be able to furnish expertise and capital goods in sufficient quantities to allow the peripheral revolutions to pass directly to a socialist phase of construction? Lenin had answered each of these questions with an absolute certitude – capitalism could *not* recover from the war, the Russian revolution *would* ignite socialist revolution in Europe which, in its turn, *would* come to the aid of Socialist construction in Russia. He knew that his party and his followers were not going to be inspired to heroic action by 'maybes' and 'perhapses'.

Lenin urged his followers on with the certainty of an idealogue, and, consequently, he had to ignore the methodological uncertainties that lay at the very heart of his analysis. This does not mean that Lenin violated the logic of Marxism in inspiring and leading the October Revolution. It merely means that Marxism could *never* supply in advance a specification of the necessary and sufficient conditions for a successful socialist revolution. Marxist revolutionary action could only be based upon a series of more or less well-informed predictions or inferences from a more or less accurate analysis of a temporally distant socio-economic structure. Its 'justification', therefore, always lies *after*, rather than *before*, the event. It is justified if, and only if, its predictions turn out to be accurate. That, precisely, was the burden of difference between making history and merely writing it. In the event, none of the principal predictions, upon which the whole Russian revolutionary venture was premised, in fact materialised. The country was forced in upon its own ruined resources and low cultural level. In these circumstances the regime, as even Lenin was prepared to admit, was bound to degenerate. But what was never conceded was Lenin's (and the Bolsheviks') huge responsibility for inaugurating a venture of total transformation that turned to cataclysm when the predictions upon which it was based proved to be false. Men can, no doubt, be inspired by ideas to heroic and self-denying action but, by a similar token, those same ideas can inspire actions that, inadvertently perhaps, lead on to barbarism. Ideologies, are, in this sense, never innocent; they always wear upon themselves the mark of Cain.

5

Imperialism and the Death Throes of Capitalism

Lenin's response to the war is impossible to square with the view that he was, *par excellence*, a doer and not a thinker, a power-seeking pragmatist who was largely unconcerned with the constraints of theory. In fact, Lenin, having exhausted the slender opportunities available to him to denounce the war and all who supported it, threw himself into a study of Hegel and the most basic methodological issues of Marxism. Thereafter he devoted himself to constructing a thorough Marxist account of the nature of modern capitalism and how it had necessarily produced militarism and war. This account, written in 1916 and first published in mid-1917 under the title *Imperialism, the Highest Stage of Capitalism*,[1] was the most fundamental text in the politics of Leninism. It encapsulated its world view and defined the global characteristics of what was held to be an entirely new epoch in human history – the epoch of the final collapse of capitalism and the advent of socialism. It also, of course, established the theoretical justification for the Bolshevik-led October Revolution of 1917.

We should recall that all of Lenin's writings, including such apparently academic texts as *Imperialism, the Highest Stage of Capitalism*, served political purposes. They were always partisan, they always demonstrated a political point, and they were always therefore simultaneously an affirmation of a general line and an assault on all alternatives. Ideologies are, in this guise, demarcations, and the crucial demarcation Leninism set out to draw was that between revolutionary Marxism and revisionist social democracy. Lenin's insistence upon dialectical methodology had set the demarcation in the sphere of philosophy (see Chapter 9), and the theory of imperialism (or monopoly capitalism) was to work similarly for economic and social theory. Acceptance of the laws of the dialectic entailed the acceptance

113

of fundamental change only being possible through 'breaks in continuity' or 'qualitative transformation'. Acceptance of the theory of imperialism was meant to render these abstractions into a present obligation to act. It too was directly concerned to deprive the social democrats of the last of their pretexts and excuses for avoiding their revolutionary responsibilities.

Ever and anon the reformists and gradualists, the adherents of piecemeal and peaceful transformation, had argued the notion of unripe time. Capitalism, they declared, had not quite exhausted all the possibilities for its further development. As good Marxists, therefore, the social democrats counselled caution. In their version of Marxism, as long as a mode of production continued to be capable of further development it remained progressive, and ought not, therefore, to be overthrown. This was, as we saw Chapter 4, the consistent position of the Mensheviks in Russia throughout 1917. The apparent failure of Marx's predictions with regard to capitalist crises and the pauperisation of the working class was, moreover, at the root of almost all schools of socialist revisionism. Bernstein, as we have seen, insisted that the workers were not becoming more and more impoverished, and society was not splitting up into two hostile camps as Marx had predicted. Revolution, the reformists argued, was therefore an implausible and unnecessary strategy. As a theory and practice of revolutionary transformation, Marxism was virtually dead by 1914. It was Lenin who, almost single-handedly, revived it, both as a revolutionary theory and as a revolutionary practice; the theory of imperialism was the very keystone of his whole enterprise.

Lenin's analysis of contemporary capitalism (set out in *Imperialism, the Highest State of Capitalism*) was written to give the lie to these complacent, social democratic and revisionist assessments of the modern economy. The simplest and most fundamental message of Lenin's *Imperialism* was: capitalism is ripe, it is rotten-ripe and decaying; its time has passed, it is living on borrowed time. An epoch is at an end. Socialism is not only its chronological successor, it is logically entailed in the very development of capitalism in its monopolistic phase; all its objective and subjective preconditions have matured within monopoly capitalism; and its triumph becomes a necessity. 'Socialism,' Lenin said in an unusually expressive phase, 'is now gazing at us through all the windows of modern capitalism.'[2] The theory of imperialism is a gloss to this conclusion. Its whole message is to point up the immediacy (or what Lukács called 'the actuality') of the revolution'.[3] *Imperialism* is, above all, concerned with defining a time.

Its audacity, and its significance, was that it located the moment of the death throes and paralysis of an entire historical epoch and the coming to birth of a new one, and this on a global scale. Leninism categorically defined a time for all humanity – now is the moment of choice between socialism and barbarism.

Just as Marx arrived at the imperative for revolution *before* he demonstrated its economic necessity, so too did Lenin. The economic analysis of finance capitalism did not anticipate Lenin's conclusion that global revolution was on the agenda; it served to justify it. In precisely the same way, Marx's *Capital* had been a belated 'scientific' vindication of his earlier revolutionary conclusions. For them both, economics was Minerva's owl.

Marxism and Capitalism

The first proposition of *Imperialism* as political economy was that in becoming monopolistic, capitalism had ceased to be progressive. Monopoly capitalism, far from serving to advance, develop and refine technological innovation, in fact tended to stymie it. This was, of course, an absolutely crucial conclusion because, in the Marxist account, modes of production, and the civilizations that they spawned, could only justify themselves historically if they served generally to advance the development and refinement of the productive forces available to mankind. As with all phenomena, modes of production contained within themselves rival forces or contradictions (especially class contradictions) and, as they moved from maturity to senility, these contradictions became ever more pronounced and irresolvable. This was the point, Lenin argued, that the capitalist mode of production (in its moribund stage of state monopoly capitalism) had now reached. The time had come for a new mode of production and a new civilisation to replace it. The final *dénouement* was at hand, the time for which all previous history had been but a preparation. Socialism as the first classless mode of production, and therefore the first truly universal civilisation, was the only possible progressive alternative to moribund capitalism. The final (and first genuinely *human*) epoch of history was at hand.

Orthodox Marxism had, in Lenin's view, correctly located the progressive drive of capitalism in its competitive market structure. In a situation where a whole number of enterprises compete for the available market there is a built-in incentive for technological innovation. On pain of failure and bankruptcy the capitalist must constantly retool and refine the machinery deployed: 'The bourgeoisie cannot exist without constantly revolutionising the instruments of production'.[4] At the minimum the capitalist must keep pace with the average level of productive efficiency in his or her area of trade, and produce goods within what Marx termed the 'socially necessary labour time'. We have, at this point, to sketch in some elements of Marx's economic analysis that Lenin rather took for granted. Unless we do so we cannot understand the novelty of his analysis and the impact it made.

According to Marx, capitalism historically signifies the triumph of commodity production. Commodities are goods with a use value expressly produced for sale in the market. Previous modes of production had, of course, produced goods for sale on the market but no other productive system had relied so universally and exclusively on the production of commodities. Under capitalism, unlike all earlier modes of production, *everything* had its market price – useful goods, labour power, skills and professions, women's favours, art and learning – all were reduced to a sordid cash nexus. The historical originality of capitalism was that virtually every major group within society depended for its survival on its ability to sell its goods, services or raw labour power on the market. The market, therefore, was that complex process of exchange where all these enormously varied commodities sought buyers and sellers and found their values relative one to another. For the whole business to work there had to be, in Marx's view, some common denominator they all shared so that an equivalence of exchange could be arrived at. And the only thing they all shared was that they embodied labour power. The volume of labour power that went into the production of any commodity was, therefore, the measure of its worth. This was, in Marx's time, considered a fairly orthodox precept of political economy (at least as old as John Locke's Second Treatise) known as the labour theory of value. In very general terms then, goods exchanged against each other according to the volume of labour power they contained.

There was, however, one unique commodity upon which the whole cycle of capitalist production intimately depended, and this was labour power itself. It was, indeed, part of Marx's definition of capitalism that it was the stage of commodity production at which labour power itself becomes a commodity. In simple terms, capitalism, according to Marx, exists wherever wage labour is the predominant form of gaining a living. People who have, as a consequence of the early processes of capitalist accumulation (sometimes called the primitive accumulation of capital), become separated from their own forces of production (small farm or artisan workshop) are forced to hire themselves out as labourers. Their survival depends upon their ability to find someone to buy their labour power. What, then, is the value of the labour power they bring for sale to the market? It is the same as that governing the value of all other commodities, namely the labour time requisite for its production. And the cost of production of labour power is the labour time that, on average, is expended in producing food, shelter and clothing for the worker. Operating the labour theory of value therefore, we should, says Marx, expect the labourer to receive no more than that minimum necessary to keep him in his condition as a labouring being. '*The price of his labour* will, therefore, be determined by the *price of the necessary means of subsistence*'.[5] In fact, this is, on average, what s/he receives – the cost price of her/his own production.

What keeps capitalism going is the difference between the stock of values the labourer *produces* and the stock of values *received* in wages. Labour power is unique among commodities in that it alone generates more value than it consumes. Until or unless it does so there could be no economically rational motive in employing anyone. Marxist (and Leninist) economics seizes upon the obvious fact that the whole motive for employing someone is precisely the calculation that the value of goods produced will be greater than the value of goods consumed (or paid as wages). This difference is known as surplus value. Now, if the value of labour power (wages) remains static, while technology increases productive efficiency, the difference between the value of goods produced by the worker and the value of goods represented by wages must grow. Surplus value should, therefore, increase. But, Marx observes, this ignores one crucial factor, namely that the costs of technical innovation have to be paid for and charged, as it were, against the surplus value extracted from the workers. Competitive capitalism is, in fact, fated to undergo a constant decrease of its rate of profit precisely because its inner dynamic compels it to invest increasingly in machines rather than in labour power. Machines, in this analysis, cannot *create* value (only living labour power does that). Machines merely transmit the 'dead' labour power that they embody.

According to Marx's classic model, labour power alone is the generator of value. It creates more than it consumes, and the greater the speed of technological innovation, the greater the disparity between the volume of production and the capacity of the market to absorb it. This process of technical change inevitably means, however, that the

capitalist has to invest ever-greater resources in plant and machinery –
or what is referred to as Constant Capital. Competitors are always
forcing the technological pace, and the capitalist has to keep up with
them to stay in the game. The problem here is that, according to the
labour theory of value, machines do not create values, they merely
transmit them. If a machine takes 200 man hours to build, it will
transmit to the products it helps to create no more than that stock of
values, expressed in labour time, that it contains. But if the volume of
expenditure on machinery constantly grows at the expense of
expenditure on wage labour (or what is called Variable Capital) then
there must be a tendency for the rate of profit to decrease. Put another
way – if labour power is the sole source of value, and expenditure on it
constitutes a constantly diminishing proportion of total capital
expenditure, then it follows that the rate of extraction of surplus value
(and therefore of profit) must show a tendency to decline.

   The capitalist, faced by this remorseless tendency of the rate of profit
to decline, has to respond. He cannot unilaterally raise the price of the
goods he produces above the general market level, for then no buyers
would be found and he would rapidly go out of business. The only
option left is to increase the rate of surplus value by increasing the
exploitation of the workforce. This can be done in three principal ways:

1. By increasing the length of the working day.
2. By decreasing the rate of pay.
3. By speeding up the work process.

In these ways the capitalist can extract a greater stock of values from
the workforce for the same (or less) expenditure on wages. There are,
however, finite limits to these devices. The working day cannot be
expanded continually: the workers have to have a modicum of rest to
replenish their energies for the next day's work. Wages cannot for long
be reduced below minimum subsistence (their normal level) without,
again, impairing the labourer's ability to maintain him/herself as a
labouring being. Nor can the pace of the work process be infinitely
speeded up – it necessarily involves a complex division of labour and
can only proceed at the pace that the average labourer can sustain.
Despite these reservations there was, Marx believed, a necessary
process at work here that led to the constant worsening of the worker's
situation. Basically, he argued that, regardless of any personal feelings
in the matter, the capitalist was forced to increase exploitation in a vain
attempt to sustain the rate of profit. One thing was certain, and this

was that 'the mass of misery, oppression, slavery, degradation and exploitation'[6] would grow rather than diminish as capitalism 'progressed'. This was the Absolute General Law of Capitalist Accumulation, according to Marx's *Capital*.

One of the large problems confronting Marxists in the early years of the twentieth century was to explain why this tendency towards impoverishment had not, in fact, occurred. There was strong evidence, from all parts of Europe, that the standard of living for most groups of workers had improved consistently in the latter part of the nineteenth century and at the beginning of the twentieth. For some there had been considerable gains, not only in material conditions, but also in security, negotiating rights, legal protection, welfare and educational provision. The growing wave of revolutionary sentiment that was predicated on the worsening of conditions had conspicuously failed to materialise.

The Export of Capital

Lenin's basic response to these problems of the Marxist model of revolution was to argue that the capitalists had, through a series of interrelated stratagems, managed to buy a little extra time for their exploitative mode of production, but only at the cost of making its internal and its international contradictions ever more flagrant and intolerable. The plasters they had applied could not cure the deep infection and nothing now could stop the boil from bursting.

The first stratagem they had adopted, in their frantic attempts to arrest the tendency of the rate of profit to decline, was to engage in wholesale export, first of manufactured goods, and then of capital. 'Typical of the old capitalism, when competition held undivided sway, was the export of *goods*. Typical of the latest stage of capitalism, when monopolies rule, is the export of *capital*.'[7]

The metropolitan capitalist countries found themselves, towards the end of the nineteenth century, with a glut of capital resources that could find no profitable outlets in the home market and was therefore compelled to explore the prospects of investment abroad:

The need to export capital arises from the fact that in a few countries Capitalism has become 'overripe' and (owing to the backward state of agriculture and the poverty of the masses) capital cannot find a field for 'profitable' investment.[8]

Capital, true to form, sought avenues of investment that would yield the highest possible return and realised that, with the saturation of the home market, these were largely to be found abroad. There the scarcity value of capital resources was far greater and the workforce had lower material expectations and no defensive organisations. There were valuable stocks of raw materials that could be exploited (or at least denied to competitors). Rail, road and harbour networks needed financing, factories needed to be built and armies equipped. If all this greatly extended the national debts of weaker peripheral countries, then so much the better, for they too provided lucrative and relatively stable outlets for super-abundant capital. Moving out of the rigours of a competitive internal market into regions where capital was scarce, and where human and natural resources could be exploited ruthlessly, yielded profit margins far above the norm. There was, consequently, according to Lenin, a flood of capital export in the last two decades of the twentieth century that coincided exactly with the enormous territorial expansion of Britain, France and Belgium. These countries had, by the end of the nineteenth century, become predominantly exporters of capital rather than exporters of commodities. Their economies were sustained by colonial exploitation and the huge returns yielded by exported capital. Their relative prosperity was almost wholly attributable to their role as international parasites. They had become rentier states living by 'clipping coupons' and pocketing the returns from foreign investments.[9] Lenin's account of the export of capital in the latter part of the nineteenth century, and the consequent development of parasitism, was, as he concedes, largely derivative of John Hobson's study *Imperialism: A Study* published in 1902.

Part of the originality of Lenin's argument (and one that was to become central to later theories of neo-colonialism) was that exploitation could no longer be conceived exclusively in *class* terms. The epoch of imperialism had produced the phenomenon of *national* exploitation. The world (which had already been appropriated and shared out between the principal capitalist countries) was divided increasingly into exploiter and exploited nations. There were rentier states, semi-colonies (outwardly independent but in fact dependent on the dictates of foreign capital) and outright dependencies or colonies: 'The world has become divided into a handful of usurer states and a vast majority of debtor states.'[10] Capital, in the imperialist phase, had become an international weapon of subjugation, and its patterns of exploitation had become universal so that the whole world was drawn into its web. The cost of extracting 'super profits' from foreign investment was, therefore, that the contradictions and oppressive nature of capitalism had become global in extent.

Super-profits, according to Lenin's analysis, sustained the imperialist bourgeoisie in a number of ways:

(i)   They helped to avert the spiralling crises that Marx had predicted would flow from the falling rate of profit – the 'Achilles' heel' of bourgeois civilization.

(ii)   They could, in part at least, be used to improve the material conditions of certain key groups of workers within the metropolitan economy – to create a 'labour aristocracy'.

(iii)   Since broad strata of the population could be shown to have benefited from colonial exploitation, fertile ground was created for the fostering of an imperialist ideology in which the 'national interest' could plausibly be conflated with the interests of finance capital.

(iv)   Protection of these 'national interests' could be projected as a matter of great state importance and campaigns for rearmament, naval superiority and so on, convincingly canvassed.

(v)   Expanded military and naval expenditure, and the consequent expansion of the national debt, themselves provided further lucrative sources of super-profits for finance capital.

State Monopoly Capitalism

It is clear just from the above list that the epoch of monopoly capitalism, or imperialism, or finance capitalism (for the three terms are used interchangeably in the canon of Leninism), signified the end of the classical liberal economics of *laisser faire, laisser passer*. The notion of the minimal night-watchman state, whose concerns were to be restricted to maintaining public order and defence against external aggressors, was no longer plausible. The old liberalism was thoroughly at odds with the ever-increasing interventionism of the modern imperialist state. Far from being wholly concerned with maintaining law internally, and providing defence against external attack, the imperialist state had emerged by the end of the nineteenth century (and even more decisively in the First World War) as the dominant economic actor within the national economy. It promoted the wholesale expansion of economic territory through colonization, it put up high tariff barriers to protect internal monopolies from foreign competition. It imposed upon the whole population high taxes to pay for the vastly increased military and naval expenditure.

The wartime imperialist state not only altered dramatically the fiscal and tariff milieu in which industry operated: it became the major productive association within the national economy. It not only set the conditions in which trade and industry developed, it also became the major trading and industrial organisation. During the war, as Bukharin,[11] and later Lenin, observed, the imperialist state qualitatively altered in nature:

the war has done more than was done for twenty-five years. State control of industry has made progress in Britain as well as in Germany. Monopoly, in general, has evolved into state monopoly.[12]

From being an enabling agency for a market economy, it became the principal owner of capital resources, employer of labour, dictator of the norms of consumption, and controller of access to credit for the whole of the economy. It emerged as the indispensable guarantor of the whole cycle of capitalist production. Without it, the cycle could not be repeated. It followed, therefore, that in its monopolistic degenerate phase, capitalism could only survive as state capitalism. The imperialist state formation was, essentially, a state capitalist trust in which the state itself featured as a trust of trusts.

As the banks had suborned manufacturing industry with their power to grant or withhold credit and investment funds, so now they used their power, as the paymasters of states, to control and dominate governments. Now the circle was complete. The personnel and policies of banking or finance capital fused with those of the state. The state capitalist trust was born which could now dictate foreign and domestic policy, the expenditures it entailed, and the supplies it demanded. As leaders of the state, the bankers could guarantee demand, and also their returns, by setting taxes on the population as citizens, and tariffs on them as consumers. They could compensate themselves generously for obsolete industries deemed to be appropriate for state control and, finally, limit by law the pretensions of trade unions for higher wages and better conditions. They came to realise, in short, that whereas the minimalist states served competition and the free market, the imperialist state, *directly* under the control of the finance capitalists, best suited monopoly capitalism. The state, like the banks, from being a modest intermediary of competing interests, now became the directing and controlling centre of monopoly capitalism. Without maintaining its control of the state, monopoly capitalism could not survive. The state therefore no longer passively reflected existing allocations of power and wealth, but was itself the principal agency for creating and reproducing them. This wholly new political/economic structure:

> turned the old capitalism, the capitalism of the free competition age, into the capitalism of giant trusts, syndicates and cartels . . . introduced the beginnings of state-controlled capitalist production, combining the colossal power of capitalism with the colossal power of the state into a single mechanism and bringing tens of millions of people within the single organisation of state capitalism.[13]

Evidence of the ever-growing intrusiveness of the state was not hard to find. The 'heights of the economy', comprising the heavy-industry infrastructure and transport, had been nationalised. The big banks had been brought under governmental control or ownership, and therewith the state controlled the whole nervous system of the modern economy, especially the crucial matter of access to investment funds and credit. The right to strike had been eliminated, and in many cases the right to move jobs had also been proscribed. Rationing had been introduced, and non-negotiable wage settlements imposed. The state had, in short, acquired awesome powers to control all the factors of production and exchange. Since it controlled resource allocation, wages, prices, taxes and tariffs, it could, to a large extent, control the volume of the social surplus at its disposal, and guarantee the profitability and survival of the finance capitalist interests that it served. This was the last stand of capitalism as an historical phenomenon. It had begun with heroic defiance to the arbitrary and despotic power of the feudal state, it had proceeded in its competitive heyday to revitalise society and, consequently, to rely upon a minimal state. Now, in the hour of its necrosis, its own social power had evaporated, it had moved to extinguish unreliable and fractious civil society and to rely wholly and exclusively on the might of a vastly expanded, armed and economically integrated state power. It had created, in Bukharin's famous words 'The New Leviathan beside which the Leviathan of Thomas Hobbes seems but a child's plaything'.[14]

This analysis of the relationship between the development of capitalism and the development of the state was absolutely central to the initial formulation of Leninism, and thereafter it continued to distinguish it from other political creeds. Its principal conclusion is that in proportion as capitalism becomes monopolistic, it becomes degenerate and parasitic, expansionist and coercive, revealing itself as state-directed violence. The more degenerate capitalism becomes, and the shallower the social base of its power, the more authoritarian and oppressive its state power becomes. All imperialist states, regardless of the constitutional garb in which they dress themselves, are, therefore, dictatorships of finance capitalism.[15] This highly theorised, essentialist analysis of the bourgeois state formation was to have the most fateful consequences for the politics of the Soviet Union, as we shall see in the next chapter.

The principal polemical point of Lenin's analysis of imperialism and finance capitalism was to give the lie to social-democratic optimists that the very processes of capitalist accumulation brought ineluctable advance towards socialisation, and therefore towards socialism. In their eyes, each advance of the state as organiser of society and of the economy was proof positive of their case that the anarchy of a market economy had finally become intolerable. The whole economy, they fondly believed, would gradually be transformed to work with the benign public purpose of the post office. Socialism would come dripping down in increments of the consistent advance of state power and democratic influence. The reformists all embraced variants of the Fabian optimism in the inevitability of gradualness. These were what Lenin contemptuously referred to as 'the socialism on credit' men who, like all opportunists, pursued the path of least resistance. But the path of least resistance was always, in Lenin's view, the path of acceptance of bourgeois dominance. Its advocates, far from building socialism, had become accomplices of the almighty imperialist state, apologists for its politics, and corrupters of the labour movement. Imperatively, they had to be exposed as the Trojan horse of imperialism within the labour movement, because it was they who had managed so successfully to convince the working class that the agencies of their incorporation into the imperialist state were in fact progressive. Leaders of this kidney were not simply mistaken, they were traitors to socialism and had to be exposed as such:

> objectively the *opportunists* are a section of the petty bourgeoisie and of a certain strata of the working class who *have been bribed* out of imperialist superprofits and converted into *watchdogs* of capitalism and *corrupters* of the labour movement.[16]

The Phasal Development of Capitalism

Capitalism was not, in Lenin's analysis, a frozen, unchanging phenomenon. It had its own natural history of turbulent early growth, settled maturity, and final decadence. During its maturity (a phase which, according to Lenin's chronology, spanned approximately the century 1770–1870), capitalism had been progressive precisely because it had been competitive. There were other aspects of this period that could also be termed progressive. On the whole, Lenin grudgingly admitted, the political culture and political structures typical of this period had provided possibilities for the emancipation of ordinary people which they had never before enjoyed. The gradual extension of the franchise had been complemented by the extension of civil and political rights which, though limited, provided the means through which the working classes could, for the first time in history, begin to organise themselves under the protection of law. At this time too, the state was generally restricted in its scope and its pretensions. It was, of course, a hollow nonsense, in Lenin's view, to maintain that the liberal state was neutral in the class struggle, but at least it had not yet spawned a great bureaucracy or extensive standing army.

All this was to change. In the forty-odd years from 1870 to 1914 the nature of capitalism and of its state form underwent, according to Lenin, profound and regressive changes. The essence of these changes was the transformation of competitive capitalism into monopoly capitalism, and finally into state monopoly capitalism. There were then, in Lenin's account, three principal epochs in the development of capitalism, each with its distinctive set of economic, social and political characteristics:

The first epoch from the Great French Revolution to the Franco-Prussian war is one of the rise of the bourgeoisie, of its triumph, of the bourgeoisie on the upgrade, an epoch of bourgeois-democratic movements in general and of bourgeois-national movements in particular, an epoch of the rapid breakdown of the obsolete feudal-absolutist institutions. The second epoch is that of the full domination and decline of the bourgeoisie, one of transition from its progressive character towards reactionary and even extra-reactionary finance capital . . . The third epoch, which has just set in, places the bourgeoisie in the same 'position' as that in which the feudal lords found themselves during the first epoch. This is the epoch of imperialism and imperialist upheavals . . . the epoch of the over-maturity and decay of the bourgeoisie, in a number of leading countries.[17]

Lenin was later to refine this periodisation somewhat and set back the commencement of the third, or decadent, phase of capitalist development to 1900. From that point on, he later concluded, competition yielded place to monopoly, entrepreneurial capital was displaced by finance or banking capital, and the export of capital prevailed over the export of goods. The chronological regression that Lenin generally held to can be schematised as follows.

First Period 1789–1870

Nascent and developing capitalism, progressive both as a mode of production (hugely more efficient than the feudalism it displaced) as well as in its relatively liberal and permissive political attitudes and constitutional arrangements.

Second Period 1870–1900

Developed and dominant capitalism turning towards monopoly and imperialism. Externally the economic territory of the entire world is appropriated by the great powers; internally confronted by mounting social contradictions (growth of socialism and organized labour) and increasingly reliant upon the power of the state for its maintenance and reproduction, free trade and the minimalist state cease to be the rallying watchwords of capitalism.

Third Period 1900–

Decadent and decaying monopoly capitalism that becomes, during the First World War, state monopoly capitalism, desperately attempting to sustain itself through colonial plunder and the bribery of an upper stratum of the workers; externally militarist and oppressive, internally monolithic and intolerant; civic and political freedoms suspended or withdrawn and the state becomes frankly dictatorial.

Finance Capital and the Banks

The process of monopolisation had begun modestly enough in the banking systems of the capitalist world and had, with growing momentum, proceeded outwards to swallow some of the most important sectors of the modern economy. The German economist Jeidells had been one of the first to notice the tendency towards monopoly within banking and his insights had been taken up and developed by the Austrian Marxist, Rudolf Hilferding.[18] Lenin was therefore, in terms of economics, hardly blazing new ground – as he freely admitted. He reported largely their evidence that, by the turn of the century, a handful of enormously powerful banks in most of the advanced capitalist countries had succeeded in swallowing up and absorbing the assets of a vast number of smaller local banks. In this way, Lenin observe, 'Scattered capitalists are transformed into a single collective capital.'[19] The big banks, from being mere intermediaries, facilitating exchange and payment, had become all-powerful institutions that controlled access to credit and investment funds on a national scale. It was but a short and inevitable step, in Lenin's account, for the banks to make use of the power they now exercised over even the largest enterprises, to create within the industries they now controlled, the same monopoly position they had developed for themselves. They began to intervene increasingly and to control whole areas of industry. In times of depression they bought out the small and less efficient enterprises 'for a mere song or promoted profitable schemes for their "reconstruction" and "reorganisation".'[20] They encouraged the establishment of the largest integrated or 'combined' plants situated with the best access to raw materials and markets. They brought to industry precisely the same devices they themselves had employed in order to guarantee their own maximum returns – absorption, annexation, cartelization and trustification. Their object was the consistent one of eliminating competition, or at least moderating its influence, within the sectors of trade and industry that they dominated.

In this way, the big banks transformed themselves from auxiliary transmission belts of entrepreneurial and manufacturing capitalism into the prime movers and motors of an historically new form of capitalism.[21] The dominance of manufacturing, or industrially based capital, gave way to that of banking or finance capital. It established a new mode of production in which it held unquestioned sway. In the process it created vast, integrated corporations (either unitary, or federated in trusts and cartels) that now saw to the extraction of raw materials on a world-wide basis, and refined and processed those materials in huge plants that developed the socialisation of labour to an extraordinary degree. It was *these* plants, Lenin maintained, that aggregated great masses of workers together in a highly complex division of labour, highly capitalised and consuming a disproportionate share of electrical power, that characterised the new mode of production: 'Tens of thousands of huge enterprises are everything; millions of small ones are nothing.'[22] But it was typical of the new mode of production that not only were the businesses of extraction, transportation and manufacture brought under single integrated control, the process of distribution was as well. The trusts and cartels built up comprehensive distributive networks of warehouses and retail outlets to oversee the marketing of their products. The significance of this qualitatively new system of production was that, for the first time in history, there had emerged the *possibility* of matching production to consumer needs. To some extent, in some countries and in some sectors of industry, the chaotic planlessness of competitive capitalism (what Marxists refer to as the anarchy of production) had been overcome. The monopolistic trusts and cartels could, at least in theory, schedule the extraction and transportation of raw materials, their processing, and the distribution of finished goods, according to informed predictions of market needs; and all this on an international scale. In this way, the potential was created for overcoming the recurrent crises of overproduction and underconsumption that had so plagued capitalism. It was, however, only a *potential*, which, Lenin emphasised, could not be realised under capitalism except in a limited and distorted manner.

There were, according to Lenin, profound and irresolvable structural imbalances in the whole system of capitalist production and market distribution that could not be overcome within the framework of private property. One of these was the disparity in development between industry and agriculture, another was a similar disparity between the developed world and the underdeveloped world. There was, finally, the long-term disparity between the capacity of the market to absorb the product and the greatly expanded volume and value of the commodities being produced. The capitalists, in short, could not reduce the rate of exploitation of their workforce because that was the source of their profit. But the more that was withheld from their employees in this way, the smaller became the capacity of consumers to absorb the product. In the long term this incapacity of the market to absorb the product would prove fatal to the whole possibility of repeating the cycle of production. It was, of course, precisely in order to offset this underconsumptionist tendency that the metropolitan capitalist countries had embarked upon programmes of export of goods (and subsequently of super-abundant capital) that could not be employed profitably on the home market. This, however, only postponed the final crisis of capitalism, it did not eradicate it. On the contrary, it exacerbated the imbalances and unevenness of the global economy.

The Uneven Development of Capitalism

The distinctive nature of Leninism as an analysis of international finance capitalism is contained in its stress upon uneven development. Some earlier Marxist theorists – Rudolf Hilferding, and especially Nikolai Bukharin – had put considerable stress upon the capacity of the banks and trusts to plan production to match output with consumption. Bukharin came perilously close to arguing that, with the advent of state monopoly capitalism, the anarchy of production had largely been overcome. An 'organised' capitalism superintended by the state, and therefore increasingly able to produce the conditions of its own stability and continuity, was in the process of evolving. The historical originality of the bourgeois state, in Bukharin's view, was that far from being the passively determined object of the economic base of society, it had itself become the central economic actor at the macro level. Bukharin's somewhat astounding conclusion (which was to be of enormous importance in later Bolshevik theory of the state) was that in the epoch of imperialism the political superstructure determined the economic base rather than the reverse.[23] To Lenin, this analysis, though brilliant in its intellectual rigour and daring in its conclusions, was overly abstracted and lacking in dialectical nuance. That there was a clear tendency for monopoly or finance capitalism to establish its sway and that it had, in fact, done so, Lenin did not doubt. But that fact ought not, he maintained, obscure the equally incontrovertible fact that *some* sectors of the economy (whether national or global) lagged far behind and were at relatively primitive stages of capitalist evolution. Nor did Lenin doubt that, especially during the war, monopoly capitalism had evolved into state monopoly capitalism where the state's role in guaranteeing the conditions for capitalist accumulation and reproduction had become decisive. But this did not mean that the imperialist state had managed to overcome the anarchy of production or to quell the social tensions of a class-divided society. On the contrary, its temporary palliatives merely exacerbated basic structural diseases.

The modern economy was, in all countries, multi-layered, in Lenin's account. Finance capital, in establishing its dominance, did not thereby liquidate industrial, manufacturing, merchant or landed capital. Similarly, the decisive international influence of Britain and France and their imperialist pre-eminence could not for ever obscure the antagonisms between exploiter and exploited, between the imperialist rentier state and the strivings for economic and political independence of their colonies and semi-colonies. According to Lenin, the crucial destabilising feature of the whole global system of capitalism was the different stages that differing sectors of industry and different countries found themselves at in the processes of capital accumulation.

There were, in the Leninist analysis, four basic phases of capital accumulation. The first is what Marx and subsequent Marxists referred to as 'the primitive accumulation of capital'. Essentially, this was accomplished through the forcible (or fiscal) extraction of a 'surplus' from agricultural production. In the second phase the emphasis is upon investment in production of the means of production – railways, machine tools, the construction of plant and communications. In the third phase, consumer goods quickly glut the market and a surplus of capital resources is generated that cannot be absorbed on the home market. It is at this point, as we have seen, that the export of capital becomes not just an adventitious device, but necessary to the maintenance of capitalist production relations. The system cannot sustain itself without such massive exports of capital. This, in turn, leads to physical intervention to protect investment and to guarantee returns. The whole world now becomes a terrain of plunder for which the principal imperialist powers compete. They are driven to expand their economic territory and do so, very roughly, in proportion to their relative economic strength at that time.

The problem is that *after* the world has been divided up and the fixed lines drawn on the globe, the process of capitalist accumulation proceeds apace and at differing rates. Relative newcomers to industrialisation (such as Germany, Japan and the United States) appear, and they too come to suffer from a glut of capital resources in search of outlets. But they encounter a world already carved up, claimed, and protected against them. The only way open for them to press their claims to 'a place in the sun' is to fight for it, since the first comers would not voluntarily relinquish their effective monopoly of the economic territory of the whole world. The battle for the economic territory of the world, for its redivision, could not, however, be conducted by trusts, cartels or banks, no matter how powerful; it could be conducted only by states. And the parties to this titanic struggle could aspire to victory only if their total resources were mobilised and organised. Once again it was only state power that had the resources and the authority to emerge as the mobiliser and organiser of the nation's resources. The more each competitor state in the global battle assumed this role, the more every other competitor took fright and justified *its* interventionism by reference to the external threat and the need to retain (or claim) international dominance. The whole process of heightened international tension and conflict was both cause and effect of an increasingly militant imperialist ideology that identified national interest with trading interest, and bolstered and legitimised itself by reference to the hostile and predatory intentions of other world actors.

Imperialism and World Politics

In the Leninist conception of international politics in the age of imperialism there is a remorseless and constantly escalating battle for economic territory. Economic territory may mean straightforward annexation as a colony. There the imperialist power will enjoy the rights of plundering natural material resources and ruthlessly exploiting the workforce. At the very least it denies these opportunities to potential competitors. It will create exclusive access for its own exports of goods or capital. Economic territory may also mean a sphere of influence where the metropolitan regime effectively controls the economic life of ostensibly politically independent regimes. These semi-colonies will be bound by treaty and commercial agreements to grant privileged access to the metropolitan country for supply of commodities and capital resources. Its industrial infrastructure, communications and even its national debt will be controlled from outside. Old-fashioned specifications of national independence, stressing as they did juridical conceptions of the enforcement of a common law over a geographically delimited area, and a monopoly of coercive power within it, were, in the epoch of imperialism, of little account. Of the many nation states in the world, only a handful could claim genuine independence in the sense that their internal and external policies were unconstrained by the economic power exerted upon them by a third party.

In the Leninist analysis, the imperialist world was divided into three leagues. In division one were the great powers, the metropolitan finance capitalist countries whose power derived, ultimately, from massive export of capital. First among these was Britain, with France not far behind. Lurking in the wings, growing apace and threatening their sovereignty, were the rapidly expanding economies of Germany, the USA and Japan. On the world stage these were the only countries that mattered – all the rest danced to their tune. Their powers, relative to one another, changed in proportion to the growth or decline of their economies. There could be no permanence or fixity in any international settlement or set of alliances – these things merely reflected relative power at a given moment and would be revised as soon as it became apparent that the relative powers of the contracting parties had altered. The great powers were, in short, locked into a remorseless competition for power that could only be resolved by war. War, Lenin concluded, was the natural condition of the epoch of monopoly capitalism or imperialism.

The second division in the international arena was made up of ostensibly independent nation states with the ritual trappings of what was called autonomy or sovereignty – legislative and executive powers, courts, prisons, police and army. But, in Lenin's analysis, these were but emperor's clothes. They disguised only from their wearers their own powerlessness to act independently. Their governments were, to all intents and purposes, proxy governments, with only a limited field of initiative in those areas which were of no immediate concern to their foreign economic backers. The social structure upon which they were built was similarly cramped and restricted in the options available to it. The indigenous bourgeoisie acted as little more than the agent of foreign capital. It had been established by foreign capital and trained to fulfil its behests. It had no autonomous roots in its local culture, and no traditions of organisation or of struggle to assert its own class interests. It was a weak and enfeebled group that hitherto had failed to display the all-important attributes of a genuinely class existence – national organisation and the ability to articulate its own interests. It was, in short, a comprador bourgeoisie. Similar strictures were advanced against the political incapacity of the swelling ranks of bureaucrats and functionaries, whose prime function it was to devise and implement ever more swingeing and comprehensive systems of taxation to finance the national debt that was itself underwritten by foreign finance capital. As with the social base of these semi-colonies, so with their political stance – dependence bred dependence.

There would, however, in Lenin's view, come a time when even this supine bourgeoisie would be roused to assert itself against the depredations of foreign capital and become a genuinely national bourgeoisie. At that moment it would become a progressive force *vis-à-vis* international finance capitalism. Any movement that threatened the interests of finance capital by denying it protected markets and a *carte blanche* for the ruthless exploitation of indigenous resources and labour would, necessarily threaten its super-profits. Then the downward spiral of the falling rate of profit would make itself felt increasingly in the metropolitan countries, along with its revolutionary consequences. The national bourgeoisie of the semi-colonies was therefore a vitally important potential ally in the world-wide struggle against imperialism. In so far as its objectives were to promote national economic independence, deny markets to monopoly capital, generate its own investment funds, and assert itself as a genuinely independent political actor, it threatened the hegemony of imperialism. In the first stages of the global battle it was therefore imperative for communists to lend their support to the movement for national liberation. In the Leninist scheme of world revolution, as we shall see, the victory of the *socialist* revolution in the developed countries was integrally connected with the victory of the *national* revolution in the colonies and semi-colonies. Together they would constitute a united front against world imperialism.

The third division was occupied by colonies and dependencies that did not even enjoy a fictional independence. They were in no sense political subjects; they were the objects of the power of others. Neither in law nor in constitutional theory did these countries enjoy even a notional independence. And yet the idea that they formed part of the 'mother country', and were to be raised to a position of material and cultural equality with it, was equally a fiction. In Lenin's view, the disparity between stated intentions (bringing civilization, dignity and order) and actual accomplishment (bloodshed, extreme exploitation and ethnic divisiveness) was too glaring to be long sustained: 'In this sense imperialism is indisputably the "negation" of *democracy in general*, of *all democracy*, and not just *one* of its demands, national self-determination.'[24] The colonial peoples would not for long stomach the indignity and oppression to which they were subject. Every movement to assert labour rights or national rights would increase the costs of imperial supervision and control of 'the natives'. There would come a point when the costs of maintaining colonial despotism would outweigh the returns, and the imperialist powers would be forced to withdraw. For the moment, Lenin agreed, this might appear a forlorn prospect when the armed might of the state capitalist trust was measured against the puny fighting forces for national liberation. But in the end sheer weight of numbers would prevail. The long-term logistics and demography of the world balance of power were, unquestionably, on the side of the oppressed and exploited nations. They comprised the overwhelming majority of the world's population and, in the long run, all the devices of the imperialist powers to suppress their quest for freedom would be in vain.

The modern world of imperialism was then, in the Leninist account, a world of profound and irresolvable contradictions. On the one hand, capitalism had, through supra-national trusts, disclosed tendencies for the internationalisation of capital. What we might today call the multinational corporations had an interest in the peaceful division of the world into spheres of interest for the exploitation of resources and as zones for the investment of surplus capital. Precisely these themes were taken up by Karl Kautsky in his theory of 'Super imperialism'. On the other hand, imperialist states recognised increasingly the imperative to expand their economic territory, and to claim colonies and semi-colonies as their exclusive preserves. To do this, and to deny access to all competitors, they mobilised all the nation's resources aggressively under the aegis of the state. International trusts and cartels might, therefore, have an interest in a sort of super-imperialism where nations would agree peacefully to a distribution or redistribution of the world. But the world of states in the epoch of imperialism was the world of gladiatorial combat between rival state capitalist trusts, armed to the teeth and ruthlessly pursuing their own individual advantage. This was a restless war of each against all that could only be resolved in armed conflict:

The question is: what means other than war could there be under Capitalism to overcome the disparity between the development of productive forces and the accumulation of capital on the one side, and the division of colonies and spheres of influence for finance capital on the other?[25]

The hostile opposition of interests among imperialist states constituted, in Lenin's view, the principal contradiction of the modern world. Where each state's gain was perceived as another state's loss, where the economic territory of the world was finite, already claimed, and hotly disputed, and where uneven development was inherent in capitalist evolution; there would be permanent wars of ever-increasing dimensions; the costs of maintaining the entire structure of oppression would become intolerable.

The subsidiary, but vitally important, contradiction besetting the modern world was the hostile opposition of interests between the imperialist powers on the one hand, and the colonies and semi-colonies on the other. The striving to free themselves from foreign economic exploitation and political domination could not long be suppressed. In universalising its contradictions, finance capitalism had assured itself of a global revolutionary explosion. Class war had become international in a qualitatively new way in the epoch of imperialism. It had become the battle for emancipation for whole nations that were exploited by other nations:

> Capitalism itself gradually provides the subjugated with the means and resources for their emancipation and they set out to achieve the goal which once seemed highest to the European nations: the creation of a limited national state as a means to economic and cultural freedom. This movement for national independence threatens European capital in its most valuable and most promising fields of exploitation, and European capital can maintain its dominance only by continually increasing its military forces.[26]

The imperialist *states* (not simply particular classes within them) had become the principal exploiting agencies *vis-à-vis* their colonies. Whole national groups now participated in exploitation, as whole national groups were subject to it. The phenomenon of rentier *states* (as distinct from a particular class of rentiers), existing parasitically by exacting tribute from other states, had qualitatively altered the nature of international exploitation and class war. The socialist revolution was intimately tied to the movement for national liberation. This was to be one of the most potent and extraordinarily successful elements of Leninism.

The final essential contradiction of the modern world was the hostile opposition of the interests of the proletariat and those of the finance capitalists. At its simplest level this expressed itself as the international striving of all those employed wholly as wage labourers to free themselves from the exploitation they suffered at the hands of monopoly capitalism. This essential contradiction was, however, obscured in the contemporary world by two inter-related factors. The first of these was the persistent tendency to regard the state as a neutral body representing the whole nation, and therefore claiming the allegiance of the whole population. The second was the dominance of social democratic or reformist ideas leading the working class to believe in the possibility of a gradual piecemeal transition to socialism within the existing political and socioeconomic conditions. This was, of course, particularly the case with the 'aristocracy of labour', whose privileged positions within the workforce derived, according to Lenin, from participating in a share of the super-profits extracted from colonial exploitation. The major thrust of Leninism in its early formulation was to dispute and to expose these illusions that so paralysed the will of the proletariat.

Lenin's theory of imperialism did a great deal more than explain the war. It provided Lenin's followers, then and since, with a comprehensive world view whose basis was the finding that capitalism, its political structures and the bourgeois values upon which they were based, was in its death throes. A civilisation, a whole epoch in the history of humanity, was finally drowning in blood. The purpose of his whole analysis was to demonstrate that this entire civilisation, this whole period of history, had declared its own bankruptcy. It could not be reformed or redeemed – it had reached its final brutal impasse and now had to be swept aside so that a new era could be born. The necrosis of capitalism coincided, therefore, with the revolution for socialism; this, for Lenin, was the central reality of the contemporary world.

Socialism as the Transcendence of Imperialism

In dialectical thought all things constitute a unity of opposites. So capitalism, in its final stage of degeneration, was, simultaneously, creating the very structures through which it was to be transcended into a new and higher civilisation – socialism. In its last desperate efforts to save itself it was, paradoxically, compelled to create the very systems of economic management that constituted, in Lenin's eyes, a halfway house to socialism. Wartime state capitalism had already nationalised the commanding heights of the economy. The big banks had been brought under the direction of the state and, therewith, the state had the effective capacity to direct all credit and investment allocation to the entire economy. Here, in Lenin's view, was an excellent apparatus, ready made and available 'at a stroke' to the socialists to introduce a nationwide system of bookkeeping and accountancy. The trusts and cartels, similarly, had already established effective monopolies in crucial areas of production and distribution that facilitated enormously the task of bringing the economy under social control. The formerly unrealisable *potential* of finance capitalism could, at last, be realised in practice. Moribund capitalism, in its very struggle to delay its demise, was compelled to create the large-scale macroeconomic administrative structures that not only facilitated their transference to social control, but made that transfer the natural and necessary next stage. The theory of imperialism demonstrated, to Lenin's followers at least, that socialism was not only desirable as a goal, and necessary to end the war, it was also immediately practicable on the basis of the organisational and administrative structures created by state capitalism. It was, indeed, as Lenin repeatedly insisted, the only way to overcome the destruction and economic ruin that the war had produced everywhere in Europe.

The dialectics of imperialism were also (by 1917 at least) applied to the imperialist state. In proportion as it struggled to contain the explosive contradictions of social unrest, colonial discontent and the ruinous costs of international war, it was obliged to come out ever more openly, as the brutal defender of the profits of the monopolists. State monopoly capitalism, in which the state intervened overtly to limit the bargaining power of trade unions, prohibit strikes, forbid movement of labour, and control wages and rations, would finally expose the sham of the state's neutrality. The prolongation of the war, and the death and destruction it wrought, would finally dissolve the basis of legitimation of the modern nation state. By bringing the world beyond the brink of madness into mutual self-destruction, the state form of the bourgeoisie, the last bastion defending its profits and its rights to colonial plunder, declared its final redundancy and forfeited its claim to the allegiance of its citizens. Without the organising, ideological and punitive power of the state, monopoly capitalism could not survive. It was, however, equally the case that without capitalism, the state (especially the discredited form of the rapacious nation state) was unnecessary and would have to be transcended by wholly new administrative forms.

We cannot even begin to understand Lenin's analysis of the nature of properly socialist administrative forms (set out in 1917 in *The State and Revolution*) unless we understand that these were directly premised on his prior (highly theorised) account of the cancerous nature of the modern nation state and its final discrediting during the war. His enthusiasm for the slogan/strategy 'All Power to the Soviets' stemmed directly from his earlier analysis of the reckless role of the state in its frenzied last stand as the guarantor of imperialist and bourgeois power and profit. Lenin came to believe, in late 1916, that capitalism and the state were twinned. The war had brought them both, locked together as one, to a final decadent and destructive terminus. There could be no destroying capitalism without the destruction of its directing centre. The demise of the one was the simultaneous death of the other. The state would have to be smashed. Such was the extraordinary radicalism into which Lenin's theoretical analysis led him. As the doctrinaire he was, he did not flinch from his conclusions despite the outrage they occasioned to even his most loyal supporters. It was, as we shall see in the next chapter, precisely his determination to act on highly theorised projects that was to impoverish the whole subsequent Leninist (and consequently Soviet) theory and practice of politics, and the very language in which it could be understood.

Another momentous conclusion of Lenin's theory of imperialism was that it redefined not merely the time, the chronology of epochal change from one system to its successor; it also fundamentally redefined the geographical space in which this transcendence was to occur. Socialism had hitherto been presented as an historical agenda relevant only to the most highly developed countries of the world. (The same, it might be said, applied to the other major ideologies of the nineteenth and early twentieth centuries – Western Europe had generated them and was their natural terrain.) Leninism introduced a wholly new geopolitical framework to ideological discourse. This was undoubtedly to be a major aspect of its cosmopolitan appeal. One of the basic axioms of the theory of international finance capital was that it could only be understood as a global system – a genuinely world-historical mode of production that universalised the basic divide of exploiter and exploited. At its most complex it set out an analysis of, on the one hand, the fundamental unity of the global economy, and, on the other, the uneven development of differing regions, countries and industries. One of its most basic postulates was that exploitation in the modern world was to be understood not simply as the extraction of surplus profits by one class from another but also, in the new global division of labour, the extraction of super-profits from one country by another. Whole nations now participated (however marginally for the majority) in the exploitation of other countries. The struggle for national independence and economic autonomy therefore became inseparable from the battle to end imperialist exploitation. Leninism touched the raw nerves of global politics in the twentieth century, and out of it, directly or indirectly, developed the pervasive contemporary analyses of neocolonialism and dependency theory.

Lenin's critique of global capitalism was tailor-made for the aspirations of colonial peoples. It provided a plausible account of the gross imbalances within their economies and fomented their growing sense of outrage at their permanent subaltern status. Lenin's theory of imperialism not only explained the motive for, and the nature of, imperial domination, it also precipitated the struggle for national independence suddenly into the forefront of the global anti-imperialist struggle. The battle for national and economic autonomy in the colonies was now presented as coextensive with, and necessary to, the struggle for socialism in the world at large. Lenin, indeed, redefined a socialist as one who, as a fundamental condition of his or her own liberation, is committed to the liberation of all peoples subjugated by one's own national state.

One of the strategic implications of Lenin's analysis of imperialism was that, given the integrity of the global system of capitalism, the analysis of the objective and subjective conditions for a revolutionary advance towards 'socialism could only be made on an *international* (rather than a narrowly national) basis. Capitalism, as a world system, would therefore break at the weakest link in its global chain. It by no means followed that this weakest link would be found in the most developed or the most highly industrialised countries. As we have seen, the Leninist analysis made this latter location for the commencement of the world revolution rather unlikely. In the most developed countries *all* classes, in their differing degrees, participated in colonial exploitation – that was the meaning of the imperialist rentier state. Whole sections even of the working class had been bought off with their paltry share of the super-profits of colonial exploitation and had fallen easy prey to traitorous labour leaders. An aristocracy of labour had effectively polluted class consciousness and dominated working class politics. In the advanced imperialist states the ideological apparatuses and coercive powers of the ruling classes had been refined and strengthened over generations.

In the semi-colonies, however, none of these countervailing factors prevailed. The native bourgeoisie was very weak: the legitimating rationale of state power did not even appeal to the fiction of popular consent. Exploitation of the indigenous workforce was severe, and unrestrained either by the moral limitations that prevailed elsewhere, or by the existence of effective trade unions. It was therefore in the periphery of the capitalist world that the beginnings of the revolution were most likely to occur, rather than in its metropolitan heartland where its defences were best developed and its contradictions less extreme. This was not, incidentally, as large a deviation from orthodox Marxism as most commentators would have us believe. Marx himself, while acknowledging that England was 'the demiurge of the bourgeois cosmos' with the most highly developed industry and most extensive and mature working class, never believed that *therefore* it fell to the English proletariat (whose very class existence he doubted) to begin the revolution. Marx, rather, believed in 1848 that France, or even thoroughly peripheral Germany, would begin the continental revolution for socialism. Whatever the dispute about the marxian propriety of Lenin's argument, there is no doubt that his theory of imperialism did provide his followers with what for them was a plausible and convincing explanation of why, in 1917, it fell to the Russians to begin the great assault on the global and epochal system of capitalism.

The theory of imperialism, and its derivative political strategies, unmistakably marked off Leninism, as an ideological statement and programme, from all competing strands of socialism. Its political point was obvious – those who contrived to maintain, however grudgingly and with whatever qualifications, that capitalism was still progressive and that, therefore, revolution was not on the immediate agenda, had become apologists for the carnage of imperialist war. On the other hand, those who agreed with the analysis of *imperialism* could not but see the continuation of capitalist civilization as the gravest threat to the existence of humanity. They would therefore also agree to the urgency of revolutionary action against it. In the dialectical logic of Leninism it therefore followed that those who were not prepared to commit themselves to revolutionary activity against imperialism, those who were not prepared to commit themselves to revolutionary activity to turn the imperialist war for plunder into a civil war for socialism, had, by their complacency, become the accomplices of degenerate imperialism. The line was drawn, the ideological hurdle set up: either assent to the propositions of imperialism and *therefore* to immediate revolutionary action to end both capitalism and war; or sustain the possibility of the further development of capitalism, postpone the revolution indefinitely, and support the war effort of one's own country. These were the dialectical poles of contemporary politics. All the so-called intermediary positions ('for a just peace', 'for a peace without annexations or indemnities') were, according to the dialectical reductionism of Leninism, no more than apologies for defencism. Objectively, as we have seen, such people were the lackeys of imperialism and the corrupters of the working class. This was the new brutalism of Leninist politics which was to be formulated in Lenin's infamous slogan 'He who is not for us is against us'.[27]

For the first time, Lenin provided his supporters with utterly distinct specifications of both the time and the space in which they were to live and act. Until that requirement had been met Leninism could not have existed as a distinctive ideological current with its own map of the contemporary world. The theory of imperialism was compass and chronometer of Leninism and contemporary communism.

6

Politics and the State

We have seen that in 1914 Lenin arrived at the conclusion that the whole historical epoch of capitalism was dissolving in internal and international contradictions. The epoch of revolutionary transformation to inaugurate the global triumph of socialism was firmly on the agenda. These findings were the distinguishing characteristics of Leninism as an emergent ideology and were theoretically vindicated in his text, *Imperialism, the Highest Stage of Capitalism*.[1] The questions that now presented themselves to Lenin was how ought socialists to restructure social, political and economic relations, and what were to be the positive content of socialism as the first genuinely human and universal form of association? Given that the international revolution for socialism was now adjudged to be imperatively necessary if humankind was to avoid a descent into barbarism, it plainly became necessary for revolutionary theory to establish, at least in outline, the principles, procedures and institutions that were to inform the construction of socialist society. There was, moreover, an immediate practical point to this task. Lenin recognised perfectly well that, in order to get the masses to act decisively, it was not enough for the revolutionaries to expose the rottenness of existing society. The withering critique of state monopoly capitalism might be sufficient to undermine the legitimacy of existing structures of power but this, of itself, would not dispose the mass of the people to act to overthrow it. Before they could have the confidence to do this, Lenin argued, they had to be persuaded that it was feasible and practicable to replace it with something better. The positive content of the socialist transformation had, therefore, to be projected as something that was not only necessary, but also practicable.

It was at this point that Lenin chose to emphasise the potentially positive aspects of imperialism or monopoly capitalism. Lenin's

142

account of the negative aspects of monopoly capitalism were explored in Chapter 5, and they were constantly rehearsed in his writings between 1914 and 1916. In late 1916, having to his own satisfaction completed the critical assault on state monopoly capitalism, Lenin's primary point of focus changed substantially. His concern now was to demonstrate that, as in all previous epochs of human history, the seeds of the future could be discerned in the present – if only in distorted form. In this perspective state monopoly capitalism simultaneously revealed itself as, on the one hand, the final degenerate form of a once-progressive mode of production and, on the other, as a complete preparation for the civilisation of socialism that was to replace it.

Monopoly Capitalism and the Transition to Socialism

The dialectics of monopoly capitalism, according to Lenin, were such that the more desperately declining capitalism struggled to preserve itself, the more it created the structures through which it could be radically transformed and superseded. The necessary process of capitalist accumulation meant that one successful capitalist killed off several who were unsuccessful. Inevitably, this meant that the process, as it proceeded, constantly diminished the social base of capitalism. Quite simply, the progress towards monopoly signified the reduction in the number of capitalists. As the social base of their hegemonic power declined, the monopoly capitalists had to resort to an ever-increasing use of state power as the direct vehicle for ensuring social compliance and the preservation of their profits. But in doing this they merely succeeded in tearing aside the mask of impartiality and neutrality that had for so long successfully disguised state power. And the more the state was revealed for what it was – the dictatorship of an ever-diminishing possessing class – the more surely it would become discredited in the popular mind. Its legitimacy would be undermined. Temporarily the monopoly capitalists might, through fostering a bogus imperialist ideology, and by fomenting foreign war, direct the animosity of the workers towards foreign targets to justify the exponential growth of a hugely expanded bureaucracy and the depredations of the militarised state. These were, however, only short-term palliatives that would exacerbate rather than cure the basic malaise. The mass of the people would eventually realise that the physical and fiscal costs of imperialist war fell disproportionately upon them – then there could be no saving the discredited imperialist state.

The political implications of monopoly capitalism were echoed, as we might expect, in Lenin's analysis of the principal features of its economic base. The growth of huge consolidated plants meant an ever-growing socialisation of labour; that is, increasing numbers of workers were aggregated together in fewer and fewer immense plants. (This was particularly the case in the peripheries of the capitalist world, like Russia, where monopolisation and the export of the most up-to-date processes of exploitation had produced a higher concentration of labour than in any of the older capitalist economies.) Two important consequences flowed from these findings. In the first place, since a small number of very large plants exercised a decisive influence over a whole sector of production, it was evidently far easier to bring these under social control than to do the same with a myriad of small workshops. Secondly, it was central to Leninist theory that the more concentrated workers became, and the larger the size of their enterprise, the more the conditions were created for the growth of revolutionary organisation and consciousness. Lenin's own experience with the workers in the vast Putilov works had confirmed this general finding. Communication among the workers was best developed in such plants, relations with other plants were easier to sustain, and, above all, the workers could sense the enormous potential of their massed power. For these reasons they were the natural foci upon which revolutionary activists could concentrate their activity and maximise their influence.

Since, under monopoly capitalism, capital resources were concentrated in fewer and fewer hands and were, in any case, concentrated overwhelmingly in the few big banks, the process of bringing them under social control had, again, been enormously simplified. The big banks were, in Lenin's account, the nerve centres of contemporary capitalism. Under their aegis, 'We see the rapid expansion of a close network of channels which cover the whole country, centralising all capital and all revenues, transforming thousands and thousands of scattered economic enterprises into a single national capitalist, and then into a world capitalist economy.'[2] They controlled not only the allocation of capital and credit resources to the whole industrial infrastructure of society; they also increasingly controlled production and distribution in whole fields of industry. To control them was, in short, to control the economic base of contemporary society. Here, in embryo, as Lenin quoted Marx, was a system that possessed 'the form of universal book-keeping and distribution of means of production on a social scale, but solely the form'.[3] The revolution could effect the socialist transformation of the economy through the very mechanisms and procedures that the big banks had introduced to establish their own economic hegemony. A similar chain of reasoning applied to the trusts and cartels. These instruments of monopoly dominance could themselves be appropriated as the simplified mechanisms for asserting social control over the industrial base. The paradox of capitalism was that its seemingly all-powerful weapons of self-defence lay readily available to be seized by its opponents and used by them to transform fundamentally every aspect of social and economic life:

> the development of capitalism, which resulted in the creation of banks, syndicates, railways and so forth, has greatly facilitated and simplified the adoption of measures of really democratic control by the workers and peasants over exploiters, the landowners and capitalists.[4]

The Leninist road to socialism emphatically ran through the terrain of monopoly capitalism. It would, according to Lenin, abolish neither its advanced technological base nor its institutionalised means for allocating resources or structuring industry. Only the motive and goal of these institutions and procedures would be transformed and, along with the change of goal, the existing irrationalities, imbalances and injustices of the productive and distributive system would be done away with. When the whole objective of the productive process had been reformulated to pursue the balanced and proportionate development of the economy as a whole, to ensure the maximum satisfaction of social needs, then the existing impediments to innovation and evenness of development would disappear. The institutional framework of advanced capitalism could, to put it shortly, be utilized for the realisation of specifically socialist goals. They were to become, indeed, the principal (almost exclusive) instruments of socialist transformation:

> Capitalism has created an accounting *apparatus* in the shape of the banks, syndicates, postal service, consumers' societies, and office employees unions. *Without big banks socialism would be impossible* . . . The big banks *are* the 'state apparatus' which we *need* to bring about socialism, and which we *take ready-made* from capitalism; our task here is merely to *lop off* what *capitalistically mutilates* this excellent apparatus, to make it *even bigger*, even more democratic, even more comprehensive. Quantity will be transformed into quality. A single State Bank, the biggest of the big, with branches in every

rural district, in every factory, will constitute as much as nine-tenths of the *socialist* apparatus. This will be country-wide *book-keeping*, country-wide *accounting* of the production and distribution of goods, this will be, so to speak, something in the nature of the *skeleton* of socialist society . . . We can 'lay hold of' and 'set in motion' this 'state apparatus' (which is not fully a state apparatus under capitalism, but which will be so with us, under socialism) at one stroke, by a single decree, because the actual work of book-keeping, control, registering, accounting and counting is performed by *employees*, the majority of whom themselves lead a proletarian or semi-proletarian existence.[5]

This was, by any standards, an extraordinary programme, the like of which had never before been contemplated, let alone recommended as the practical programme of a socialist party on the verge of a successful revolution. These were, we should recall, the substance of Lenin's recommendations to the Bolsheviks on the eve of the October Revolution ('Can the Bolsheviks Retain State Power?', September/October 1917).[6] His train of thought was so far removed from anything in the Western political tradition that we need to pause and reconstruct the line of argument that led Lenin to the apparently heretical and apolitical proposition that a single state bank could be as much as nine-tenths of the state apparatus needed to bring about socialism.

Lenin was always the diligent student of Marx and never more so than in the last months of 1916 and early months of 1917, which he devoted to a scrupulous study of Marx and Engels on the state. He was prompted to do so partly because he was dissatisfied with what he believed to be the dangerous ruminations of his fellow Bolshevik, Bukharin, but also because he recognised the need to confront the crucial issue of any revolutionary theory or practice – that of state power.

State Capitalism and the Commune/Soviet Alternative

Up to this point Lenin had reflected little on the nature of state power or on the problem of what a successful revolution was to do with it. His attitudes on these matters, up to late 1916, had been entirely orthodox and rather predictable. He had merely repeated the left Marxist line that the bourgeois state was nothing other than the punitive and coercive instrument of the owners of capital. It was, in the last resort, 'separate bodies of armed men' with exclusive right to bear arms and the will to use them in defence of existing allocations of power, wealth and status within society.

As we have seen, according to the Marxist theorists of imperialism, the further capitalism slid into monopoly and the concentration of capital, the more its social base shrank and it was obliged to rely upon the naked power of the state to sustain its power and profits. Capitalism, particularly in its final degenerate stage, would itself expose the illusory neutrality of the state. At that point, in order to keep in check the mounting tide of internal popular discontent, as well as the growing assertions of independence from colonies and dependencies, the imperialist state would have to increase its armed forces immeasurably as well as extend its authoritarian control of every aspect of social life. It would be obliged to suppress all hitherto independent associations or absorb them into itself. It would bring increasingly under state control and ownership the crucial strategic areas of the economy such as transport, communications, steel, munitions and banking. Nationalisation was, in Lenin's view, a typical feature of state capitalism. Through rationing the state would control distribution, and through draconian legislation to limit the powers of the trade union and labour movements, it would control wages and the conditions of labour. Finally, by controlling tariffs it would protect indigenous industries (and profit margins) from the threat of foreign competition. The imperialist state now became absolutely central to creating and reproducing the conditions for the perpetuation of capitalism itself. Monopoly capitalism became state monopoly capitalism and the historical originality of this phase of history (as Bukharin had pointed out) was that the state, far from being determined by the economic base of society and responsive to its demands, now emerged as *the principal economic actor*. The political superstructure now determined the economic base rather than vice versa. At the point of the final necrosis of capitalism, the state emerged as its hideously swollen, autocratic and militarist guarantor, with pretensions to control everything and everyone. It had become, in Bukharin's words the 'new Leviathan'[7] – a monstrous armed power that threatened to destroy individual and group autonomy, indeed to destroy civilisation itself in bloody wars in pursuit of its profits. It demonstrated finally that the career of the state in history had issued in barbarism and madness – it would have to be destroyed.

Although initially he was scandalised by Bukharin's conclusions (Lenin accused him of dangerously confusing Marxism and anarchism), Lenin himself came to agree with them by late 1916. He had by this time resurrected Marx's writings on the Commune of Paris of 1871 from the oblivion into which they had fallen and in which, he observed, Marx had arrived at substantially the same position.[8] The hugely inflated bureaucratic and military regime of Louis Bonaparte had, in Marx's view, become thoroughly parasitic and oppressive. It not only consumed a disproportionate amount of the national product, it also stifled private and social initiatives. It represented, according to Marx, the final and absurd culmination of the state's historical role.

State and society had always, in Marx's account, been locked in a remorseless struggle in which the state represented coercion and control, and society stood for free expression and spontaneity. Over long periods of history the pretensions of the state to control and dominate society had been held in check by the state's financial or technological inability to realise these aims. With the coming of the industrial revolution, however, the intrusive possibilities of the state to suborn society grew enormously. Railways, steamships and the telegraph transformed communications, enabling the checking, registering and monitoring procedures of state bureaucracies to become far more refined. Advances in military technology, communications and training gave national armies an insuperable advantage over the unarmed citizenry. And this remorseless expansion of state power could now be paid for out of the expanded product of industrialised work processes and efficient nationwide structures for the collection of taxes. The state, at last, had the capacity to intrude itself into every part of social life and, in France under Louis Bonaparte from 1851 to 1871, it attained its finally 'perfected' form:

> This executive power with its enormous bureaucratic and military organisation, with its ingenious state machinery, embracing wide strata, with a host of officials numbering half a million, besides an army of another half a million, this appalling parasitic body, which enmeshes the body of French society like a net and chokes all its pores.[9]

The mistake of all previous revolutions, Marx concluded, was that they had attempted to perfect this machine instead of smashing it.[10] It was to take twenty years for this lesson to be learned and then, in March 1871, with unerring instinct, the revolutionaries of the Paris Commune began their assault on the state. Their first act, Marx reported enthusiastically, was to declare the abolition of the standing army, bureaucracy and the police. The state – as separate bodies of men blessed with exclusive jurisdictions that were conferred by their office – was shattered: 'Public functions ceased to be the private property of the tools of the Central Government. Not only municipal administration, but the whole initiative hitherto exercised by the State was laid into the hands of the Commune.'[11] This was a revolution against the whole 'horrid machinery' of the state itself, and its object was to restore to the people in arms all the powers and prerogatives hitherto arrogated to state bodies and officials. The people in their own assemblies were to discuss and decide upon public policy, and implement and police it. They were to re-find their lost powers – their own control over every aspect of social policy.

Society at last was to emancipate itself from the state and this alone constituted the claim of the Paris Commune of 1871 to be a socialist form of organisation. It did not propose any far-reaching changes to the ownership of *property* or the direction of the work process. Its proposals were almost exclusively concerned with transforming power relations within society – the manner in which people related to their fellows. The Commune represented for Marx the empowerment of society, of ordinary men and women, to exert effective and continuous control over the deliberation and execution of public business:

> The Communal Constitution would have restored to the social body all the forces hitherto absorbed by the State parasite feeding upon, and clogging the free movement of, society. By this one act it would have initiated the regeneration of France.[12]

The conclusions that Marx arrived at in *The Civil War in France* were to have profound effects on Leninism and on subsequent Soviet theory of the state. In the first place, Marx insisted unequivocally that the modern state had nothing whatever to do with freedom or justice. It was, on the contrary, the executive and punitive instrument enforcing the domination of a particular class; it could not be used as a vehicle of genuine human emancipation. Second, the growth of the state had been accomplished only at the cost of society. Augmenting its powers necessarily debilitated the autonomy and initiative of individuals and social groups; society and the state, in this analysis, were locked into a zero sum game. The state could accomplish its perfected form (the Bonapartist imperial state for Marx; the imperialist state capitalist trust for Lenin) only by emasculating the autonomous sphere of social life. State and society, in Lenin's account, constituted a dialectical pairing: unity of opposites locked in remorseless conflict.

In the period from late 1916 until early 1918, Lenin became a fervent convert to these radically theorised propositions on the state. In 1871, Marx had declared the redundancy of the state, so how much more apposite his recommendations were in the heyday of the wartime state capitalist trust. Under the pretext of national defence, the imperialist states had mobilised everyone and everything to serve their purposes. They had summarily suspended democratic and civic rights, and had instituted national control over labour, wages, rationing and supply. The media of communication meekly did their bidding, industries were brought under their control, and the whole of society was subjected to military-style discipline. In this situation, Lenin reflected, Marx's injunctions to the revolutionaries to smash the bureaucratic/military apparatus of the state applied with particular force. The revolution against decadent monopoly capitalism, he now agreed with Bukharin, could not possibly be accomplished without a simultaneous assault on the parasitic state power that sustained it, and neither goal could be accomplished without the radical regeneration of society.

From February 1917 Lenin increasingly came to view the soviets as the authentic embodiment of social initiative and action. They were the contemporary bearers of the commune idea. They had initially been created to defend workers against lock-outs and wage cuts but, in the months following February, their concerns and their standing broadened considerably. They rapidly became a proto-government, uneasily coexisting with the self-selected Provisional Government. The soviets that had emerged in Russia in the early spring of 1917 were, Lenin insisted, an advance on the Paris Commune in that they comprised only the working people. They were, potentially at least, the expression of proletarian political dominance. They were businesslike and action-orientated bodies in which, just like the Paris Commune, public policy was deliberated at once, executed and enforced. They were, in these respects, infinitely superior to the talking shops of bourgeois parliaments with their complex divisions of legislative, executive and judicial prerogatives and powers. Unlike conventional states they had neither a professional bureaucracy nor a standing army, nor complex division of powers. Public business was implemented by elected officials answerable to their constituents, able to be re-called at any time, and paid at average workmen's wages. The policing and defensive functions of the soviets were to be discharged by a universal militia in which all were to take part. Socialism here was co-extensive with 'democracy from below, without a police, without a standing army, voluntary social duty by a *militia* formed from a universally armed people'.[13] In brief, all the mediations, institutional arrangements and cultivated mystique that had isolated the mass of the people from direct control over public affairs were to be done away with. Socialism, in this guise, meant social (rather than state) control of all public affairs, exercised through the soviets. In the light of the professedly statist theory and practice of modern communism it is paradoxical that Lenin's insistence, in April 1917, that the Bolsheviks should change the name of their party to 'Communist' stemmed from his infatuation with the Paris Commune, whose whole aim was to dissolve the state into society.[14]

The long-term implications of Lenin's virulent anti-statism in 1917 have been somewhat underestimated by Western commentators, and almost wholly ignored in Soviet analyses. The tacit implication, on both sides, is that this Utopian rush of blood had little to do with what subsequently happened in the Soviet experience. We are led to believe that these attitudes had little permanent impact. These judgements, like so many others on Leninism, seriously underestimate the debilitating effects upon Soviet practice that resulted from Lenin's doctrinal fixations. A. J. Polan has given a convincing account of the 'criminal career' that Lenin's ideas during this period were to exert upon subsequent soviet history.[15] Lenin's contemptuous dismissal of the state as a mere engine of oppression became so much an article of faith that the crucial questions of politics, in the whole subsequent career of communism, were put outside the bounds of discussion. The simplistic argument that the state was the evil genius of the contemporary world – organiser of internal and international exploitation, divisive and militarist – rendered redundant any discussion about improving its institutions and procedures, guaranteeing the accountability of its officers, or subjecting its actions and policies to judicial review. There was in the subsequent history of modern communism a similar silence concerning such crucial political concerns as the detailed procedures for the conduct of elections, access to the media, the immunity of elected representatives and so on. Prohibitions similarly covered any discussion of the meaningfulness of individual civic and political rights that expressly could *not* be exercised against the executive, nor further defined and protected by appeal to independent tribunal or constitutional court. The tireless response of Lenin, and subsequent Leninists, to these sorts of question was that they had to do with a discredited politics of an age now past and gone – the politics of exploitation and coercion. They only made sense if one accepted the entirely bogus self-justification of the bourgeois state that it was the neutral arbiter of

competing interests and the guarantor of equality of legal and civic
rights and the rule of law. It was one thing for Marx, and subsequently
Lenin, to expose the weakness of these claims, and to demonstrate that
they were often honoured more in theory than reality; it was quite
another for the Leninist tradition to deny the whole possibility of the
state being an agent of emancipation or guarantor of individual or
social freedoms. For the Leninist the state (and politics) had no
autonomy and no permanence. Both reflected the contradictions of a
class-divided society. Both were fated to disappear in proportion as
exploitation of one man by another was brought to an end. It followed,
therefore, that the crucial objective of Leninists in power was economic
rather than political – to eliminate exploitation was to eliminate classes
and therewith the need for politics and the state.

Lenin's Utopian and anti-statist ideas were not, therefore, an
irrelevant and fleeting pipe-dream. Of course, the Soviet state that
was in the process of being built stood in flagrant contradiction to this
programme. A state power more intrusive and more total in its
aspirations to control and mould its citizenry than any in history was in
the process of being constructed. Yet the conventional political
language, and the conceptual framework in terms of which its
institutions and procedures might have been discussed and debated,
had already been discredited and rejected by Lenin. The vocabulary
and grammar of the Western tradition of politics was abruptly
dispensed with, and no alternatives were proposed to replace them.
Lenin had effectively emptied of meaning a tradition of political
theorizing, and a turbulent history of the practical renegotiation of the
relationship between Church and state, society and state, and the
individual and society, that stretched back to the Middle Ages. From
Marsillius to Hobbes and Locke, and from Rousseau to Montesquieu
and Mill, was, for Lenin, a tale of frivolities, a tale that had no
resonances for a properly *human* society. The consequent impoverishment of the discourse of politics in the entire career of the Soviet Union
was to have grave practical consequences for its citizens and eventually
for its own stability. Lenin's own responsibility in these matters is clear
and inescapable.

We have seen that, in 1917, Lenin believed that the primary
institutions for realising socialism were economic rather than political.
The single national bank was to comprise nine-tenths of the
institutional apparatus necessary to this task. Lying behind this
assertion were a set of assumptions that were to have deep implications
for what was subsequently to pass for the Soviet theory of the state.

There was, in the first place, the foundation principle of orthodox Marxist historical materialism – that the economic base of society determines its political superstructure. Politics, in this view, is no more than concentrated economics, and the state is no more than the agency that preserves the exploitative privileges of the ruling class. The positive content of the Leninist project for socialism consisted in this: it proposed to transform the present (coercive and statist) domination of the vast majority by a small minority, into the co-operative and voluntary participation of all to realize a more efficient system of production and a just distribution of rewards. The assumptions that made this project plausible were:

(a) The planned and rational allocation of resources (both capital and labour) in order to realise an optimal outcome, could be arrived at scientifically and should not, therefore, be a matter for serious disputation or political debate; and

(b) The principles governing the allocation of rewards within society were, similarly, amenable to positive (that is, quantifiable) resolution by basing them upon the contribution of individuals and groups to the productive endeavours of society.

In these crucial matters of public policy, as Lenin consistently maintained, broad-ranging public debate was inherently unlikely to make any significant contribution. The compilation of data and statistics, the patient monitoring of the implementation of plans, proper measures of checking and accounting, the widespread advertising of model or exemplary best practice; these were the unglamorous and uncontentious means through which these socialist objectives were to be attained. At no point in his career, either in or out of power, did Lenin ever recommend that the principles that informed economic priorities, should be debated widely by the population as a whole, or that vital orderings of priorities should be adjudicated by popular democratic decision. He set an example that all communist regimes were to follow. These matters were outside the pale of politics – they were not to be part of the domain of public deliberation. They were arrived at administratively by the party leadership and such experts as it chose to consult, and their decisions had the force of law. Politics was, in this way, deprived of its central concerns.

By the early 1920s Lenin's contempt for politics had become increasingly clear. There were, without doubt, inescapable economic problems to attend to, and it was natural that the communists should concentrate their energies on resolving them. The manner in which they *were* resolved, however, and the measured justifications that were now offered for the monopolisation of state power by the communists, were to narrow the sphere of politics even further.

By this time the regime was faced with an accumulation of crises that had brought the exchange of goods between town and country to a virtual standstill. Industrial production had slumped to less than a third of pre-war levels, the peasants were withholding their grain, transportation was in chaos, and famine stalked the land. Everything, Lenin concluded, now had to be subordinated to the central task of regenerating industry and restoring the exchange between town and country. By this time, Lenin concluded, the proletariat had all but disappeared. It had been decimated in defence of the revolution during the civil war and had melted away into the countryside during the awful years from 1918 to 1921. Its remnants were ravaged by disease, cold and hunger. Small wonder, then, that it was demoralised and disorientated. It had effectively been declassed. In those three and a half years, 'it has suffered distress, want, starvation and a worsening of the economic position such as no other class in history has suffered. It is not surprising that it is uncommonly weary, exhausted and strained'.[16] Lenin was forced to concede that the state power that the communists had built up was devoid of a solid class base: 'The proletariat has become declassed, i.e. dislodged from its class groove and has ceased to exist as a proletariat.'[17] The peasants were either sullenly resentful or in open conflict with the regime. It was in these circumstances of profound economic dislocation and crisis, when the social base of the regime had effectively disappeared, that the dictatorship of the proletariat was theorised. Its themes were to constitute the foundation mythology of the Soviet state and they were to resonate throughout its structure up to its demise in 1991.

The Dictatorship of the Proletariat

The foundation proposition of the dictatorship of the proletariat was that all states in the modern world were obliged to be authoritarian and dictatorial:

> Either the dictatorship (i.e. the iron rule) of the landowners and capitalists, or the dictatorship of the working class . . . There is no

middle course . . . There is no middle course anywhere in the world, nor can there be.[18]

The central reality of the current epoch was, according to Lenin's analysis, the unremitting war between the progressive forces of socialism and the degenerate forces of capitalism. There might be periods of uneasy truce between the two, when both were exhausted and neither had the power nor the will to defeat the other (and this, Lenin concluded in 1920, was the current situation). But such periods were merely interludes before the struggle was rejoined on a broader scale. The situation of the Soviet state at that time was that it had, through titanic effort and commitment, survived the initial capitalist onslaught, loss of territory, and an externally funded civil war, but the costs had been enormous. The country was ravaged, the towns depopulated, industry and transport were in ruins, and the people were suffering from hunger and privation. To exacerbate its agony, the revolution in Russia had not sparked off the anticipated European revolution. The beleaguered and diminished resources of Russia were not, in the immediate future, to be redeemed by the accession to the revolutionary fold of the industrially advanced countries of the West. Russia was forced in upon her own ruined resources. The socialist revolution in Russia had survived the first furious onslaught, but it was alone in the world. The regime was set about by powerful opponents on the international stage and had virtually no resources to secure the loyalties of its own population. Its own social base had, as we have seen, been effectively destroyed. Lenin's sombre conclusion was that, although the imperialist powers had not succeeded in toppling the Soviet regime, they had managed to contain it and to damage it so severely that its inspirational appeal to other peoples (as well as to its own citizens) had been profoundly weakened.

In this situation of crisis, Lenin and his colleagues were obliged to undertake a fundamental re-evaluation of the whole nature of the revolution – its justification, its goals, and the institutions necessary for their implementation. The initial anti-statism of the Soviet/commune idea had been premised upon the rapid spread of the international revolution. It was, indeed, intended as the inspirational focal point for that world revolution. Its message to the peoples of the world was: follow the soviet example, take power into your own hands and dispense with state-licensed bureaucrats, judges, ministers and police; dissolve the whole parasitic apparatus of the imperialist state; and reclaim control over your own lives. In the first flush of the revolution, socialism was projected as people power – an end to being bossed. It signified, above all, the radical transformation of power relations, of all the relations of domination and subordination that had hitherto characterised class-divided societies.

Lenin had now to face the unpalatable fact that the revolutionary dissolution of the imperialist states had not occurred, and was not likely to do so in the immediate future. Against all his predictions they had managed to stabilise their currencies, had arrived at a post-war settlement and demobilised their armies without massive unrest.

In this environment of internal and international isolation (encircled within by the peasantry and outside by imperialist powers) socialism in Russia could only survive as a frank dictatorship. In order to justify this fundamental change of stance, Lenin resorted to a political relativism that was quite in keeping with orthodox Marxism but which was to be the stigmata that the Soviet state would never wash away. He constructed a set of arguments that were harsh, cynical and deeply apolitical, to justify the sole power of the communists. He created what now came to be promulgated as the foundation myth of the Soviet state, in extraordinary circumstances, with justificatory arguments that were to have a thoroughly criminal career.

We can, with few qualms, recognise that *any* political regime in Russia in 1920, in order to fulfil the elemental responsibilities of government (to defend its territory and feed its population), would have had to resort to authoritarian measures. The accumulation of crises and the scale of suffering (for which, no doubt, the communists were themselves in large part responsible) made decisive, even ruthless, action necessary. The crises themselves could well have provided sufficient justification for draconian government action to remedy them. Lenin might well, at this juncture, have said: we can do no other, these things are regrettable, our actions and policies are severe, and difficult to justify in terms of socialist norms, but desperate times demand desperate remedies. This would have been a conventional and plausible response; the sort that politicians have ever routinely made.

It is precisely the fact that Lenin was never content with the unreflective stock-in-trade responses of ordinary politicians that makes him at once intellectually interesting and deeply dangerous. Current predicaments for him had always to be set in their more general and universal contexts; that is, they had to be theoretically resolved. What this meant effectively was that virtue had to be made out of necessity, the unforeseen and the calamitous had to be presented as parts of an intelligible process; and errors and abrupt changes of policy had to be integrated into a new characterisation of the nature of the epoch and the goals of socialism.

Lenin at this time openly admitted that the communists were but a drop in the ocean of the people and that the entire burden of running the administrative apparatus was shouldered by an incredibly small number of activists: 'A few thousand throughout Russia and no more'.[19] The communists could not, or would not, give up power, yet they could not possibly justify their power either by appeal to popular sovereignty exercised through free elections, or by democratising the actual business of public administration through a revitalisation of the soviets. Either of these options, Lenin clearly recognised, would have swept them from power. This was the decisive turning point of the revolution, when the fatal reassessment of the content of socialism and the means of its realisation was arrived at. It was the moment when theory, from being an explanatory system of ideas, became a poisonous apologetic that was to corrupt and disfigure the Soviet socialist idea for the rest of its life. Theory, hereafter, was no more than the vindication of the power of a self-selected band of the elect.

Let us for the moment return to our starting point. The contemporary epoch was a time of remorseless conflict between socialism struggling to be born and capitalism's rabid responses to approaching death. In order to stave off their own mounting internal crises, the restive assertiveness of their colonies and the aggressive intentions of their competitors, the imperialist states had no choice but to become increasingly authoritarian and dictatorial. This had been revealed graphically during the First World War, but these features would not disappear during the years of phoney peace. However they dressed themselves, whatever constitutional goals they adopted, *all* capitalist states had become dictatorships: to preserve their powers, privileges, possessions and profits they had no other recourse. Lenin's simplistic relativism with regard to the *forms* in which political power is exercised now came to the fore. It was, he said, a matter of consummate indifference whether bourgeois states chose to present themselves as parliamentary democracies, constitutional monarchies, republics or militarist dictatorships. The outward forms in which they decked themselves were of no significance. What mattered was the objective content of their policies. They existed to serve the interests of monopoly capitalism. The dictatorship of the imperialist bourgeoisie could, in short, be just as surely accomplished by the assembly of a democratic republic as it could be by a military autocrat. There was indeed a sense, Lenin argued, in which democracy was the most perfected form of bourgeois dictatorship:

> Marxists have always maintained that the more developed, the 'purer' democracy is, the more naked, acute and merciless the class struggle becomes, and the 'purer' the capitalist oppression and bourgeois dictatorship.[20]

This, for Lenin, was doing no more than give voice to Marx's own essentialist argument that the differing *forms* of the bourgeois state ought never to obscure the truth that they were all purely external variations on the *essential* reality of the class power of the capitalists. Lenin was, however, to take this argument a further fatal step forward (if 'forward' is the right word). From 1920 onwards, he argued that what applied to the state form of bourgeois rule applied equally to the class rule of the proletariat. It too could be exercised by the many or the few. It too could, as occasion demanded, be justified by appeal to popular mandate or, quite simply, by appeal to the *force majeure* necessary to sustain a mode of production. Socialism, Lenin argued, could cloak itself in diverse garb. Its *form* of rule and its mode of justification were of no importance so long as the essential class content of its policies remained intact: '*The form of government,*' he concluded fatefully, 'has absolutely nothing to do with it.'[21]

The speciousness of Lenin's relativist position, and its crude apoliticism, was echoed at the time in the writings of both Bukharin and Trotsky. They too agreed that the content of socialism could no longer be identified with the early goals of mass popular participation in the management of all social, economic and political affairs. Proletarian power was not, henceforth, to be expressed or exercised through factory and regimental committees, soviets and local communal organisations, people's militias, trades unions or co-operative organisations. The spontaneous revolutionary upsurge of popular initiative that had characterised the early period of the revolution amounted, all three now agreed, to no more than the preliminary destructive phase of the revolution. It was a necessary phase in that it destroyed old structures of power and discredited the value systems on which they had been based – but it had created nothing *positive* to provide the values and structures of the future. According to Trotsky: 'The more perfect the revolution, the greater are the masses it draws in; and the longer it is prolonged, the greater is the destruction it achieves in the apparatus of production, and the more terrible inroads does it make upon public resources.'[22] Bukharin, similarly, had by the summer of 1920 come to the conclusion that the revolution, thus far, had merely resulted in the decomposition of the old and not the construction of the principles and structures of the new.[23] It had, Lenin asserts implicitly, been a mistake to identify the substantive content of socialism with administrative patterns catering for maximum public involvement. Socialism, he now concluded, had nothing to do with altering the relationship of *power* among men, but with transforming their *productive* relations so that, in the long run, the realm of necessity could be overcome and, with that, genuine social freedom realised. Only under far distant *communism* would it be possible to transform power relations radically within society and to create the opportunities for universal participation in public administration. It was only in 1920–1 that Lenin and the other Bolshevik leaders began to make clear and consistent distinctions between socialism and communism. Hitherto the terms had been used almost interchangeably and there certainly had not been any great emphasis upon socialism as a distinct historical phase preparatory to communism.

Political Monopoly and the Slide to Terror

Lenin, and the other principal theorists of Bolshevism, quite self-consciously in the summer of 1920, set about constructing the theoretical vindication of a prolonged 'transitional period' that was to be known as 'the dictatorship of the proletariat'. Until this point the dictatorship of the proletariat had not figured very largely in Bolshevik theory of the state and it had (as in Lenin's own *The State and Revolution*) been identified frequently with the Paris Commune type of administration which, in turn, was identified with the soviets. There was, in the early period of the revolution, no perceptible difference between the slogans 'for a state form of the Commune type', 'All Power to the Soviets', and 'the dictatorship of the proletariat'.

All this was to change very abruptly in the period between the summer of 1918 and that of 1920. The regime was faced with a series of acute crises. Problems of grain and food supply were exacerbated by the collapse of the railway system. Fuel and raw materials supply was similarly affected, and these problems added to the severe downturn in production consequent on the aggressive campaign for workers' control. Then the civil war broke out and the government lost its access to oil from the south, and huge regions of Russia were outside its control. The Germans occupied the Ukraine, armies of intervention played havoc in the north and east, while the White armies roamed the south and west. The very survival of the regime, it was argued plausibly, demanded the utmost centralisation and efficient use of its slender remaining resources. Everything and everyone should be mobilised for the defence of Soviet power. This meant that the whole country had to be placed on a war footing, with men and materials mobilised for the several fronts of the civil war. 'The Soviet Republic is besieged by the enemy. It must become *a single military camp*, not in word but in deed. All the work of all institutions must be adapted to the war and placed on a military footing!'[24] It followed consequently that the revolutionary practices of debate, discussion and collegial decisions, by factory and regimental committees and soviets, was now quite out of place:

> Collegiate methods must not exceed an absolute indispensable minimum in respect both to the number of members in the committees and to the efficient conduct of work; 'speechifying' must be prohibited, opinions must be exchanged as rapidly as possible and confined to information and precisely formulated practical proposals . . . Whenever there is the slightest possibility, such methods must be reduced to the briefest discussion of only the most important questions in the narrowest collegiate bodies, while the *practical management* of institutions, enterprises, undertakings or tasks should be entrusted to one comrade.[25]

The new watchwords were iron discipline; ruthless and firm direction; one-man management and accountability; and universal labour mobilisation. It would, Lenin advised, 'be a good thing to eliminate the word "Commune" from common use'.[26] All this presumed, of course, an authoritative directing centre to prioritise allocations of men and material. Only the state could assume this role, and only the Communist Party could supply the discipline and resolve to make it an effective vehicle for the salvation of the revolution.

The dictatorship of the proletariat was now cast in a quite different light, as was the role of the Party within it. Faced with such a profusion of internal and external enemies bent on the military destruction of socialism, Lenin now maintained that only a regime as militarised, centralised and dictatorial as its opponents could survive. 'Military discipline in military and all other matters!'[27] It was equally clear, he now maintained, that the dictatorship could not be exercised by the whole of the class. The Commune dream of universal participatory democracy would no longer serve. Only the advanced sector of the class, those blessed with knowledge, commitment and experience, were capable of leading the proletariat and administering the state. The finest of the class's representatives, its disciplined and tested cadres, were the party members. It fell to the party, therefore, to exercise the dictatorship on behalf of the class: 'To govern you need an army of steeled revolutionary Communists. We have it, and it is called the Party.'[28]

It was during the civil war that the party became identified with the highly centralised and militarised state formation that was emerging in Russia. This government – the Council of People's Commissars headed by Lenin – rapidly usurped the powers of the Central Executive Committee of Soviets to which it was notionally responsible. The whole Soviet system (with one or two local exceptions) rapidly declined in vitality. The Soviets were either dominated by Communist placemen or they voluntarily relinquished their powers to the Council of People's Commissars. In the whole subsequent history of the Soviet Union they were never to regain their old powers, confidence or vitality. Paradoxically, it was the proposed revitalisation of the Soviets by Mikhail Gorbachev with the elections of March 1989, that led directly to the growth of potent national constituencies that were swiftly to dismember the Soviet Union itself.

By 1921 the fundamental contours of the Party/State's role in the transition to Socialism had been fairly well defined. It was frankly acknowledged that the transition to Communism would take a long, long time. After war and civil war, the country was on its knees. Industrial production had all but collapsed, the urban proletariat had disappeared, famine threatened and, above all, there was now little prospect of the international revolution redeeming Russia's backwardness. In this bleak situation, the role and responsibilities of the Party/State grew immeasurably.

It was abundantly clear that the dictatorship of the proletariat could not be exercised by the (non-existent) proletariat. Only the party could assume its historic role and act on the proletariat's behalf as the governing power in the land. Because 'the proletariat is still so divided, so degraded, so corrupted in parts . . . that an organisation taking in the whole proletariat cannot directly exercise proletarian dictatorship. It can be exercised only by a vanguard that has absorbed the revolutionary energy of the class.'[29]

By late 1920 the wheel had turned full circle. The content of socialism had been redefined and, along with that, the nature and role of the state had been utterly transformed. So long as socialism was defined in terms of transforming the relationships of domination within society and encouraging the whole population to resume control over its lost powers, neither party nor state could claim a preponderant role. Socialism here was self-activity; it was now possible 'to cast bossing aside' as Lenin cryptically put it. By late 1920 Lenin, Bukharin and Trotsky were all agreed that socialism had nothing whatever to do with those procedural norms that were meant to guarantee popular power – the election and recall of *all* office holders and their payment at workmen's wages. Nor did socialism, in the new notation, have anything to do with freedom of political association or freedom of the press. In the parlous situation of 1920–1, with their urban proletarian base dismembered and the remnants of the working class disaffected, Lenin was clear that to allow political competition would mean the political extinction of the Bolsheviks. To permit freedom of the press 'means facilitating the enemy's task, means helping the class enemy. We have no wish to commit suicide,' Lenin frankly wrote to Myasnikov 'and therefore, we will not do this'.[30] 'The scientific term "dictatorship",' Lenin explained towards the end of 1920:

> means nothing more nor less than authority untrammeled by any laws, absolutely unrestricted by any rules whatever, and based directly on force. The term 'dictatorship' *has no other meaning but this.*[31]

All states were, however, class states. In the contemporary epoch, as we have seen, they became, in Lenin's analysis, class dictatorships. The dictatorship of the proletariat was, therefore, '*won and maintained by the use of violence against the bourgeoisie*'. It was, he went on, 'violence against the bourgeoisie'.[32] In these terms, it was obvious that any arbitrary action of the party/state could be justified, for the regime itself was the sole judge of who it was that constituted the ill-defined 'bourgeoisie' that was so easily read as a synonym for all the regime's opponents. In the dialectical logic of Leninism, after all, those who are not with us are against us: they form, objectively, the camp of the enemy. In this oppressive logic it is, as we have remarked, particularly the moderates, the conciliators and consensus men who are, in fact, the most dangerous of antagonists. They are of the type of the reformist socialists and labour aristocracy who pose as socialists but are, objectively, '*the real agents of the bourgeoisie in the working class movement*, the labour lieutenants of the capitalist class . . .'[33]. Into this camp, of course, fell the 'petty bourgeois' Mensheviks and Socialist Revolutionaries,[34] and all who supported them. In this reductionist way the terms 'bourgeois' and 'opponent' are run together, and together they merit unrestrained suppression by the proletarian state.

It was unambiguously Lenin who not only condoned but actively encouraged the growth of the political police (the Cheka) and, as opposition mounted to the regime, vindicated its resort to terrorist methods against all the varied opponents of the regime – liberals and social democrats, peasants who withheld grain, speculators, hooligans, idlers or drunken workers. The severity of punishment he invoked varied from time to time and according to the group concerned, from deprivation of ration card to compulsory labour, from imprisonment to summary exemplary execution. The thesis of the 'declassing of the proletariat', coinciding as it did with the theorised consensus of Lenin, Trotsky and Bukharin in 1920, that the proletarian state would have to have recourse to coercion to re-educate the (corrupted) remnants of the working class, was a grim anticipation of the wholesale state-directed terror that was to come. Kronstadt was the Rubicon. Here, in March 1921, the terrible logic of Lenin's either/or (either the dictatorship of the proletariat exercised by the Communist Party, or the dictatorship of the bourgeoisie exercised by the White Guardists) was visited upon the hero city of the revolution itself.

The Kronstadt workers and sailors of the Baltic fleet had impeccable grounds for claiming, at the end of the civil war, the restitution of the revolutionary rights and revolutionary institutions for which they had sacrificed so much. They had, after all, been the legendary loyalists and shock forces of the revolution. In the July days of 1917 they had mobilised *en masse*, in October they had led the assault on the Winter Palace, and they had been called to the crucial fronts of the civil war to stiffen the resolve of the Red Forces, to save Soviet power. Now that it was all over, now the revolution had defeated all its enemies, they demanded what they had fought for – freely elected soviets which entailed freedom for all socialist parties to compete. The famous resolution of the battleship *Petropavlovsk*, which was to become the Kronstadters' manifesto, summarised their simple programme:

> Because the present day Soviets do not express the will of the workers and peasants, new elections should immediately be held, after a period of free agitation . . . Freedom of speech and press for

workers, peasants, anarchists and leftist socialist parties; freedom of assembly for the trade unions and peasant associations; release of all socialist political prisoners and of all workers, peasants, soldiers and sailors arrested on account of their political activity. Abolition of all political units in the army, since no single party should have special rights to propagandize. Equalization of all workers' rations. Peasants' free right to control their soil and to keep livestock as long as they do not employed paid workmen.[35]

This was, no doubt, a revolt against the 'commissarocracy', against the growth of bureaucratic high-handedness and political intolerance. It did not, however, begin as an expressly anti-communist rebellion. It was simply a heroic last statement of the Soviet ideal – 'Free elections to free soviets' and 'All power to the soviets and not the parties' were its endlessly repeated slogans which, it was hoped, would spark similar risings throughout Russia and oblige the communists to give up their stranglehold on power.

For Lenin, the Kronstadt revolt was more dangerous to the régime than all the military threats of the previous two years put together.[36] He acknowledged that its campaign against bureaucratism and for real democracy 'has had a wide influence on the proletariat,' and that government policies had antagonised the peasants, bringing them into open revolt against the regime. None the less, objectively 'the movement was reduced to petty-bourgeois counter-revolution and petty-bourgeois anarchism. 'It was,' he maintained, 'the work of Socialist Revolutionaries and white-guard emigrés'.[37] It traded upon a general mood of exhaustion, and a situation of extreme deprivation already turning into mass hunger, a situation exacerbated by the demobilisation of the army and the effective collapse of industry and, therewith, of organised exchange between town and country. The workers, Lenin conceded, 'were starving', they were forced into becoming petty traders in order to survive: 'That is the economic source of the proletariat's declassing and the inevitable rise of petty-bourgeois, anarchist trends.'[38] In these circumstances of universal deprivation, isolation and general political disorientation:

Whoever brings about even the slightest weakening of the iron discipline of the party of the proletariat (especially during its dictatorship), is actually aiding the bourgeoisie against the proletariat.[39]

In suppressing the Kronstadt revolt, in shooting the insurgents down 'like partridges' (as Trotsky instructed his troops), the Bolsheviks could rationalise their repression – it was directed not against proletarians, sailors, and the hero city of the revolution, but against the petty bourgeois contagion that everywhere was exploited by White Guardists and wreckers. The Bolshevik leaders, with Lenin in the lead, were obliged, in order to hold on to power at this critical moment, to lie to themselves and to their shrinking band of followers. Their language, both in public and in private, becomes more extreme and more vindictive. This was certainly the case with Trotsky, and the opening of the archives reveals new evidence that Lenin, too, pressed increasingly for the use of terror to be increased against all perceived opponents.[40]

Lenin had, once again, rejected as counter-revolutionary any suggestion that the communists might relinquish their monopoly hold on power. Insisting upon monopoly of power in the absence of public support led, ineluctably, to state coercion and terror. The Soviet state was, as Lenin and Bukharin acknowledged, now mimicking the forms of the imperialist state formation it had initially set out to destroy.

Lenin and the End of Politics

State power could, evidently, no longer be grounded in popular consent, nor hold as its objective the broadening and deepening of popular democratic participation. A new set of grounding principles, and a new legitimating rationale, had to be found. It was no accident that it was these tasks that pre-eminently absorbed Lenin, Bukharin and Trotsky in 1920–1. They now unanimously agreed that socialism had nothing to do with collegial administration or popular involvement – *it now defined itself not in procedural but in substantive terms*. Socialism was defined as the most efficient allocation of capital and labour resources to guarantee maximal efficiency of production. It was not merely agnostic to administrative forms – it in fact had a strong preference for authoritarian one-person direction at every level of industry and of the state. Far from being hidden and apologised for, dictatorial power was of the essence of the proletarian state, and it could not be otherwise. There was no alternative means of delivering Russia from internal economic crises. There was no alternative to the strictest punitive discipline for the demoralised and declassed remnants of the working class (still less for the restive peasants). Above all, in an international climate of continuous hostility and aggressive capitalist encirclement, the Soviet state could do no more than grasp the dictatorial powers long assumed by its capitalist opponents.

The relativism of Lenin's position had now become plainly apparent. He had reverted to a thoroughly reductionist Marxism, in terms of which the state has no autonomy – it was merely the agency for executing class power. The *form* the state assumes was, according to Lenin, just as irrelevant to the proletariat as it was to the bourgeoisie. As the bourgeoisie had, according to time, place and international conditions, rapidly adapted its practices, conventions and constitutional forms, so the proletarian state had to do likewise, 'the form of democracy is one thing and the class content of the given institution is another'.[41] There was, in short, nothing sacrosanct about democracy. It was no more tied to the essential interests of proletarian power than it had been to bourgeois political dominance. Lenin poured scorn on all those who would make a fetish of democratic procedure: 'We do not believe in "absolutes". We laugh at "pure democracy".'[42] In the current situation, the maximisation of production in order to satisfy elemental human needs was all that mattered. Everything else, democracy included, would if necessary have to be sacrificed: 'Industry,' Lenin reminded his followers, 'is indispensable, democracy is not.'[43] The dictatorship of the proletariat (unambiguously exercised by the party) was emphatic that neither in the workplace nor in the state would democratic principles apply. Lenin was perfectly clear 'that formal democracy must be subordinate to the revolutionary interest'.[44] So long as the conflict between capitalism and socialism persisted 'we do not promise any freedom or any democracy'.[45] 'In the final analysis every kind of democracy, as political superstructure in general . . . serves production and is ultimately determined by the relations of production in a given society.'[46] We should be clear that there was nothing inherently anti-Marxist about Lenin's position. Marx too had displayed a thoroughly ambiguous attitude to democracy and the politics of pluralism.[47] It was entirely consonant with the general tenor of Marx's analysis that Lenin (and subsequent Leninists) should view the state in purely instrumental terms as that organisation of coercive and administrative powers that best conduced to the maintenance and reproduction of class dominance.

True to his Marxist fundamentalism, Lenin also displayed a strongly relativist attitude towards politics. Politics, Lenin asserted frequently, was no more than a concentrated expression of economics.[48] Its role was to distil and articulate, in the public arena, the fundamental economic antagonisms within society. Politics was that sphere of human activity in which antagonistic class interests were openly expressed in rival and incommensurable formulations about public policy. In modern society it reduced itself to the articulation of the interests of those who sought to retain and strengthen the existing relationship between wage labour and capital, and those who sought to destroy it. Just as the classes of contemporary society reduced themselves to two essential classes – proletariat and bourgeoisie, so the political struggle essentially expressed itself in the struggle of their respective parties. The process of consolidation and differentiation of economic groupings within society would be reflected naturally in the emergence of two hostile political parties. As we shall see in Chapter 7, political consolidation into a single political party was an essential part of the class formation of the proletariat for Marx, as for Lenin. It was the party that would bring proper socialist consciousness and national organisation to the workers – without which they could not exist as a class. The party would purge the workers of their illusions and, through its propaganda and practical engagement, guide them towards a truly revolutionary awareness of the impossibility of reconciling their interests with those of the possessing classes. At that point, in the Marxist account of history that Lenin so dutifully followed, politics effectively came to an end. It was no more than the war of words that could clarify and illuminate, but never terminate, the essential economic oppositions of contemporary society. To effect fundamental changes in the distribution of economic and social power, debate, propaganda and political struggle would have to yield place to armed conflict: 'when history places the dictatorship of the proletariat on the order of the day it is not voting but civil war that decides *all* serious political problems'.[49] Since politics was no more than the tale of consciously articulated economic interests (that is, the distillation of class differences), it followed that, after the revolution, with the swift elimination of private property, its very basis would cease to exist. Where there were no separate groups of hirers of labour and those obliged to sell their labour, there were no classes, and where there were no classes there could be no politics.

It was not, however, solely the Marxist metaphysic of history that consigned politics to the oblivion of man's pre-history; its metaphysic of science did the same. Lenin, particularly in the last years of his active political life (1920–2), repeatedly bemoaned the tendency within and outside his party, to lapse into endless debate and theoretical controversy: 'We have so many resolutions that nobody even takes the trouble to file them, let alone read them. We must devote our attention to business and not to resolutions.'[50] The time for such distractions, he insisted, had passed. And this not simply for the reason that urgent affairs of state demanded full-time attention but, more significantly, because the very mode of reasoning and attitudes of mind on which all this argumentation was based had become outmoded. In the post-revolutionary epoch these 'political fireworks' were no more than the recitation of personal prejudices and projects, thinly disguising motives of personal advancement, or self-advertisement. Politics of this sort, was, in Lenin's eyes, mere idle and vainglorious chatter. Lenin's intemperance with it grew year by year. It expressed for him everything that was emotive, flashy and outmoded in revolutionary discourse. It was, in short, the language of those who had not ascended to the calm precision and certainty of science. Introducing the results of the State Commission for the Electrification of Russia, which he extolled as 'the second programme of our Party'[51] Lenin invited the 8th All-Russia Congress of Soviets to consider and accept the change of style in the conduct of public business that this connoted:

> Henceforth the rostrum at All-Russia Congresses will be mounted, not only by politicians and administrators but also by engineers and agronomists. This marks the beginning of that very happy time when politics will recede into the background, when politics will be discussed less often and at shorter length, and engineers and agronomists will do most of the talking. To really proceed with the work of economic development, this custom must be initiated at the All-Russia Congress of Soviets and in all Soviets and organisations, newspapers, organs of propaganda and agitation, and all institutions, from top to bottom . . . Henceforth, less politics will be the best politics.[52]

Science now emerged as an alternative legitimating rationale for state power. In proportion as Lenin's faith in the creative capacities of the mass (or even of the proletariat) declined, and in proportion as he emphasised the appalling lack of culture that impeded Russian development, so he vaunted the role of science and of scientists. As a mode of reasoning science was greatly to be preferred to the disputations of party theoreticians or the vain ramblings of the mass. Its findings, like those of dialectical thought (the very heart of science, according to Lenin) could not be improved upon by subjecting them to popular approval. The authority of the expert was, in this way, conjoined to that of the party. The party, being the guardian of the dialectic, was duty-bound to guard the prestige and authority of science and, similarly, those who disposed of authority sought for themselves the protective blessing of science.

Lenin, in the last years of his active political life, was a principal contributor to the trends that were to characterise Soviet politics for decades to come. Philosophically and temperamentally he could not abide pluralism or eclecticism. He was, like his mentor Plekhanov, a determined votary of the monist view of history. He fervently believed (against all evidence to the contrary) that the working class had but one will to realize in history, one vision and one path to its realisation, and that the party and the party alone could articulate it. There was never any room within Lenin's world-view for a genuine principled and continuing *debate* between different, but equally authentic, formulations of the proletarian mission. In this he closely followed Marx, who was similarly intolerant of divergent or eccentric working class projects and theories. In both cases, the denial of authenticity to rival formulations stemmed from the profoundly arrogant disposition of the *doctrinaire*. It was precisely because Lenin and his followers were so firm in their theoretical rectitude that they were able to reject and condemn deviants and dissenters. If the working class has but one will, and science one outcome, and if the party is the guardian of the thought process and development of both, then it had to follow that opposition to the party was not only anti-class, but also anti-science. This tightly oppressive logic was to characterise the subsequent development of the Soviet state and the Communist Party. By the time of Lenin's death both had been, to all intents and purposes, emptied of their properly political content.

7
Party, Class and Consciousness

In the historical career of Leninism the theory and practice of party organisation proved to be at once its greatest asset and its greatest liability. Its assets were obvious. It set out to establish (and sometimes succeeded in doing so) a disciplined, tightly-structured organisation of dedicated activists utilising front organisations and modern media of communication to mobilise mass action. Its members were to have the satisfaction of knowing that, because of these factors, their political potency was out of all proportion to their actual numbers. Its liabilities were less immediately apparent, but manifested themselves with increasing force as Leninist parties became more mature, and especially where their unchallengeable tenure of state power produced, as it was bound to, internal degeneration.

At many different levels, Leninism was either agnostic to democracy or actually hostile towards it. The contextual setting for the emergence of Lenin's early ideas on the party was pre-revolutionary Russia, in which political activity was proscribed and democracy rejected by the tsar as a senseless dream. None of the Russian Marxists had any effective experience (at least until the overthrow of the tsar in February 1917) of the operation of democratic mass parties. In any case, by this time Lenin felt that the mass parties of European Social Democracy had finally discredited themselves by voting war credits. The historical methodology of Leninism flatly rejected the basic supposition of democracy, that political differences within society could and should be negotiated peacefully.

As we have seen, the Leninist metaphysic of science was, from first to last, radically at odds with democratic theory or practice. Objective truth, it maintained, was in no way advanced by undertaking a canvass of popular opinion. Since that truth was a single and unique truth,

170

procedural means had to be arrived at whereby unanimity of outcome could be guaranteed. The monolithic organisational structures of the party were, in this way, legitimated by the twin axioms that the working class had but one real will in any historical situation, and that science yielded indisputable propositions about all phenomena. Deviants were therefore either ignorant, miscreant or alien to the ethos of the working class. They needed either re-education or discipline. Only when Leninist parties became governing parties in single party states were the enormities of this circular reasoning made apparent. Not only party members, but the whole of society was subjected to its version of reality and the punitive discipline that was the fate of all dissenters. There was established not only a circularity of thought but of social and political power. The top leadership of the party not only defined the truth but appointed all those, within both the party and the state, who were charged with policing it and punishing heretics. In this incestuous round, in which the party was answerable only to itself, arbitrariness and corruption of power were equally inevitable. Lenin himself, in his last writings, came close to recognising this impasse, but by then he was effectively powerless.[1] After him, only Gorbachev tried to emancipate the party from its arrogant presumption of a monopoly of truth and its concomitant rejection of contested elections and uncensored media. The predictable paradox of Gorbachev's endeavours was that, proportionate to his success, the power of the party and the integrity of the Soviet Union collapsed. By their history, ethos, and organisational structure, Leninist parties proved unable to effect the transition from legitimating themselves as vehicles of science and objective truth, to justifying and sustaining their power through genuine popular consent.

The Party and Proletarian Consciousness

The essential function of the party, according to both Marx and Lenin, was to articulate the historical goals of the working class and to enthuse and mobilise the workers to fulfil them. Its ultimate objective was to eliminate private ownership of the means of production through revolutionary action and thereby finally eliminate exploitation and class divisions within society. We have, however, already seen that, according to Lenin, the working class was not a uniform, undifferentiated mass. It was itself comprised of differing strata at differing levels of organisational and theoretical development. It therefore articulated, from within its own midst, a wide variety of rival projects. The problem immediately presented itself of how to distil, from this diversity, a coherent, unifying goal? To answer this question Lenin closely followed Marx in invoking the shadowy notion of historical immanence. Put very baldly, this notion of immanence had it that thorough study of the development of society would disclose certain general tendencies which, once established and dominant, propelled men to act in given ways. The great majority, of course, could not properly grasp these tendencies or laws of development, and consequently had little conception of how they might alter their situation. For the majority of workers, the most they might consider possible was a modest amelioration of their existing situation as wage workers – a reduction of the hours of work perhaps, or an increase in pay. They had little idea that they might aspire to change their very status and become masters and co-owners of their own plants. And yet the laws of history, in the Marxist formulation, demonstrated that as capitalism matured, so the antagonism and opposition of interests between capital and labour would intensify constantly. History showed that temporary ameliorations of the workers' conditions were never more than that – they were eroded by the next slump. Historical experience would drive home into the minds of men that it was precisely the partial and limited dreams of improving their conditions under capitalism that were Utopian, and they would increasingly make it clear that only the revolutionary overthrow of the power of capital and its replacement by socialism could realize the workers' yearning for a decent and civilised life.

The workers themselves could not, in general, anticipate these future developments. Unaided they could not discern, in the apparent chaos of everyday events, the trends and tendencies that were propelling them in the direction of revolutionary confrontation with their masters and the state. The accumulated experience of generations, their frustrated hopes and worsening conditions, would finally convince them of the necessity of effecting fundamental changes in power and property relations. But in the long meanwhile they would be fated to suffer for want of awareness of their goals and lack of resolve that stemmed, in no small part, from the absence of effective organisation.

This was the point at which Marx, and more expressly Lenin, inserted the party into the process of history. In Marx's account, the communists 'have over the great mass of the proletariat the advantage of clearly understanding the line of march, the conditions, and the ultimate general results of the proletarian movement'. Their immediate aim, he went on, was the 'formation of the proletariat into a class, overthrow of the bourgeois supremacy, conquest of political power by the proletariat'.[2] There is little in Lenin's account of the party that is much more than a gloss to Marx's original. In the first place, Lenin took up the central assumption that Marx also made but seldom elaborated – the communists (or members of the party) knew the goals of the proletarian movement better by far than did the proletariat itself. Blessed with knowledge of the laws of history they could anticipate the future. Armed with this prescient awareness they could so lead the proletariat, to maximise its influence and guard it from failure.

There were a number of very basic axioms that lay at the very heart of the theory and practice of Leninism with regard to the party that we have to note before proceeding further. We are obliged, at this point, to accept on trust some propositions that will be developed more fully in Chapter 9. As a philosophical system, Leninism affirmed the world to be knowable and law-bound. It also maintained that there were two ways of knowing, and that the systematic, generalised (or 'objective') knowledge of science was privileged over the 'subjective' knowledge conveyed by immediate experience. It was the party that disposed of scientific or objective knowledge. Its analysis of the strivings of the proletariat was, therefore, privileged over the proletariat's own awareness of its goals. That there was but one cohesive set of class goals and a single discernible class will was, similarly, axiomatic to both Marxism and Leninism. Both maintained that it was the communists who alone articulated these goals and this will – that was the party's principal historical role.

At this point, Leninism (again faithful to the Marxian original) resorted to a little-noticed definitional conjuring trick – one that proved to be of crucial importance for the mesmeric effect of the ideology. The trick was spectacularly simple and audacious – the class was defined as class only to the extent that it conformed to the *party's* account of its objectives, and mobilised itself to fulfil them. The proletariat could, it was maintained, only ascend to class existence to the extent that it was organised on at least a national plane and capable of articulating its objectives. To accomplish these tasks it urgently needed a political organisation – the Communist Party. The party now not only enters into the *definition* of class existence but becomes *the essential expression of it*. Without effective articulation and political organisation in pursuit of its objectives, the proletariat did not exist as a class. Marx cryptically put it in this way when defining the tasks of the Communists' 'formation of the proletarians into a class and consequently into a political party'.[3] It was a definitional proposition that flowed from his more general assertion (much quoted by Plekhanov and subsequently by Lenin) that 'every class struggle is a political struggle'.[4]

Leninist literature is, of course, full of references to the party's responsibilities and obligations to the class. What is rarely mentioned, but is much more fundamental, is the responsibility of the class to the party. It was now to be held to account for any waverings, whoring after non-party doctrines or leaders, and any failure to conform to party expectations. The messy, real proletarians – the aggregation of wage workers with all their diverse projects and aspirations – were to be judged in their progress towards a properly class existence by the party that had itself devised the criteria for their class existence. A further paradox of this situation was that the class background of the party leaders, and of the theoreticians that defined the nature of proletarian existence, was not a matter of importance. It was very likely, indeed, that they would be 'a portion of the bourgeois ideologists'[5] (as Marx put it) rather than workers who, after all, had neither the training nor the leisure to consider such matters scientifically. Kautsky was, as we have seen, even more adamant that it was the bourgeois intelligentsia rather than the working class that was the vehicle of science,[6] that is, the body that defined the content of the socialist project and the role of the working class in implementing it.

Leninism is wholly a child of Marxism in respect to the basic foundations of its theory of the party. It bases itself on a similar claim to a special sort of knowledge and a similar arrogant contention that the proletarian cause cannot be discovered merely by taking a poll among workers. As Trotsky observed, 'even the proletarian psychology includes in itself a terrible inertia of conservatism'.[7] The views of the majority have nothing to do with it. The majority are ill-organised and suffer from false consciousness. The lowest common denominator of their ideas would represent more an aggregation of ignorance than a display of wisdom. Proletarian purpose, Lenin frequently asserted, cannot be forwarded merely by 'counting heads'.

Party and Parliament

This elitist and anti-democratic disposition of Leninism was reinforced powerfully by the Marxist metaphysic of history that it set out explicitly to revive and purify. History, Leninism faithfully intoned, was no more than the history of class struggle. Successive classes had emerged that had been obliged, in order to guarantee their monopoly access to wealth and status within society, to seize the power of the state. They used the law, prisons, police and army to justify and defend their own privileges. In each case, however, emergent classes had to confront the power of existing power holders. The principal lesson of the Marxist theory of history was that dominant classes never relinquish voluntarily their control over access to wealth and power within society. They have to be overthrown forcibly. 'Revolutions are the locomotives of history', Marx insisted,[8] only through revolutionary action were the fundamental transitions in history accomplished. Such fundamental transformations – in which one group of claimants for wealth, status and power displaced another – could not be effected in a peaceful manner. The fallacy of all other ideologies and political parties was that their theoretical assumptions, as well as their political practice, assumed that rival claims within society could and should be reconciled peacefully. They presumed that rational discussion and compromise, conducted by elected representatives according to the gentlemanly etiquette of parliamentary debate, could and should resolve social disputes and attend to the grievances of the electorate. The presuppositions of democracy, and of all the democratic parties (including the reformist social democrats) were, in Lenin's view, out of joint with the logic of Marxism. They were no doubt superficially attractive, but they were flabby and philistine. They all dealt in the honeyed hypocrisies of national unity, class conciliation and political compromise. In the final analysis, however, history demonstrated that only force and organised revolutionary action had effected the transition from one epoch to another and that, in the pre-revolutionary period, was the principal message that the Leninist party had to imprint upon the masses: 'In the long run we know that the problems of social life are resolved by the class struggle in its bitterest and fiercest form – civil war.'[9]

The party's aim was, therefore, unlike that of any other political party. It did not aspire to power within the existing system. It sought to overthrow it. It did not accept existing states as legitimate sources of authority, nor their laws as anything other than the codification of the interests of the ruling class. It was a party with an ideology of militant rejectionism or separatism, whose object was to undermine the legitimacy of existing allocations of power and wealth, and all the institutions and ideologies that supported them. Its essential terrain of struggle was outside parliament, outside existing constitutions, and therefore outside the law.

This rejectionist stance of Leninism did not mean that the party should wholly abstain from conventional politics – that was the stance of anarchism with which, Lenin insisted, revolutionary Marxism had nothing in common. There were, of course, times when the revolutionary tide was running with full force, when it was entirely proper for the party to withdraw entirely from the impotent 'talking shops' of bourgeois parliaments and to expose them for the shams they were. At such moments in history the party's place was in the streets, the industrial plants and the garrisons. These were the real loci of power and they, rather than parliament, constituted the decisive terrain. The activity of the party within parliaments and in everyday political struggle was none the less important in educating and preparing the class for the time of revolutionary assault. The party's role here was to dispel the widespread illusions that the mass continued to cherish – illusions about the possibility of a peaceful reconciliation of opposing interests.

No matter how cramped and restricted bourgeois parliaments were, they ought to be used to demonstrate to the mass of the people how illusory it was to expect from such bodies fundamental changes in their conditions. 'Bourgeois democracy,' Lenin reminded his followers, 'which is invaluable in educating the proletariat and training it in the struggle, is always narrow, hypocritical, spurious and false; it always remains democracy for the rich and a swindle for the poor.'[10] Politics, even the restricted politics of the bourgeois state, none the less served a number of educative and organisational purposes that Leninist parties ought not to neglect. In the first place they would, as we have seen, purge the masses of their illusory hopes that substantial change could be accomplished *within* the existing structures of political and economic power. They would demonstrate, moreover, the true class configuration of contemporary society. It would become abundantly clear which parties, speaking on behalf of which social groups and classes, supported or opposed progressive reforming legislation. The party's responsibility here was clear. It was to promote precisely those issues that would exemplify and reveal the antagonism between the possessing classes and the dispossessed. Its object was never to canvass those issues that invited the maximum consensus between political groups, but to seize on those that obliged the supporters and the opponents of labour emancipation to take diametrically opposed and highly visible public stances.

It was the antagonism of interests that needed constantly to be emphasised and teased out, and for that to be successful the party imperatively had to adopt the politics of confrontation and undermine the efforts of all those on the 'left' or the 'right' who espoused a politics of conciliation. For the Leninist party, the most iniquitous and dangerous forces were always those of the centre. The siren calls of the advocates of class harmony and social peace, the seductive message of reformists and conciliators – these were always the most insidious of voices, because they made people believe what they wanted to believe – that they could get what they needed and wanted without struggle:

> In a society based upon class divisions, the struggle between the hostile classes is bound, at a certain stage of its development, to become a political struggle. The most purposeful, most comprehensive and specific expression of the political struggle of classes is the struggle of parties. The non-party principle means indifference to the struggle of parties. But this indifference is not equivalent to neutrality, to abstention from the struggle, for in the class struggle there can be no neutrals; . . . Indifference is tacit support of the strong, of those who rule.[11]

The object of the communists was therefore not to reform an unreformable system of power, but rather to demonstrate the impossibility of meaningful and lasting changes within the system, and to expose the vain claims of those who maintained the reverse. It was to reveal and accentuate the class orientation of all political groupings by choosing those issues that would polarise political life by obliging parties to declare themselves for or against the preservation of existing structures of power.

There was, finally, a limited utility to parliamentary politics in that it provided a medium through which the party could reach its targeted constituency. It could and should use all the opportunities and limited freedoms of bourgeois election campaigns to get its message through to the working masses. It could and should extract every last ounce of advantage from the immunity afforded to parliamentary representatives to use parliament as a megaphone of the class war. The utility of parliament in this respect was not that it offered an opportunity to convince one's opponents through rational argument of the desirability of change, but rather that, within the central institutions of state, the voice of the militant proletariat might find one protected place from which it could reverberate throughout the land. Communist deputies should therefore pay little heed to the impact of their proposals upon their fellow legislators. They were there not to speak *to* parliament but to speak (as Bebel had put it) through its windows to the land outside. Above all, they were never to be seduced by notions of the independence of representatives, responding as personal conscience dictated, to informed debate. They were unambiguously tribunes, delegated to fulfil a brief that was not theirs to temporise or extemporise. They ought never be allowed to forget that they were nothing but the voice of the party in parliament.

We have seen that, for good Leninists, the decisive terrains of party activity lay not inside, but outside parliament, and there were many levels to the arguments they adduced to vindicate their stance. Historically, they argued, it was a matter of fact that the great issues concerning fundamental changes to structures of power and property had been resolved not by debates but by force of arms: witness the great bourgeois revolutions against feudal and monarchical power. More basically, historical materialism demonstrated that it was social status, wealth and power that dictated political attitudes, and that sustained them as non-negotiable claims. Those, in short, who believed that the rich might be persuaded by moral or intellectual argument to give up their privilege were, at best, hopeless Utopians. The *real* sites of power within bourgeois civilisation were located neither in parliaments nor in cabinets, but in concentrations of capital and armed power. It was in those locations that the power of capitalism had to be confronted if the party was ever to become a serious revolutionary force. The factories and garrisons had to be politicised, they had to become the fundamental centres of class struggle within society, because in the one exploitation (that sustained the whole system) was systematically pursued, and in the other it was backed by the sanction of state force: 'Not a single great revolution has taken place, or ever can take place, without the disorganisation of the army.'[12] If the bourgeois state was, in the Leninist analysis, no more than the purposeful organisation of coercive power to sustain exploitative economic relations, then it followed that rather than being mesmerised by the illusory histrionics of political debate, the Leninist should seek to penetrate its *real* basis.

Party and Class

It was within the factories and workshops that the material values sustaining capitalism were produced and reproduced. Here workers were hired, and here surplus value was extracted from them and converted into profit – the lifeblood of the whole system. It was in the factories and workshops that the workers were brought together in numbers that increased with each refinement of the division of labour within the work process. Here they could feel the potential strength of their combined numbers. And here, above all, only workers were concentrated – men and women who were exclusively dependent upon selling their labour power. Within the factories, mines and workshops there were, by definition, no small traders, peasant farmers, small-scale entrepreneurs, bureaucrats, teachers or petty functionaries: only the working class, pure and undiluted. It was therefore within the industrial enterprise that the party should concentrate its resources and establish its primary organisations. In the whole history of the Soviet Union it was, of course, on industrial and vocational constituencies that the party was based. Belief in the primacy of territorial or parliamentary constituencies was for those who continued to accept the illusion that parliament really was the seat of effective power within society. For the communists, however, industrial organisation took precedence. Their 'natural' constituency was the industrial working class or proletariat. It was, they contended, this class, and this class alone, that could lead society along the road to the overthrow of bourgeois civilisation. But before it could do so effectively the proletariat had to be organised, unified and made conscious of its great historical role. It was the responsibility of the party to bring to the class these vital elements of organisation and consciousness – on these the future of the revolution (indeed, of all humanity) depended.

It was a central tenet of Leninism that although the party expressed the interests of the working class unambiguously and was, indeed, the natural representative of *all* who were exploited by capital, it could never be identified with the class. It was imperative that it kept itself ideologically and organisationally distinct from the class. The party was, as we have seen, charged with the responsibility to articulate the *general* and the *long-term* interests of all wage workers. It was therefore obliged to represent and articulate not merely an existing and already achieved level of consciousness and organisation amongst the working class, but to guide and lead it towards its next phase of development. If it did not do so, then, in Lenin's view, the party had no *raison d'être*. It would condemn itself to voicing the disparate (and sometimes conflicting) grievances of differing groups of wage workers. Trades unions were the proper vehicles for this sort of work. If the party was to restrict itself to the battle for minor economic improvements, its message, and its membership, would be diluted rapidly. In this case, it would sink to the level of following behind in the tail of the workers ('tailism'), its political goals would be obscured by over-concentration on bread-and-butter issues of the pay and conditions of labour ('economism'). It would leave the field wide open to bourgeois liberals and radicals to posture as the friends of labour and its political mouthpiece. Unless a resolute and theoretically informed party of the proletariat aggressively prosecuted its long-term goals and relentlessly exposed the hypocrisy of all the bourgeois parties, the working class was fated to be led by radical opportunists who would exploit the political vacuum they found, in order to emasculate the revolutionary mission of the working class.

In Chapter 1 we examined, at some length, the inadequacy of the prevalent line of interpretation that has it that Lenin uniquely is responsible for the noxious consequences of insisting upon the separation of Party and class. I argued that this was not only intrinsic to Marxism it was a foundation precept of the orthodoxy of Russian Marxism that Lenin inherited from Plekhanov. Evidence was cited from Marx, Plekhanov and the immaculate Kautsky, to the effect that without the theoretical and organisational initiatives of the socialist intelligentsia, at the head of an independent proletarian political party, the working class would be doomed to historical impotence. None of those with a claim to represent Marxist orthodoxy ever maintained that adequate revolutionary consciousness was a natural or spontaneous product of the workers' movement itself. We need not, at this point, reconstruct once again the contexts in which Lenin, in 1902, arrived at his conception of the 'Party of the new type' outlined in *What Is to Be Done?*

We have already observed that, in the Leninist formulation, party membership entailed far more than mere adherence to a programme and preparedness to pay membership dues. It involved a continuing activist commitment to serve the party in an appropriate functional role. It was conceived, from the outset, as a mobilizing elite of the most dedicated, from whom special qualities were expected. We have, similarly, observed that the party's targeted constituency could not be the undifferentiated mass of wage workers as a whole. The party ought rather to concentrate its attention on the advanced section – the *avant-garde* – of the proletariat. It would be wholly wrong, in Lenin's view, to dissolve the party into the class as a whole. To do so would only dilute its forces by spreading them impossibly thin. It would, moreover, lead ineluctably to the great majority of average and backward workers dictating the tasks of the movement and would thereby emasculate the potency of the party as a historic force. It would become bogged down in local, transient and petty demands, and forfeit its generalising and forward-looking role.

The party and the class could never be an amalgam; they could never be fused, precisely because it was the party's duty to lead the class. Ideally, the party, the advanced workers, and the class as a whole, were in constant reciprocal upward motion. Here, Lenin did insert a truly original note into contemporary politics that was to be fundamental to the morale and self-image of Leninists. It was the notion of the party as an accelerator or multiplier of forces. The basic idea was simple enough: that efficient organisation can increase immeasurably the political and social impact of relatively small numbers of activists. A small but disciplined group, working according to a common plan, possessing a clear command structure and a well-elaborated division of labour can therefore have a disproportionate, even decisive, effect upon the politics of a country. The measurement of the likely impact of any group or party cannot therefore be properly assessed simply by totalling its adherents or voters. On the contrary the political potency of any organisation is, in large part, a function of its effective organisation. Lenin often invoked the model of large-scale enterprises, operating a sophisticated division of labour with authoritative managerial allocation of function, to show how the productivity of such a system was hugely greater than that of larger numbers of workers working in scattered handicraft workshops. The party, he concluded, must model itself on the factory. At other times he made the comparison between the power of a small professional army and that of a mass of ill-organised insurgents. From both comparisons, the Leninist party was to absorb a vocabulary and an imagery that was far from insignificant to its later development. The martial metaphors of war, battles, advance guard and general staff were complemented by productivist metaphors of division of labour, motive-force, transmission belts, cogwheels and so on.

Whichever set of metaphors was adopted, the central point remained constant:

> My argument is that in all countries, everywhere and always, there exists, *in addition* to the party, a 'broad section' of people *close to the party* and the huge mass of the *class* that founds the party causes it to emerge and nurtures it . . .
> The party is the politically conscious, advanced section of the

class, it is its vanguard. The strength of that vanguard is ten times, a hundred times, more than a hundred times, greater than its members. Is that possible? Can the strength of hundreds be greater than the strength of thousands? It can be, and is, *when the hundreds are organised.* Organisation increases strength tenfold.[13]

The party ought therefore to be as concerned with the intensity of commitment of its members, and the efficient articulation of their differing functional responsibilities, as with the extensiveness of its broader-based support. In part, that broad-based support would itself be generated precisely by the confidence the mass would come to have in an efficient, disciplined organization that in fact delivered its promises – 'Better Fewer but Better!'[14] This did not mean that the relatively small party could, of itself, transform society or effect a revolution: that would be sheer adventurism. Rather, the party would act upon the 'broad section' of its supporters and voters through a whole series of intermediate organisations and through the medium of its tightly-controlled press and propaganda units. The 'broad section' would, in its turn, draw in the bulk of the whole working class and, after them, the wavering or marginal strata of society. This was, as we shall see later, the importance of such groups as the non-party trade unions – they would become the 'transmission belts' of party influence upon the wider working class.

The crucial thing, in the Leninist account of the relationship between party and class, was not to conflate the two, but to grasp the fundamental importance of the linkages between them. In all Leninist parties, these mobilising linkages were the same: the central party authority directed the full-time party cadres who, in turn, mobilised the local, functional or trade union cells of the party to activate the advanced workers, whose assertiveness would then draw in the average and the backward strata of the working class through their influence over trade unions, cultural organisations and other front organisations or transmission belts.

Without mass involvement, Lenin recognised only too well, the party would be impotent. If, in its slogans and practical policies, it ran too far ahead of the advanced workers, its influence would be nil. The dangers of adventurism or Jacobinism of this sort stood at the opposite pole from the sins of economism, spontaneism, tailism or reformism at the other end of the spectrum. Both extremes threatened disaster, which only close and detailed analysis, combined with astute political leadership, could avoid. In any event, and in almost any conceivable circumstance, the Leninist parties of the Communist International could, if Moscow so minded, be found guilty of falling for one or other 'deviation' and consequently needing to be purged or 'renewed'.

Democratic Centralism and the Universalisation of Bolshevik Tactics

For the Leninist, a secret underground party structure was as vital to defensive as it was to offensive strategy. Leninists reposed no faith in the permanence of 'bourgeois' democracy or 'bourgeois' civil rights. They would be sustained only so long as they served to disguise, and thereby protect, capitalist exploitation. It followed, therefore, that the more successful the party was at exposing them as shams and illusions, and the more social tensions became exacerbated within society, the more the bourgeoisie would be obliged to rely upon the naked coercion of army and police to defend their power. Given this scenario, it would be impossibly Utopian for the revolutionary party to rely exclusively upon open, publicly-accessible organisational structures. They were, after all, likely to be singled out for particularly repressive treatment, as would all the militant leaders of the labour movement. It was imperative therefore that the party should prepare itself for this eventuality. The party had to construct parallel power structures and secret lines of communication and propaganda to duplicate its open ones. Its underground agents must therefore be 'professionals' skilled in the use of codes and ciphers, scrupulous in protecting their contacts, and trustworthy beyond reproach. Secrecy and professionalism was particularly important in such crucial areas of party activity as infiltrating the armed forces.

Lenin's original justification for a secretive, hierarchical party, staffed (or at least commanded) by 'professionals' was that the conditions of tsarist autocracy in Russia, where *all* political activity was proscribed, left no other realistic option open. He did not, at that time (1902), nor at any time up to the October Revolution of 1917, presume to recommend the Russian model for more general international adoption. On the contrary, he looked forward to the happy time when civic and political rights and the rule of law would allow the party to reform itself into a structure more like that of the model party for the whole of Europe – the German Social Democratic Party (SPD). During the First World War his attitude began to stiffen. How was it that so many of the leading members of European social democratic parties had succumbed to nationalist and reformist views? How was militant socialism to be protected against such contagion? Hesitantly, Lenin began to arrive at the conclusion that organisational control had been far too lax. The European socialist parties had, in retrospect, been far too permissive and broad-church. They had allowed, for far too long within their midst, frank apologists of imperialism; moderates who counselled alliances with radical or liberal bourgeois parties, as well as notorious proponents of a peaceful and gradualist road to socialism, such as Eduard Bernstein. In part this had been caused by the avarice for votes and the unwarranted measurement of socialist advance in terms of parliamentary seats secured. The result had been the dilution of the revolutionary and proletarian message of marxian socialism through appeals for electoral support to the most diverse social strata. The parliamentary tail had ended up wagging the party dog. All sorts of careerists and adventurers with a marginal commitment to socialism, and often even a frank disavowal of revolutionary politics, had entered the socialist parties and corroded their revolutionary message:

> during the decades of comparatively 'peaceful' capitalism between 1871 and 1914, the Augean stables of philistinism, imbecility, and apostasy accumulated in the socialist parties which were adapting themselves to opportunism.[15]

The moral was clear. The socialist movement must rid itself of its opportunist fellow travellers and it could only do so by establishing a far clearer and more emphatic statement of its goals, and by instituting procedural rules and strict discipline to ensure that these goals were adhered to. It could maintain its purity only through periodic cleansing or purging of its membership. Regular re-registration, in which each member was obliged to demonstrate his or her dedication and commitment as a condition for acquiring a new party card, were to become a typical feature of Leninist parties.

It was not until the Second Congress of the Communist International in 1920 that Lenin was able to lay down, in some detail, the organisational structures appropriate to Communist Party organisation. By this time, his earlier modesty about the relevance of the Russian experience, and his reluctance to generalise from it, had wholly disappeared. The Russian communists (the ex-Bolsheviks) had been the only socialists in Europe to overthrow their government; they alone had established a soviet regime and now, alone, they confronted the concerted armed might and propaganda onslaught of the imperialist world.

It was now entirely clear to Lenin why the Russians had succeeded where the others had failed: the Russians had maintained both theoretical and organisational integrity, whereas the others had not. They had purged themselves of fellow-travelling revisionists, 'economists' and social pacifists, while other so-called socialist parties had maintained a permissive ideological broad church. They had developed the compulsory organisational discipline of a party of genuine activists, whereas the others had diluted party membership to include anyone who merely paid subscriptions. The Bolshevik Party (now the Communist Party) had insisted upon iron discipline and the firm accountability of all its sections to an authoritative centre, while other parties were content with a loose, almost federal, structure. It was clear to Lenin that there would be no spread of the revolution unless and until frankly revolutionary vanguard parties were created, and there was no other model of success apart from that of the Russian Communists: 'Bolshevism *has created* the ideological and tactical foundations of a Third International . . . Bolshevism *can serve as a model of tactics for all.*'[16]

Lenin's twenty-one Conditions of Admission into the Communist International were drafted for the Second Congress of the International in July 1920. They still remain as canons of orthodoxy for the surviving Leninist parties. Many of these conditions repeated the basic message that a split from the reformist and centrist leadership of the old socialist parties was absolutely obligatory. The whole foundational logic of the Communist International, and of all its constituent parties, was that the gradualist moderate social democrats had become traitors to the working class. They had become the principal enemies of militant communism. They were class enemies. Every Communist Party was obliged therefore to 'consistently and systematically dismiss them from "positions of any responsibility" in the working-class movement and to unmask their treachery'.[17] This would not, however, be a one-off operation. The dangers of dilution and infiltration were permanent, and so Communist Party branches were obliged to 'carry out periodic membership purges with the aim of systematically ridding the party of petty-bourgeois elements that inevitably percolate into it'. Constituent sections were obliged to conduct 'persistent and systematic propaganda and agitation' in the army and the countryside, and they were to 'place no trust in bourgeois legality. They must everywhere build up a parallel illegal organisation.'[18] Above all, the parties of the Communist International must be 'marked by an iron discipline bordering on military discipline, and have strong and authoritative party centres invested with wide powers and enjoying the unanimous confidence of the membership'.[19] This could only be effected if they organised themselves according to the precepts of democratic centralism.[20]

Ever since 1920, Communist or Leninist Parties have prided themselves on being vanguard parties of action. A party of action must, they maintain, exhibit at least two basic features. It must, in the first place, group together only those who are not only of like mind, but who also are prepared to devote their time and energy to its cause. In the second place, for the effectiveness of individual members and its several specialised sections to be maximised, the party must have a truly authoritative centre to co-ordinate and direct them. A party that is preparing for war must be organised for war; it must have clear command structures and definite procedures for deciding upon and implementing its strategy and tactics. The party must, in short, speak with one voice and act with one will. Democratic centralism was the shorthand term used to describe the package of organisational provisions (and prohibitions) through which that unity was to be secured and preserved.

According to the official formulation, democratic centralism is to be distinguished from bureaucratic centralism. This latter implies high-handed application of general formulas, without discussion and taking no heed of particular circumstance. The former takes as its ideal starting point the broadest and fullest debate and consultation, and a generalised system of election in which the mass of party members elect their local committee, the local committees elect a regional committee, and the regional committees in their turn elect the Central Committee, which, finally, elects the Presidium (later to become the Politburo) of the party. When, however, the process of periodic consultation and debate has produced a clear general line on policy matters, articulated by the authoritative and highest organs of the party, then debate and discussion must cease. No individual or lower party organ could dissent from or countermand instructions proceeding from a superior level of authority. The penalty for deviance was expulsion. This was made clear in 1921 at the Tenth Congress of the Russian Communist Party. Exasperated by the continuing organised opposition to his policies by such groups as the democratic centralists and the workers' opposition, Lenin declared that 'the opposition's time has run out and that the lid's on it. We want no more oppositions!'[21] 'We are not,' he declared, 'a debating society.'[22] The party and the regime were, according to Lenin, facing an accumulation of economic and political crises exacerbated by its internal weakness and external isolation. It was beset with internal and external enemies who attempted to profit from the deprivations that economic crisis had produced. In these circumstances they took advantage of every dissension or sign of a split within the party, fomenting divisions to weaken its resolve. In such circumstances, factions were impermissible – they were potentially fatal to the party's integrity and therefore to its hold on power. In his 'Draft Resolution on Party Unity' Lenin insisted that 'The Congress, therefore, hereby declares dissolved and orders the immediate dissolution of all groups without exception formed on the basis of one platform or another . . . Non-observance of this decision of the Congress shall entail unconditional and instant expulsion from the Party.'[23] This was the so-called 'ban on factions' first introduced in the Russian party and then extended to all the constituent sections of the Communist International.

The system of democratic centralism that prevailed under the Russian party was extended to all the parties of the Communist International (often known by its shortened name – the Comintern). Although they could, for purposes of democratic propaganda, style themselves Communist Party of France, Germany, Italy, Great Britain and so on, it was made clear, from the outset, that they were merely the sections of a larger, integral whole – the Third (or Communist) International. Their national congresses and their national Central and Executive Committees were not sovereign bodies. On the contrary, they were subordinate to the World Congress of the International which, in turn, elected its all-powerful Executive Committee. As in the Russian party, so too in the International, effective power and control of all policy decisions, allocation of key personnel and of finance were vested in the central executive bodies. To ensure that this control was not diluted by local or national considerations, or by the preferences of powerful 'national' figures, the Executive Committee of the Communist International took to appointing its own agents who were dispatched to all those countries where there was a significant Communist Party. The Comintern agents were responsible for ensuring that the policy directives of the International were adhered to undeviatingly. They reported directly to the Comintern Executive Committee on all aspects of the work, the personnel and the activities of the parties for which they were responsible. They were the guardians of the 'general line' and it was largely through their direct influence (not least their control of the purse strings) that the emergent Communist Parties of the world (particularly of Europe) were 'Bolshevised' successfully in the early 1920s.

Declassing of the Proletariat and Party Dictatorship

In 1921 a studied and harsh attitude towards internal and external criticism and debate came to typify Leninism. As a current of thought it finally broke with the democratic traditions of the European left with which it had always been ill at ease. It poured scorn on all those leaders who continued to cherish the illusion that the workers might achieve their emancipation through the existing democratic, parliamentary and legal institutions of bourgeois society. It dismissed contemptuously those who argued that freedom of the press and freedom for other political groupings might serve to renew the Russian Communist Party and the administration of the socialist state – that way, Lenin responded, the party was being asked to commit suicide.[24] It was made abundantly clear that in the prolonged period of the dictatorship of the proletariat, the party could not allow political competition. The state was to be a one-party state. In the past, Lenin had felt the need to justify 'temporary' restrictions upon democracy by appealing to the extraordinary crises faced by the regime. By 1921 he had given up this apologetic and defensive stance: he was proud of the fact that the Communists were honest and unambiguous. They were exercising a class dictatorship: only the party was capable of governing, because only it possessed the necessary resolve, unity of will, and tried and tested leadership. The proletarians as a whole, by contrast, had suffered more than any ruling class in history from the effects of their own revolution. In material terms they had not benefited at all. They had suffered 'want and privation unprecedented in history'.[25] They had sacrificed themselves on the battlefields of the civil war and had been driven by starvation, cold and epidemics out of their urban strongholds. They had been decimated by typhus and cholera. They had, in consequence, become demoralised and prey to all sorts of petty bourgeois and anarchist slogans. The proletariat was, Lenin maintained repeatedly, divided, degraded and corrupted:

> so divided, so degraded, and so corrupted in parts . . . that an organisation taking in the whole proletariat cannot directly exercise

proletarian dictatorship. It can be exercised only by a vanguard that has absorbed the revolutionary energy of the class[26]

The proletariat had become declassed.[27] It lay bleeding and prostrate. In this situation only the party, that had absorbed into itself the conscious vanguard of the working class, was fit to exercise power:

> only the political party of the working class, i.e. the Communist Party, is capable of uniting, training and organising a vanguard of the proletariat and of the whole mass of the working people . . . Without this the dictatorship of the proletariat is impossible.[28]

All socialist revolutions, Lenin now insisted, would have to go through a ruthlessly dictatorial period in which the party would be obliged to use the full coercive power of the state to put down its internal enemies – even within the working class. It could tolerate no political opposition and ought frankly to declare that, in a situation of desperate struggle, democracy had to be sacrificed. These were the negative, coercive aspects of the dictatorship of the proletariat – the utilisation of state power to crush all opposition to socialism. The dictatorship of the proletariat also had positive, constructive roles to play. Foremost among these was the task of economic reconstruction. That was the new front to which everything and everyone must be mobilised. That was the long-term goal for which the party had to prepare and reform itself. Upon it depended the future of the regime and of socialism itself.

The imperative to restructure the economy had many interlinked facets. Historically, it arose from the communists' recognition that the economic costs of revolution were directly proportionate to its radicalness. The deeper and more extensive a revolution, the more profound and severe the costs it inflicted upon the economic structure of society. As Bukharin neatly put it 'The extent of the expenses of Communist revolution is determined by the depth of communist revolution . . . All *actual* costs of revolution are based on a *diminution of the process of reproduction* and a decline of productive powers.'[29] Lenin now recognised that the slogans of 1917, through which the energies of the masses were supposed to be mobilised to repair the deficiencies of the economy, had, in fact, produced dislocation and collapse. The movement for workers' control of the factories had destroyed authority patterns within the workplace and produced intense worker suspicion of 'bourgeois' technical specialists or managers. The old relations of production had been destroyed, but no new system of accountability and discipline put in their place. The result was a catastrophic drop in production, a dearth of consumer goods and a consequent reluctance of the peasants to market their produce. By 1921 the situation was desperate. Industrial production had all but ceased; famine and starvation stalked the country. As a condition for the physical survival of people and of the towns, the economy had to be got working again. Only the party could lead this revival, but it too lacked experience and expertise. From now until his last writings in 1923, Lenin repeatedly and bitterly criticised the communists for their inability to manage the economy. The party was full of useless theoreticians, spinners of theses and resolutions, men who were bold, self-sacrificing and daring, but who had neither the training nor the temperament to get on with the patient, painstaking work of administering, checking, husbanding resources, and encouraging the exemplary production units. In the times of revolutionary onslaught such men had been paragons, now they had become superfluous; worse, they had become harmful because they could not learn new ways. They continued to invent disputes and theoretical debate when the job in hand was to revive production and exchange between town and country. They refused even to acknowledge their own ignorance and ineptitude, and dealt contemptuously with those who alone could teach them – the bourgeois specialists, managers and businessmen: 'It must be admitted, and we must not be afraid to admit, that in ninety nine cases out of a hundred the responsible Communists are not in the jobs they are now fit for; that they are unable to perform their duties, and that they must sit down to learn.'[30]

Lenin was already, in 1921, signalling the turn that was to characterise the party for the rest of its life – its future role was to be economic and administrative rather than political in any meaningful sense. Its urgent goals were, as we have seen, economic. To these ends, all else, the party included, must be subordinated. Only by rebuilding large-scale industry as 'the only possible economic foundation for socialism'[31] could the party re-create the urban industrial working class – the party's own social base. Until then, the party would be hanging in the air, without visible social support. '*The production of the proletariat is the "essence" of the period of primitive accumulation*' was how Bukharin put it.[32] We now are presented with the somewhat bizarre proposition that one of the party's primary tasks was to use the power of the state to recreate the proletariat in the places and proportions and with the attitudes necessary to ensure the party's own survival. The party's principal task, as the governing power of the dictatorship of the proletariat, was to re-create the vanished proletariat. The state was to restructure the economic base with the express purpose of guaranteeing the continuity and reproducibility of its own power. This was exactly what the imperialist state had done. With no extensive social base to rely upon, the imperialist bourgeoisie (as Bukharin had pointed out in 1916[33]) had also lit upon the idea of utilising the economic, fiscal and coercive powers of the state to guarantee their own economic survival and to put down all political rivals.

In 1920 it was again Bukharin who invoked this model of the bourgeois state as the only effective organisational structure, both to guarantee the power of the Communists (who were a tiny minority in Russia) and to ensure the transition to a socialist economy: 'State capitalism saved the *capitalist* state by an active and conscious intervention in production relations. Socialist methods will be a continuation of this active process of organisation.'[34]

In his *Economics of the Transition Period* (which had a profound effect on Lenin's whole conception of the dictatorship of the proletariat and the party's role within it), Bukharin went on to elaborate his meaning:

Now we must raise the question as to the general principle of the system of organization of the proletarian apparatus . . . It is clear that the same method is formally necessary for the working class as for the bourgeoisie at the time of state capitalism. This organisational method exists in the co-ordination of all proletarian organizations with one all-encompassing organization, i.e. with the state organization of the working class, with the *soviet state of the proletariat*. The 'nationalization' of the trades unions and the effectual nationalization of all mass organizations of the proletariat, result from the internal logic of the process of transformation itself. The minutest cells of the labor apparatus must transform themselves into agents of the general process of organization, which is systematically directed and led by the collective reason of the working class, which finds its material embodiment in the highest and most all-encompassing organization, in its state apparatus. Thus the system of state capitalism dialectically transforms itself into its own inversion, into the state form of workers' socialism.[35]

Lenin had, in the crises of 1921, moved to embrace a directly similar conception of the role of the party state as a purely instrumental force through which a minority of power holders could ensure the continuity of their power. All other institutions, groups and systems of values were to be expressly subordinated to this objective – none of them was to be allowed an autonomous existence.

In 1920–1 Lenin produced a comprehensive re-examination of the socialist project, not only for Russia but for all the emergent communist parties of Europe. The dictatorship of the proletariat, exercised by the party, displaced the original version of commune/soviet-style democracy. Within society at large, politics and democracy had effectively been proscribed. Even within the party it was precisely the inappropriate continuation of debate and theoretical dispute that most exasperated Lenin. Far from encouraging it, as some suggest, he insisted repeatedly that it must cease: 'Henceforth less politics will be the best politics.'[36] His intemperance, even with opponents within the party, reached new depths of savagery as when he told Shlyapnikov that the appropriate response to his criticisms was a gun.[37] By this time the party had emasculated the trade unions and Lenin saw no larger purpose for them than to act as the 'transmission belts' or 'cogwheels' through which party and state policy was transmitted to the masses. The last potential obstacle to the untrammelled power of the party had been removed. The trade unions had been obliged (as had all other social bodies) to accept the party's right to insert its own nominees in key union posts and to make industrial management solely answerable to the state, and not at all to the workers: 'So long as we, the Party in Central Committee and the whole party, continue to run things, that is, govern, we shall never – we cannot – dispense with the "shake-up", that is, removals, transfers, appointments, dismissals, etc.'[38] Above all, Lenin had insisted upon the party's need to reform and re-educate itself to meet the wholly new challenges of directing the state and managing the economy.

The virtues and values he now prized in party members were almost the inverse of those that had commended communists during the earlier revolutionary periods. The party had no need now of charismatic, impetuous orators. It needed diligent, thorough and decisive administrators who would stick to the unglamorous jobs of retailing production propaganda and following, in detail, the performance of work schedules. Men like Stalin. Not only was this the year of Stalin's accelerated promotion to head the crucial Secretariat and Orgburo of the party, more importantly it was the year in which the new ethos of the ruling elite was established, and its qualities and goals defined. All of them were to enter directly into the construction of Stalinism. It was, further, the fulfilment of the Leninist plan to use the state to regenerate industry and re-create the proletariat that Stalin was to pursue so ruthlessly in the late 1920s and 1930s.

Myth, Party and Power

It was Stalin who, within a week of Lenin's death in January 1924, arrogated to himself the responsibility for defining the new term 'Leninism' that he was largely responsible for coining. It was no accident that the first two articles of the new litany he invented apostrophised the party and its unity as the most sacred elements of the Leninist inheritance:

> Departing from us, Comrade Lenin enjoined us to hold high and guard the purity of the great title of Member of the Party. WE VOW TO YOU, COMRADE LENIN, THAT WE SHALL FULFIL YOUR BEHEST WITH HONOUR! Departing from us, Comrade Lenin enjoined us to guard the unity of our Party as the apple of our eye. WE VOW TO YOU, COMRADE LENIN, THAT THIS BEHEST, TOO, SHALL BE FULFILLED WITH HONOUR![39]

The mythic qualities of the Leninist party were, undoubtedly, a source of quasi-religious comfort to the converted, and of awe to the outsider. The poetry and prose in which it was celebrated, the ritual and theatre in which it presented itself, all combined to create the aura of a transcendent body that was larger by far than the mere sum of its parts. Loyalty and submission to its great cause gave the humble individual the chance to play a part in the development of the sublime. The party, and it alone, authoritatively interpreted the dialectic, the will of the class, and the laws of history. It defined the General Line, and against its collective wisdom no individual could be right. It required of its members not only political loyalty but also a code of conduct that required them, whenever called, to sacrifice personal ambition, friendships, and even their own honour and lives to its cause. This was the meaning of *partiinost* or party-mindedness – putting the party first, above all personal or individual inclinations. *Partiinost*, in this sense, exemplified in practice, in everyday life, that members had rejected the self-seeking individualism of bourgeois philosophy and culture. The party *was* the expression of communal, collaborative values in which the individual, as evidence of his or her commitment, subordinated persona; strivings to its collective will. For generations, the sanctity of the party and unflinching acceptance of its policies and demands became *the* distinctive marks of the true Leninist. Its discipline and constraints were willingly accepted by many as necessary antidotes to the old Adam of individual self-concern. The awful paradoxes of this situation were most graphically revealed in the great show trials of the early 1930s where Stalin, with apparent ease, was able to extract from life-long Communist militants and prominent leaders, lurid confessions about their wrecking and criminal activities within the party which, they knew full well, would result in their execution.

The more the party was glorified as all-seeing, omnipotent and irreproachable, the more the individual felt his or her limitations and individual insignificance. It came to serve the same functions that, in Marx's account, God and the Church had performed in earlier times. In proportion as the party and its General Secretary were endowed with transcendent qualities, the ordinary rank-and-file member was reminded of his or her inadequacies. Their only escape from frailty was to realise some small measure of a finer self through total identification with the goals of history and all humanity, expressed and realised through the party.

The veneration of the party and its sanctification as the central element of Leninism was conceived of by the man who would, within ten years, decimate it in mass purges and execute virtually all its veteran leaders and intellectuals. The capricious and barbarous manner in which Stalin, as head of the party, was to deal with all opposition, real or imagined, raised in high relief a problem that Lenin himself, towards the end of his life, had painfully recognised but failed to resolve. In the whole history of communist power it proved to be a problem that was, both theoretically and in practical terms, incapable of resolution. Cryptically stated, it was the ancient problem of *quis custodiet ipsos custodes* – who is to guard against the guards? More intelligibly we might reformulate this as, who or what is to restrain the Communist Party? To whom or to what are its leaders accountable? If the party was not to be held accountable periodically through democratic procedures, nor face the challenge of competing political parties or the scrutiny of critical media of mass communication, how was it to prevent its own deterioration? Who or what could guard it against corruption, nepotism or excess?

These problems troubled Lenin insistently during the last years of his life. All around him he saw, and bitterly complained about, the incompetence, high-handedness and bureaucratic inertia of large numbers of party members and state officials. The ineffective antidotes he prescribed were those that subsequent generations were to resort to with similar lack of success. in dealing with the same systemic problem. In the first place, he proposed a wholesale purge of the careerists, place-seekers and speculators. The party would cleanse itself – Better Fewer but Better. The threat of expulsion would, it was believed, concentrate the minds of party members wonderfully on the proper discharge of their duties. In the second place, the party would purify itself and its state administration by establishing scrutinising committees comprised of dedicated and honest proletarians and peasants.[40] This would establish a form of limited or proxy external accountability. In the third place, the party must guard against abuse, by establishing firm and stringent norms of conduct and behaviour that would be enforced by a Party Control Commission. Here, the party would institute a rigorous form of self-policing. Cumulatively, Lenin wanted to believe, these procedures and institutions would guarantee the purity and probity of the party and its members. He was, however, enough of a realist to acknowledge that, even during his own tenure of power, each of these seemingly fail-safe mechanisms had been perverted to such an extent that, in their actual operation, they served to exacerbate the malaise they were intended to cure, not least because Stalin effectively controlled them. Already by 1922 and 1923 he was obliged to think the unthinkable: what if unscrupulous and malevolent men succeeded in capturing even these institutions and manipulated them to cover up or condone their own abuses of power? The problem was not academic. On the contrary, it threatened the whole future of the socialist project, and Lenin was poignantly aware of his personal responsibility for having failed to alert the party to the potentially disastrous consequences of this danger.

The party that Lenin bequeathed to his successors was already monolithic and increasingly bureaucratised. It had proscribed all internal and external opposition, it permeated every department of state and dominated all those social organisations whose continued existence it was prepared to tolerate. It was responsible to no one. Contested elections to state and other bodies had long since ceased, and all important positions were filled by appointment rather than by election. In the very success of its own dominance the party created the grounds of its own degeneration. Through the powers the central bodies of the party (Secretariat and Organisation Bureau) now possessed and exercised, to place their nominees in all subordinate bodies of party, state and society, they could guarantee the perpetuation of their own power.

Democratic centralism – the vaunted organisational code of contemporary communism that was to save it from the corruption and indecisiveness of Western socialism, proved in practice to be a prime factor in the degeneration of communist parties and the regimes they led. The process whereby lower party bodies elected the next level, which in turn elected the next, and so on up to the party's highest bodies, the Politburo and the General Secretary was, evidently, one of vertically structured indirect election. It was premised on the view that there were distinct levels of induction within the party that implied gradations of commitment, experience, reliability and theoretical awareness within the membership. The implicit rationale was that only appropriate peer groups could judge the leadership qualities of their peers. Thus only members of the Central Committee of the party were entitled to vote for the members of the Politburo and they, in turn, selected the General Secretary. Ordinary members of the party played no role whatever in these crucial deliberations – their vote for the membership of their local party bureau was four or five times removed from the leadership selection process at the national level. So ingrained was the attachment to indirect election, and the presuppositions upon which it was based, that to the last, and despite cogent advice, Gorbachev fatally refused to conform his pre-eminence by seeking a direct popular mandate as president of the Union of Socialist Soviet Republics. The notion of direct popular mandate was, from first to last, foreign and dangerous to the legitimating norms of the party, and even its most reform-minded leaders could not escape their residual antipathy to this mere 'arithmetical' calculation of the popular will. It offended against the very *raison d'être* of the party and consequently, with spectacular rapidity, the party was swept aside by it.

8

Nationalism and Internationalism

In the grand panorama of the Marxist account of history, the tale that is told is of man's growing consciousness of a shared humanity. It is, in a sense, the last gasp of Enlightenment optimism that when at last people escaped from thraldom to religions and empires, that set them artificially one against another, then they might realise their common project of improving the moral and material life of all. This solidarism had been part of the fabric of socialist thought since the French Revolution and it was expressed in the extravagant yearning for a world without strangers in which 'men to men should brothers be'. It was a central part of the Utopianism of the socialist project. For Marx, and for the Leninist tradition, each epoch of human history, each new civilisation, had contributed to this tendency to break down the barriers of local, regional, national and religious differentiation. Each epoch had contributed, sometimes unconsciously and often against its better judgement, to the development of a common *species* awareness which it was the objective of communism finally to realise.

In his Paris Manuscripts of 1844, Marx developed the themes of universality and immediacy that were to be so central to his whole scheme of thought even if these particular writings were to be hidden from his disciples for almost a century. Man, Marx insisted, could only be free when he transcended the narrow confines of self, family and locality, and came to grasp his oneness with all humanity – when he 'in practice and in theory adopts the species as his object' and 'treats himself as a *universal* and therefore a free being'.[1] The whole of history, in this account, has been but a preparation for the dawning of an age in which all the distances that had separated men, all the identifiers that had set them one against another, would finally disappear. Communism was conceived of as the end of man's pre-history; it was the point at which the last great antagonism dividing mankind – the class antagonism between owners of the means of production and wage labourers – was finally done away with. Mankind could then enter into a genuinely *human* existence. Each would recognise that the free and full development of the potentialities of everyone else was a condition for one's own development. Mankind would, at last, lead a species life freed of the divisiveness and antagonisms of ancient signifiers of identity:

This communism, as fully-developed naturalism, equals humanism, and as fully-developed humans equals naturalism: it is the *genuine* resolution of the conflict between man and nature and between man and man – the true resolution of the strife between . . . freedom and necessity, between the individual and the species.[2]

The basic problem that Leninism inherited from Marx was that this project of attaining the undivided human, or species existence of mankind, was held to be attainable only through an historical period in which the exacerbation of differences was to reach the pitch of actual civil war. It would come only after the utmost accentuation of the antagonism between the polarised classes of modern society. Only after the bourgeoisie, on a world scale, had been eliminated was it possible for the proletariat to emerge as the class that embodied the universal strivings of humanity. In the meantime, divisiveness and antagonism would have to be its strategy.

The matter was further complicated by Lenin's own global analysis that located exploiter and exploited nations. The boundaries between class and nation now became obscured, and the success of the universalist project of all mankind came to be identified with the defeat of the world's great imperialist powers. From this it was only a small step to identify the universal project with that national group that emerged as the foremost protagonist and organiser of the anti-imperialist struggle (synonymous now with the struggle of all mankind). Through this process of elision, the universal strivings of all mankind became identified with the universal class – the proletariat – whose foremost representative in the battle with imperialism was, of course, the Russian working class acting under the direction of its Communist Party.

Capitalism as World-Historical Mode of Production

A large part of the historically progressive role of emergent capitalism was that its very mode of production drove it to break down the complex web of baronial, municipal and guild prerogatives; the duchies, dukedoms and petty principalities, each with its own trade barriers and laws, that set up so many obstacles to the circulation of ideas, goods and people. The scale of production under capitalism imperatively demanded a market on at least the national scale but it could not, of course, enlist the mass support it needed for its own victory under the vulgar watchwords of trade and manufacture. The bourgeoisie, in its contest with feudalism and narrow localism, had dressed its cause in grander colours. It proclaimed the equality of civic and political rights, and the freedom of all under the law. It fought for freedom of association and travel, and of expression and religion. It broke down the barriers of both trade, and intellectual obscurantism, and created the broader basis of political identity in the modern nation state. The market, in short, demanded that people be drawn into more extensive patterns of exchange, and therefore into larger communities.

Part of the paradox of capitalist development was, however, that the more mature it became, the more it found itself cramped and constrained both by its initial spatial dimensions and by its self-chosen civic and political ideals. The scale and volume of its productive outputs rapidly outgrew the limited capacities of nation states to accommodate them. The political unit of the nation state proved too small to absorb the product of capitalist industry which increasingly required an international, global market. Capitalism, in order to survive, had to become expansionist, militarist and aggressive. It had, in its late maturity, to expand its economic territory and it could do so only by subjugating other nations. In its final epoch of finance capitalism or imperialism, it was evident that capitalism had long outgrown its national shell. The nation state was no longer commensurate with the volume of productive output.

External subjugation was complemented by internal oppression and a rapid shift from the liberal, legal and politically egalitarian ideals that had typified its youth and early maturity. Imperialist nationalism of the 'white man's burden' and 'manifest destiny' type was decadent, parasitic and oppressive nationalism, that could only be fed by denying its client and dependent national groups all rights to their own self-determination. In the epoch of imperialism, according to Lenin, the nationalism of the imperialist powers was the negation of freedom, democracy and equality, both at home and abroad: 'Both in foreign and home policy imperialism strives towards violations of democracy, towards reaction. In this sense imperialism is indisputably the "negation" of *democracy in general*, of *all democracy*, and not just of *one* of its demands, national self-determination.'[3]

It was primarily the changed scale and nature of capitalist production, in the last decades of the nineteenth century, that led to this metamorphosis. Its productive techniques led to the exponential growth of a stock of excess commodities on a scale that was without precedent in man's history. Its goods were of a quantity, quality and price that no other productive system could remotely match. These goods, Marx maintained, were the heavy artillery of capitalism, by means of which it battered down all Chinese walls[4] and within decades reduced to subservience civilisations that had for millennia remained unchanged:

The need of a constantly expanding market for its products chases the bourgeoisie over the whole surface of the globe. It must nestle everywhere, settle everywhere, establish connexions everywhere . . . The bourgeoisie has through its exploitation of the world market given a cosmopolitan character to production and consumption in every country.[5]

Capitalism, in Marx's account, accelerated spectacularly the process of mankind's coming together. Sophisticated and hitherto timeless ancient empires in the East, hunter and gatherer tribes in Africa and Australia, petty princedoms in Germany, and even obscurantist despotisms in Russia, had all been brought under its sway. It had driven railroads, cut canals, launched a thousand steamships and created instantaneous communications through the telegraph, so that the physical scale of the world had been rapidly reduced. The whole world had been brought abruptly, for the very first time in human history, into global patterns of exchange and communications. There was nowhere of significance in the whole world where international trade (and the culture that went with it) did not penetrate. Here was the first world-historical mode of production, the first to universalise itself, the first to draw all countries of the world, without exception, into common patterns of intercourse. Global capitalism was, in Lenin's view, the necessary precondition for global socialism:

What is left is capitalism's world-historical tendency to break down national barriers, obliterate national distinctions, and to *assimilate* nations – a tendency which manifests itself more and more powerfully with every passing decade, and is one of the greatest driving forces transforming capitalism into socialism.[6]

It was, in Marx's view, under capitalism that the transition from nationalism to cosmopolitanism would increasingly be accomplished. Capitalism would create not only a universal exchange of goods but of ideas as well: 'National one-sidedness and narrow-mindedness becomes more and more impossible, and from the numerous national local literatures, there arises a world literature.'[7] The mass of the people – the workers – were, in any case, in all countries virtually excluded from the domain of their national culture. They were neither sufficiently educated to appreciate its resonances nor did they possess the leisure or finance to enjoy its fruits. Their culture, Marx seems to say, was the culture of labour, and it was that which bound them together across national boundaries: 'The working men have no country. We cannot take from them what they have not got.'[8]

The universal potential of capitalism as a global system was, however, bound to be frustrated by its own internal dynamics and its allocations of wealth and power. Far from putting an end to the division and antagonism between human beings, capitalism merely universalised its own relations of domination and subordination. In place of the myriad local and specific divisions of the pre-capitalist world, the modern world witnessed the emergence and exacerbation of the last great divide within humanity – the opposition of those exploited by capital to those who owned and disposed of capital. In place of the complex of ancient signifiers of identity – craft, caste, tribe, region, state, empire, religion or gender, the whole social world had been reduced to one essential conflict – the antagonism of interest between those obliged to sell their labour power and those who hired it. This was, according to Marx, the last great arrest in man's progress towards the recovery of a genuine humanity. The class divide of contemporary capitalism, had, by becoming universal, enormously simplified and clarified the ascent from multiform particularity to global generality. History (which, as we have seen, was moving at breakneck speed in comparison to all previous epochs), would rapidly expose the reality of this last great antagonism. The exploited of the world would quickly develop common organisational structures and a common conviction that only by ending the sway of private property in the means of production could they end their exploitation and usher in the final phase of a genuinely human and universal existence.

Progressive Potential of National Self-Determination

Lenin's preoccupation with questions of nationalism and internationalism coincides with his adoption of the theory of finance capitalism or imperialism. Up to that point, in common with most socialist intellectuals in Europe, he had hewed fairly closely to the Marxist line of the Socialist International that proclaimed the sacred right of every nation to self-determination. There were some, the so-called Austro-Marxists particularly, who felt that it would be a retrograde step to dissolve entirely the political and economic bonds of large states such as the Austro-Hungarian empire. The important thing, they argued, was to allow a significant degree of cultural autonomy to each constituent national group, while preserving the advantages of large economic units. Others, particularly some on the Eastern fringe of Europe, argued forcibly that given the accelerated drive towards the internationalisation of trade and the wholesale export of capital typical of the new epoch of finance capitalism (or monopoly capitalism), a return to the politics of nationalism would be not only outmoded, it would be reactionary. Thinkers such as Rosa Luxemburg believed passionately that nationalism had become reactionary in a dual sense. In the first place, it pandered to and fomented divisiveness and smallness of political and economic units, while modern productive forces demanded an international and global market. Economically, therefore, the siren calls of nationalism were retrogressive. In the second place, those best situated to promote national separatism were the bourgeoisie, or even the reactionary aristocracy, in alignment with the 'national' Church. The national card, she concluded, was a dangerous card to play. It undermined the militant solidarity of the international working class and threatened to make national, rather than class affiliation, the primary signifier of identity.

Similarly powerful arguments were advanced by Bukharin, who in many respects anticipated much of Lenin's own intellectual development in the period from 1914 to 1917. It was Bukharin who had been the first Bolshevik to advance a comprehensive theory of finance capital, in which he concluded that the era of nation states as self-sufficient economic units had gone for ever. Nationalism, therefore, was a thing of the past – it was fundamentally out of tune with the necessary internationalisation of production, trade and credit that were the typical features of international finance capitalism. History now presented only one alternative to rotten-ripe international finance capitalism, and that was the international proletarian revolution. This revolution could not aspire to the instant break-up of the world into a host of particularistic nation states – that would be reaction, not progress. It ought to do its utmost before, during, and after the proletarian revolution, to canvass the desirability of a United States of Europe that would become a United States of the whole world.

These were potent arguments. They seemed to accord not only with the tendencies of the modern world but were evidently consistent with Marx's universalist metaphysic. The basic problem with such arguments, in Lenin's view, was that they presented a *tendency* as an accomplished *fact*. That there were important, perhaps predominant, forces in the modern world that made nationalism increasingly redundant, Lenin did not doubt. This did not, however, mean to say that national self-determination was already a thing of the past. That would be to mistake the first month of pregnancy for the last. The trend that Bukharin and Luxemburg observed was profoundly important, but it was, in concrete reality, patchy in its impact. It affected different industries differently within a particular country and was even more variegated in its impact upon differing countries. Some industries had already been brought under the monopolistic control of banking or finance capital, others had not. Some countries had had their economies effectively annexed to, or directly controlled by, the capital-exporting imperialist countries, others were only just beginning to be penetrated by finance capital. In some countries, the extinction of competition by monopoly signified that capitalism itself had outlived its progressive potential; in others, the very early phases of capitalist accumulation were barely under way.

In concrete terms, therefore, the world presented a most variegated map of the developmental phases of capitalism. This is what Lenin meant by his all-important phrase 'the uneven development of capitalism'. From all this it followed, in the Leninist account, that there were indeed areas of the world in which capitalism had become retrogressive and where, therefore, nationalism had become a thing of the past. There were, equally, areas of the world where capitalism was just attaining predominance over more ancient modes of production and distribution. Here, nationalism was a thing of the present. Finally, there were large areas of the world where the processes of capitalist accumulation had only just begun and where capitalist productive and distributive relations were far from dominant. Here nationalism was a thing of the future.

There were, according to the Leninist analysis, three distinct groups of countries in which the progressive significance of the national question (or the rights of nations to self-determination) was markedly different. It is worth quoting Lenin at length, because this analysis was to be crucial to the global strategy of modern communism. Countries must, he argued, be divided into three main types:

> First, the advanced capitalist countries of Western Europe and the United States. In these countries progressive bourgeois national movements came to an end long ago. Every one of these 'great' nations oppresses other nations both in the colonies and at home . . .
>
> Secondly, Eastern Europe: Austria, the Balkans and particularly Russia. Here it was the twentieth century that particularly developed the bourgeois-democratic national movements and intensified the national struggle. The tasks of the proletariat in these countries, both in completing their bourgeois-democratic reforms, and rendering assistance to the socialist revolution in other countries, cannot be carried out without championing the right of nations to self-determination.
>
> Thirdly, the semi-colonial countries, such as China, Persia and Turkey, and all the colonies, which have a combined population of 1,000 million. In these countries the bourgeois-democratic movements either have hardly begun, or have still a long way to go. Socialists must not only demand the unconditional and immediate liberation of the colonies without compensation . . . they must also render determined support to the more revolutionary elements in the bourgeois-democratic movements for national liberation.[9]

Whether national self-determination was progressive or retrogressive depended, therefore, upon the context which had to be explored in the concrete detail of the particular case. On one thing Lenin was clear: it could not be maintained *a priori* and as an invariable truth, that national self-determination had objectively become reactionary·in the contemporary world.

Lenin was also clear that, tactically and strategically, it by no means followed that the promotion of national liberation played into the hands of the class enemies of the proletariat. On the contrary, it would do the proletarian revolution no good at all to be seen putting down the aspirations of nations that had never enjoyed autonomy. Better by far, strategically speaking, to allow them to taste the illusory benefits of political independence and let experience teach them the larger economic benefits of voluntarily rejoining a much more extensive economic entity. More importantly, the potential for the movements for national liberation in the colonies and semi-colonies was, in Lenin's view, a crucial factor both in the breakdown of imperialism and finance capitalism, as well as in the global triumph of the international revolution for socialism. It was, he maintained, too simplistic by far to categorise and assess such movements simply on the basis of the class composition of their leadership groups. Of much more basic significance were the kinds of policies they were bound to pursue.

Rentier State, Super-Profits and Labour Aristocracy

The national question, according to Lenin, had to be seen in the context of a world that had changed radically since Marx's day. The crucial new factor in world politics was the division between exploiter and exploited nations. Marx had talked only of exploiting classes. He could not have anticipated the situation that prevailed increasingly from 1900 onwards, in which whole national groups participated in the exploitation of other national groups. Britain, in particular, had emerged as the foremost 'rentier state'. Its principal export was, from the turn of the century at least, not finished goods, but capital resources. British capitalism survived and flourished not by the production and export of useful commodities, but by the export of super-abundant capital that could not be employed profitably on the domestic market. Having created, through the colonial policies of the British state, protected markets for the export of capital, the British could guarantee for themselves an optimal return. A whole class of wealthy rentiers grew up who lived from the tribute extracted from their foreign investments. A whole country's economy was sustained by 'clipping coupons'.[10] It was, however, not only the rentier capitalists and the barons of finance capital who profited from colonial exploitation. The originality in Lenin's argument was the contention that, in varying degrees, all classes were accomplices in this enterprise. The super-rich surrounded themselves with armies of domestic servants – butlers, valets, chauffeurs, gardeners, housekeepers, maids – ranked in servile hierarchy. But the rot went deeper still. It was not simply a matter of the exponential growth of a section of wage-workers tied by bonds of personal, almost feudal, dependency to their masters, it was the more serious matter of the industrial proletariat (or at least some of their significant strata) being drawn into the web of complicity in colonial exploitation.

Colonial exploitation conferred upon the imperialist powers evident economic benefits. It created closed and protected markets for the export of goods and capital, on both of which premium rates of return could be guaranteed – where necessary by the use of the coercive force of the state. Exclusive access to raw materials, and to the indigenous workforce, could, similarly, be enforced. Since the expectations of the indigenous workers were lower, and since the cultural restraints upon excessive exploitation that prevailed in the 'home' country did not apply, they could be exploited more ruthlessly. For all these reasons colonial investment attracted a rate of return much higher than that of the metropolitan market. This was the source of what Lenin termed 'super-profits', which had become of crucial importance in sustaining the reproducibility of the capitalist mode of production. Without these super-profits the metropolitan economies could not have avoided the tendency that Marx had predicted for the rate of profit to decline. When the rate of profit declined, the capitalists would, again as Marx had predicted, have to increase the rate of exploitation of their workers. They would have to increase the length of the working day, speed up and intensify the work process, or reduce wage rates to below the minimum. The declining rate of profit was at the heart of Marx's account of capitalist crises. It would, eventually, make the reproducibility of the cycle of 'investment – production – sale – profit – investment', untenable. It would, further, give rise to such impoverishment, discontent and organised opposition from the industrial workers that the whole system would be swept away by revolution. Denying finance capital access to super-profits from colonial exploitation was therefore the key strategic goal of the world revolutionary process. It would fatally undermine the political economy of imperialism and restore the revolutionary fervour of the metropolitan working classes.

In the epoch of international finance capitalism or imperialism, capitalism had discovered a short-term solution to its systemic problems. Through the extraction of super-profits from colonial exploitation, it could temporarily buoy up the rate of profit within the home economy. It could, moreover, use part of the residue of its super-profits to improve the security and the living standards of certain selected groups of workers. These skilled workers, often those who already had strong protective trades unions, could be bought off with the crumbs from the rich man's table. A wholly new phenomenon now began to emerge: a labour aristocracy whose standard of living, security, expectations, and social mores became almost indistinguishable from those of the lower middle class. Their share of the pickings from colonial exploitation might well be relatively modest, but they did participate objectively in what now had become the systematic exploitation of one national group by another.

The idea of a labour aristocracy, whose economic roots lay in imperialist policies, was to become a central feature of Leninist politics. It helped to explain why, despite Marx's predictions, that the working class of the major industrialized countries seemed to have become more bourgeois than revolutionary; it was central to Lenin's post-1914 accounts of the growth of social democratic gradualness and reformism. The skilled workers of the labour aristocracy wielded, in Lenin's account, a disproportionate influence upon the class as a whole. They were better organised, more articulate, more confident and better educated, and it was to this constituency that the reformist 'socialist' leaders addressed themselves. This was their natural constituency, and through them bourgeois ideas penetrated into the proletariat, corrupting its consciousness and paralysing its will:

the opportunists (social chauvinists) are working hand in glove with the imperialist bourgeoisie *precisely* towards creating an imperialist Europe on the backs of Asia and Africa, and that objectively the *opportunists* are a section of the petty bourgeoisie and of a certain strata of the working class who *have been bribed* out of imperialist super profits and converted into *watchdogs* of capitalism and *corrupters* of the labour movement.[11]

The proletariat of the advanced industrial countries could not, therefore, recover their vitality and revolutionary mission unless and until they were successful in ending their own countries' participation in colonial exploitation. Marx's conclusion that English workers could never be free until Ireland was free, anticipated a far more complex and extended web of British colonial exploitation. Lenin's conclusion was clear and forthright: 'no nation can be free if it oppresses other nations'.[12] The corruption of the metropolitan working classes could only be remedied by the ending of colonialism.

It was, in his view, the First World War (that was a necessary consequence of imperialist competition for economic territory) that would finally teach the metropolitan workers that the meagre returns they received from participating in colonial exploitation were dearly bought with their own blood. They were the cannon fodder of the imperialist armies, suffering death and mutilation on a prodigious scale. They would finally recognize that the dole they received amounted to no more than widows' mites. The struggle against imperialism within the metropolitan countries was then, in the Leninist account, a condition for the recovery of the revolutionary mission of the proletariat. As defeat of one's own country as the lesser evil had become the mark of the genuine socialist and revolutionary, so too did the emancipation of one's own colonial dependencies. Far from being a sign of bourgeois opportunism, the cause of national self-determination for the colonies was the *conditio sine qua non* of revolutionary progress.

The Achilles' heel of finance capitalism was, therefore, in the colonies. Every successful national liberation movement would deny the imperialists economic territory. It would deny access to their goods and capital. It would deny their exclusive free access to raw materials and an easily exploitable workforce. Each successful assertion of economic and political independence would thereby diminish the volume of super-profits available and assist in precipitating capitalist crisis. Even unsuccessful assertions of the right to national independence were important in contributing to the global struggle. They would increase the costs of administration by forcing the imperialists to send a greater armed presence, more naval support, more police, judges, jailers and civil servants. The greater the costs of administration, the lower the net return. Whether successful or not, every significant movement for national self-determination undermined the capacity of imperialism to maintain and reproduce itself. The national movement in the colonies was therefore fighting the same enemy as the proletariat in the advanced countries. Theirs was a common anti-imperialist cause and it was, in Lenin's view, absolutely central to the prospects of world revolution that they should be linked indissolubly.

As far as the colonies and semi-colonies were concerned (and they comprised the great majority of the world's population) the desirability of political and economic freedom was self-evident to all but a tiny minority of their population. They could not but have an interest in resuming control of their own national resources and in putting an end to the subordination of their economies to those of the imperialists. Their raw materials were extracted on a vast scale but almost never refined *in situ*, and the same applied to many of the cash crops they were forced increasingly to specialise in: the cotton, tobacco, tea and rubber plantations had nothing to do with local needs but everything to do with the demands of the home economy. Their own traditional industries had been devastated by the incursion of cheap manufactured goods and their workforce reduced to helot status under the control of alien managers. Both the workers and the emergent national bourgeoisie had an interest in self-determination. It might well be the case, Lenin freely conceded, that it was the national bourgeoisie that would be the dominant force in the anti-imperialist struggles. Nor did he doubt that, if successful, they would manipulate the new national states in their own narrow class interests. That was to be expected. It did not, however, contradict the essential strategic significance of the movement for national liberation as an anti-imperialist struggle.

The potency of Leninism as an ideology in the twentieth century derived in large measure from its fusion of the national democratic revolutionary process in the colonies with the project for socialist revolution in the advanced countries. They were two sides of the same war for the overthrow of international finance capitalism, and Lenin took heart that, in the long run, victory would lie with the world's exploited, who comprised the overwhelming majority of its population. Leninism was the first ideology to embrace the peoples of the non-European world as co-participants in a common endeavour. They were not the disciples or younger brethren obliged patiently to learn and accommodate themselves to more 'developed' and sophisticated Western models of parliamentarianism and liberalism. They were not for ever more to respond to the initiatives and designs of others and permanently to have to apologise for their own economic, political and cultural backwardness. The Leninist programme of world revolution suggested, on the contrary, that the West had become degenerate, parasitic and corrupt in all these respects. *Its* values and institutions had become prostituted, and whole strata of its populations had degenerated into servility and parasitism. The impetus for regeneration would most probably come not from within itself but from outside – from the East, or from the colonies. Leninism spoke a language of psychological empowerment to colonized and economically-dominated peoples. They were at last to emancipate themselves from subservience. From being bit-part actors in a script written in a foreign language, they were now invited to play principal roles in a 'progressive' drama of their own creation.

The global strategy of revolutionary socialists was clear – with the (bourgeois) national democratic movements, especially those in lands dominated by one's own country, expose the treachery of the reformists who pander to the labour aristocracy, and reveal the true nature of the war as an imperialist war for the division of colonial spoils, in order to prepare the workers for the revolution that will finally put an end to all exploitation, both class and national.

Socialism and Internationalism

Perhaps the most original and influential element of Leninism as a modern ideology was its global perspective. As capitalism had become international in scope, so too the appraisal of the prospects for revolution had to be based upon the global balance of forces and could not be national-specific. Within this general appraisal it was crucial to Leninism that the battles for socialism and national liberation were to be seen not as being chronologically and theoretically distinct and separate but, on the contrary, as being mutually intertwined and mutually supportive. They were parts of the same revolutionary dynamic. It followed, therefore, that the colonies and semi-colonies would not have to wait for all the latent possibilities of capitalist development to have been exhausted before making their bid for independence. They were not to be consigned to being a footnote in the history of mankind; rather, they might well be the initiators and catalysts of a global explosion that would sweep imperialism away. The anti-imperialist revolution might begin in the colonies, though it could not be consummated there. To the extent that it was successful, it would induce economic and social crises within the imperialist countries. They would then take the path of properly socialist revolution and this, in its turn, would greatly radicalise the working masses of the ex-colonial regimes. Recognising that revolutionary socialist regimes had no interest in perpetuating exploitation or national subjugation but were, on the contrary, champions of the welfare of all peoples, the ex-colonies would quickly recognise the advantages of a larger universal union of free and equal peoples. This was the revolutionary progression that Lenin spelled out, to realise, in the modern world, Marx's project of a genuinely human universalism that would, for all time, put an end to the divisiveness of class and nation. The ultimate objective was not the permanent presence of a multitude of nation states but, on the contrary, the creation of a comprehensive confederation of all peoples.

During, and immediately after, the October ·Revolution, Lenin insisted that the guarantee of independence for all national groups oppressed by the old tsarist empire had to feature as a central plank of Bolshevik policy. There could be no tolerance of great power chauvinism or for taking a patronising attitude towards the national question. The nations of the East, the Trans-Caucasian peoples of the South, and the more developed peoples of Russia's Western border, must all openly be granted their rights of national self-determination which, to be meaningful, had to include the right of secession – the right to create their own independent state. In 1913, in his 'Theses on the National Question', Lenin put it in this way: 'our programme cannot be interpreted to mean anything but *political* self-determination, i.e. the right to secede and form a separate state'.[13]

Lenin was unambiguous (or so it would seem from his repeated and emphatic declarations) that all oppressed national groups had an absolute right to self-determination. There could, he insisted, be no question of a socialist regime using state violence to suppress national rights. People, he observed, cannot be driven into paradise with a cudgel.[14] That being said, there were, however, some highly significant qualifications to be made. The first was that to advertise a right did not mean advocacy of its exercise. The comparison Lenin made was with the right to divorce. In any civilised union of a man with a woman the condition for the relationship remaining civilised was that either party might, after due notice, have the right to end it. The existence of this right, however, in no way inferred that divorce was the 'normal' or typical resolution of problems between two parties.

The second reservation was fraught with more serious implications. Ever since the Second Congress of the Russian Social Democratic Labour Party in 1903, Lenin had insisted that the party of the proletariat must be thoroughly agnostic to issues of national differentiation. It admitted members in their status as workers and fighters for socialism and not at all as members of particular ethnic or national groups. He (along with the majority of the Congress) therefore stoutly resisted the claims of the Bund to represent exclusively the interest of Jewish workers in a federal party. There could be no question of federalism or of 'national sections' *within* the party. The party was duty bound to represent and articulate the interests and universal strivings of all wage workers. Thus, while it was inevitable that demands for national liberation and self-determination would be voiced, and natural for the party to be sympathetic to them, it could never itself be organisationally broken down into separate national groupings. The international organisational integrity of the party had to be maintained at all costs. It was, in any case, the party's duty constantly to point up the pitfalls of narrow nationalism, always to point out the dangers of setting workers against workers, and always to emphasise the benefits of unity in ever-larger and more embracing economic and political units. The party ought never to forget that it stood, in the long term, for the common cause of all humanity: 'In place of all forms of nationalism Marxism advances internationalism, the amalgamation of all nations in the higher unity . . . . '[15]

This higher unity, Lenin fondly believed, could only be attained by adopting a permissive and understanding attitude to the sensitivities of minority oppressed peoples. After their first taste of economic, political and cultural independence, their very conditions of life and work would lead them into an awareness of the advantages of participating in larger economic and political units. Those ties would, he insisted, have to be voluntary and freely entered into. Any attempts at imposing an obligatory language, or using force to prevent secession, must be ruled out absolutely. Such actions, he asserted, would play straight into the hands of bourgeois separatists – the proponents of exclusivist nationalism. Marxists, by contrast, were supporters of the integrative national sentiment of the working population which, far from being inconsistent with proletarian internationalism, was fundamentally expressive of it. The properly democratic or socialist state 'must grant autonomy to its various regions, especially to regions with mixed populations. This form of autonomy in no way contradicts democratic centralism; a democratic state is bound to grant *complete freedom* for the various languages and annul *all* privileges for any one language. A democratic state will not permit the oppression of any one nationality by another, either in any particular region or in any branch of public affairs'.[16]

After the October Revolution, Lenin devoted very little time to his elaboration of the national question. His writings on the subject were sporadic and relatively sparse. They amounted, in any case, to a repetition of the general themes developed in 1913–14. He insisted, of course, that the iniquities of the tsarist Empire, 'the charnel house of the peoples', should be flatly condemned and rectified. *All* subject nations were to be offered the right to secede. The Russian communists could not present themselves to the world as champions of the anti-imperialist struggle so long as they continued to oppress their own subject peoples. There must be an end to great power chauvinism, an end to the compulsory official language, and an end to the patronising or bullying stance the Russians had hitherto adopted towards all the 'lesser' nations of the old Empire. Only by granting them the greatest measure of freedom, up to and including secession, only by displaying sensitivity towards their sense of outrage for the enormities of the past; only in this way would the smaller national groups become convinced of the good intentions of the new socialist state to treat them as equals. The new Soviet state ought not to fear secessionist movements. They were entirely natural reactions to past oppression. But Lenin was optimistic that this natural flowering of national sentiment, leading to the creation of separate states, would be of brief duration. When the hitherto oppressed nations of the old tsarist empire came to recognise and appreciate the fraternal tolerance of socialist Russia, and when economic realities taught them the benefits of an enlarged association, then they would participate enthusiastically in a larger union.

The complex ambiguities of Lenin's position on the national question are in marked contrast to the blunt decisiveness of his policies on most other questions. He was absolutely for the right of nations to self-determination which, to be real, had to include the right of secession. He was, however, absolutely against the proliferation of outmoded small states. He believed in large and ever-growing political and economic units, yet seemed to convince himself that this process could be accelerated by tolerating and encouraging the widest self-determination for nations. The proletariat, he argued, could never participate in suppressing the people of another country. They were duty bound to support the people's liberation and independence. Simultaneously, however, the proletariat of both oppressor and oppressed countries must absolutely insist upon maintaining the closest ideological and organisational unity.

There were, in Lenin's mind, two nations in every modern nation[17] and two cultures within every country:

> The elements of democratic and socialist culture are present, if only in rudimentary form, in *every* national culture, since in *every* nation there are toiling and exploited masses . . . But *every* nation also possesses a bourgeois culture . . . in the form not only of 'elements' but of the *dominant* culture. Therefore, the dominant general 'national culture' *is* the culture of the landlords, the clergy and the bourgeoisie.

The task of the revolutionary proletariat was, he went on 'to take *from each* national culture *only* its democratic and socialist elements; we take them *only* and *absolutely* in opposition to the bourgeois culture and the bourgeois nationalism of *each* nation'.[18] Bourgeois nationalism was, by its nature, exclusivist, separatist and domineering. Its assertion in any one country constituted, therefore, a permanent threat to all others. Proletarian internationalism, by contrast, was to be secured by granting to all national groups local self-government, absolute equality in the status of their language with all others, autonomous control over 'all the cultural and educational needs of the population' and, of course, the right of secession. With such iron-clad guarantees (later bolstered by Lenin's acceptance of the federal principle as the organisational basis for a multinational state) it was confidently expected that the 'closer union of the proletarians and working masses of all nations and countries'[19] could be attained peacefully. But federation itself was but 'a transitional form to the complete unity of the working people of different nations'.[20]

There remained, however, fundamental and irresolvable ambiguities in this whole analysis. The proletariat alone was, axiomatically, the sole class representing the universal interests of all humanity and standing for genuine internationalism. Yet Communists were obliged to 'assist the bourgeois-democratic liberation movements'[21] in all oppressed countries, even when it was evident that the leading role would be played by bourgeois (and therefore reactionary) nationalists. At other times Lenin was insistent, as we have noted above, that only the socialist and democratic elements of any nation deserved support. It was, in any case, always made clear that the commitment to the cause of national independence was only a temporary tactic that could never command the unambiguous support of the proletarian party. From the moment independence was achieved it was to strive for socialist transformation, which entailed the fusion of all 'national' movements into the broader current of proletarian internationalism. National independence was, therefore, just the prelude to international unity; it could never be valued as an end in itself. For this reason, Leninism insisted, the communists must, at all times, jealously preserve their organisational autonomy within the general movement for national liberation:

we, as Communists, should and will support bourgeois-liberation movements in the colonies only when they are genuinely revolutionary and when their exponents do not hinder our work of educating and organising in a revolutionary spirit the peasants and the masses of the exploited.[22]

While making common cause with the national bourgeoisie in the struggle for liberation the communists were, simultaneously, to undermine their social bases of support and turn the movement into a social struggle against the power of the landlords and the priests and, where possible, to assume direct leadership of the liberation struggle. They were expected to do this in overwhelmingly peasant societies where, as Lenin admitted, 'There is practically no industrial proletariat in those countries.'[23] Their tasks were, to say the least, complex and potentially contradictory.

Internationalism in One Country

There is general agreement among commentators that Lenin was genuinely, and as a matter of principle, wedded to the view that any display of Russian arrogance or chauvinism towards the former subject peoples of the Russian empire would be disastrous for the emergent Soviet Union. There were, however, men close to him, particularly his own Commissar for Nationalities – Joseph Stalin, who took a far less tolerant and permissive view.

It is clear that Stalin, neither by inclination nor by intellect, could appreciate the sophistication of Lenin's account of the relationship between nationalism and internationalism, and for this good reason Lenin himself had closely supervised the writing of Stalin's text on *Marxism and the National Question* in 1913.[24] After the revolution, however, as Commissar for Nationalities, Stalin reverted increasingly to the simple sureties for which he could find at least some warrant in Lenin's thought. It was, for him, unambiguously clear that it was the Russian proletariat that had made the revolution and had been the driving force of socialist transformation. All the other classes and all the less developed national groups had wavered, prevaricated or actually opposed their initiatives – they were therefore potential sources of counter-revolution. A strong hand was needed to keep them in check until such time as the virtues of a unitary socialist state and economy persuaded them that their own interests were best secured by accepting proletarian (and Russian) leadership. It was, in his version of Leninism, the proletariat alone that expressed the universal strivings of all humanity and it therefore had a privileged voice in expressing the strivings of any community. In assessing claims to national independence, pride of place had to be given to the expressed wishes of the indigenous working class. From this it was just a short step (and one that was entirely consonant with the spirit of Leninism) to assert that the only articulator of proletarian purpose was the Communist Party.

In short, the final arbiter of whether or not movements for national independence were or were not progressive was the Communist Party.

It was this circular argument that dominated subsequent Soviet nationalities policy, despite the fact that Lenin, in the last ineffective political campaign of his life, fought vigorously against it. It was a measure of his isolation that none of the prominent leaders of the Communist Party came to his aid over the notorious Georgian question. Stalin had brutally crushed the Georgians' attempts to create their own state and Lenin had vowed to support them. Weak and disabled as he was, he recruited Trotsky as his agent to expose Stalin's chauvinism and brutality in this affair and to get him removed from his position of power. Trotsky did virtually nothing to pursue these matters. By his own inaction he shielded Stalin and ultimately sealed his own fate. Trotsky, like almost all the prominent communist leaders, evidently had little sympathy with Lenin's softer line on the national aspirations of the minority peoples of the old empire. At Lenin's insistence, the first Constitution of the Soviet Union contained (as did all subsequent versions) a clause expressly granting the right of secession to all constituent Republics, but like many constitutional rights it was made plain from the outset that its exercise was hedged about with qualifications that effectively negated it.

After Lenin's death his disciples simultaneously pursued twin strategies that proved increasingly difficult to reconcile. Within the Soviet Union the consistent objective was the drawing together (*sblizheniye*) of the heterogeneous national and ethnic groups so as to accomplish, eventually, their fusion one with another (*sliyaniye*). Within a socialist commonwealth, it was argued, separatist or aggressively nationalist movements were outmoded and fundamentally reactionary. The degree to which cultural and linguistic autonomy was permitted varied widely over time and was, in any case, generally subordinated to the larger goal of creating an historically new community of the Soviet people. In the larger world, however, it remained a fundamental plank of Soviet policy to encourage all movements of national liberation from colonial or imperialist domination. These were, definitionally, 'progressive' movements and it was through them that the Leninist parties were to win such spectacular success in China, Yugoslavia, Vietnam and Cuba. Financing and arming such movements, and supporting their successful communist governments became, however, an immense drain on Soviet resources, contributing to the final break-up of the Soviet Union.

The dialectics of success were such that the more extensive the spread of communism became in largely impoverished countries decimated by civil war, the greater the demands on the economy of its Soviet heartland, and the greater too the threatening response of the West. To withdraw support would have been a break with the Leninist faith and be seen as capitulation to imperialism, yet to sustain it and to defend the gains that had been made was ruinously costly. It proved to be one of the factors that stymied Soviet efforts to demonstrate to the world that their planned economy could deliver to its citizens greater material benefits than all competitor systems. In the name of Leninist orthodoxy and attachment to anti-imperialist solidarity with the oppressed peoples of the world, Soviet citizens were, in effect, asked to forgo material improvements and increased living standards. The fruits of socialism, it seemed, were mortgaged elsewhere and their enjoyment constantly postponed.

As with every other feature of Leninism, its resolution of the national question was premised upon the rapid spread of the revolution to at least the economically advanced and culturally developed countries of Europe. The accession to the proletarian cause of the German, French and British workers would, in Lenin's optimistic prognosis, offset the relatively backward economic and cultural situation of Russia and Eastern Europe. A genuine proletarian cosmopolitanism would be born which would, moreover, be techno-logically advanced, culturally tolerant and well able to supply the extended needs of its people. The benefits of participation in so large, tolerant and prosperous an international association would be so obvious that the smaller and less developed nations would swiftly recognize the overwhelming advantages of membership. Their under-standable desire to savour the advantages of national independence and separateness would rapidly give way to enthusiasm to participate in the larger whole. Culturally specific forms of national life would, no doubt, continue to thrive for some time, but they would no longer be identified with the dangerous and divisive political forms of national states.

In the event, it became clear, even during Lenin's lifetime, that the USSR was likely to remain isolated for a long time from the culturally and technologically advanced West. Within the Union itself (as distinct from the one ideally projected) it was the Russians who were not only the overwhelmingly preponderant national group – more to the point, they comprised an even more overwhelming majority of the urban, technically skilled, and proletarian population of the whole. Far from the cultural and technical backwardness of the Russian workers being redeemed by the accession of the Western workers to the international cause, it was the Russian workers who were, *faut de mieux* credited with being the bearers of revolutionary virtue. Since, in the logic of Leninism, it was the proletariat and it alone that could articulate genuine internationalism, within the USSR it fell largely to Russian workers to define the nature and objectives of the new transnational association. It was not surprising that, for all the other national groupings, socialist internationalism came to be viewed as a slender pretext for Russian domination and a perpetuation of Russian imperial designs.

In the wider world, the same 'arrested development' and isolation of the revolution each year increased the tendency to identify both socialism and proletarian internationalism with the fortunes of the Soviet Republic. Lenin himself had, as we have seen, universalized the experience of the Russian Revolution in the conditions for admission to the Communist International. Before he died, and with increasing force thereafter, an internationalist was defined as one who unreservedly and without qualification supported the policies of the Soviet regime. The cause of the international proletarian revolution became, step by step, identified with what Isaac Deutscher referred to as 'the sacred egoism of the Soviet state'. What had begun as a universal transformative mission to create the global conditions for a properly human existence lapsed into an apology for the provincialism of an isolated and backward state.

9

A Philosophy of Certainty: Dialectical Materialism

Lenin first began to take an interest in philosophy in the years following the failure of the revolution of 1905. This period saw the culmination of a process of critical self-examination that the Russian intelligentsia undertook, prompted partly by developments in contemporary European thought and partly by a resurgence of native religious philosophy led by such prominent thinkers as Berdyaev, Bulgakov, Frank, Struve and Gershenzon. The publication in 1903 of an influential collection entitled *Problems of Idealism* stands at the beginning of this phase, which culminated in 1909 with the publication of the celebrated *Vekhi* or 'Landmarks' collection. This latter collection was, from its first essay to its last, a denunciation of the barrenness of the whole socialist tradition in both the theory and the practice of the Russian intelligentsia. The militant materialism of Chernyshevsky and Plekhanov had, the contributors maintained, imposed upon Russian populists and Marxists alike an obligatory endorsement of science as the liberator of mankind and the objective criterion of truth. No amount of science, no weight of empirical experience could, however, yield the smallest moral precept – 'scientific' socialism of this sort was, they argued, ethically bankrupt. The other great rallying cry of the Russian intelligentsia – service to the popular masses (or the proletariat) was, similarly, an abnegation of the intelligentsia's role of educating and improving the people.

The socialist intelligentsia had, *Vekhi* argued, been overwhelmingly concerned with the mere material demands of the people and had ignored their cultural and spiritual needs. 'In summary,' Frank concluded, 'we can define the classic Russian *intelligent* as a *militant monk of the nihilistic religion of earthly contentment*'.[1] Their careless mystique of the common people exalted mediocrity, reducing values and objectives to those of the common herd. It also produced a suffocating communalism which 'repudiates the idea of individual responsibility'[2] so essential for a meaningfully moral existence. It was time, according to Struve, for it to renounce 'its irreverent, anti-governmental dissociation' and to recover its proper spiritual and educative role. This, we should recall, was the man who, just eleven years previously, had composed the Manifesto of the First Congress of the RSDLP.

Lenin was, at first, little concerned with the great ferment of ideas that swept through the intelligentsia in the early years of the twentieth century. It was, after all, entirely natural in Lenin's view for the economic instability and social ambiguity of the 'petty bourgeois' intelligentsia to manifest itself in fleeting enthusiams for the latest imported or home-grown fads. Bergson, Nietzsche, Freud, James, Avenarius and Mach all had their coteries of fellow thinkers and, of course, the resurgence of orthodox spirituality in the works of Vladimir Solovyov and his followers was very influential. This climate of intellectual experimentation and the challenging of all the old orthodoxies at first left Lenin almost untouched. He felt no need to stray from the straight and narrow path of Marxism. He was proud to identify with Marx and Engels who 'despised pedantic, playing with new words erudite terms, and subtle "isms" '[3] – hardly words to gladden the hearts of conventional philosophers.

1908 – Restating the Orthodoxy, Mind and Matter

It was the philosophical waywardness of his Bolshevik disciples, Bogdanov and Lunacharsky, that obliged him to take up the cudgels (and, in his hands, cudgels they were) of materialist orthodoxy to put them to rout. Even then, as he freely conceded in a letter to Gorki in February 1908:

> I am fully aware of my unpreparedness in this sphere, which prevents me from speaking about it in public. But, as a rank and file Marxist, I read attentively our Party philosophers . . . and they drive me to give *all* my sympathy to Plekhanov . . . His tactics are the height of ineptitude and baseness. In philosophy, however, he upholds the right cause. I am for materialism against 'empirio – ', etc.[4]

Lenin was reacting, somewhat belatedly, to the publication of Bogdanov's three-volume *Empiriomonism*, published between 1904 and

1906. Bogdanov's intent was to update and reinforce Marxism with the scientific and philosophical findings of Ernest Mach. According to Bogdanov, empirio criticism finally resolved the dualism between thought processes and natural objects, and it did so by postulating humankind as the creators and organisers of their world. In this view, all reality was anchored in the specifically human experience of co-operative endeavour to secure humanity's material existence. What aided this process of liberating humans from the vagaries and insecurity of nature was useful in the emancipatory project, and therefore true to the goals of the human association. It was, in many ways, a stance reminiscent of the early Marx, in which socialism was equated with humanism. Here people came to know both their own limitations, as well as those of their materials, through activity in working with the raw materials furnished by nature. This was an activist and goal-orientated epistemology in which the learning process of associated labour was of paramount importance. In work, people came to know themselves, the extensiveness and limits of their skills in collaborative productive work, and the qualities of the objects with which they mixed their labour.[5]

It was Bogdanov's resolution of the relationship of mind to matter that particularly distressed Lenin. Bogdanov was, in his view, flying too close to the idealist proposition that without a subject there can be no object. Things, in Bogdanov's account, were no more than 'crystallisations of human projections governed by practical ends . . . they are components of collective experience'.[6] In Lenin's view, Bogdanov had yielded far too much, he had blurred the fundamental proposition of materialism that things emphatically do exist prior to and independent of a sentient observer. The distinction between mind and matter, their separability as categories, was fundamental to Lenin's materialism at this time. Bogdanov's error was to retail the confusion of his mentor Mach, 'that things or bodies are complexes of sensations'.[7] Lenin summarised this mistaken position as follows:

1. All that exists is declared to be sensation.
2. Sensations are called elements.
3. Elements are divided into the physical and the psychical; the latter is that which depends on the human nerves and the human organism generally; the former does not depend on them.
4. The connections of physical elements and the connection of psychical elements, it is declared, do not exist separately from each other; they exist only in conjunction.[8]

It was, Lenin argued, precisely this confusion (arising from the simple semantic trick of eroding the distinction between mind and matter by reducing both to 'elements')[9] that Bogdanov had fallen for. In his book he conceded that he had indeed borrowed from Mach 'the idea of the neutrality of the elements of experience in relation to the "physical" and the "psychical", and the dependence of these characteristics solely on the *connection* of experience'. Bogdanov had thereby 'abandoned the materialist standpoint and has inevitably condemned himself to confusion and idealist aberrations'.[10] Worst of all, Bogdanov was now reduced to maintaining the impossibility of objective truth: 'The criterion of objective truth . . . does not exist; truth is an ideological form, an organising form of human experience.'[11]

Lenin did not, of course, wish to dispute the crucial importance of experience or practice as the only sure means of verifying, or correcting, our ideas of the world. With Engels, he agreed that before there was argumentation there was action: '*Im Anfang war die Tat* . . . The proof of the pudding is in the eating. From the moment we turn to our own use these objects, according to the qualities we perceive in them, we put to an infallible test the correctness or otherwise of our sense-perceptions.'[12] The truth-revealing functions of experience were, therefore, not in dispute. What was in dispute was Lenin's insistence (which he takes to be the orthodoxy bequeathed by Engels and Plekhanov) that there is an irreducible dualism in the relationship of mind to matter, and that, in this relationship matter is, logically and historically, the prior category. He had, further, to vindicate the contention of materialism that objective truth was attainable – that it was indeed the one essential condition of human progress.

It was not difficult, Lenin felt, to establish the obviousness of these materialist propositions. The sciences of geology and biology amply demonstrated the fact that the world existed prior to the development of *Homo sapiens*. 'Natural science leaves no room for doubt that its assertion that the earth existed prior to man is a truth.'[13] This was, Lenin maintained, neither a subjective nor an ideological proposition; it was, on the contrary, objectively demonstrable. There were, almost daily, fresh scientific 'discoveries' revealing hitherto unsuspected properties of the natural world. Coal tar had, for instance, lately been found to contain alizarin.[14] It would, Lenin argued, be absurd to argue that, before this discovery, coal tar had not contained alizarin. The fundamental proposition that posits the primacy of matter is, according to Lenin and the whole Leninist tradition, the only one compatible with the actual practice of science.

The scientist first observes and studies the object of his or her attention, reflecting it in his or her sensations and pondering its structure. S/he construes an hypothesis about that structure but the hypothesis itself, as a construct of mind, is quite worthless unless s/he can demonstrate its adequacy by showing conclusively through experimentation that the object in question does indeed manifest the truth of the hypothesis. If it does, then the scientist has not, through his or her *idea* of the object, *constructed* it. S/he has, on the contrary, correctly understood the object's own internal construction. The proof of this is that others may repeat the experiments and gain the same results. The referent here is always the material object of study and not the ideas that others may have of it. In this way, according to Lenin, materialism 'in full agreement with natural science, takes matter as primary and regards consciousness, thought, sensation as secondary'.[15] Lenin asserted that there was no other way of comprehending the world except through the brain processing reflections received from the exercise of the senses of seeing, touching, hearing and tasting. But, as Lenin observed, 'Sensation depends on the brain, nerves, retina etc., i.e. on matter organised in a definite way.'[16] The process of knowing was, in this account, itself amenable to materialist analysis. Science would eventually unravel the complex interaction of chemical, electrical and physical processes through which sensations themselves were produced and subsequently processed by the brain.

'Materialism,' according to Lenin, 'is the recognition of "objects in themselves" or outside the mind; ideas and sensations are copies or images of those objects';[17] 'Matter is a philosophical category denoting the objective reality which is given to man by his sensations, and which is copied, photographed and reflected by our sensations, while existing independently of them.'[18] The mind creates an 'image', picture, or reflection of an object that 'exists independently of the subject'.[19] Materialist theory was, in short 'the theory of the reflection of objects by our mind'.[20] 'Matter is a philosophical category denoting the objective reality which is given to man by his sensations, and which is copied, photographed and reflected by our sensations, while existing independently of them.'[21]

It follows that, for Lenin, materialism specified the primal reality of an external objective world. Our ideas 'reflect' this objective world more or less adequately and are refined through practice: that is, through human appropriation of, and experimentation with, the objects of the natural environment. In the course of this interaction human beings come to recognise 'the existence of objective law, causality and necessity in nature'.[22] These laws of nature, as Marx had pointed out, act '*independently* of our will and our mind', but once grasped by humans enable them to become 'masters of nature'.[23]

Against the epistemological relativism of Bogdanov and his circle, Lenin insisted that objective truth, indeed absolute truth, was attainable. There are, admittedly, some confusing qualifications that Lenin inserted at this point. We learn, for instance, that absolute truth is (following Engels' 'dialectical' analysis of the matter) 'compounded from relative truths'.[24] In *Materialism and Empiro-Criticism* it would indeed seem to be the case that the dialectic has a very restricted purview and a modest role to play in the development (or construction) of knowledge – it is rarely mentioned and never expanded upon. Its principal role is the cautionary one of reminding ourselves that knowledge is always incomplete and, dare one say it, relative:

> In the theory of knowledge, as in every other sphere of science, we must think dialectically, that is, we must not regard our knowledge as ready-made and unalterable, but must determine how *knowledge* emerges from *ignorance*, how incomplete, inexact knowledge becomes more complete and more exact.[25]

There is, then, as Lenin is prepared to concede, an element of relativism even in the materialist dialectics of Marx and Engels to the extent that they recognised the historically conditional nature of all truth but 'not in the sense of denying objective truth'.[26]

It is, perhaps, hardly profitable to pursue much further the substance of Lenin's excursion into theories of knowledge. We would miss the point if we were to regard it as a dispassionate attempt to distil the merits and deficiencies of the great variety of epistemologies then on offer. It was no such thing. His object was to reveal that all philosophy was partial and partisan. It was either reactionary (denying the possibility of an objective world, objective truth, causality, and laws of nature), or it was progressive and affirmed their reality. It was either integrally materialist or idealist. It either endorsed the inequities and injustices of the present, or envisaged a future in which society and nature would be reconstituted to meet the needs of humankind. Lenin's book was, as Kolakowski points out, above all concerned to demonstrate that 'there can be no middle ground between materialism and idealism' and that 'philosophical theories are not neutral in the class struggle but are instruments of it. Every philosophy is in the service of some class interest.'[27] According to the Marxist philosopher Louis Althusser, Lenin's great contributions were that the history of philosophy reduces itself to the clash between materialism and idealism, and that philosophy has no autonomy, it is merely 'a continuation of politics, a certain rumination of politics'.[28] Philosophy, in this account, was a matter of drawing lines and demarcating.[29]

Any dereliction from consistent materialism was, Lenin was sure, fraught with grievous political consequences:

> From this Marxist philosophy, which is cast from a single piece of steel, you cannot eliminate one basic premise, one essential part, without departing from objective truth, without falling prey to bourgeois-reactionary falsehood.[30]

This, Lenin noted, had been the fate of Lunacharsky and Gorki: they began by questioning the existence of an objective external reality and ended up embracing a religion of humanity;[31] and similarly, 'Bogdanov's denial of objective truth completely "harmonises" with fideism.'[32]

In philosophy, as in politics, the most insidious and dangerous of enemies was not the frank opponent but the middle-of-the-roader, the reconciler and the neutral. It was the 'claim to be non-partisan in philosophy and in social science'[33] that most enraged Lenin about the proponents of empirio-criticism: 'Of all Parties,' our Joseph Dietzgen justly said, 'the middle party is the most repulsive.'[34] The Machists were, in Lenin's view, 'a contemptible middle party, who confuse the materialist and idealist trends on every question'.[35] They 'clear the way for idealism and fideism',[36] and their proponents become 'learned salesmen of the theologians'.[37] It was the 'objective, class role of empirio-criticism' to render 'faithful service to the fideists in their struggle against materialism in general and historical materialism in particular'.[38]

1914 – Hegel, Dialectics and Proper Marxist Method

As we have seen, Lenin's 1908 reflections on philosophy were almost wholly concerned with restating the compelling simplicities of materialism as transmitted from Feuerbach to Marx and Plekhanov, but especially as developed by Engels. It was several times repeated in the text that the materialism aspired to was neither mechanistic nor positivist, but dialectical.[39] Dietzgen, and particularly Engels,[40] are credited with being 'dialectical materialists'. We are told that 'Engels was able to discard Hegelian idealism and *to grasp* the great and true kernel of Hegelian dialetics. Engels rejected the old metaphysical materialism for dialectical materialism'.[41] Quite what this means was, at the time, left largely undiscussed. For all his professions to be dialectical in his approach, Lenin's materialism was, at this time, decidedly static. There was no concern with such complex questions as the inter-relationships of things that were, moreover, themselves in constant flux. Dialectics, as the exploration both of these connections and of quantitative and qualitative change, was conspicuous by its absence in Lenin's *Materialism and Empirio-Criticism*. It was not until 1914, when new threats to the militant integrity of Marxism appeared, that Lenin turned in earnest to Hegel for guidance on proper dialectical method.

It was, in Lenin's view, Hegel's great genius that revealed the operation of the dialectic in the field of ideas (and Lenin steeped himself in Hegel more thoroughly than did any Marxist of his time). Early in his career, while in exile in Siberia, he fell under Hegel's spell and thereafter, wherever he went, his Hegel volumes went with him.[42] It was a matter of pride that it was Chernyshevsky who had consistently radicalised the materialism of Feuerbach, and that his own mentor, Plekhanov, had first coined the term and systematically developed the philosophy of dialectical materialism.[43] Lenin was indeed to make considerable play of the authentically Russian roots of what was to become the international philosophy of communism.

The dialetic, according to Marx, 'is a scandal to bourgeoisdom and its doctrinaire professors'[44] and it was so because it radically contested their complacent and ordered conceptions of the physical, natural and social worlds. It was, in a word, an inherently *revolutionary* philosophy:

it includes in its comprehension an affirmative recognition of the existing state of things, at the same time also, the recognition of the negation of that state, of its inevitable breaking up; because it regards every historically developed social form as in fluid movement, and therefore takes into account its transient nature not less than its momentary existence; because it lets nothing impose upon it, and is, in its essence, critical and revolutionary.[45]

It was, of course, precisely the revolutionary quality of dialectical thought that made it so attractive to Lenin, and the obligatory philosophical stance of his followers. At the end of this chapter we shall explore the function that dialectical materialism fulfilled in the general structure of Leninist ideology, but for the moment let us try to unpack the meanings in the above quotation from Marx.

We should perhaps notice that, in Marx's account, the object of investigation is an 'historically developed social form'. The sphere in which the dialectic operated was the economic, social, political and ideological life of humankind. From his doctoral study of the development of Greek philosophy,[46] Marx was evidently aware of the role of dialectic as a mode of argumentation, particularly in the examination of phenomena that were in constant flux. He was, further, indebted to Hegel (who he re-read in the course of preparing *Capital*) for his elaboration of the dialectical clash of rival ideas being the central theme of the philosophy of history. In this account, every significant idea (or thesis) had its counter idea (or antithesis) and the debate between them was eventually resolved in the formulation of a new synthesis that preserved, on a higher level, the positive or progressive elements of both thesis and antithesis. The process did not, however, end there, because the new synthesis assumed the role of the old thesis and it would, in time, be confronted with a new antithesis, from which a synthesis on a higher plane would eventually emerge. The dialectic is here presented as intrinsic to 'the self development of thought'.[47]

Marx's own estimate of his originality in utilising the dialectic was that he had traced the deeper roots of the clash of antagonistic ideas back to the economic and social roots whence they sprang. Marx's claim was contained in his findings that the differing ideas of individuals are, in general, a reflection of where they stand in relation to the allocation of material goods and status within society. It is, in short, not ideas that construct material reality, but material reality that constructs ideas. Whether one is an exploiter of the labour of others, or is oneself exploited by another, is for Marx of primary significance in determining the nature of ideas about economic, social and political matters. This is not to say (as Marx sometimes comes close to asserting) that ideas have no autonomy whatever, but it does mean that important ideas on the organisation or reorganisation of society are significant in their impact upon history only to the extent that they articulate the interests of economically determined classes. It is therefore the extent to which such ideas reflect these material realities that gives them their currency and their ability to influence history.

For Hegel, according to Marx, the idea is the demiurge of the real world 'and the real world is only the external, phenomenal form of "the Idea". With me, on the contrary, the ideal is nothing else than the material world reflected by the human mind, and translated into forms of thought'. It was a matter of turning the dialectic 'right side up again'.[48] In and of themselves, however, 'Ideas *cannot carry out anything* at all'.[49] They merely articulate the real opposition of material interests of classes in history. The real location of the dialectic is, therefore, in the clash between class interests. All of history was the history of class struggle, and in the modern world this reduced itself to the clash between proletariat and bourgeoisie. Early in his career, Marx had (as Lenin approvingly notes in his *Philosophical Notebooks*) located classes (rather than ideas) as the real protagonists of the dialectical struggle:

> Proletariat and wealth are opposites: as such they form a single whole. They are both creations of the world of private property. The question is exactly what place each occupies in the antithesis . . . Within this antithesis the private property owner is therefore the *conservative* side, the proletarian the *destructive* side. From the former arises the action of preserving the antithesis, from the latter the action of annihilating it.[50]

Marx's later historical works, *The Class Struggles in France* and *The Eighteenth Brumaire of Louis Bonaparte*, elaborated in some detail and with considerable finesse, this dialectical analysis of the clash of class forces and their constantly changing forms (although we might well reflect that classes, for both Marx and Lenin, were merely surrogates for ideas). Marx himself, however, almost never sought evidence for the operation of the dialectic in the natural or physical world.[51]

Engels: Dialectics as the Science of Nature

It was Engels who, in his *Anti Duhring*, effected a fundamental shift in the purview and pretensions of dialectical thinking. For Marx, as we have seen, the dialectic remained a set of interpretative hypotheses about the nature of historical and social reality which 'Viewed apart from real history . . . have in themselves no value whatsoever . . . they by no means afford a recipe or schema, as does philosophy, for neatly trimming the epochs of history.'[52] The dialectic here remains a reflection upon history rather than constitutive of it (for that, after all, had been Hegel's error). For Engels, by contrast, matter itself, *all* matter, was dialectically constructed. Engels is categorical where Marx is hypothetical:

Nature is the test of dialectics, and it must be said for modern natural science that it has furnished extremely rich and daily increasing materials for this test, and has thus proved that in the last analysis Nature's process is dialectical and not metaphysical.[53]

It was precisely the dialectic, in Engels's account, that signified the ascent of socialism from mere ethical inspiration to a science: 'Dialectics is nothing more than the science of the general laws of motion and development of Nature, human society and thought.'[54] All phenomena, in Engels's account, conformed to such general laws as the negation of the negation and the law of the transformation of quantity into quality.[55] 'To me,' Engels boasts, 'there could be no question of building the laws of dialectics into Nature, but of discovering them in it and evolving them from it.'[56] It is true that Engels does make important disclaimers and distinguishes the exact sciences from other natural sciences, and both of these from such 'human' sciences as history and politics.[57] Only in the first category of science was it possible to distil 'eternal truths, final and ultimate truths'[58] but he none the less did bequeath to subsequent Marxists the conviction that dialectics was a special science of sciences. It was, in this rendering, universal in scope and explanatory of the very constitution of the whole natural world.

Lenin had already, in his 1908 book *Materialism and Empirio-Criticism*, lavished praise on Engels as being in the forefront of developing Hegel's dialectical ideas in a materialist way[59] and when he returned to a study of the dialectic in 1914 he was, like Engels, concerned to show that all phenomena are dialectically constituted and therefore conform to its laws. His sixteen-point codification of the essentials of dialectical thinking seem to bear the imprint of his teacher:

(1) The *objectivity* of consideration (not examples, not divergences, but the Thing-in-itself).

(2) The entire totality of the manifold *relations* of this thing to others.

(3)   The *development* of this thing (phenomenon, respectively), its own movement, its own life.

(4)   The internally contradictory *tendencies* (*and* sides) in this thing.

(5)   The thing (phenomenon, etc.) as the sum *and unity of opposites*.

(6)   The *struggle*, respectively unfolding, of these opposites, contradictory strivings, etc.

(7)   The union of analysis and synthesis – the break-down of the separate parts and the totality, the summation of these parts.

(8)   The relations of each thing (phenomenon, etc.) are not only manifold, but general, universal. Each thing (phenomenon, process, etc.) is connected with *every other*.

(9)   Not only the unity of opposites, but the *transitions* of *every* determination, quality, feature, side, property into *every* other (into its opposite?).

(10)   The endless process of the discovery of *new* sides, relations, etc.

(11)   The endless process of the deepening of man's knowledge of the thing, of phenomena, processes, etc., from appearance to essence and from less profound to more profound essence.

(12)   From co-existence to causality and from one form of connection and reciprocal dependence to another, deeper, more general form.

(13)   The repetition at a higher stage of certain features, properties, etc., of the lower and

(14)   The apparent return to the old (negation of the negation).

(15)   The struggle of content with form and conversely. The throwing off of the form, the transformation of the content.

(16)   The transition of quantity into quality and *vice versa*. (15 and 16 are *examples* of 9)[60]

One of the themes to which Lenin returns time and again, and which he finds brilliantly confirmed in Hegel, is the priority of theoretical (or abstract) reasoning over pragmatic (or concrete) reasoning. Lenin's account speaks of two differing layers of experience – the immediately lived and the theoretically reflected, and one is tempted to think that these correspond closely to his earlier distinction between spontaneity and consciousness. In both cases the distinction is between knowledge that is the product of everyday, lived experience that is uninformed by deep reflection or purposive experimentation, and knowledge that is abstractly theorised and demonstrable in practice. The first has little conception of the interrelatedness of things and ideas, while the second sees the universal in the particular and vice versa: 'Every individual is (in one way or another) a universal. Every universal is (a fragment, or an aspect, or the essence of) an individual'. More simply and forcefully, Lenin put it that 'the *individual is the universal*'.[61] The first sort of knowledge is the province of public opinion and the marketplace as the second is the domain of science and the laboratory. These distinct modes of knowing were characterised by Lenin and subsequent Leninists as the subjective and the objective.[62] The point to be made is not that the former is necessarily wrong, but more that it is incomplete and inadequate. It grasps appearances, is disjointed, discontinuous and unable to generalise.

The path of the dialectic, by contrast, is always from the particular to the general or universal. It moves, as Lenin notes approvingly from Hegel: 'from appearance to essence, from essence of the first order, as it were, to essence of the second order, and so on without end. Dialectics in the proper sense is the study of contradiction in the very essence of objects'.[63] The study of the contradictions internal to all phenomena and the placement of all phenomena in relation to all others was the dialectical path from subjective to objective knowledge and it was attainable only through the medium of abstraction:

> Thought proceeding from the concrete to the abstract . . . does not get away *from* the truth but comes closer to it . . . *all* scientific (correct, serious, not absurd) abstractions reflect nature more deeply, truly and *completely*. From living perception to abstract thought, *and from this to practice* – such is the dialectical path of the cognition of *truth*, of the cognition of objective reality.[64]

Here we have a process, what Lenin terms the process of truth, that takes us from the particular and the subjective 'towards objective truth *through* "practice" '.[65]

An essential component of dialectical reasoning was the analysis of the contradictory elements locked up in every phenomenon: 'The splitting of a single whole and the cognition of its contradictory parts.'[66] Everything is, therefore, to be understood as a unity of contradictory or opposed elements; everything, in the language of dialectics, is a unity of opposites. Beneath the appearance of every seemingly stable and unified thing there lies constant tension and opposition which it is the job of the dialectician to tease out and reveal. This was central to the revolutionary progressive role of dialectics because, unlike bourgeois science, its focus was not stability and permanence, but internal conflict and permanent movement. 'Contradiction,' according to Hegel, 'is the *root of all movement and vitality*, and it is only insofar as it contains a contradiction that anything moves and *has impulse and activity*.'[67] Lenin emphasises this passage approvingly, with three thick lines, as he did Hegel's further reflection that the negative was 'the *principle of all self-movement*'.[68]

Only he was a dialectician (and revolutionary) who constantly highlighted the basic clash of antagonistic class forces within society – that was the principal political point of Lenin's researches and writings on the dialectic. Those who, like the renegade leaders of the Second International, talked of social peace, *union sacrée* or *burgfrieden* at the crisis point of capitalist civilisation, were apostates to the dialectic, and therefore to the essence of Marxism. Such people attempted to wish away the objective constitution of society simply because it did not suit their subjective political purposes: because it might incur the wrath of the authorities or be unpopular. In a supreme act of wilfulness they therefore 'decreed' the temporary suspension of the very process they had hitherto asserted to be constitutive of society. In the end, Lenin had to believe, the objective realities of a class-polarised society would reassert themselves and exact vengeance on all those who had forgotten that the essence of dialectics was 'the unity of opposites'[69] and that 'Development is the "struggle of opposites".'[70] Dialectics was, moreover, 'the theory of knowledge of (Hegel and) Marxism. This is the "aspect" of the matter (it is not "an aspect" but the *essence* of the matter) to which Plekhanov, not to speak of other Marxists, paid no attention'.[71]

To the unity of opposites Lenin added another cardinal element of the dialectic which, once again, the ex-socialists of the Second International had sedulously ignored. This was what Engels had called the law of the transformation of quantity into quality which was noted in the last of the sixteen characteristic points of the dialectic quoted above. Engels' famous example of the law was the transformation of water into steam. The phenomenon water, as a liquid, conformed to the rules of hydraulics (it could not, for example, be compressed) but it could, without violating its properties as a liquid, be raised progressively in temperature. There came a point, however (what Engels calls a 'nodal' point), at which the addition of a further quantum of heat abruptly transformed the liquid water into steam which no longer obeyed the laws applicable to liquids, but conformed to those applicable to gases. Here, at 100 °C, we have a qualitative change in the nature of the object being examined, produced by a small incremental change, that is, the addition of a small quantum of heat. Much the same happens if the temperature of water is reduced. There again comes a point (0 °C) at which the liquid, water, becomes the solid, ice.

It is clear then that 'quantitative change suddenly produces, at certain points, a qualitative difference'.[72] The dialectician must therefore seek to locate those crucial nodal points (or 'nodal lines', 'leaps in nature', 'breaks in gradualness')[73] at which sudden qualitative (or revolutionary) change can no longer be avoided. This, in turn, entailed the need to define the outer limits of change which existing structures or institutions could accommodate and to predict the time-scale for their dissolution. In this analysis, of course, the relative strengths of the internal contradictions constitutive of the structure under examination would be a crucial consideration.

The political point of the law of the transformation of quantity into quality was to reject the arguments of all proponents of gradual or purely evolutionary change. It was, as we have seen, central to all revisionist schools of thought that abrupt or revolutionary change was neither rational nor desirable. It offended, moreover, the precepts of evolutionary development which were held to be the last word in science. Against this philistine and timorous science, Lenin launched the dialectic which 'alone furnishes the key to the "leaps", to the "break in continuity", to the "transformation into the opposite", to the destruction of the old and the emergence of the new'.[74] The distinctive mark of dialectical thinking, of Marxism, was, Lenin insisted, recognition of the fact that in all processes, natural and social, moments occur when there is an abrupt break in continuity. He quotes Hegel approvingly: 'What distinguishes the dialectical transition from the undialectical transition? The leap. The contradiction. The inter-ruption of gradualness.'[75] Dialectical thought is therefore not a denial of evolutionary or quantitative change; it is, rather, the insistence that such change must eventually confront the finite elasticity of all things and all structures. It discerns the limits beyond which things cannot evolve without effecting a fundamental transformation of their nature.

It is clear that Lenin, in his close examination of Hegel's works in 1914, was engaged in a process of self-clarification. He, more than any other contemporary Marxist, felt that in August 1914 the militant and revolutionary ethos of Marxism had been betrayed wholesale by the leaders of the Second International (and especially by his old mentor in philosophy, George Plekhanov). They could, and did, justify their actions by utilising some of Marx's own references on the propriety, in certain circumstances, of a 'just war'. Where, then, lay the deeper sources of their error? It lay, Lenin instinctively felt, in their ignorance or wilful avoidance of Marx's *method*. They selectively appropriated those conclusions of Marx that suited their present purposes while simultaneously rejecting the logic of his thought and its application to the contemporary world. This was precisely why open and consistent revisionists such as Bernstein had poured such scorn on the dialectic – because Marx's method, his logic and his dialectic were radically corrosive of Bernstein's whole strategy and the presuppositions upon which it was based.

There is something of a disparity between the burden that the dialectic was meant to bear as the foundational theory of knowledge of Marxism (and Leninism) and the meagre outline of its content that was publicly available to Lenin's supporters. Lenin's 1908 book on materialism had, as we have noted, little to say on the matter of dialectics, while his 1914 reflections on Hegel were private ruminations, not intended for publication; they did not see the light of day until 1928–9. Until that time, they were simply not in the public domain and can therefore hardly count as elements of Leninism as ideology. Even when, as in the pages above, we attempt to construct an overview of Lenin's position on dialectics, the texts themselves are difficult to construe. It is often difficult to disentangle what is Hegel from what is Lenin. Lenin's interjections are scattered and discontinuous, they take the form either of summaries or cryptic comments at a high level of abstraction. In the whole of the *Philosophical Notebooks* there are only five pages of continuous narrative – Lenin's brief essay 'On the Question of Dialectics'[76] which was all he completed of a projected book on dialectical materialism.

Reflecting or Transforming Reality?

It may well be the case that Lenin held back, once again, from venturing into print on these matters because he was diffident about his competence in philosophy. That had not stopped him in 1908, however, when he felt that the *political* integrity of Marxism had to be defended against any dilution of its materialist basis. In 1914 he had, surely, touched on a subject of even more fundamental importance – he now seemed to be arguing that the very method that Marxists had hitherto adopted in their analysis of matter had itself been inadequate and mistaken. The notion that the mind simply 'reflects' or 'photographs' matter now seemed far too simplistic and static; it appears to give no autonomy to the mind itself as an active and transformative subject. Dialectical thought is, by contrast, more dynamic and, notionally at least, less dogmatic. It must be less categorical about the nature of reality precisely because it now saw all phenomena (a) in a ceaseless process of inner dissolution and reconstitution; and (b) as reciprocally connected, so that the internal changes in any one phenomenon causally affected all adjacent phenomena, and changes in these in turn reverberated upon the thing initially observed. Causes become effects and vice versa. Faced with this inherent fluidity and complexity of things, the demands made upon the activity of perception and cognition are now greatly increased, along with the number of possible hypotheses:

Cognition is the eternal, endless approximation of thought to the object. The *reflection* of nature in man's thought must be understood not 'lifelessly', not 'abstractly', not *devoid of movement*, not without contradictions, but in the eternal process of movement, the arising of contradictions and their solution.[77]

The dialectician was forced to grasp that there was a 'continuity of space and time',[78] that things were both in a place and not in it, that they never simply were but were becoming something different. They had to be grasped 'not as dead, rigid, but as living, conditional, mobile, becoming transformed into one another'.[79] In this more fluid and complex universe, a universe which seemed far less determinate than the one sketched by Lenin in 1908, it was entirely clear that man's conceptions had, similarly, to become fluid, complex and less determinate. Human concepts, in order to 'reflect living life', had to conform to its mutability; they 'are not fixed but are eternally in movement, they pass into one another, they flow into one another'.[80] Lenin here is coming precariously close to the proposition that concepts may indeed play an active role in *constructing* reality (even if practice still had to confirm the veracity and adequacy of that construction). He is, finally, led precisely to this position:

Practice in the theory of Knowledge	Alias Man's consciousness not only reflects the objective world, but creates it.[81]

Lenin must have been aware that this formulation (which, as we have seen, appears as a natural entailment of dialectical thinking) was radically at odds with much of his earlier philippic against the Empiriocritics. If, in his revised assessment, there is no longer a radical disjunction between mind and matter, if mind is credited with some capacity to create or constitute the objective world, then where now is the sharp dividing line between idealism and materialism that Lenin still wished to insist upon? The old materialist separation of mind and object becomes the dialectical symbiosis in which 'The world is the other being of the Idea.'[82]

Lenin, it would seem, has broken the spell of Engels' more deterministic materialism and come far closer to the early Marx's dialectical Prometheanism which, like his own current labours, began with an appropriation and critique of Hegel. He now seems committed to the view that ideas themselves have a part in the construction (and therefore the transformation) of reality. He is, in this sense, returning to an earlier fount of inspiration (and a source much quoted by Lenin): Marx's 'Contribution to the Critique of Hegel's Philosophy of Law – Introduction'. He invoked Marx's own odyssey of 1844–7 in which he moved from Hegel to Feuerbach and thence 'to historical (and dialectical) materialism'.[83] The first major work of this transition was, precisely, Marx's 'Introduction'. Here he had insisted that 'it is not enough for thought to strive for realisation, reality must itself strive towards thought',[84] and here Marx maintained that 'theory also becomes a material force as soon as it has gripped the masses'.[85] Lenin's whole life had, after all, been dedicated to the truth of these propositions, and in 1914 he needed their solace more than ever. What he could hardly admit to himself (still less to others) was the disjunction between the methodology that yielded these conclusions, and that which he had earlier taken over from Engels.

Both intellectually and instinctively Lenin, in 1914, had to believe in the power of ideas to transform an existing economic, social and political reality. This ' "activity of man" that *changes* external actuality, abolishes its determinateness . . . and thus removes from it the features of Semblance, externality and nullity'[86] had, of course, to acknowledge Marx's rather obvious caveat that ideas, in and of themselves, 'cannot *carry anything out* at all. In order to carry out ideas men are needed who dispose of a certain practical force.'[87] This, in turn, was no more than a restatement of the thesis that theory becomes a material force when it has gripped the masses. He had to believe that radical theory could and would play an active, if not decisive, role in transforming that reality. He was intellectually, politically and psychologically disposed to recognise (at least in the secrecy of his private notes) that 'Intelligent idealism is closer to intelligent materialism than stupid materialism.'[88] He goes on to make his preferences clear: Hegel wins hands down over 'the vulgar-materialist' Plekhanov who, in a thousand pages on philosophy, had contributed nothing to 'dialectics *proper*'.[89] It was, Lenin concluded, 'completely impossible to understand Marx's *Capital* . . . without having thoroughly studied and understood the *whole* of Hegel's *Logic*. Consequently, half a century later none of the Marxists understood Marx!!'[90]

These conclusions were, clearly, too explosive to publish. They were also, as Lenin must have recognised, too critical of his own 'vulgar-materialist' standpoint of five years previously. There was clearly a tension between the new theory of knowledge (or epistemology) and the old conception of the objectivity of the material world that Lenin could not bring himself to state openly but which he recognised implicitly by keeping them separated in different books. *Materialism and Empirio-Criticism* had almost nothing to say on the structure and intent of dialectical thought, while the *Philosophical Notebooks* were notably cautious about the priority of the material world. It is, above all, significant that Lenin never returned to these themes, and that his *Philosophical Notebooks* were not published until five years after his death. By that time less fastidious minds than his, and men less captivated by the subtlety of Hegel's thought, had already put together a new universal explanatory system that made materialism into a metaphysic and the dialectic into an invariable set of 'scientific' laws. Armed with such weapons, communists could storm any fortress, overcome every obstacle. The dialectic became, in due course, an apologetic for Stalin's ruthless voluntarism in forcing a recalcitrant reality to dress by the requirements of thought. Dialectics became a 'science of sciences', fated to walk hand in hand with socialism as planned economy and planned society, and the party leadership was, of course, its oracle.

Philosophy – Political Functions and Entailments

Despite the patchiness of Lenin's reflections there can be no doubt that the dialectic was crucial to his mind-set and to his self-belief in the period from 1914 to 1917. It provided, after all, a philosophical anchorage for virtually all his principal political strategies. At the broadest level, the struggle of antagonistic classes that Lenin took to be constitutive of Marxian history was merely a manifestation of the unity and identity of opposites. The transformation of quantity into quality was, in the modern world, evident in the struggle of socialism to emerge from of a moribund capitalism that had arrived at the limits of its evolutionary development. The nodal point for the dissolution of the one and the emergence of the other was signalled by the incapacity of capitalism to rule in the old way, and the revolutionary assertiveness of socialism in creating alternative values and institutions. The dialectic, finally, served the highly important ideological function of drawing a sharp line of distinction between renegade social democrats, reformists and apostles of social peace on the one hand, and genuinely revolutionary Marxists on the other. Above all, there is the unquantifiable impact that Lenin's study in the dialectic had upon his own sense of certitude. He was, after all, in every sense isolated – from his Russian environment, his emigré colleagues, and of course from all the European Marxist leaders he had hitherto esteemed. Psychologically and intellectually he needed as never before to be certain of his grounds, not only for condemning as traitors to Marxism the old leaders of the Second International, but also for formulating the methodological basis upon which a new and purified revolutionary international was to be founded. It was this problematic that drew him to reformulate Marxist method in his dialectical materialism, and it was hardly adventitious that it supplied him with certain philosophical backing for the political strategies he had in mind. Chronologically, this was the birth of Leninism.

The dialectic was, in Lenin, pressed to the service of proletarian (that is, revolutionary) politics and this should in no way surprise us for he made no bones about the partisan nature of all philosophy. All political ideologies, as Marx astutely observed, projected as natural, foundational and eternal, precisely those characteristics of man, society and the state that suited their political purposes and vindicated the economic interests of the classes that were privileged by these ideologies. Philosophy, as Marxist scholars repeatedly insisted, had no autonomy; it merely served class purposes. For Althusser, as we have seen, philosophy drew lines and made demarcations – it served the classic functions of ideology.

It is too easy to conclude from all this that Leninism privileges the interests and the discourse of the working class. The problem here is that Lenin, in both his political and his philosophical writings, was clear that the vehicle of science cannot be the proletariat. Only the intelligentsia that has undergone an arduous apprenticeship in philosophical practice[91] was capable of acquiring and extending objective or scientific knowledge. The intelligentsia alone were capable of grasping, at a necessarily high level of abstraction, the interconnectedness of things, the identity of the universal and the particular, the unity of opposites and so on. The mass of the people were, as we have seen, restricted to the narrow confines of unreflective and undemonstrable subjective knowledge. It was, however, only objective knowledge that could guide revolutionary politics, for it alone had a purchase on the future. The intellectuals were (as in Marx's original sketch of their functions in the *Manifesto*) able to lead precisely because they had 'over the great mass of the proletariat the advantage of clearly understanding the line of march, the conditions, and the ultimate general results of the proletarian movement'.[92] They were able to lead because the scientific understanding of society meant the formulation of laws of development with predictive power. To know science was therefore to know the future, or, at the least, to have a prescient awareness of what was coming into being.

The practical consequence of this stance is fairly obvious. Of all modern ideologies, Leninism, more than any other, gives far more credence and authority to the role of intellectuals. No other ideological current makes attachment to a particular philosophical position a condition for membership and an obligatory part of the curriculum at every level of education. Indeed, almost all other ideologies are thoroughly eclectic in matters of epistemology. Few other ideologies so clearly and overtly credit the discourse of intellectuals on the grounds that they articulate a moment of truth beyond the grasp of ordinary people, as Leninism does, and in so doing it confers on its theoretical leaders a crucial and unchallengeable authority. The price to be paid by anyone in pursuit of certainty is unquestioning acceptance. It follows equally that the discourse of its political leaders must be credited by its followers with a special authority that, even if inscrutable (and perhaps especially if this is so), is definitive of their true or essential interests. Leninist leaders must always and invariably present themselves to their followers as eminent theorists and philosophers. As in no other ideology, their power is that of the word. No single Leninist leader has spent any considerable period in power without his selected or collected writings being trumpeted as major contributions to the theory of Marxism–Leninism. This is an ideology created wholly by intellectuals and, some would argue, not only by them, but for them and in their interests.

The dialectic was a highly important element in the legitimation of the Communist Party and its leadership groups. It is significant that Lenin believed that of all the Communist Party leaders, he alone understood the intricacies of the dialectic. Bukharin, for all his brilliance as a principal theoretician of the movement, had never, according to Lenin's 'Testament', mastered it.[93] It is even more significant (though at first sight bizarre) that Stalin, as leader of the party, insisted upon his prerogative to feature as the author of the chapter on dialectics in the authoritative *History of the Communist Party of the Soviet Union* (the 'Short Course')[94] which was the handbook of communists for a whole generation. So valuable and central a property was never allowed to escape the control of the party and its top leadership.

We should not, however, be left with the impression that the philosophical preoccupations of Leninism were wholly a one-way process and that, therefore, the rank and file followers of Leninist parties derive no comfort or satisfaction from what might be seen, from the outside, as the intellectual tutelage of their leaders. On the contrary, there is testimony enough in the biographies of Leninist militants that they rejoiced in the power of the materialist dialectic whose agents they believed themselves to be. They might unwillingly confess that to explain and justify its propositions about the materiality of the world and its dialectical evolution was beyond them. But they were sublimely confident that there were people of their party who *could*, with the best of them, confront and answer such problems and confound all opponents, and this was long a source of enormous pride and almost bewitching self-confidence.

The importance of dialectical materialism for the practical politics of Leninism has generally been understated or even ignored. One way of illustrating its very practical significance is to pursue the implications of its counter-factual – suppose a widespread rejection of the possibility of there being such a thing as objective truth. Suppose that all we can hope for is to muddle our way to more or less adequate and acceptable propositions about nature, society and social policies. In this case we could not, in principle, be against widespread debate about all of these matters, and we would probably in fact actually think it desirable that there should be encouragement (or, at the barest minimum, no prohibition) to voicing of divergent and even eccentric views. Holding to such a sceptical or relativist position, we would perhaps want to go further and insist upon rules and conventions that guaranteed that this diversity of views would be respected and adhered to – within and between political parties, in electoral procedures, in Parliament, in the press, in academic life, on radio and television, in philosophy, science, history and so on.

If, on the other hand, we assent to the paired propositions (a) that there is such a thing as objective or scientific truth in matters natural, social, historical and economic; and that (b) those blessed with thorough knowledge of the laws of development of those phenomena have privileged access to the truth – then the practical consequences are very different. Those who disagree with the demonstrable pronouncements of science, far from deserving protection, must be presumed to be either ignorant or malevolent. In any case, they must be presumed to be agents of hostile class views, because there is only proletarian philosophy and bourgeois philosophy: 'those who are not with us are therefore against us'. It is clear that widespread public debate would allow the voicing of mistaken views and give undue credence to them, thereby undermining the authority of science and the integrity of the proletarian idea. This conception of truth, and the path to its attainment, not only has no need of the dense network of rules, conventions and forbearances regarding toleration and protection of dissenting voices, but must see them as being misguided, if not actually harmful. Science, Leninism concluded, is not advanced by taking straw polls, counting heads or conducting elections. The materialist metaphysic of Leninism came to insist that *all* problems are amenable to scientific resolution. By this it is meant that all those disposing of the requisite dialectical skills, armed with the appropriate data, and experienced in exploring and analysing the phenomenon under consideration, would come to the same conclusion. After the revolution this was, increasingly, Lenin's stance; it is at the root of his intemperance with respect to continued debate within the party and his contempt for 'politics'. For Leninists, proper science speaks with one voice. Its status and repute are diminished by dispute. It is a body of demonstrable truths.

It follows that bodies must be established whose business is to provide authoritative 'scientific' pronouncements on all matters. Academies of Sciences embracing all fields of knowledge did this at an academic level, and the party did so in practical and policy spheres. In order to ensure that throughout all these agencies just one authoritative voice emerges, it obviously becomes necessary to create organisational and administrative procedures, rules and norms, to guarantee unanimity of outcome. Faction cannot be allowed, or rival platforms tolerated, contested elections are considered to be counter-productive. Decisions of the authoritative utterers ought to be seen to be taken unanimously, and endorsed unanimously by those most affected by them. Decisions of the most authoritative bodies: party, state, trades union, academic or whatever, must therefore be adopted unanimously and be binding upon all lower and less authoritative bodies. The whole justification for Leninist organisational models of democratic centralism, and the pervasive Leninist style of unanimity in decision-making, derives from its philosophical starting point. We could, again, put this in a different way. When communist regimes begin to allow, or even encourage, wide-ranging debate within and outside the party; when they tolerate or even begin to protect, the rights of dissident voices, they thereby begin to disavow the Leninist conception of the party as the bearer of science and truth. They can justify such actions only by recourse to a relativist notion of truth which must threaten the metaphysic upon which their *own* claim to power is based. In short, they then cease to be Leninists and dissolve the integrity of the structures of power on which modern communism is based. That is precisely what happened in the Soviet Union. In no other modern ideology was the relationship between metaphysical principle and actual power relations so intimate.

10
Leninism and Stalinism

If the relationship of Leninism to Marxism is a hotly contested matter, so too is the relationship of Leninism to Stalinism. Theorists of totalitarianism assert that the theoretical, psychological and institutional bases of the Stalinist aspiration for total control over society and individuals was firmly established by Lenin. On the other hand, there is a persistent line of interpretation offered not only by Trotskyists but also by a fairly broad spectrum on the left, that Stalinism was, in all essential respects, the illegitimate offspring of Leninism. The two phenomena are, in this interpretation, quite distinct in purpose, style and method, and it is maintained there is considerable evidence to support the view that Lenin himself was not only aware of the dangers of Stalinist 'degeneration', but tried to rouse the party to purge itself of it.

Let us deal, first of all, with some factors that are not vehemently contested. There is, in the first place, considerable agreement that Lenin and Stalin were widely different in terms of their backgrounds and personal attributes, and consequently their general political styles. Lenin was brought up in a large, affluent and cultured family that was exceptionally supportive and stable. Stalin was brought up in poverty as an only child whose brutal and drunken father was largely absent from the home.[1] Throughout his life, Lenin retained the discipline and exactitude of a scholar; Stalin effectively ceased serious study at the age of fourteen. Lenin was a good linguist, his early distinction as a scholar of Greek and Latin carrying over into his later familiarity with French, German and English. He was a cosmopolitan who had lived in most of the principal cities of Europe. Stalin had virtually no experience of life outside his native Georgia and adopted Russia; he developed a strong suspicion of all things foreign.

Even Lenin's harshest critics concede that he was, personally, extraordinarily modest and self-effacing. He stamped hard on post-

243

revolutionary attempts to lionise him, to memorialise his greatness, or to invoke religious imagery to conjure up a godlike being. The papers, he complained, had been full of such insulting rubbish while he was on the verge of death after the assassination attempt on him in 1918. Upon his recovery, he immediately sent his top aides to the offices of Soviet newspapers with forthright instructions that such vulgar glorification of the personality was to cease forthwith. Stalin's brief show of modesty was, by contrast, false and contrived. During his rise to power, he found it convenient to play the part of honest broker and modest disciple of Lenin. He profited at this stage precisely from a comparatively low public profile, and because his competitors tended to disparage the unglamorous backroom tasks of party administration that Stalin had concentrated in his hands. When, however, Stalin had ousted all his rivals and secured to himself undivided sway over the party, no encomium to him could be too extravagant and no praise too fawning. A condition of membership of the Soviet élite now became an attitude of compliance and servility towards Stalin and a preparedness to laud his genius.

It is fairly widely agreed that the differences of background and temperament made for considerable differences between the two men in their political styles – in how they presented themselves to their colleagues and the wider world. Lenin's authority was that of an exacting headmaster, looked up to and respected for the breadth of his knowledge and for the clarity with which he could present it. He impressed and convinced through the force of his logic, and the frankness and persistence with which he put his arguments. Stalin, by contrast, was more devious and dissimulating. With him, arguments of political principle degenerated rapidly into personal attacks, administrative manoeuvres and, eventually, the physical elimination of real and imagined opponents. For Lenin, the party had a corporate significance that transcended the sum of the personalities that comprised it. He might, at crucial moments, insist upon his right to fight for fundamental reorientations of its political strategy but, equally, he always sought and won the approval of the Central Committee and the Party Congress for all these changes. Procedural formalities, at least as far as the party was concerned, mattered to him. While he lived, Party Congresses were convened every year, and Lenin attached great importance to them. After Stalin effectively consolidated his power at the 15th Party Congress in 1927, he tolerated only three further congresses until he died in 1952. Fundamental redefinitions of the strategic goals of socialism (and of the party) such as the collectivisation of agriculture and the rapid industrialisation of the country, were not even put before a Party Congress. In his rise to power, Stalin had adroitly used his control over appointments to local, regional and national party bodies to marginalise opponents and secure his own pre-eminence. When that objective had been secured, he treated the party veterans, the Bolshevik 'Old Guard', as his bitterest enemies and wiped them out in the purges of the 1930s. Proportionately, the party suffered more executions and imprisonments than any other sector of Soviet society. Stalin decimated its leadership, rode roughshod over its rules and conventions, and extinguished the last sparks of autonomous life within it.

Lenin's Last Struggle - The Assault on Stalin

Perhaps the most compelling evidence for the case that there is a fundamental distinction between the content and styles of Leninism and Stalinism appears in Lenin's last writings. The 'Letter to Congress' (Lenin's 'Testament') was explicit that 'Comrade Stalin, having become Secretary-General, has unlimited authority concentrated in his hands, and I am not sure whether he will always be capable of using that authority with sufficient caution.'[2] Lenin's codicil found Stalin to be too coarse (*gruby*) for a general secretary of the party, and called for the Congress to 'think about a way of removing Stalin from that post and appointing another man in his stead' – that unnamed man, Lenin went on, differs from Stalin in 'being more tolerant, more loyal, more polite and more considerate to the comrades, less capricious, etc.'[3] That this was not the careless slight of a dying man was evident in virtually everything that Lenin concerned himself with, and wrote about, in the last eighteen months of his life. His investigations into the affairs of the Georgian Communist Party, and his deep opposition to the high-handed and chauvinist attitudes of Stalin and his appointees (such as Ordzhonikidze), had convinced him that, personally and politically, Stalin was not only untrustworthy and rude; he had become a real threat to socialism. It is no exaggeration to say that Lenin devoted almost all his energy, in the period following the two strokes he suffered in December 1923, to the battle against Stalin.

Lenin's last two articles, dictated to his secretaries in brief periods when he was at the limits of his physical and mental capabilities (and under ban from the Central Committee from engaging in political work of any sort) were both, very obviously, directed against Stalin. 'How

We Should Reorganise the Workers' and Peasants' Inspection'[4] and 'Better Fewer but Better'[5] were virulent critiques of bureaucracy and incompetence in the state administration as a whole, and of Stalin's empires in particular. The Workers' and Peasants' Inspection (WPI) had been established under Stalin's auspices in 1919 and he had been its commissar since its inception. It was supposed to act as a body that would, on the one hand, train workers and peasants to assume leading roles in the administration, and, on the other, act as the regime's most potent instrument of public accountability, ensuring that *all* the activities of all the other departments of government were exposed to careful scrutiny. It had, Lenin concluded, failed lamentably in both respects:

> Let us say frankly that the People's Commissariat of the Workers' and Peasants' Inspection does not at present enjoy the slightest authority. Everybody knows that no other institutions are worse organised than those of our Workers' and Peasants' Inspection, and that under present conditions nothing can be expected from this People's Commissariat.[6]

There was a double sting in Lenin's article, because not only did it point an accusing finger at Stalin for his scandalous neglect of the WPI, it also advocated that this very body should now be revitalised, merged with the party's own Central Control Commission, and vested with powers to call even the Politburo of the party to account. The reconstituted WPI would, in this way, become a check not only upon the incompetence and arrogance of state administrations but would, Lenin added pointedly, root out 'bureaucrats in our Party offices as well as in Soviet offices'.[7] It would, by inference, act as the most powerful check upon the ever-growing power of the party's General Secretary – Stalin himself. It was little wonder, therefore, that Stalin and his entourage (supported by Bukharin at *Pravda*), fought against the publication of Lenin's last article right through the meeting of the Politburo that had to be convened by Trotsky to press the matter.[8] The article duly appeared in *Pravda* on 4 March 1923, but it is clear that Lenin had no intention of letting the matter rest there. He had informed his secretary that 'he would move the question of the Workers' and Peasants' Inspection at the congress'[9] (the forthcoming 12th Congress of the party that convened in April 1923). The day following the appearance of 'Better Fewer but Better' (5 March 1923), Lenin wrote a uniquely sharp note to Stalin formally requesting an apology for the latter's rudeness in a telephone conversation with Lenin's wife Krupskaya: 'I ask you, therefore, to think it over whether you are prepared to withdraw what you have said and to make your apologies or whether you prefer that relations between us should be broken off.'[10] Stalin had, it seems, brusquely accused Krupskaya of breaking the rules laid down by the Politburo (and supervised by Stalin) that forbade Lenin 'newspapers, visitors and political information'[11] and allowed him access to his secretaries for only five minutes a day to dictate his personal diary. Lenin despatched his secretary with his note to Stalin, having first covered himself by sending copies to Zinoviev and Kamenev – itself an indication of how little he now trusted Stalin. Stalin, cornered, backed down and yielded the necessary apology which has, however, never come to light.

It is quite clear that Lenin was preparing a major theoretical, organisational and personal assault on Stalin. He was convinced that Stalin constituted the largest threat to the unity of the party and that this was a matter 'which can assume decisive importance'.[12] His coarseness made him unfit to be General Secretary, and his great Russian chauvinism made him unsuited to the Commissariat of the Nationalities. There is in this, 'Lenin's Last Struggle',[13] a large measure of heroism. Nothing became Lenin's tenure of office so much as the leaving of it – a frail, terminally-ill man, confined as a prisoner to his rooms in the Kremlin, denied access to information and spied on by a team of doctors answerable solely to the man he was bent on destroying. (There is, indeed, a full-length study propounding the view that, with the assistance of Lenin's doctors, Stalin finally succeeded in poisoning Lenin.)[14] Not even his old comrades seemed prepared to come to his aid, partly because they feared that, at the last, he would promote Trotsky as his successor. And Trotsky too, even though entrusted with Lenin's papers on the Georgian question,[15] and a damning brief against Stalin for the forthcoming Congress, even Trotsky would not fight his corner. At every critical turn he prevaricated, fell ill or, out of real or mock modesty, refused to display himself as Lenin's anointed. Lenin's sole remaining allies were his own Krupskaya and the faithful and indomitable women of his private office (who included, bizarrely enough, Stalin's wife, Nadya Alliluyeva).

We would be cold of soul to recognise nothing of the heroic in the last stand of the stricken old man. But, equally, we would be blind not to recognise, in Lenin's unequal confrontation with Stalin, the pathos of a self-induced tragedy. His own past sins of omission and commission were coming home to haunt him; his own creature was destroying him. We come now to the other side of the story that sees Stalin as Lenin's natural, and perhaps necessary, successor.

Stalin as Lenin's Creature

There could be no doubt in the mind of anyone of any prominence in the party, that Stalin was Lenin's man. It is clear from Robert Tucker's biography[16] that, early in his career as a revolutionary, Stalin developed a hero fixation with Lenin – a desire to prove himself to be Lenin's closest comrade in arms and most assiduous supporter. For his part, Lenin welcomed this 'marvellous Georgian' who was evidently quite well read in Marxism and was, more to the point, a vital organisational link to the Trans-Caucasian revolutionary movement. Stalin seemed to Lenin to encapsulate all the qualities of a revolutionary activist. He was a good organiser and was well trained in conspiratorial technique. He was, during the hard period of reaction following the failure of the rising of 1905, invaluable to Lenin as a source of funds for the party, being the main conduit to the armed fighting squads that carried out large-scale expropriations to fill the Bolsheviks' coffers. It was Stalin and his Bolshevik Committee who basked in the reflected glory of the 1907-8 strikes and workers' congress that made his fiefdom in Baku uniquely active in this period. Their tenacity and resolve, and their uncompromising stance towards the Menshevik liquidators, made a considerable impact on Lenin, who referred to the Caucasian Bolsheviks as the 'last Mohicans of the political mass strike'.[17] By 1912, at a point when Lenin had effectively broken with the intellectuals of his party, who had been seduced by the philosophical wanderings of Bogdanov, Lunacharsky and Gorky, it was to the practical men of the Caucausian underground that Lenin turned to reconstitute his Bolshevik Central Committee. Both Stalin and his assistant Ordjonikidze were co-opted into the five-man directing centre; in addition they were appointed to the four-man Russian Bureau which was charged with directing the party's activities in Russia.[18] We should note that Stalin's rapid elevation to the directing bodies of the party was wholly at Lenin's personal insistence.

It was at Lenin's prompting that Stalin embarked on the writing up of an article/pamphlet on the subject of the national question. Stalin's 'Marxism and the National Question' was written in January 1913 and published a few months later.[19] It was a very creditable survey and critique of a wide range of social-democratic material from the Leninist standpoint. It decried federalism and national cultural autonomy, and it stood firm on the principle of national self-determination, while simultaneously professing the larger goal of international proletarian unity. It is said that Lenin himself gently guided his protégé in the themes he should cover and in the general organisation of the pamphlet (Stalin's sole contribution to what might be termed 'theory' prior to the October Revolution), and that Lenin carefully edited out its infelicities before publication. It may have been the case that Lenin was anxious that his rapidly-promoted lieutenant should, in the intellectually snobbish milieu of the Russian socialist movement, be seen to have at least some theoretical bona fides. None of this should, however, lead us to suppose that Stalin was wholly without knowledge or ability in these matters, or that the pamphlet he wrote was not substantially his own work. He may have been something of a journeyman as far as theory was concerned, and he was understandably overawed by Lenin's own voluminous pronouncements on the national question, but the conventional view that he was a dunce in matters of theory hardly bears examination.

Lenin's 'marvellous Georgian'[20] was, almost as soon as he returned to Russia in early 1913, betrayed by his fellow Bolshevik (and secret police agent) Malinovsky, and he remained in Siberian exile until the overthrow of the tsar in February 1917. Upon his return to Petrograd in March 1917, as the most senior Bolshevik in Russia, he took control of the party committee and of the editorship of *Pravda*. It was, again, a mark of Lenin's esteem that, despite Stalin's waverings in the months before Lenin's return in April 1917, he was retained in his post as editor of *Pravda*, the party's principal journal. When Lenin and Zinoviev were forced to flee Petrograd, and with Trotsky and Kamenev arrested after the abortive rising of the July Days, it was Stalin who resumed the leadership of the party in their absence.

After the revolution, Stalin was made Commissar for Nationalities, and, in 1919, Commissar for the WPI. He was, simultaneously, a member of the Central Committee and the only one of its members to sit on the Central Committee, the policy-making Politburo, and its organisational or executive arm, the organisation bureau or Orgburo.[21] Through the WPI he could maintain his agents and monitoring systems within each of the departments of state, and through the party's Orgburo (established in March 1919, according to a plan jointly prepared by Lenin and Stalin) he directed the recruitment and placement of party cadres throughout the country. Fate here played a large part. The organisational life of the party had, hitherto, been in the hands of an exceptionally gifted and energetic young man, Jacob Sverdlov, who was well liked throughout the party. It was only after Sverdlov's sudden death from typhus at the end of 1918 that Stalin was able to insinuate himself into the centre of the party organisation. His pre-eminence as the organiser of the party was confirmed officially with his election in March 1922 to the new post of general secretary of the Central Committee. He was then responsible not merely for the placement and promotion of all responsible party officials, but also for preparing the agenda and attendant papers for meetings of the Politburo. He now, quite literally, set the agenda for the ruling elite of the Soviet regime and increasingly controlled its recruitment and placement. Finally, he was responsible for party discipline and the purging of careerists, via the Central Control Commission established in September 1920.

We should be clear that, at each step of this remorseless accumulation of power, Lenin not only endorsed or suggested Stalin's nomination, he also vigorously defended Stalin against those who protested against his multiple job-holding. 'Who among us', Lenin asked his colleagues rhetorically, 'has not sinned in this way?'[22] It was only at the very end of 1922, shortly before his second stroke in mid-December, that circumstances combined to force Lenin, for the first time, to question seriously Stalin's fitness for the power he wielded. By that time, as in all real tragedy, the time was too late and the proto-hero had, through his own sins of omission and commission, fatally flawed his own defence.

Lenin – Building the Monolith

Lenin had himself been the most determined destroyer of all political opposition, both within and outside the party. He had, in the months following the October Revolution, rejected the appeals for a broad-based socialist coalition government that had extensive support even within his own party. He had, with equanimity, authorised the closure of the opposition parties' premises, and the harassment and arrest of their activists.[23] Most ominously for the future of Russia, Lenin applauded the summary dissolution of the Constituent Assembly that had been elected by universal suffrage in November 1917 and that had been convened briefly in January 1918.

The Bolsheviks, with Lenin in the van, had, in the run-up to the October Revolution, claimed that they alone would guarantee the convocation of the cherished and long-awaited Constituent Assembly. Trotsky, indeed, claimed that October was 'the salvation of the Constituent Assembly'.[24] Up to that point all parties, the Bolsheviks included, maintained that only the Constituent Assembly had the unchallengeable authority and legitimacy to re-create the constitutional, legal, power, and property relations of post-imperial Russia. With the Bolsheviks installed in power, however, the emphasis changed rapidly. It was pointedly claimed by Lenin that soviet democracy was infinitely more democratic than 'bourgeois' representative democracy. Soviet democracy was, he argued, activist and participatory; it involved millions in the educative experience of their own self-administration and was, therefore, 'a million times more democratic than the most democratic bourgeois republic'.[25] There could be, he cautioned, no going back to the outmoded and discredited bourgeois parliaments. He was no doubt banking heavily on the strong 'Soviet patriotism' of the worker and soldier masses.

The elections to the Constituent yielded, in round figures, 40 per cent support for the peasant party (the Socialist Revolutionaries – SRs), and 25 per cent for the Bolsheviks – 15.8 million votes and 410 seats in the Constituent Assembly (an absolute majority) as against 9.8 million votes and 175 seats. The Bolsheviks nevertheless dominated the principal urban areas and the most important armies.[26] Lenin argued from contingent factors that the vote was not representative – it could not have reflected the dramatic split between left SRs (close to the Bolsheviks) and right SRs that had occurred with the October Revolution. The response to this was obvious, and as it was pertly put by Rosa Luxemburg: if indeed the composition of the Constituent inaccurately reflected popular opinion, then 'new elections to a new Constituent Assembly should have been arranged'.[27] The Bolshevik strategy of eliminating democracy, retaining sole control, and riding roughshod over all opponents was, Luxemburg concluded:

> worse than the disease it is supposed to cure; for it stops up the very living source from which alone can come the correction of all the innate shortcomings of social institutions. That source is the active, untrammelled, energetic political life of the broadest masses of the people.[28]

She was equally clear that the rule of the masses was entirely unthinkable 'without a free and untrammelled press, without the unlimited right of association and assemblage'.[29] In the absence of these conditions, the Bolshevik experiment was, she prophesied, bound to degenerate into a 'clique affair – a dictatorship . . . of a handful of politicians' and the inevitable brutalization of public life.[30]

This was the prognosis of one of the handful of foreign socialists that Lenin still considered to be true to the revolutionary spirit of Marxism. It was a judgement echoed by the Mensheviks and taken up by the more civilised voices within his own party. In the absence of a free press, in the absence of freely elected and sovereign representative assemblies, what remedies could citizens dispose of against the incompetence or arbitrariness of the administration?

Lenin's objections to the Constituent Assembly were increasingly presented in theoretical rather than contingent terms. (If these latter had been Lenin's main grounds for rejecting the results of the election, then he would have had no real answer to Rosa Luxemburg's challenge.) The time for traditional parliamentary regimes was, he asserted, now over:

> The working classes learned by experience that the old bourgeois parliamentary system had outlived its purpose and was absolutely incompatible with the aim of achieving socialism, and that not national institutions, but only class institutions (such as the Soviets) were capable of overcoming the resistance of the propertied classes and of laying the foundations of socialist society.[31]

The soviets were, he maintained, in every way superior as agencies of revolutionary democracy. They were not only class-specific bodies but also pre-eminently active rather than deliberative institutions. The success of democracy was to be measured in terms of the numbers of people who participated in the practical running of public affairs rather than in the token action of voting. The soviets, by combining legislative, judicial, administrative and policing functions, made the business of public administration, for the first time in history, a truly mass affair. There could therefore be no reversion to a more primitive constitutional form that had, in any case, universally demonstrated itself to be the chosen instrument of bourgeois dictatorship: 'To hand over power to the Constituent Assembly would again be compromising with the malignant bourgeoisie.'[32] Such, at least, was the Bolsheviks' main defence for the summary dismissal of the long-awaited Constituent Assembly (though Lenin, as we have seen, in his propaganda sallies immediately before the October Revolution, had maintained repeatedly that only a Bolshevik-led soviet revolution could save the Constituent Assembly from the treacherous intentions of the right: 'Our Party alone, on taking power, can secure the Constituent Assembly's Convocation.'[33]

In practice, however, the Bolsheviks hewed far more closely to Lenin's words at the end of September: 'Only the development of this war can bring *us* to power but we must *speak* about this as little as possible in our agitation (remembering very well that even tomorrow events may put us in power and then we will not let it go)'.[34] The Council of People's Commissars (or Sovnarkom) confirmed by the Second Congress of Soviets, was wholly Bolshevik, and the party overwhelmingly dominated the Central Executive Committee to which the Council was officially responsible. On 30 October, Sovnarkom unilaterally arrogated to itself legislative powers simply by promulgating a decree to this effect. This was, effectively, a Bolshevik *coup d'état* that made clear the government's (and party's) pre-eminence over the soviets and their executive organs. Increasingly, the Bolsheviks relied upon the appointment from above of commissars with plenipotentiary powers, and they split and reconstituted fractious Soviets and intimidated political opponents. Within six weeks of the October revolution, Gorky's paper *Novaya Zhizn* lamented the rapidity with which life had run out of the Soviet movement: 'The slogan "All power to the Soviets",' it concluded, 'had actually been transformed into the slogan "All power to the few Bolsheviks"... The Soviets decay, become enervated, and from day to day lose more of their prestige in the ranks of democracy.'[35] The initial heroic stage – the stage of mass involvement and unsullied dreams – was already over.

It was unambiguously Lenin who (with Trotsky now as his most strident supporter) rejected coalition, rejected power-sharing and rejected the democratic road. His ruthlessness with political opponents, his refusal to acknowledge the legitimacy of their alternative formulations of public policy, and his destruction of the public forums in which they might be expressed was, undoubtedly, one of the precipitants of the civil war. The dissolution of the Constituent Assembly was viewed by many as the first blow struck in this war – the Bolshevik declaration of the commencement of hostilities against the Russian people. It was, of course, out of civil war that the brutalisation of public life spread, infected the party and the state apparatuses and created a milieu, a style of work and an attitude of mind in which Stalinism could live and thrive.

The End of Opposition

It was Lenin who had prided himself upon being the hammer of all the 'deviations' and 'oppositions' within the party. The Democratic Centralists and the Workers' Opposition had suffered the same fate as the trades unions and the co-operative movement, in their claims for a measure of freedom and autonomy, for a space in which to put their alternative specifications of public policy. Each in turn was told by Lenin that, in the epoch of mortal struggle between the emergent proletariat and the moribund (and therefore desperate) bourgeoisie, the choice was between one dictatorship or the other.[36]

In this acute international situation, in 'this besieged fortress'[37] neither freedom nor democracy was possible. The slightest deviation, the smallest breach of discipline, could only serve the enemy. Whatever the intentions or professed motives of the perpetrators, such actions were counter-revolutionary. This distinction between the stated motives of people and the 'objective' significance of their utterances or activities was routinely invoked by Lenin to discredit any opposition, or even any claim to a protected space. There was, of course, no defence against this imputation of a hidden and dangerous meaning to words or actions. Only the party leadership was the judge of what did or did not promote the interests of the proletariat and/or the revolution, and these things changed according to internal and international situations. It was precisely this logic that Stalin was to apply in his wholesale liquidation of 'spies, wreckers and provocateurs' in the 1930s. Lenin anticipated both the arbitrariness of defining culpable groups, as well as Stalin's ruthlessness in dealing with them. In March 1918, Lenin was already calling for the setting up of 'a really revolutionary court that is rapid and mercilessly severe in dealing with counter-revolutionaries, hooligans, idlers and disorganisers'.[38]

There were to be, in Lenin's dictatorship of the proletariat exercised by the party, no hidden places or empty spaces in which individuals or groups could exercise their independence. The claim of the trades unions, for example, to a measure of autonomy and neutrality *vis-à-vis* the party and the state Lenin condemned as 'either a hypocritical screen for counter-revolution, or a complete lack of class-consciousness'.[39] The co-operators, similarly, were told that 'it is quite hopeless to expect any vestige of independence to remain. This cannot be, and it is no use dreaming of it'.[40] 'There can and must be no question of any kind of independence for individual groups'; 'Everything,' Lenin insisted, 'must come under the Soviet government.'[41]

By March 1921, at the very time when the regime was undertaking the relaxation of economic measures against the peasants, at the very time when the last elements of armed resistance had been put down, Lenin resolved to impose a new regime of severe discipline and obligatory unanimity upon the party. He had, as we have seen, become increasingly exasperated with internal dissension and debate, both of which he considered to be factors of morbidity. The party, he complained, was sick, it was down with the fever.[42] It had allowed itself 'the luxury of discussions and disputes within the Party. This was an amazing luxury for a Party shouldering unprecedented responsibilities and surrounded by mighty and powerful enemies uniting the whole Capitalist world'.[43] The threat of a hostile exterior combined with the parlous situation of internal isolation, was enough for Lenin to insist that the Tenth Congress of the party 'take strict measures to prevent all factional actions'. It was at his insistence that:

> The Congress, therefore, hereby declares dissolved and orders the immediate dissolution of all groups without exception formed on the basis of one platform or another (such as the Workers' Opposition group, the Democratic Centralist group, etc.). Non-observance of this decision of the Congress shall entail unconditional and instant dismissal from the Party.[44]

This was the notorious 'ban on factions', the objective of which was to give formal backing to Lenin's personal conclusion 'that the opposition's time has run out and that the lid's on it. We want no more oppositions'.[45]

The party, as a governing party beset by enemies, want, privation, and consequent political vacillation, could not be waylaid by 'arguments about freedom of speech and freedom to criticise'. These were not absolute values; far from it, whether they could be exercised and the extent to which they could be exercised, was wholly contingent upon political circumstances as evaluated by the party leadership. The import of Lenin's campaign for unity and unanimity was that it was impossible for any individual or group to be right against the party. That was the content of *partiinost*. This was the doctrine that was later to disarm Stalin's critics such as Trotsky and Bukharin. The party was elevated to the highest focus of loyalty. It expressed the mission of the working class, the revolution and all progressive humanity, and to fight against it was to fight one's better self.

Lenin himself, at the last, fell prey to this, his own doctrine. It was he who had insisted that there was no more authoritative court of appeal than the party's own leading centre. How could he complain when it fell outside his control? In what terms, what language could his complaints be put, for he had himself consistently poured contempt upon plaintiffs claiming rights of freedom of speech, freedom to propagandise? Could he complain of arbitrariness when he had extolled rule based wholly and exclusively on force unrestrained by any rules or laws? He had himself frequently upbraided subordinates for their squeamishness about exacting exemplary punishment and their reluctance to resort to terror. Above all, to whom was he to make his appeal, and with what credibility? All the potential supporters of a campaign against bureaucratic high-handedness and party authoritarianism had been smashed at his express promptings. His putative supporters, and the very language and media through which he might appeal to them, had been neutered by his own past intolerance. His last struggle and his defiant and heroic words were, in retrospect, hollow gestures and crocodile tears. As with Trotsky's later outpourings against Stalin's excesses and the bureaucratization and brutalization of public life,[46] there was never a moment when Lenin frankly acknowledged the extensiveness of his responsibility for creating the institutions, the attitudes of mind, the political intolerance, and the institutional and moral relativism whose bitter fruit was Stalinism.

The final line of defence for the Stalin-as-betrayer-of-Leninism school of thought is that the top Bolshevik leaders were, with the exception of Stalin, intellectuals with a typical intellectualist disdain for organisational matters. We are asked to believe that these trusting, high-minded (but organisationally naïve) dilettantes were hoodwinked by the *apparatchik*, Stalin. They could, therefore, be forgiven for failing to recognise the awesome personal power that was disguised behind the organisational façade. Of Bukharin, this was, perhaps, half true. His was a restless mind little given to the tidiness of administrative practice – and for this good reason, Lenin kept him clear of departmental responsibilities. Bukharin apart, few others could plausibly claim such naïvety. Trotsky certainly could not. He was a veteran of party intrigue during his long pre-revolutionary career. He was the principal co-ordinator and organiser, first of the revolution itself and then of the Red Army and the civil war. At every stage he recognised the importance of the placement of party personnel and he was one of the first to insist that non-party bodies, such as the trades unions and the soviets, should have all their leading personnel nominated by the party. He was so excessive and ruthless in subordinating everyone and everything to the untrammelled power of the party/state that Lenin had to rein him in and caution the party, in his 'Testament' against the excessively 'administrative' style of Trotsky in dealing with problems.[47]

It could hardly be said of Lenin himself that he discounted the importance of the power of organisation – particularly that of the party. Stalin, as Lenin's long-term lieutenant in running the party, had learned the tricks of the trade from the master himself. It was Lenin who had, in his tireless polemics, taught Stalin how to apply Plekhanov's aphorism that the way to deal with an opponent was to stick the badge of a traitor on him. The tactic was to exaggerate any and all deviations so that dissenters, often with very different views, were bunched together under one derogatory label. They became 'economists', 'tailists', 'liquidators', 'god builders' or 'white guardists'. Before the revolution, Lenin had had no compunction about utilizing the party apparatus to isolate and marginalise his opponents. After the revolution, oppositionists such as the Democratic Centralists and the Workers' Opposition were broken up systematically by the party machine – they were reallocated to jobs in distant parts of the country, or sent abroad. The Kronstadt rebels, for their part, were machine-gunned in their hundreds, perhaps thousands.

All the prominent party cadres shared a common guilt. They had all actively participated in, or passively condoned, the suppression of successive groups and factions. They had, all alike, been vehemently dismissive of opposition protests that opponents of the regime were summarily and arbitrarily dealt with. Appeals to due process of law; demands for checks and balances and limits to administrative prerogatives were, according to Lenin, appeals to alien class principles – to bourgeois legality. As there was no loyalty higher than that to the party, so there was no law higher than the interests of the revolution. All of this stemmed, of course, from the institutional relativism that lay within the whole Marxist tradition. Institutions (and the patterns of regulation and restraint, checks and balances that constituted them) could, in the Marxist view, claim no real autonomy. They were all instruments of one class or another. They were agencies through which class power was exercised. It was Lenin who had insisted repeatedly that the crucial characteristic of state power, as exercised by the proletariat, was that it was a dictatorship that rested wholly and exclusively on force. This was far from an abstract proposition, because the regime, almost from the outset, could only maintain itself through the organisation of coercive power. The civil war experience was itself a prolonged and brutalising loss of innocence for the revolution and its revolutionaries. Its arbitrary violence, retribution and exemplary executions bred a disposition to settle matters through the exercise of force. It accentuated (and partly created) an imperious management style, rigid centralisation, and unquestioning obedience to authority. It was the civil war that also transformed the political/ institutional life of the country. The soviets abnegated their powers or were emasculated by the party. The agencies of state, throughout much of the country, were primarily the Army and the Cheka; dissidents were already being confined to concentration camps. Terror was, in Lenin's time, embraced unambiguously as an instrument of state policy. The regime, even under Lenin, had begun to devour its own children. The Kronstadt rising of March 1921 was, clearly, a turning point: the regime declared war not only on its erstwhile supporters but also on the heresy of attempting to make the power of the Soviets a reality.

Institutional Relativism and the Re-definition of Socialism

This leads us straight to the heart of the relationship between Leninism and Stalinism – the respecification of the character of the socialist project that Lenin initiated and that, eventually, Stalin was to implement. In the initial flush of revolutionary fervour, buoyed up by Lenin's *The State and Revolution*, all was supposed to be transparent. Government was to be accessible to the masses and exercised by them. Here procedural rules had been located as the very essence of socialist administration. The determining question had been *how* government and administration were to be conducted – were all its elected officials subject to recall and paid at workmen's wages? Socialism was, as we have seen, then interpreted as a condition in which all were (or potentially were) participants in their own self-administration. Socialism here was understood to be a radical restructuring of all relationships of domination and subordination within society – an end to bossing.

That was exactly what the Kronstadters were reclaiming as their revolutionary birthright in 1921. By this time, however, Lenin, Trotsky and Bukharin were reformulating the foundation mythology of the regime and, in the process, dramatically redefining socialism. A fateful respecification of the nature of soviet socialism was unquestionably orchestrated by Lenin and was already under way by the late spring and summer of 1918. Lenin (and Trotsky and Bukharin) became increasingly convinced that the people's lack of culture, their impoverishment due to internal industrial breakdown and international isolation, and their brutalisation during the civil war, made the dream of self-administration an impossible one to realise. Socialism was redefined as maximal efficiency and productivity. The elemental goals of re-establishing industry, transport and exchange between town and country were placed at the top of the agenda for the party and the state. All that promoted these objectives was now hailed as progressive and revolutionary; even if it meant the subjugation of the unions and the soviets to the dictates of the communist commissar; even if it meant that coercion had to be applied to the working class itself. One-man management, discipline, and a patterned hierarchy of control and power, were now acknowledged to be necessary to meet the newly redefined goals of socialism. Here, above all, was the entry point for what was to develop as Stalinism. The future had been sold. The idea of socialism as state-directed control of the economy, of the state as the allocator of resources to all enterprises and to all individuals, was not Stalin's creation. It was, on the contrary, a project generally accepted by the Soviet regime and its leaders. In 1920 Trotsky declared that:

> The dictatorship of the proletariat is expressed in the abolition of private property in the means of production, in the supremacy over the whole Soviet mechanism of the collective will of the workers, and not at all in the form in which individual enterprises are administered.[48]

Lenin himself, also in response to the criticisms of Karl Kautsky, had been even more sweeping, '*The form of government*,' he declared, 'has absolutely nothing to do with it.'[49] By mid-1919, at the time he proposed to 'eliminate the word "commune" from common use',[50] he was insisting upon a purely productivist definition of socialism:

> In the last analysis, productivity of labour is the most important, the principal thing for the victory of the new social system . . . Communism is the higher productivity of labour – compared with that existing under capitalism.[51]

Stalin did not have to pen a novel theory of the overweening power of the Soviet state, or invent a conception of socialism as productivism. He inherited the idea from Trotsky, Bukharin and Lenin. It was merely left to him to implement them in his ferocious onslaught against the peasantry after 1929.

There has been a considerable debate over the question 'was Stalin really necessary?'[52] The terms of this debate are largely drawn around the abrupt ending of the New Economic Policy in 1929, and the rapid collectivization of the entire peasant population that ensued. Simultaneously, the drive for rapid industrialization began and the whole of the Soviet Union was thrown into a state-orchestrated turmoil, arguably more extensive, more profound and more brutal than any society had hitherto undergone. We can, of course, ponder whether this frontal assault on a settled and ancestral pattern of life was, in the medium term or the long term, rational in social or economic terms. We can ask whether other strategies might not have yielded greater returns (however measured). Historians will forever disagree about whether, had Lenin lived, he would have supported Stalin's shock tactics or Bukharin's plans for more balanced and moderate development of all spheres of production and exchange. There can be no doubting that the assessment of the status of the New Economic Policy was, and remains, a highly important historiographical issue, but it far from exhausts the nature of the relationship between Leninism and Stalinism. It can indeed be argued that over-concentration upon this intrinsically unresolvable issue of policy preferences detracts from the more substantial bonds of filiation.

I have, throughout this book, argued that Leninism was suffused with a dual metaphysic of history and science that gave it its quality of certainty. It also made it methodologically ill-disposed to democracy in the sense of widespread mass participation in, or adjudication of, rival public projects. The mass of the people could never be the vehicle of science, nor could it adequately comprehend its own past or, therefore, its own future. This philosophical arrogance Stalin faithfully took over from Lenin, expressly incorporating it in his own work, on *Dialectical and Historical Materialism*.[53] As was the case with Lenin, the laws of the dialectic could be, and were, deployed to explain (or justify) all sorts of extreme practical policies: 'if development proceeds by way of the disclosure of internal contradictions, by way of collisions between opposite forces . . . then it is quite clear that the class struggle of the proletariat is a quite natural and inevitable phenomenon'. Such struggle, Stalin went on, 'we must not try to check . . . but carry to its conclusion'.[54] This was, Stalin correctly noted, no more than a restatement of Lenin's central axiom that 'Development is the "struggle" of opposites.'[55] The path of development, the Leninist path, could therefore plausibly be shown to lead through the exacerbation and fighting through of class antagonisms within society.

Stalin's ruthlessly severe programme of class against class could be shown to have sound dialectical warrant. It was, moreover, entirely in accord with Leninist principles and practice that this process could only by supervised by the party, because it alone properly comprehended both the science of society and the science of history.

Given the common starting points, it is hardly surprising that, at every turn, Stalin could find warrant for his policies in Leninist ideas or Leninist practice. His insistent claims to be no more than a good Leninist are sound enough. Like Lenin, he found criticism or opposition to the party line to be objectively counter-revolutionary. Like Lenin, he attached to real or imagined oppositionists pejorative labels, and arraigned them through guilt by association. Like Lenin, he allowed them no due process of law to defend themselves. It was, we must recall, Lenin who had insisted repeatedly upon the irrelevance of the particular *forms* through which class power (or state power) was exercised. It could, Lenin maintained, be realised by a single dictator as well as by a democratic collegium. It might have the deceptive trappings of an 'independent' judiciary or it might operate through martial law and summary tribunals. The particular *forms* in which state and class power dressed itself was, according to Lenin, a matter of little significance; what mattered was the class *content* of the policies it pursued. Stalin did not invent the institutional relativism that was at the heart of the Soviet contempt for due process and constitutional and legal propriety – it was, on the contrary, thoroughly developed as a central feature of Leninism.

The same can be said about the substantive content of the project for socialism in Russia. It was Lenin who had, before the forced retreat of the New Economic Policy, re-defined socialism as the maximization of output and productivity. To achieve this, he made unambiguously clear, would entail the end of collegial forms of administration and their replacement by the unchallengeable authority of one man. Within the work process too, Lenin insisted, the forms of administration have absolutely nothing to do with it. It followed that if extensive coercion and/or re-education of the workforce was necessary to achieve the goals of increased production then that too was not only compatible with socialism but necessary to its implementations. According to Lenin's tortuous logic:

> Soviet socialist democracy and individual management and dictatorship are in no way contradictory . . . the will of a class may sometimes be carried out by a dictator, who sometimes does more alone and is frequently more necessary.[56]

In conditions of isolation, with a ravaged industry, and a diminished, declassed proletariat 'We need more discipline, more individual authority and more dictatorship.'[57] Lenin had long before taken the fateful step of arguing that socialism was not only agnostic to the patterns of domination and subordination within society, it was also unconcerned about *how* authority was exercised. Leninism therefore could see no good purpose in limiting prerogatives of power-holders or providing redress to those who felt aggrieved by their actions. The whole baggage of European political thought was, in this casual and disastrous way, thrown overboard – its preoccupations had, long before Stalin arrived on the scene, been declared to be irrelevant and its language no part of socialist discourse. It was quite clearly Lenin who had decisively and definitively terminated the dialogue between Marxism and liberal patterns of thought.

Lenin was, in short, complicit in all that made Stalin and Stalinism possible. At every stage (until the very last, when it was far to late) Lenin had personally supervised Stalin's ascent to power within the party and the state, and silenced his anxious critics. More significantly, he had overseen the liquidation of politics as principled disputation in the early years of Soviet power, and had approved the elimination of all centres of opposition, both within the party and outside it. The whole logic of both his philosophical position and political disposition inclined towards unanimity of outcomes. He did not only condone he positively encouraged terrorism against all who opposed the party line, and vigorously insisted upon the party's right to dominate all officially licensed agencies of political power and social representation.

It may well have been the case that, had Lenin lived longer, the course of the Russian Revolution would have been less bloody, and more civilized and humane. It is clear beyond doubt that Lenin was altogether more balanced, more self-confident and more cultured than Stalin. It is quite plausible, therefore, to argue that he would not have been drawn into the excesses, personal vindictiveness and disastrous war against the peasantry that Stalin pursued. All this is, however, sadly beside the point. The point is that the Western tradition of politics had, for hundreds of years, earnestly engaged precisely the problem of how to limit and control the impact of persons upon the political process. From the French and American revolutions onwards, political theorists (as well as individuals and social groups), had looked to such means as the powers of popular mandate, constitutional diffusion of powers, and redress through independent judiciary, to limit the tendencies towards the arbitrary exercise of power. It was, unambiguously, Lenin who had dismissed that whole tradition of thought as being mere bourgeois apologetics. It was he who had lauded the unrestrained and unbounded power of the proletarian dictatorship which, he had fatefully argued, could be as well exercised by a single dictator as by a democratic collegium. He left his colleagues and the Soviet people with neither the vocabulary nor the forums through which a stand against the arbitrary power of persons could even be challenged.

11
Conclusion

I have argued throughout this book that Leninism, as a distinctive ideology of the modern world, grew out of Lenin's response to the outbreak of the First World War. It was this event that led Lenin to reappraise the nature of contemporary capitalism and its historical evolution; it was this event that led to a radical redefinition of the nature of socialism and the road to its realisation; and it was, finally, this event that led to a radical redefinition of who now were his friends and who his foes.

Lenin's conviction that the war signified that capitalism had finally exhausted its progressive potential was no doubt shared by many socialists. What he now had to do was to convince them that the prospects for a 'growing over' of capitalism into socialism was neither possible nor compatible with basic Marxist method with regard to epochal transformation. If capitalism had indeed reached its historical terminus, then it followed, for Lenin, that its internal contradictions could no longer be accommodated within the framework of bourgeois society. Every epoch had, of course, its own contradictions. Within each epoch these contradictions became ever more acute until they became irresolvable. They emerged, finally, as directly antagonistic and non-negotiable claims. This, for Lenin, defined the moment of *revolutionary* transition which, far from being able to avoid or postpone, Marxists were duty bound to press to its conclusion. At this point it became, in his view, otiose and redundant to continue to press for gradual, incremental change *within* the system. The idea of a breaking point at which society (as with all natural phenomena) underwent rapid qualitative changes, in the course of which its character was altered radically, was clearly fundamental and necessary to Lenin's standpoint. It was for this good reason that, with the outbreak of the First World War, Lenin threw himself into the study of

Hegel's and Marx's dialectic. He had to convince himself that his conclusions were methodologically correct and that, conversely, his opponents had ignored or traduced Marx's method. The gradualists, the opportunists, had become trapped in vulgar bourgeois evolutionism. It was, in the circumstances, hardly surprising that Lenin emerged from his researches believing that the concept of the break, the leap – the nodal point – was the essence of Marx's teaching.

It would be far too easy to assume that Lenin was doing no more than adopting a philosophical stance that suited his polemical position, that is, the urgency and necessity of revolutionary overthrow. This was not simply a convenient stance. It had, in the first place, impeccable foundations in Marx's thought. It was, second, a profoundly innovative interpretation of the Hegelian roots of Marxism that had been conveniently forgotten in the Marxism of the Second International. Finally, once embraced, it assumed a powerful life of its own as a way of seeing the world; as a mental map that was unique to Lenin. The ideology he was beginning to articulate was suffused with the categories of the dialectic. It was both the methodological basis of Leninism and its chronological starting point as a comprehensive alternative to all existing ideologies. Lenin's dialectical materialism, like every aspect of his emergent ideology, expressed its own decisive closures and demarcations. Proper Marxist method was now identified exclusively with acceptance of the laws of the dialectic. Whoever did not endorse the law of the transformation of quantity into quality and its attendant insistence upon the break in continuity (the revolutionary leap) was no Marxist. Axiomatic borders were established between Leninism and every other species of socialism or Marxism. The line was drawn between revolutionary Marxists and those gradualists, reformists, Fabians and Possiblistes who inhabited what Lenin contemptuously referred to as 'the marsh'.

Philosophy may be (although is certainly not always) the starting point of an ideology but it can never, by its overly-abstracted nature, be the foundation of the ideology's popular appeal. Here the abstract has to be rendered more concrete in an economic, social and historical account of contemporary reality that is recognisable and convincing to its targeted constituency. Western civilisation had its ample complement of Cassandras, on both the left and the right, who had ferociously assaulted its self-seeking narrowness and its moral decadence and decline. To establish its claim as a distinctive ideology, Leninism had to go beyond abstracted (but commonplace) predictions of impending doom. It had to establish that the means to establish a superior civilization had already been created within the rotting structures of the bourgeois order. Here, again, the dialectic did good service, unmasking the present as a unity of opposites: moribund and degenerate, yet, simultaneously, pregnant with transformative progressive potential.

The dialectical method was both the notional and the chronological starting point of Leninism, but, as we have already observed, it is not proper method that forms the basis of the appeal and mobilising power of an ideology. These features are, rather, conferred by the utility of its map of the contemporary world – how accurately it seems to draw the contours and mark the great divides, the plausibility of the tale it tells of how its constituents came to occupy their present blighted place, and how they might, with some effort, move at last to lands of dignity and prosperity. Philosophy has to be rendered as history, geography and economics. Those, precisely, were the functions of the theory of imperialism.

The theory of imperialism as developed by Lenin contained a number of complementary narratives, all of which were important to the mental map of the contemporary world that it furnished to its followers. It was, in the first place, emphatically a history. It not only characterised the phasal evolution of capitalism as a civilization and a mode of production, it also gave a complementary account of the development of the labour movement and how it too had been undermined in the period of capitalism's final decadence. For the first time in the career of Marxism, Leninism also set an exact timetable for the realisation of its goals – the time for revolutionary socialist transformation was *now*. All those who cavilled at these conclusions, all those who promised to be revolutionaries tomorrow, Lenin consigned to the camp of counter-revolution. At every point the demarcating line was drawn and this, precisely, is what a distinctive ideological statement entailed.

Imperialism contained too, as we have seen, a highly distinctive narrative about political space as well as political time. It was geopolitics as much as it was calendar and almanac. It defined the cores and peripheries of the capitalist cosmos that became so influential in subsequent 'dependency theory'. It described the developed North and West exploiting directly an impoverished South and East, setting terms of trade and conditions attaching to access to capital that would ensure their continued subservience within the global economy. Above all, it linked the national democratic revolution of the colonies and semi-colonies with the socialist revolution in the advanced countries, as integral parts of a unified assault on imperialism. For the first time, socialism emerged as a global ideology that gave to non-Europeans crucial, perhaps decisive, roles in the development of what was portrayed as the movement of progressive humanity. The geographical narrative, as with all the component parts of Leninism, contains its own demarcations. Only he could now claim title to be a socialist who renounced all the annexations and colonial dependencies of his own country. Indeed, Lenin went further: only he was a socialist who actively assisted and encouraged the movement for national independence in his own country's colonies and who, in the course of the war, pronounced the defeat of his own country as the lesser evil.

The economics of imperialism are, perhaps, more obvious and better-rehearsed, but crucial none the less to the structure of Leninism. The role of the banks as monopoly controllers of credit and capital resources was, for Lenin, symptomatic both of the decadence of capitalism and of the urgency for socialist transformation. It was, further, a token of the ease with which socialization would be accomplished and popularly administered. The economics of state monopoly capitalism as the last stand of the domination of finance capitalism in the mightiest, most dictatorial and most intrusive state structure known to man, presaged, simultaneously, the transcendence of the nation state. Only he was a Marxist who now acknowledged the final decadence and parasitism of capitalism as a civilization and as a mode of production. Only he was a Marxist who now accepted not only the need for its immediate transcendence by a new mode of production, but who also worked for the revolutionary overthrow of the state structure that was its last redoubt. Smashing capitalism involved smashing the imperialist state, and the soviets were the *only* administrative form that could replace it – they were of universal significance. Later, of course, the soviets were equated with the dictatorship of the proletariat, and that shibboleth too served the function of differentiating friend and foe, believer and non-believer.

Leninism was, in its emergence and development, a series of ever-more refined closures and delineations because it chose to define itself in militant opposition not only to all existing liberal, conservative and moderate socialist ideologies, but specifically to all other species of revolutionary socialism and all other variants of Marxism. In order to reach his targeted constituencies, however, his somewhat abstracted theorisations had to be rendered into programmatic statements and then into concrete political slogans that would prompt the mass to act. Ideologies (at least, *successful* ideologies) have a sure grasp of the importance of these differing levels of articulation – from methodology and philosophy to general theory, from programmatic statements to day to day agitation. In the case of Leninism, this progression (or regression, perhaps) might be presented as the line from the *Philosophical Notebooks* to *Imperialism, the Highest Stage of Capitalism* and *The State and Revolution*, the *April Theses* and *Can the Bolsheviks Retain State Power?* The final agitational thrust was, of course, conveyed in his uniquely radical political slogans 'Down with the War', 'Land to the Peasants', 'Freedom to the Nationalities' and 'All Power to the Soviets'.

That all this was new, not only to Lenin but also to Marxism, is entirely evident from an examination of the reception that Lenin's theoretical and agitational propositions received. Scandal, outrage and incomprehension were the reactions – even from his own most devoted followers. To pretend that the demarcating features of Leninism as a distinctive ideology and mental map of the contemporary world were articulated and well known before April 1917, is to fly in the face of all the evidence.

It was only then that Leninism emerged as a rounded, more or less coherent, and more or less comprehensive ideology of the modern world. For the first time, Leninism had satisfied all the necessary conditions of a distinctive ideological statement. It had now:

(i)   *Set out a new methodology for understanding and changing the world.* Though not an essential component of ideology *per se*, Leninism made attachment to correct method a condition for adherents. Dialectical materialism was, it was claimed, capable of comprehending the inner composition and future evolution of all that is or was. Science was, in this way, paired with prediction.

(ii)   *Defined a new time for mankind.* It asserted that capitalism, as a mode of production and civilization, manifested its terminal contradictions in oppression and war, but it created simultaneously the conditions for global prosperity, peace and harmony in socialism. The time of transition from class-bound to genuinely human society was now.

(iii)   *Located its constituencies.* That is, the urban industrial workers of the developed countries supported by the poor peasants and the national democratic movements of the colonial and semi-colonial areas of the world. It was, explicitly, a *global* ideology, integrating uneven levels of development into a common assault on international finance capitalism.

(iv)   *Given its targeted constituencies an historical account of how they came to occupy their present situation* and how they shared common interests in its revolutionary overthrow. It had also shown how and when capitalism had entered a terminal, degenerate and oppressive phase in which class enemies, bribed with a portion of super-profits from colonial exploitation, had penetrated the working class and sapped its revolutionary will.

(v)   *Presented an inspirational vision of the desired future* – a world without war, national oppression, private ownership of the means of production, or coercive state formations. It was the naïve but perennially attractive dream of social and personal liberation: what Lenin referred to as 'an end to bossing'.

(vi)   *Provided a plausible account of how to get from the despised present to the desired future.* The role of the party as mobiliser and articulator of the class was, clearly, a necessary feature of the revolutionary transformation, but not a sufficient condition. Finance capitalism itself created the administrative systems for its own supersession (banks, trusts, consolidated enterprises and so on), while the people themselves spontaneously reclaimed their lost powers by establishing their soviets.

(vii)   *Translated complex theorisations into accessible practical programmes and distinctive slogans* capable of galvanizing the masses into action. Ideology here moulds as much as responds to a constantly changing political reality. It is the level at which it bids for support and therefore assaults the claims of all competitors. For Leninism, the appropriate slogans were therefore divisive and confrontational.

(viii)   *Distinguished itself clearly from all competitor ideologies.* At every level of its discourse, from basic methodology to day-to-day slogans, from the national question to analysis of the war, Leninism had established its demarcations and delineations. Across a broad range of significant historical, economic, social and political issues it could with ease test whether one was friend or foe. It had finally marked itself off, as all ideologies have to do, from all competitors.

It seems evident that each of the above elements was necessary to the synthesis of ideas that was to become known to the world as Leninism. It seems equally clear, therefore, that this synthesis, this breadth and simultaneous articulation at differing levels of generality and accessibility, not only did not exist before 1914, it was not even contemplated.

The need for it had not arisen. To that point, it appeared to Lenin, the revolutionary essence of Marxism, though challenged, had not been betrayed.

Part of the strength (and even more of the frailty) of Leninism was precisely that it felt obliged to provide a satisfactory theoretical explanation of the existing. Satisfactory theory, in its account, could never rest content with the contingent and accidental. The nature of contemporary capitalism and its wartime state form had, therefore, to be presented as *necessary* in the sense that the whole capitalist system could no longer guarantee its stability, or reproduce its own power, without the features it displayed at the time. They represented, according to Lenin, the termination of a prolonged process of development that was neither accidental nor temporary, but necessarily given. Lenin's determinist methodology itself disposed him to assert that capitalism, and the imperialist state, could be no other than what they were. Their wartime forms were their finally accomplished forms that merely revealed what had hitherto been immanent but shrouded. In particular, bourgeois states could exist in the future only as brutal dictatorships. Whatever constitutional forms they might drape themselves in, bourgeois states in the modern epoch were, in the Leninist analysis, structurally compelled to pursue goals that were the inverse of the original progressive goals of liberalism. Free trade and market sovereignty had given way to monopoly and state direction, the autonomy of individuals and of groups had been extinguished by the swollen powers of the executive. Finance or monopoly capitalism could only reproduce itself and guarantee its continual power as state monopoly capitalism. Democratic and civic rights had been extinguished in order to guarantee the continued power of a handful of monopolists. Internally oppressive and externally aggressive, the imperialist states had brought death and destruction to the world in their remorseless struggle to maximise their spheres of exploitation. They were all unalloyed dictatorships that had nothing to do with democracy, peace or freedom.

There was no doubt that dialectical method played a large role in the Manichaean structure of Leninism: consummate evil was counterpoised to unsullied good; exploitation and tyranny to freedom of work and activity; militarism and war to peace and international cooperation; omnipotent state to the empowerment of society; anarchy and waste to conscious planning; colonial subjugation to national self-determination. In the one camp flew the flags of darkness and oppression, and in the other the banners of light and freedom. The historical, dialectical and rhetorical structures of Leninism conspired to eliminate nuance or qualification. The whole thrust of its politics, as Lenin repeatedly boasted, was indeed to destroy the middle ground; to eliminate the dangerous utopians who imagined that there might be a negotiable compromise between the values and institutions of capitalism and those of socialism. This was the most dangerous group of all, precisely because it challenged the absoluteness of the Leninist analysis and the politics of confrontation that derived from it. In political terms, therefore, a foundational precept of Leninism was that the gradualist, reformist social democrats were, in fact, the worst enemies of socialism and the working class. They had, according to Leninism, become the lackeys and agents of the bourgeoisie within the labour movement and they were therefore, from first to last, the prime targets of communist parties. This dogmatic insistence upon the treacherous nature of social democracy, its identification with the camp of the enemy, was to leave its awful scars upon the politics of the twentieth century. In the fateful inter-war years that saw the rise of European Fascism, the potential for resistance from the left was fatally weakened by the split between communists and social democrats that increased in bitterness and intensity the closer Hitler came to power.

The battle between communism and social democracy that was, as we have seen, so fundamental to Leninism, broaches the issue of the relationship of Leninism to Marxism. There are, of course, numerous commentaries that discount the relevance of Marxism to the understanding of Leninism. This book has, as part of its object, maintained that the restitution of the Marxist doctrines of class war, and the immediate necessity of revolutionary struggle to overthrow capitalism, were of the very essence of the self-definition of Leninism, especially in its fight with social democracy. It was, after all, the moderate, reformist social democrats who maintained openly that Marx had to be 'corrected'. His historical predictions, they maintained, had not materialised and were increasingly less likely to do so. The workers were not becoming increasingly impoverished, the middle classes were not disappearing, consequently class 'contradictions' were diminishing rather than increasing. In any case, it was argued, it was time to drop the habit of talking about 'contradictions' which expressed a mode of dialectical thinking that was arbitrary and outmoded, and, above all, no longer corresponded to contemporary reality. As Marx's conclusions were found in error, so his method was found wanting. The bogus 'scientific' determinist, and inevitabilist elements of Marx's doctrine, should therefore be replaced by attachment to the moral superiority of socialism as a more just and more desirable system of society. The complementary metaphysics of history and of science should, in short, be dropped, exactly because they distorted reality and impeded socialist politics from adapting to a changing reality.

The passion and commitment of Leninism, by contrast, derived from its insistence that, in all essentials, Marx was right. The social and economic projections he made might well, for a time, be disguised by unanticipated countervailing factors, but they would re-emerge with renewed vigour. The frailty of economic, democratic, or political pressures to transform capitalism and secure even minimal decency to every worker, would increasingly become apparent. Despite all the treachery of so-called labour 'leaders' and the blandishments of 'progressive' bourgeois politicians, the Marxist revolutionary imperative would assert itself. This would, of course, require the forceful restatement of Marxist revolutionary objectives, it would require the unmasking of all those who opposed them. It would require the creation of an organisation which would take the tasks of mobilising and preparing for the revolution entirely seriously. It would purge itself, and the labour movement, of non-believers. It would, finally, have to construct a satisfactory economic and social analysis that would both explain the apparent failure of Marx's predictions (and the apostasy of the so-called 'leaders' of the working class) as well as show that, in fact, capitalism was heading for its final global disintegration. The Leninist party and the Leninist theory of imperialism were explicitly intended to restore the immediacy and actuality of the revolutionary essence of Marxism. It was precisely Lenin's axiomatic acceptance of undiluted Marxism that led him to formulate his characteristic findings on false consciousness and the role of the party in remedying it.

If it was the case (and the evidence for it was overwhelming) that the working classes of Europe were inclined to pursue a moderate and integrationist economic and political programme, then there were, very crudely, two possible conclusions to be drawn:

either (a) Marx had been mistaken in his economic and social analysis and so his programme for revolutionary transformation would have to be amended

or (b) the inadequate theoretical resources of the working classes had produced a mistaken appraisal of their current situation and future prospects that had been manipulated by their treacherous leaders.

To give the lie to the first (broadly social-democratic) conclusion and to restore the integrity of revolutionary Marxism, Lenin was obliged to emphasise the dangerous notion of false consciousness. Far from being a departure from orthodox Marxism, the notion of false consciousness became of central importance in defending it in the modern world. Marxists had to show how and why the working class had been diverted from its socialist and revolutionary mission, and how and why it had fallen prey to bourgeois values and bourgeois politics. The English experience had, in a word, to be explained. But to explain it, contemporary Marxists like Lenin (and Kautsky for that matter), had to maintain that revolutionary socialism was not a natural, necessary or spontaneous product of the collective experience of the working class. Lenin was obliged, therefore, to resort to the notion of false consciousness being the natural product of the working classes' mode of knowing. It followed that true or adequate consciousness could not be generated solely from within the experience of the working class, nor could it be distilled out of its communal thought processes. It had to arise rather, from a separate and distinctive experience and mode of knowing. The socialist intelligentsia, Lenin agreed with Kautsky, had initially *formulated* the ideas of socialism, and they alone could save it from its contemporary distortions. Their determined activism alone could restore to history the conditions necessary for the enactment of Marx's transformative project.

The party, however, in the Leninist account, attains its significance not from its raw activism and mobilising effectiveness. Its activism is, rather, significant only insofar as it serves to uncover the true nature of reality to which the party has privileged access. Activism that is uninformed by the party's special knowledge would be as unproductive as quiet resignation. The science to which the party laid claim was, of course, the science of materialist dialectics. We have earlier seen how this permeated the structure and the pretensions of Leninism and here we can only recount some of the conclusions and consequences of the party's superior mode of knowing. Materialist dialectics asserted that all things that were and are, were and are composed of matter and nothing else. They were, therefore, amenable to scientific investigation that explored both the internal dynamics of their evolution as well as the relations in which they stood to other phenomena. From these investigations it was the purpose of science to construe general laws about the behaviour of things. The behaviour of matter was therefore knowable and law bound; that is predictions could be made about it. The general laws of the dialectic – the unity of opposites and the transformation of quantity into quality, applied just as surely to the economic and social worlds as to the material. In these spheres too, development signified the irreconcilability of contradictory forces and the eventual transcendence of one phenomenon by another. The findings of 'science' in this way happily coincided with the demands of the revolutionary process, providing it with the mystique of scientific inevitability. What the working class itself could not apprehend as its own destiny would be revealed to it through the intercession of the Party armed with the science of materialist dialectics.

The dialectical (or 'scientific') mode of reasoning was, of course, difficult of access to the ordinary activist but it would be quite mistaken to discount its importance within Leninist ideology. For the believer it expressed precisely the universal and all-encompassing nature of Leninism as a systematic explanation of all phenomena. More to the point its mode of explanation was held to be radically distinct from, and superior to, all 'bourgeois' modes of knowing or thinking. Dialectical materialism, it was constantly asserted, was the privileged system of thought of the working class. It was not only a philosophy of certainties, it was also a philosophy of militant separateness. There were other consequences that flowed from the adoption of this dialectical metaphysic. In the first place it gave a particularly prominent role to those who, by intellect or authoritative position within the movement, were able successfully to establish their claim to interpret its complexities. Having once established their claim, the metaphysic itself gave warrant to their utterances. More ominously, however, the contention that all phenomena of the natural and social worlds were amenable to scientific exploration that would yield objective and verifiable propositions about their nature, led easily to the conclusion that for any given problem, only one solution was scientifically possible. This, in its turn, demanded that decision-making procedures be so structured as to guarantee unanimity of outcome. Science, in this formulation, would be devalued and discredited by permanent debate and dissension. The monolithic nature of the party, therefore, in part derived from, and was certainly sustained by, the bogus certainties of dialectical science.

The metaphysic of science ran through the whole corpus of Leninism. It formed the basis of the party's claim to lead the class since it disposed of a special body of knowledge that was inaccessible to the class itself. For this reason it would, Lenin consistently maintained, be futile to fuse the party with the class – that would be an abnegation of its special responsibilities and would weaken rather than strengthen the vitality of the class. It was equally clear, given the specially privileged discourse of the party, and the incapacity of the class to formulate its own ideology independently of it, that the party could in no way be bound by the predominant or majoritarian views of the working class. For Leninism neither the goals of the movement, nor the means appropriate to their realisation, could be advanced by opinion polls or the results of electoral ballots. As with almost all schemes of thought that distinguished between the wavering and insubstantial opinions of the mass, and the positive, demonstrable knowledge of trained initiates, it was not merely agnostic but actually hostile to democratic procedures.

Leninism was, indeed, hostile, not only to democracy but also to politics; and science was to be the antidote to both. When once the most effective optimal allocation of resources to guarantee the optimal return had been arrived at, and when technological innovation had been allowed free rein from the restraints of monopoly capitalism, then politics as disputation and politics as envy about the distribution of scarce resources would wither away. Less politics, as Lenin put it, would be the best politics. Lenin, in power, was repeatedly captivated by the latest technical innovation. He variously extolled Taylorism, electrification, and revolutionary techniques for extracting gas from coal without mining it. The most spectacular example of this technological Utopianism was, of course, Lenin's extravagant estimation of the transformational potential of electrification of the whole country. He presented this grandiose project as the 'third programme of the Party' that was set to overcome the distinction between rural and urban life and end the menial slavery of women to household work. Every power station, Lenin insisted, was to be not only a utility generating power but, far more significantly, a sort of popular university for new technique, a centre of enlightenment for the whole district. Here was the most up to date and modern productive force that would not only allow Russia to leap directly into the twentieth century but would simultaneously create a cultural transformation of her people. 'Communism', in short, was now expressed in the Utopian formula 'Soviet power plus the electrification of Russia'. The displacement and emasculation of politics in Leninism and the whole Leninist tradition is, in this account, directly attributable to its fixation with an outmoded metaphysic of science.

The metaphysic of science was complemented by a metaphysic of history that pretended to know not only the final goal of all human endeavour but also the forces that propelled it and the very moment of its denouement. History, Leninism maintained, knew only class actors and, in the modern world, there were only two essential classes: bourgeoisie and proletariat. History also demonstrated that the irresolvable conflict between class interests could be overcome only through revolutionary confrontation. The theory of imperialism situated the final battle between the two antagonistic classes of modern society to be coincident with the outbreak of the First World War. Leninism specified precisely in temporal terms the commencement of a new epoch in human history – the epoch of socialist transformation of the whole globe which was to begin immediately and was to progress with uninterrupted vigour to consume all of bourgeois civilisation. On this highly theorised analysis, the Bolshevik Revolution of October 1917 was premised. It was justified as the commencement of a world revolution for socialism as the only alternative to a political and economic system that could not possibly re-establish itself after its final crisis in world war.

When it became apparent that capitalist regimes *were* able to stabilise themselves, demobilise, negotiate a post-war settlement, and effect the transition to a peacetime economy, Leninism was presented with a fundamental problem. Just as with the failure of Marx's revolutionary predictions, so in the 1920s, Lenin and his followers could either admit frankly that their prognosis about the necessary collapse of capitalism and the world revolution had been analytically flawed, or they could attempt to explain this apparent failure by attributing blame to third parties. To have conceded the former would, effectively, have been to renounce their own claim to power and the whole justification for the October Revolution. They resorted, there-fore, to the thesis that the rest of the European working class, and particularly its leaders, had failed in their socialist duty. They had failed for want of adequate theoretical preparation and they had failed because they lacked a purposive, structured and disciplined organisa-tion to lead them. Far from conceding error on his own part, Lenin then resolved to make Bolshevik theory and practice a model for all parties subscribing to the Communist International. Only at this point did the organisational structure of the party (and of the International) become a factor of the highest significance in the history of Leninism. As time wore on and the Soviet Republic remained isolated in the world, so foreign leaders were made to feel an ever-increasing burden of guilt for 'failing' their Russian comrades. With each 'failure' in the West, and with each year that passed, the lesson was drummed home ever more insistently – the failure of the world revolution could not be attributed to analytical failings of Leninism, but to political short-comings of the Western working classes and their leaders. Once again, it was not the metaphysic of history, nor its substantive elaboration by Lenin, that was found in any way wanting, but the false consciousness of the mass and the treachery or ineptness of its leaders.

The predicament of Leninism, as an explanatory ideology, became more and more precarious as the twentieth century progressed. It could no more satisfactorily explain the evident failure of the world revolution to mature (at least in the crucial highly-developed countries of the West), than it could the mounting evidence of the failure of scientific state planning to emerge as more productive and equitable than its capitalist competitors. Just as Leninism, in its original formulation, had implicitly used the values and promises of liberalism as an immanent critique of what the wartime imperialist state had, in fact, created, so now the gap between the promise and actual performance of Leninism in power proved to be profoundly corrosive. The promises of genuine democracy within the workshops and the popularly elected soviets were the first victims of communist power, justified by Lenin in terms of the exigencies of civil war. Far from being restored thereafter, Leninism prided itself on a tough-minded relativism towards all institutional arrangements. It now maintained that the institutional forms through which a class exercises power are as irrelevant to socialism as they are to capitalism. Bourgeois dictatorship finds its natural complement in proletarian dictatorship that can only be exercised by its vanguard – the Communist Party. The realm of freedom proved to be a cruel illusion made the crueller by the tireless repetition that 'soviet democracy' was a million times more democratic than bourgeois democracy. In similar fashion, the insistant promise that the superiority of the conscious and planned allocation of resources would unleash the enormous potential of technology so cruelly restricted under monopoly capitalism, equally failed to materialise. On the contrary, the technological gap between the 'planned' economies and those of Western capitalism grew larger and the promised realm of plenty was, in fact, a regime of endemic shortages of even the most basic basic commodities.

The very persistence, adaptability and continued vitality of capitalism could not be explained by the logic of Leninism. The one feature of its system of thought that made the whole intelligible was, as we have seen, the contention that by 1914 capitalism was moribund: it could no longer reproduce itself; its epoch was over. It was entirely evident that the longer capitalism survived this prognosis, the more empirical evidence undermined the Leninist metaphysic of history. It was equally clear that the more the defects of centralised state planning revealed themselves (after the hugely impressive figures in the early period of Stalinist industrialisation) the more the metaphysic of science, upon which the party based its claim to rule, would be discredited.

History did not bear out the predictions of Leninism, nor was science its great redeemer. On the contrary, the contemptuous disregard that both of these arrogant metaphysics had engendered for democracy and due process was finally to come home to roost. In its Russian heartland and East European peripheries it was swept aside by popular movements that had long been disenchanted by their permanent subordination to the great historic goal of constructing communism, and their subservience to the dictates of science and its party spokesman. Leninism, as we have seen, was fundamentally incapable of adjusting itself to the precepts and practices of democracy. Its belated attempts to master the overwhelming movement in its favour were finally recognised for what they were – the desperate attempts of men whose own grounding principles and imperious habits were incompatible with popular sovereignty.

Like all other ideologies, Leninism invented its own world: creating, structuring and simplifying it to render it intelligible to itself and to its followers. Unlike the other principal ideologies of the contemporary world it was, however, the product of one man's mind during a very brief period of time. It therefore had none of the apparent disadvantages that 'broad-church' ideologies such as liberalism, conservatism or socialism notoriously suffer from. These bodies of ideas had been developing for about a century before Leninism made its appearance. They became, consequently, highly synthetic, complex and contradictory bodies of ideas that engaged in persistent internal disputes about objectives and strategy. Philosophically, they were eclectic and messy, with adherents of the same ideology professing the most varied first principles. The internal complexities of these ideologies make them, no doubt, often ambiguous and even opaque, as much to the academic commentator as to the prospective voter. Their messages are necessarily diffuse, for the reason that each must try to do justice to the variety of intellectual traditions contributing to their formation, and for the reason that in a democratic polity the objective must be to win majority support. In this situation ideologies are condemned constantly to the difficult task of balancing decisiveness and distinctiveness of message against the 'catch all' imperatives of securing power. Too broadly-based an appeal may distress its own activists and confuse the electorate, yet too narrow a platform will leave it easy prey to accusations of sectarianism. The internal eclecticism and variety characteristic of the mainstream ideologies is, no doubt, a fertile source of confusion in the popular mind and of disdainful critique by intellectuals. It is, on the other hand, a vital source for the continuous adaptability and responsiveness of all broad ideological currents. They are able to find, within the wide range of their intellectual inheritance, new constellations of objectives and supportive arguments that can, without too much loss of consistency, be presented as a coherent response to a changed situation.

Leninism was not conceived as a broad-church ideology of this sort. It did not emerge out of the constraints of democratic discourse, nor did it sympathise with its presuppositions. Being the product of one man's mind it had, undoubtedly, a tight internal consistency. Philosophically, methodologically, politically and organisationally it was all of one piece, or, as Lenin liked to say 'moulded from one block of steel' and this no doubt was part of its appeal to intellectuals. Not only was it the product of just one man's thought, it was also, as we have seen, formulated in an extraordinarily compressed time-scale. Its critical formative years were 1914 to 1917; by March 1923 its founder had written his last word and made his last speech, and by the end of January 1924 he was dead. He was reflecting and theorising what was, by any measure, an extraordinary period in world history – a period of international war, devastation and disruption, collapse of empires, civil war and rebuilding. The process of theorisation, for Lenin, was, as we have seen, the process in which the extraordinary became the normal and the necessary. As its philosophy dealt in the sureties of objective knowledge, so its politics dealt in categorical assertions about class, economic structures, forms of state and international relations. It was, as we have seen, the absolute surety of Lenin's convictions that impressed (or distressed) his contemporaries and which certainly induced in his followers an esteem bordering on veneration. Upon his death he became a secular saint obscenely celebrated as 'the most living of all men alive'. His writings assumed the status of canonical texts and the measure of a communist became his fidelity to the behests of Lenin. Stalin went to the vulgar extreme of catechizing Lenin's thoughts as commandments enjoined upon the faithful. More poignantly, even as sophisticated and sensitive a follower as Georg Lukács could reflect that, after Lenin, Marxism had stood still.

What this sombre and damning judgement amounted to was that the space for theoretical innovation was extremely narrow, precisely because the body of unchallengeable postulates was so extensive. Leninism was the prisoner of its own creator's 'eternally valid' categorical, and it was anchored in a time frame from which it could not escape. It was, finally, arrogant and dogmatic in its rejection of all eclecticism and eccentricity. It could not therefore either renew and revitalise itself, nor meet the challenge of a genuinely democratic politics which, at the last, swept all its pretensions away.

Appendix 1
Chronology of Major Events and Lenin's Principal Writings, 1870–1924

Dates given to 30 January 1918 are those of the Russian Old Style calendar, which was twelve days behind the West European calendar in the nineteenth century, and thirteen in the twentieth. From 1 February 1918 the Russian Calendar conformed to the Western.

References to texts are to Lenin's *Collected Works*, the English translation of the fourth Russian edition in 45 vols, Moscow, 1960–70. In the shorthand notation that follows volume number is given in bold type directly followed by page number. References to Harding, 1983 are to the present author's *Marxism in Russia: Key Documents* (Cambridge, 1983).

1870	10 April	Vladimir Illich Ulyanov (Lenin) born in Simbirsk.
1879		Lenin begins as pupil in Simbirsk classical grammar school. His headmaster, Fyodor Kerensky, is the father of Alexander Kerensky, whose government Lenin is to overthrow in October 1917.
1881	1 March	Tsar Alexander II assassinated by the terrorist organisation *Norodnaya Volya* (People's Will).
1883		Formation in Geneva of the first Russian Marxist group – The Emancipation of Labour and the publication of *Socialism and the Political Struggle* by its leader, George Plekhanov. (Extracts in Harding, 1983, pp. 44–54.)
1886	January	Lenin's father dies.
1887	March	Lenin's elder brother, Alexander, arrested in plot to kill Tsar Alexander III.
	8 May	Lenin's brother and his accomplices executed.

281

	August	Lenin enters Kazan University.
	December	Participates in minor student protest, is arrested and expelled from University.
1888–1893		Begins to study Marx and participates in revolutionary discussion circles in Samara; studies externally for law degree from St Petersburg University; involved in controversy with leading Populists; begins collecting data on capitalism in agriculture.
1893	Autumn–Winter	Arrives St Petersburg, joins leading Marxist circle at Technological Institute; and tutors workingmen's discussion circles in the Nevsky Gate area of the city.
1894	March–June	Writes his first significant text, *What the "Friends of the People" Are and How They Fight the Social-Democrats* 1, 133–332; this lengthy Marxist rebuttal of the economic and social arguments of the Russian Populists was the first publication of the social democrats within Russia.
1895	Spring	Arrival of the brochure *On Agitation* in St Petersburg (in Harding, 1983, pp. 192–205).
	April–May	Goes abroad to contact emigré Emancipation of Labour Group in Geneva; greatly impresses Plekhanov and Akselrod.
	May–September	In France, Switzerland and Germany meeting prominent Marxists; returns to Russia, visiting working-class centres to arrange publication and distribution of projected journal *Rabotnik*.
	November–December	Strike wave in St Petersburg and elsewhere; writes a number of agitational leaflets and prepares copy for underground newspaper. Writes his *Draft and Explanation of a Programme for the Social-Democratic Party*, 2, 95–121.
	8 December	Lenin and other prominent leaders of the St Petersburg Union of Struggle for the Emancipation of the Working Class arrested.
1896	Spring	Begins preparations for a comprehensive study of the evolution of capitalism in Russia.
	June	Most extensive strikes to date in St Petersburg textile industry.

1897	January	Renewed strikes in textile industry; Lenin exiled to Shushenskoye for three years.
	May	Arrives at place of exile; continues to write agitational pamphlets and articles on economic theory.
	Winter	Writes *The Tasks of the Russian Social Democrats*, **2**, 327–51; continues drafting his major study on capitalism in Russia.
1898	1 March	Foundation Congress of the Russian Social Democratic Labour Party (RSDLP) in Minsk, its *Manifesto* written by Peter Struve (in Harding, 1983, pp. 223–6).
	July	Lenin marries Nadezhda Krupskaya; they work together translating *History of Trade Unionism* by Sidney and Beatrice Webb.
	August	Lenin completes the draft of his major study *The Development of Capitalism in Russia*, **3**, 25–632. This text was published in March 1899 and constitutes arguably his single most original contribution to Marxist theory. It gives a detailed account of the development of capitalism out of feudalism through distinctive phases of usury, merchant, manufacturing and industrial capitalism, and attempts to place differing regions of the country and different trades along this progression.
	August	Publication in Geneva of Akselrod's influential programmatic statement *Present Tasks and Tactics of the Russian Social Democrats* (in Harding, 1983, pp. 227–41).
	November	At the First Congress of the Union of Social Democrats Abroad, the veteran Emancipation of Labour Group is defeated by the 'young' opposition.
1899	March	Publication of Lenin's *The Development of Capitalism in Russia*. Eduard Bernstein publishes his seminal revisionist book *The Preconditions of Socialism and the Tasks of Social Democracy* (English translation entitled *Evolutionary Socialism*).
	Spring	Publication of E. D. Kuskova's *Credo*, the first manifestation of revisionism in Russia (in Harding, 1983, pp. 250–3). This provoked an angry riposte by Lenin, *A Protest by Russian Social Democrats*, **4**, 171–82.
	September	Publication of the 'Separate Supplement' to *Rabochaya Mysl* (Workers Thought) no. 7 –

		the most developed statement or Russian revisionism (extracts from its leading article in Harding, 1983, pp. 242–50).
1900	January	Lenin's term of exile ends.
	February–July	Much travelling between social democratic centres in Russia to establish connections for the publication of an 'orthodox' newspaper to counter the influence of 'revisionist' journals such as *Rabochaya Mysl* and to prepare for a Second Party Congress.
	May Day	Large-scale street demonstrations in Kharkhov.
	August	Lenin in Zurich for discussions with Plekhanov and Akselrod for the publication of a new journal *Iskra* (The Spark).
	11 December	First issue of *Iskra* appears, edited by Lenin and carrying his leading article, 'The Urgent Tasks of Our Movement', **4**, 366–71 which broached many of the ideas later elaborated in *What Is To Be Done?*
1901	January–March	Composes a series of articles for *Iskra* and *Zarya* (The Dawn) outlining the need for comprehensive reorganisation of the party for it to fulfil its role as leader of the democratic revolution.
	May Day	Widespread demonstrations throughout Russia culminating in the pitched battle of the Obukhov Defence in St Petersburg.
1902		Throughout the year constant editorial work for *Iskra*; organising *Iskra* representatives for forthcoming Second Party Congress.
	February–March	Writes his *The Agrarian Programme of Russian Social Democracy*, **6**, 109–150.
	March	Publication in Stuttgart of *What Is To Be Done?*, **5**, 349–520. This was intended (and used) as the common platform of the veteran leadership of *Iskra* in their battle for predominance at the Second Party Congress. It stressed the centrality of the all-Russia struggle against tsarism and the consequent need for a centralised, disciplined, and professionally organised party whose leading core would be the editorial board of the party newspaper.
1903		Continuing editorial and journalistic work for *Iskra*; leading role on the Organising

		Committee established to oversee the convocation of the Party Congress.
	March–June	Strikes and demonstrations on unprecedented scale in most major cities, particularly prolonged in the south.
	June–July	Drafts standing orders and agenda, prepares draft rules and resolutions for forthcoming Congress.
	17 July	Second Congress of Russian Social Democratic Labour Party convened in Brussels; Lenin elected vice-chairman.
	24 July	Congress moves to London.
	2 August	Speaks on his formulation of Article 1 of the Party Rules (defining the conditions for membership); Martov's rival formulation is carried (extracts from this debate in Harding, 1983, pp. 279–87).
	2 or 3 August	*Iskra* caucus splits over candidates for election to Central Committee.
	7 August	Fierce debate over composition of editorial board of party newspaper. Lenin supported by Plekhanov; their adherents now take title *Bolsheviki* (men of the majority); the minority, with Martov as their principal spokesman, now known as *Mensheviki*.
	19 October	Lenin resigns from editorial board of *Iskra* over Plekhanov's decision to expand the editorial board to include the three editors ousted at the Second Congress.
1904	February	Outbreak of Russo-Japanese War; constant polemics within the party throughout the year; Lenin reviews the crisis of the Second Congress and its aftermath in *One Step Forward, Two Steps Back*, 7, 205–425.
	July	The 'new' Menshevik-dominated *Iskra* publishes Rosa Luxemburg's *Organisational Questions of Russian Social Democracy*, in which she concludes that Lenin's 'concept of organisation presents the greatest danger to Russian Social Democracy' (in Harding, 1983, pp. 295–309).
	November	Zemstvo Conference of local government activists; Russian liberals begin to stir.
	December	Fall of Port Arthur to Japanese; general strike in Baku.
1905	9 January	Bloody Sunday; Father Gapon leads huge, peaceful demonstration to the tsar's Winter Palace in St Petersburg massacre of

		hundreds by Guards regiments; massive strike movement begins; Lenin calls for determined revolutionary action to overthrow tsar.
	12–17 April	Third Congress of RSDLP; Lenin speaks of need for armed uprising, relations with peasantry and nature of future revolutionary government.
	June–July	Writes his *Two Tactics of Social Democracy in the Democratic Revolution*, 9, 17–140.
	August	The tsar finally promises to convoke an Imperial Duma or representative assembly; its limited purview rejected by almost all sections of society.
	October	Arrest of delegates to railwaymen's Congress leads to near universal general strike and formation of workers' Soviets, or Councils; tsar is forced to promise civic and political rights and a democratic constitution.
	7 or 8 November	Lenin arrives in St Petersburg and calls for the Party to lead an armed rising.
	December	General strike and insurrection in Moscow.
1906	January	Urges boycott of Duma; active in preparation for Congress of RSDLP.
	10–25 April	Fourth (Unity) Congress of RSDLP convenes in Stockholm. Lenin delivers speeches and reports on the agrarian question, the Duma, and an armed uprising; his formulation of Article 1 of the Party Rules is carried.
	8 July	Tsar dissolves First Duma; Stolypin begins to establish firm control for the autocracy.
	December	Kautsky's *The Driving Forces and Prospects of the Russian Revolution* largely vindicates Lenin's radical stance.
1907	January	Polemic between Lenin and Mensheviks over tactics for election of representatives to Second Duma; the Mensheviks prepared to cede leading role to bourgeois political parties.
	April–May	Fifth Congress of RSDLP.
	3 June	Tsar peremptorily dissolves Second Duma.
	August	Stuttgart Congress of the Second (or Socialist) International; Lenin, with Rosa Luxemburg and Martov, involved in giving radical sting to resolution 'On Militarism and International Conflicts'.
	December	Lenin again goes into exile.

1908		Principally concerned to counter the philosophical 'revisionism' of some prominent followers (Bogdanov and Lunacharsky) and with establishment of new Bolshevik journal. Writes his restatement of 'orthodox' Marxist philosophy, *Materialism and Empirio-Criticism*, **14**, 19–361.
1909		Continuing polemics with 'god builders' against factions calling for the recall of Bolshevik deputies from the Duma (the so-called *otzovists*).
1910		More polemics within the Bolshevik faction on matters of philosophy and political tactics.
	September–November	Works on *Strike Statistics in Russia* and writes an important article published in two parts, December 1910 and January 1911, using extensive data to vindicate his policies of 1905–7 and to support the contention that the vanguard workers (particularly the metal workers) and advanced regions draw the more backward strata and regions into economic, then political struggle. This, arguably Lenin's most important article on political strategy since 1905, sets out to provide empirical demonstration of the disproportionately significant role of the industrial proletariat in the political struggle with autocracy, **16**, 395–421.
1911		Lenin, now re-joined by Plekhanov, in journalistic campaign against all who sought to downgrade the importance of the underground party (the so-called 'Liquidators').
	December	Presides over meeting of Bolshevik groups abroad, where preparations are made for a final split from the Mensheviks.
1912	January	Prague Conference of RSDLP in Prague organised wholly by Bolsheviks, at which the Liquidators (that is, the Menshevik leadership) are declared to be outside the Party.
	April	Massacre of hundreds of striking workers in Lena goldfields prompts large-scale sympathetic strikes throughout Russia; first issue of Bolshevik daily newspaper *Pravda* (Truth).

1913	January–April	Strikes and demonstrations grow in size.
	June–December	Principally concerned with lectures and articles on the national question: *Critical Remarks on the National Question*, **20**, 19–51.
1914	January	Lectures on the national question in Paris, Brussels, Liège and Leipzig.
	February–May	Writes *The Right of Nations to Self-Determination*, **20**, 395–454 attacking the arguments of those (particularly Rosa Luxemburg) who denied the significance of the national question in the contemporary world.
	May–July	Brussels Conference of the International Socialist Bureau – the executive of the Second International – convened to settle a common programme to avoid the war that appears to be imminent.
	23 July (4 August Western Calendar)	The socialist parties of France and Germany vote for war credits for their governments – effective collapse of the Second International.
	26 July	Arrested in Austrian Galicia.
	23 August	Arrives Berne after Austrian social democrats had interceded to secure his release and safe conduct to Switzerland; immediately denounces all socialists who support national defence and urges propaganda for turning the war into a civil war for socialism: *Tasks of Revolutionary Social-Democracy in the War*, **21**, 15–19.
	September 1914– May 1915	Detailed study of Aristotle, Hegel and Feuerbach, material later published as *Philosophical Notebooks*, **38**.
	October	Resumption of publication of *Sotsial Demokrat* (The Social Democrat) under Lenin's editorship; this was to be the principal vehicle for his views for the next three years.
1915	February–July	Writes a stream of anti-war articles for *Sotsial Demokrat* and strengthens cohesion of Bolshevik emigré groups.
	June–July	Lenin begins his study of the literature on imperialism incorporated in *Imperialism, the Highest State of Capitalism*; his notes later published as *Notebooks on Imperialism* (**39**).

	July–August	Begins in earnest to establish international contacts with anti-war groups in preparation for the International Conference of Socialists Opposed to the War, to be convened in Zimmerwald.
	20–26 August	In Zimmerwald, rallying left wing, writes 'Draft Resolution Proposed by the Left Wing at Zimmerwald', 21, 345–8, but his appeals are ill-supported.
	August–December	Continues journalistic activity; desperate attempts to disseminate Bolshevik views on the war internationally.
	December	Writes preface to Bukharin's *Imperialism and the World Economy*, 22, 103–8; begins writing his own book on imperialism.
1916	January–February	Active in organising the Zimmerwald left and founding its journal, Vorbote, for which he writes *Opportunism and the Collapse of the Second International*, 22, 108–21, and *The Socialist Revolution and the Right of Nations to Self-Determination* (22, 143–57).
	11–17 April	Second international conference of anti-war socialists at Kienthal, in which Lenin emerges as principal organiser of the left wing and secures broader support than at Zimmerwald.
	19 June	Completes the manuscript of *Imperialism, the Highest Stage of Capitalism*, 22, 185–305; arguably the single most important text of Leninism, it concluded that global capitalism had become parasitic and militarist and had forfeited its historical right to exist; it provided the theoretical basis for the integration of national and socialist revolutions on a global scale.
	October	Writes a succinct and important statement of his views, *Imperialism and the Split in Socialism* 22, 105–20.
	December	Begins work in the Zurich Library on Marxism and the state which he pursues until the outbreak of the October Revolution.
1917	9 January	Lenin delivers his *Lecture on the 1905 Revolution* (23, 236–53) on the anniversary of 'Bloody Sunday'.
	24 January– 8 February	The February Revolution in Russia; mass strikes and demonstrations throughout Russia joined by the soldiers; sudden

	emergence of the powerful Petrograd Soviet followed by others in main cities; arrest of the tsar's ministers; establishment of a Provisional Government (Provisional Committee of the Duma).
2 March	The tsar abdicates in favour of Grand Duke Mikhail; Lenin receives news of February Revolution and begins to make arrangements for a return to Russia.
4–26 March	Defines his attitude towards the February Revolution in his 'Draft Theses' of 4 March, 23, 287–91, the themes of which were amplified in his five *Letters from Afar* 23, 297–342.
12 March	Stalin and Kamenev return from Siberian exile to resume control over *Pravda* and to steer the Bolsheviks into a more conciliatory position *vis-à-vis* the Mensheviks and the Provisional Government.
27 March–3 April	Lenin and Krupskaya leave Berne for Zurich, having earlier completed the arrangements for the 'sealed train' journey during which Lenin prepared his *The Tasks of the Proletariat in the Present Revolution* (the *April Theses*, 24, 21–6); arrive to tumultuous welcome at the Finland Station in Petrograd; in the night, Lenin presents his theses to the incredulous and unsympathetic party workers of Petrograd.
April–May	Furious organisational and journalistic work to convince the Bolshevik Party of his new strategy; undermining the Provisional Government, the influence of the Mensheviks and the continuation of the war; more than ninety articles in these two months.
4 May	Trotsky returns from America and joins forces with Lenin.
5 May	Formation of a new coalition government with participation of socialist and soviet leaders; Kerensky becomes Minister of War.
3–24 June	First All-Russia Congress of Soviets of Workers' and Soldiers' Deputies.
9 June	Bolshevik call for mass street demonstrations countermanded by Congress of Soviets.
10 June	Large-scale demonstration in Petrograd mounted by rank and file Bolsheviks; vacillation of Bolshevik leadership.

18 June	Renewed anti-government demonstrations protesting against the Russian offensive in Galicia.
20 June	Lenin elected to Central Executive Committee of All-Russia Congress of Soviets.
3–5 July	Riots and demonstrations in Petrograd against mobilisation of units for the front supported by Bolshevik rank and file and, initially, by the Central Committee, who called up the Kronstadt sailors but failed to provide effective leadership; improvised coup; fizzled out; Lenin forced to go underground.
7 July	An order for Lenin's arrest issued by the Provisional Government.
8 July	Kerensky becomes head of the Ministry.
10 July-8 August	Lenin, hiding at Razliv, continues intensive journalistic work and the writing of *The State and Revolution*, **25**, 387–496. This, the most 'anarchist' of Lenin's writings, elaborated his earlier conclusion that, in the final phase of state monopoly capitalism, the nation state as the unit of government, and representative government as its characteristic mode of governing, had both become redundant. The model to replace them in the construction of socialism was the commune, whose contemporary forms were the Soviets.
16 July	General Kornilov appointed Commander-in-Chief of the Army.
23 July	Arrest of Trotsky.
26 July–3 August	Sixth Congress of the Russian Communist Party (Bolsheviks).
Late August	The attempted putsch by the Commander-in-Chief of the Army, Lavr Kornilov; transformation of Bolshevik fortunes and growth of the Red Guard.
10 August–17 September	Lenin in Finland.
4 September	Trotsky freed on bail.
15 September	Bolshevik Central Committee discuss Lenin's letters, 'The Bolsheviks Must Assume Power', **26**, 19–21 and 'Marxism and Insurrection', **26**, 22–7; by this time, Bolsheviks were in a majority in the Petrograd and Moscow Soviets.

17 September	Lenin moves from Helsingfors, Finland to Vyborg to exert more direct influence on the Party's Central Committee which refused, for the time being, to authorise his return to Petrograd.
22–24 September	Lenin writes the article 'From a Publicist's Diary. The Mistakes of Our Party', **26**, 52–8.
26 September	Lenin writes to I. T. Smilga on the military aspects of the revolution **26**, 69–73.
29 September	Lenin writes *The Crisis has Matured*, **26**, 74–85.
End September– 1 October	Writes *Can the Bolsheviks Retain State Power?*, **26**, 89–136; this was Lenin's most extended programmatic statement on the approaching socialist revolution; theorised from his analysis of finance capitalism itself creating the mechanisms for socialist transformation, and extremely radical in proposing the substitution of people's power for state power.
6–8 October	Lenin writes the article 'Revision of the Party Programme', **26**, 151–78.
7 October	Lenin returns from Vyborg to Petrograd.
9 October	Formation of the Military Revolutionary Committee of the Petrograd Soviets under Trotsky's energetic leadership.
10 October	At a meeting of the Central Committee, Lenin calls for an armed uprising; the majority formally commits itself to this course of action; Zinoviev and Kamenev abstain.
14 October	Lenin meets leading Bolsheviks to discuss preparations for the rising.
15 October	Petrograd Committee of the party pessimistic about the prospects for a rising.
17 October	Lenin writes his 'Letter to Comrades' attacking Kamenev and Zinoviev for publicly opposing the uprising, **26**, 195–215.
20 October	The Military Revolutionary Committee begins to muster its forces.
23 October	The Provisional Government orders the closing down of the Bolshevik press.
24 October	Lenin writes the 'Letter to Central Committee Members' urging an immediate armed uprising; in the night, Lenin arrives at Smolny to assist in co-ordinating the revolutionary forces and to prepare the formation of a Soviet Government.

25 October	At 10 am, Lenin issues the announcement *To the Citizens of Russia*, **26**, 236, proclaiming the overthrow of the Provisional Government and the transfer of power to the Petrograd Soviet and the Military Revolutionary Committee; attends the Petrograd Soviet, writes the draft decrees on peace, on land, and the formation of the Soviet Government, **26**, 249–63; convocation of the Second Congress of Soviets; Bolshevik majority approves Lenin's measures and decides to install a new government.
26 October	Installation of a new Government of People's Commissars; Lenin drafts the *Regulations on Workers' Control*, **26**, 264–5.
27 October–1 November	Kerensky rallies his forces under General Krasnov; marches on Petrograd; defeated and flees.
29 October	Ultimatum from the Executive Committee of the Railway Union for a united socialist coalition government.
2 November	Bolsheviks seize power in Moscow after considerable fighting.
4 November	Resignations from the Council of People's Commissars, protesting against Lenin's refusal to include representatives of other socialist parties in the government.
13 November	Decree establishing workers' control over all industrial enterprises.
29 November	Establishment of Politburo within the Central Committee to deal with urgent matters.
7 December	Establishment of the All-Russia Extraordinary Commission to Combat Counter Revolution and Sabotage (Cheka).
9 December	Negotiations begin in Brest Litovsk for a peace settlement with Germany.
14 December	Lenin writes the *Draft Decree on the Nationalisation of the Banks*, **26**, 391–4.
24–27 December	Lenin, on short rest in Finland, writes *How to Organise Competition*, **26**, 404–15.
1918 5 January	Convocation of Constituent Assembly attended by Lenin before Bolshevik walk-out and summary dismissal of the Assembly.
6 January	Lenin writes the *Draft Decree on the Dissolution of the Constituent Assembly*, **26**, 434–6.

7 January	Lenin writes his 'Theses on the Question of a Separate Peace', **26**, 442–50.
8–9 January	Central Committee rejects Lenin's proposals for a separate peace and endorses Bukharin's project for a revolutionary war against Germany.
10–18 January	Third Congress of Soviets.
30 January	Deadlock in peace negotiations; at Brest Litovsk, Trotsky refuses to sign peace term but declares the war ended.

* From the beginning of February, Russia adopted the New Style Calendar; dates hereafter are the same as those prevailing in the West.

18 February	Resumption of German offensive and Lenin's insistence that peace be signed.
20 February	Establishment of Provisional Executive Committee to handle urgent business between government meetings; government decree establishing Red Army.
23 February	The government and the Bolshevik Central Committee agree to sign peace terms.
3 March	Peace Treaty of Brest Litovsk signed.
10–11 March	Lenin and the other members of the government move from Petrograd to Moscow.
8 March	The Bolsheviks adopt the title 'Communist'.
14–16 March	Fourth Congress of Soviets.
15 March	Ratification of the peace treaty with Germany and resignation of left SRs and left communists from the government.
23–28 March	Lenin dictates the original version of the article *The Immediate Tasks of the Soviet Government*, **27**, 203–18.
1 April	Establishment of a Supreme Military Council to direct defence and organise the armed forces.
5 May	Writes the article *Left-Wing Childishness and the Petty-bourgeois Mentality*, **27**, 325–54.
26 May	Convocation of the First All-Russia Congress of Economic Councils.
May–June	Lenin preoccupied with critical food supply and fuel situation; mutiny of the Czechoslovak regiments; anti-Soviet rebellion in Tambov; collapse of the transport system.

4–10 July	Lenin reports to the Fifth All-Russia Congress of Workers, Peasants, Soldiers and Red Army Deputies (**27**, 507–28).
6 July	Assassination of Mirbach, the German Ambassador; revolt of left SRs.
16 July	The tsar and members of his family shot in Ekaterinberg.
30 August	Lenin shot and wounded by Fanny Kaplan; critically ill for a fortnight; Uritsky assassinated.
10 September	Red Army takes Kazan.
24 September–Mid October	Lenin convalescing at Gorki, near Moscow.
8 October	Red Army takes Samara.
3 November	The outbreak of the Hungarian Soviet Revolution.
6–9 November	Convocation of the Extraordinary Sixth All-Russia Congress of Soviet Deputies.
10 November	Lenin finishes writing his book *The Proletarian Revolution and the Renegade Kautsky*, **28**, 229–325.
December 1918–January 1919	Lenin drafts theses for the Central Committee of the party, *Tasks of the Trade Unions*, **28**, 382–5.
1919 January	Abortive coup by German Spartacists and subsequent murders of Luxemburg and Liebknecht.
16–25 January	Second Congress of Trade Unions.
6 February	Red Army takes Kiev.
22 February	Closure of the remaining Menshevik newspapers (**28**, 447–8).
2–6 March	First Congress of the Communist International in Moscow for which Lenin prepares *Theses and Report on Bourgeois Democracy and the Dictatorship of the Proletariat*, 28, 457–74.
18–23 March	Eighth Congress of RCP(b). Denikin's advance in the south; Yudenich's advance on Petrograd; Lenin preoccupied with military matters and the strengthening of the party to meet this threat.
21 March	Soviet regime, headed by Bela Kun, established in Hungary.
September–October	Lenin works on his article 'Economics and Politics in the Era of the Dictatorship of the Proletariat', **30**, 107–17.
November–December	Red Army regroups and goes over to successful offensive against Yudenich, Kolchak and Denikin.

	2–4 December	Eighth All-Russia Conference of the Russian Communist Party; Lenin delivers the Political Report of the Central Committee (**30**, 170–88).
	5–9 December	Seventh All-Russia Congress of Soviets.
	12 December	Red Army takes Kharkov.
	16 December	Lenin writes *The Constituent Assembly Elections and the Dictatorship of the Proletariat*, **30**, 253–75.
	30 December	Red Army takes Ekaterinoslav.
1920	Early January	Red Army takes Tsaritsin and Rostov.
	25 January	In a speech to the Third all-Russia Congress of Economic Councils, Lenin vindicates one-man management and the establishment of labour armies (**30**, 309–13).
	February	Units of Red Army translated into 'labour armies'.
	29 March–5 April	Ninth Congress of the Russian Communist Party (Bolsheviks). Lenin gives the *Report of the Central Committee*, **30**, 443–62; Congress decides to issue Lenin's *Collected Works.*
	3–7 April	Third Congress of Trade Unions addressed by Lenin (**30**, 502–15).
	April–May	Writes *Left-Wing Communism – an Infantile Disorder*, **31**, 21–117.
	1 May	Lenin participates in the first All-Russia May Day Subbotnik.
	Beginning June	Writes his *Draft Theses on the National and Colonial Questions* and *Preliminary Draft Theses on the Agrarian Question for the forthcoming Second Congress of the Comintern*, **31**, 144–64; beginning of war with Poland.
	4 July	Writes his 'Theses on the Fundamental Tasks for the Communist International', **31**, 184–201.
	11 July	Red Army captures Minsk in the offensive against Poland.
	19 July–4 August	Second Congress of the Communist International; Lenin delivers *Report on the International Situation*, **31**, 215–34; Congress approves Lenin's Conditions for Admission to the Communist International, **31**, 206–12.
	15 August	Polish counter-attack begins – rapid retreat of Red Army.
	22–25 September	Ninth All-Russia Conference of the RCP(b).

	12 October	Attends the funeral of his one close friend, Inessa Armand.
	20 October	Writes the article *A Contribution to the History of the Question of the Dictatorship*, **31**, 340–61.
	21 November	Addresses the Moscow Party Organisation on *Our Foreign and Domestic Position and the Tasks of the Party*, **31**, 408–26.
	22–29 December	Eighth All-Russia Congress of Soviets. Lenin reports on the work of the Council of People's Commissars on concessions and on electrification (**31**, 461–518, 532–3).
	30 December	Delivers a speech, *The Trade Unions, the Present Situation and Trotsky's Mistakes*, **32**, 19–42.
1921	25 January	Completes his pamphlet, *Once Again on the Trade Unions, the Current Situation and the Mistakes of Trotsky and Bukharin*, **32**, 70–107: acknowledges the need for trade unions to protect their members against the 'bureaucratic distortions' of the Soviet state.
	End February	Large-scale strikes in Petrograd; severe reaction of the City Party under Zinoviev; state of siege declared.
	8–16 March	Tenth Congress of RCP(b); Lenin's *Report of the Political Work of the Central Committee* and Summing Up Speech on the Report (**32**, 170–209); his speech on the Trade Unions (**32**, 210–13); his *Report on the Substitution of a Tax in Kind for the Surplus-Grain Appropriation System* – the beginnings of the New Economic Policy (**32**, 214–28); his 'Preliminary Draft Resolution . . . on Party Unity' – banning factionalism and separate 'platforms' (**32**, 241–4).
	8 March	The outbreak of the Kronstadt rebellion; overthrow of Bolshevik power in the Baltic Fleet.
	20 March	Petrograd put under martial law at Lenin's instructions.
	21 April	Completes the pamphlet *The Tax in Kind* (The Significance of the New Economic Policy and its Conditions), **32**, 329–65.
	26–28 May	Presides at the Tenth All-Russia Conference of the RCP(b).
	22 June–12 July	Third Congress of the Communist International; Lenin defends the tactics of the Communist International and reports on the tactics of the RCP, **32**, 468–96.

	20 August	Writes the article *New Times and Old Mistakes in a New Guise* in which he bemoans the declassing of the proletariat, **33**, 21–9.
	20 September	Writes the article 'Purging the Party', **33**, 39–41.
	27 September	Writes the letters 'Tasks of the Workers' and 'Peasants' Inspection . . .' **33**, 42–8.
	17 October	Delivers an important policy statement, *The New Economic Policy and the Tasks of the Political Education Departments*, **33**, 60–78.
	23–28 December	Ninth All-Russia Congress of Soviets; Lenin reports on 'The Home and Foreign Policy of the Republic', **33**, 143–77.
	31 December	The Political Bureau of the Party directs Lenin to take six weeks' leave, extended in February 1922 until the end of March.
1922	12 January	Lenin's *The Role and Function of the Trade Unions under the New Economic Policy*, **33**, 184–96 approved by the Central Committee.
	12 March	Writes the article 'On the Significance of Militant Materialism', **33**, 227–36.
	24 March	Submits to the Central Committee his proposals for toughening the conditions for admission to the party (**33**, 254–5).
	27 March–2 April	Eleventh Congress of the RCP(b); Lenin delivers the *Political Report of the Central Committee*, **33**, 263–310.
	23 May–1 October	Living at Gorki.
	26 May	Suffers his first stroke.
	13 July	Instructs his secretary that he is well enough to read.
	2 October	Returns to Moscow and resumes work.
	5 November–5 December	Fourth Congress of the Communist International; Lenin reports on *Five Years of the Russian Revolution and the Prospects of the World Revolution*, **33**, 418–32.
	23 December	Suffers his second stroke.
	23–26 December	Dictates *Letter to The Congress* – his so-called *Testament* – in which he called for an increase in numbers of the Central Committee, gave an appreciation of its leading personnel and demand the removal of Stalin (**36**, 593–7); for the circumstances in which this was dictated, see his secretary's diary (**42**, 481–2).

	30 December	Dictates notes on *The Question of Nationalities or Autonomisation* (**36**, 605–11).
1923	4 and 6 January	Dictates the article *On Co-operation* calling for a reorganisation of the state machinery and a new emphasis on peasant co-operatives (**33**, 467–75).
	9 and 13 January	Dictates the plan of an article What should we do with the Workers' and Peasants' Inspection, **42**, 433–40.
	19–23 January	Dictates the article 'How We Should Reorganise the Workers' and Peasants' Inspection', **33**, 481–6; the articles written in 1923 are frank and often agonised appraisals of the regime's shortcomings; Lenin questions the fitness of the party to rule, reflects on the unchecked growth of the state and bureaucracy, and points to the dangers of the weaknesses of leading personnel in a situation of cultural backwardness and internal and external isolation.
	2–9 March	Dictates his last article, 'Better Fewer, But Better', **33**, 487–502.
	9 March	Suffers a third stroke.
	15 May	Moved to Gorki.
	Second half of July	His health improves.
	19 October	Pays last fleeting visit to Moscow.
1924	21 January	Lenin dies.
	23 January	Lenin's body brought to Moscow; lies in state at the House of Trade Unions.
	27 January	Lenin's body installed in a temporary mausoleum in Red Square.

Appendix 2
Guide to Lenin's *Collected Works*

References throughout are to the fullest edition available in English, the translation of the fourth Russian edition, V.I. Lenin, *Collected Works*, Moscow, 1960–70, 45 vols, plus an Index in two volumes. Vols 41–45 of this edition contain additional material drawn from the Fifth Russian edition of Lenin's *Complete Works*.

Vol. 1, 1893–4

Principal texts: *On the So-Called Market Question*; *What the Friends of the People Are and How They Fight the Social Democrats*; *The Economic Content of Narodism*. Lenin's main concern throughout these texts was to demonstrate the superiority of Marxist economic and social analyses over those of the Russian Socialists or populists. The growth of commodity production and of attendant social differentiation is chronicled, and the key strategic political finding (contrast Populist attachment to the peasant) is already clearly stated: 'the Russian worker is the sole and natural representative of Russia's entire working and exploited population' (p. 299).

Vol. 2, 1895–7

The writings of 1895 reflect the changed orientation towards 'economic agitation' and the expectation that political consciousness (and organisation) will emerge from prosecuting and extending the economic struggle. *The Draft and Explanation of a Programme for the Social Democratic Party* clearly articulates this phasal account of the development of consciousness and organisation. Lenin returns to questions of political practice in his 1897 *The Tasks of the Russian Social Democrats* where he insists that the proletariat must lead the democratic revolution against autocracy (p. 335) and that its political organisation must be disciplined, secret and based on specialized division of labour (p. 349). The lengthy texts *A Characterisation of Economic Romanticism* and *Gems of Narodnik Project – Mongering* develop his earlier arguments against populist economists, particularly on the manner in which the capitalist market expands, and he begins to refine the phasal account of the development of capitalism, better developed in volume 3 (see below).

Vol. 3, 1899

The whole of this weighty volume (658 pp.) is taken up by a single text: *The Development of Capitalism in Russia*. It was the culmination of six years' work compiling data and refining a methodology that traced the evolution of successive (and concurrent) phases of usury, merchant, manufacturing and industrial capital in different trades and different regions of Russia. It remained Lenin's most exhaustive and original contribution to Marxist theory and it defined the limits to his proposals for social-democratic political practice until the articulation of a new global analysis of finance capitalism in 1914–16. Useful digests of some of Lenin's main themes can be found at pp. 192–3, 310–18, 380–3, 541–51, 581–6, 596–9.

Vol. 4, 1898–1901

The first part of this volume contains numerous reviews of books by socialists on economic themes – there is little here that adds to Lenin's earlier analyses. The rest is taken up with a number of important articles in which Lenin stridently attacks the first appearances of 'revisionism' in Russia (*A Protest by Russian Social Democrats* and *A Retrograde Trend in Russian Social Democracy*). His articles for *Rabochaya Gazeta* (particularly 'Our Immediate Task' and An 'Urgent Question') anticipate his programmatic statement *The Urgent Tasks of Our Movement* (leading article for issue No. 1 of *Iskra*) with its stress on the urgency of assuming the leadership of the political struggle and the consequent necessity of organising a disciplined political party, with clear division of labour, and an authoritative central journal. Lenin concluded that 'Isolated from Social-Democracy the working-class movement becomes petty and inevitably becomes bourgeois' (p. 368).

Vol. 5, 1901–2

The volume begins with the words 'In recent years the question of "what is to be done?" has confronted Russian Social Democrats with particular insistence'. Lenin's *Where To Begin* reiterates the claim of the veteran leadership to resume control of the fragmented movement and to establish their journal, *Iskra*, as the authoritative voice of the party – its collective propagandist, agitator and organiser (p. 22). The role of the party in bringing consciousness and organisation into the working-class movement and its (hitherto neglected) role of accelerating this process through mass engagement in nationwide political struggle is developed as the central argument of *What Is To Be Done?* (see particularly pp. 368–441). Lenin notes repeatedly that the 'leadership' has fallen behind the spontaneous movement (tailism), and concludes that the period of 'disunity, dissolution, and vacillation' (p. 518) must be terminated. The organisational entailments for the party assuming this role, and leading the cross-class struggle for democracy, are developed in very general terms (pp. 451–92) where the importance of centralisation, specialisation, division of labour and trained professional revolutionaries, in augmenting the auxiliary or 'broad' organisations of workers are stressed. The text was written as the express platform of the *Iskra* group for the forthcoming Second Congress of the RSDLP (Russian Social Democratic Labour Party).

Vol. 6, 1902–3

The *Draft Programme of the RSDLP* provides a terse exposition of socialist objectives in the democratic revolution; pp. 29–33 contain a classic exposition of the 'minimum programme'; The *Agrarian Programme of Russian Social Democracy* pursues these implications, concluding that nationalisation of the land (p. 141) is the measure that will best accelerate capitalism in agriculture and the consequent class differentiation of the peasantry. *To the Rural Poor* sets out to demonstrate that the economic oppression and political power-lessness of the peasants can only be remedied through strengthening the alliance between 'the rural proletarians and semi proletarians' with the 'urban proletarians' (p. 423). The *National Question in Our Programme* is largely a polemic with the Polish Socialist Party; it endorses 'freedom of self-determination' for the proletariat rather than for peoples or nations, and insists upon the need for a single, non-federal party within the Russian empire. *A Letter to a Comrade on Our Organisational Tasks* is Lenin's fullest exposition of proposed patterns of accountability and organisational structure in national and local party work. The *Draft Rules of the RSDLP* include Lenin's definition of a party member (Clause 1, p. 476) that was hotly debated at the Second Party Congress and split the *Iskra* caucus.

Vol. 7, 1903–4

The *Account of the Second Congress of the RSDLP* reviews the Second Party Congress splits over the party rules, the composition of the editorial board of *Iskra*, and the appearance of 'Bolshevik' and 'Menshevik' tendencies. A greatly expanded (and rather turgid) account of these disputes (and vindication of Lenin's role in them) is given in *One Step Forward, Two Steps Back*; the substance of Lenin's case is more crisply put in his *Reply* to Rosa Luxemburg's critique of this book (pp. 474–85).

Vol. 8, January–July 1905

Contains a large number of short articles on the beginnings and development of the 'revolution' against tsarism in which Lenin argues that the party must assume the leadership of an armed insurrection, that political agitation has given way to civil war (p. 211) and that, consequently, the party must provide leadership to the armed struggle and simultaneously open its ranks to the politically undeveloped since revolutionary engagement will itself rapidly educate them (*Revolutionary Days, New Tasks and New Forces, Letter to Bogdanov and Gusev*) Lenin's proposal for a *Revolutionary–Democratic Dictatorship of the Proletariat and the Peasantry* is set out on pp. 293–303, and the importance of 'the siding of part of the army' to achieve this outcome is elaborated (pp. 560–8). His *Plan of a Lecture on the Commune* anticipates the themes of *The State and Revolution* (vol. 25) and his radical stance on the state in 1917. *A Brief Outline of the Split in the RSDLP* is a useful potted survey.

Vol. 9, June–November 1905

The principal text is *Two Tactics of Social-Democracy in the Democratic Revolution* – either the party actively leads the revolutionary overthrow of landlordism and autocracy, effected by the proletariat and poor peasantry, or it attempts to placate the bourgeoisie and the liberals who will betray the revolution and settle for a constitutional compromise with tsarism. The pamphlet is notable also for its firm rejection of an immediate transition to socialism (pp. 28–9) and its insistence that 'revolution will teach Social-Democratism to the masses of the workers in Russia' (p. 17). Instructions on how to organise combat groups and army contingents emphasise Lenin's concern that armed revolution must be adequately prepared (pp. 344–6, 420–4).

Vol. 10, November 1905–June 1906

Our Tasks and the Soviet of Workers' Deputies was Lenin's first appraisal of the Soviets as 'the embryo of a *provisional revolutionary government*' (p. 21) which should organise the arming of the people, transfer the land to the peasants, and grant freedom to the nationalities (p. 25). *The Reorganisation of the Party* reiterated earlier demands that, in a revolutionary situation, the party should immediately open its ranks to the masses to overcome the stagnation of its underground style of work. A useful summary digest of *The Stages, the Trend and the Prospects of the Revolution* is given on pp. 91–2 and a refreshingly brief synopsis of the *Draft Agrarian Programme* is on pp. 194–5.

Vol. 11, June 1906–January 1907

The Dissolution of the Duma and the Tasks of the Proletariat vindicated Lenin's prognosis in *Two Tactics* . . . (see vol. 9) that constitutional tinkering could not produce genuine democracy, and reinforced the view that only a co-ordinated armed uprising could do so. In *The Boycott* Lenin none the less called on his followers to make use of the (Second) Duma as a platform for agitation (p. 145). *Lessons of the Moscow Uprising* and *Guerilla Warfare* (pp. 171–8 and 213–23) point up Lenin's insistence that 'in a period of civil war the ideal party of the proletariat is a *fighting party*' (p. 220) and laments the fact that, in the defeat of the December Moscow rising, the party had not been equal to its tasks. It had failed for want of numbers and military competence, squeamishness about using terror, and inability to organise small, mobile guerilla units. *An Attempt at a Classification of the Political Parties of Russia* is the long title of a concise demonstration of how political parties emerge, in the course of revolutionary turmoil, as the more or less adequate representatives of economic classes.

Vol. 12, 1907

Contains a great number of short articles, resolutions and speeches. Some urge active participation in the elections for the State Duma and analyse the significance of the results (for example, pp. 15–131); others are directed against the 'opportunism' of the Mensheviks in courting the support of the liberal Kadets and renouncing both the armed struggle and the leading role of the proletariat, see for example, *The Menshevik Tactical Platform*. Lenin's prognosis of two possible outcomes of the democratic revolution now characterised as the choice between the 'American' path or the 'Prussian' – full democracy and free capitalism, or despotism 'embellished in parliamentary forms' with a capitalist economy retaining feudal landownership (pp. 355–6).

Vol. 13, 1907–8

There is little in this volume that is not said better in earlier or later writings. The exception, perhaps, is the important *Preface to the Collection Twelve Years* – a self-conscious auto-critique of Lenin's own major writings to date. In particular, Lenin cautions against taking the themes of *What Is To Be Done?* out of context; it was a summary of the *Iskra* position, no more and no less (p. 102); it was at times 'bitter and destructive' (p. 204); and a 'controversial correction of Economist distortions' (p. 108). *The Agrarian Programme of Social Democracy in the First Russian Revolution* (pp. 219–429) is a discursive elaboration of earlier analyses; pp. 295–300 and 313–22 on the nationalisation of land, and pp. 421–9, the Conclusion, would probably suffice for most. The *Lessons of the Commune* (pp. 475–8) reminds revolutionaries once again of the dangers of stopping half way and being magnanimous to enemies, but demonstrated, none the less, the potency of civil war in purging patriotic illusions.

Vol. 14, 1908

Virtually the whole volume is taken up with Lenin's one major text on philosophy: *Materialism and Empirio-Criticism* (pp. 19–361). It is concerned to restate the truths of the materialist theory of knowledge against all who set out to refute or 'improve' upon it. Among the latter were erstwhile followers (particularly Bogdanov and Lunacharsky) who became influenced by the theories of Ernst Mach and developed what was known as 'empirio-monism'. Lenin considered that this deviation would lead to 'god-building', neglect for both materialism and dialectics and, eventually, to the jettisoning of revolutionary ideology. Chapter 6 (pp. 314–58) is perhaps the most digestible and significant part of the book, reaffirming Lenin's faith that Marxist philosophy 'is cast from a single piece of steel', from which no part could be eliminated 'without departing from objective truth, without falling prey to bourgeois-reactionary falsehood' (p. 326).

Vol. 15, 1908–9

Marxism and Revisionism (pp. 31–9) is one of the few pieces in which Lenin states, and attempts to confront, Bernstein's general arguments against the 'theory of collapse'. At the other pole of socialist discourse, Lenin rejects the stance of the aggressive anti-militarists such as Gustav Hervé. *The Assessment of the Present Situation* is a sober assessment of the unfinished tasks of the revolution but takes heart that economic and political cleavages have been clarified. *The Aim of the Proletarian Struggle in the Revolution* is an overview of the development and current state of the Bolshevik/Menshevik divide on political strategies and class analysis. *The Attitude of the Workers' Party to Religion* repeats the orthodox Marxist position that capitalism creates the conditions of abasement and impoverishment that generate the need for religion but points to the peculiar situation of Russia where the absence of a radical anti-clerical bourgeoisie leaves the task of combatting religion to the proletariat and its party.

Vol. 16, 1909–10

Continuing bitter and tiresome polemics, against the *otzovists* (recallists) within Bolshevik ranks, and against Mensheviks, who are now dubbed 'liquidators' because some played down the importance of the illegal underground party organisation. Only one really important article in this volume under the anodyne title *Strike Statistics in Russia* (pp. 395–421). The article utilises extensive statistical data to demonstrate the 'objective' validity of Bolshevik theory and practice in 1905–7 and to vindicate some of the themes of *What Is To Be Done?* – the role of vanguard workers (particularly metal workers) initiating economic and political struggles, providing a catalyst to the less developed; party responsibility to respond to and lead *this* section of class. In *Concerning Vekhi* (landmarks) Lenin lambasts the liberal/Kadet intellectuals, and in *Two Worlds* he finds solace in the firm stance of the leadership of the SPD against all species of revisionism.

Vol. 17, 1910–12

There is little that is of importance or interest (save to the keen historian) in this volume. Repeated lamentations about the deplorable state of the party and the destruction of its organisations (see, for example, pp. 188, 453) does not prevent the Bolshevik coup in 1912, claiming exclusive right to party name (p. 454). *Certain Features of the Historical Development of Marxism* (pp. 39–44) provides a brief account of the tasks and difficulties of the period of reaction the party was living through.

Vol. 18, 1912–13

Lenin's writings reflect a new optimism consequent upon the strike wave following the massacre of workers in the Lena goldfields, and political mobilisation for the elections to the 4th Duma. Lenin revives his radical programme of 1905 and calls for regeneration of party organisations, see, for example, *The Revolutionary Upswing* (pp. 102–9), *The Situation in the RSDLP*, and *The Immediate Tasks of the Party* (pp. 150–7). Continuing polemics against 'liquidators' and emphasis on centrality of illegal underground: *The Illegal Party and Legal Work* (pp. 387–96). The importance of mass political strikes to stir the peasants and the army is stressed in *The Development of Revolutionary Strikes* . . . (pp. 471–77, cf. 541–2). *On Bolshevism* is a potted summary of the split in the RSDLP (pp. 485–6). *The Historical Destiny of the Doctrine of Karl Marx* (pp. 582–5) briefly anticipates themes to be developed in the following few years – periodisation of world history, the Asiatic revolutions, bankruptcy of liberalism, and dangers of imperialism.

Vol. 19, 1913

The Three Sources . . . *of Marxism* (pp. 23–2 8) is a popular simplified exposition at the level of 'The Marxist exposition is omnipotent because it is true' (p. 23). *The Bourgeoisie and Peace* contends that power is in the hands of the banks and big capitalists and that the bourgeoisie is turning towards reaction and militarism (pp. 83–4, cf. 106–7). *Controversial Issues* (pp. 149–69) is Lenin's best summary of the controversy with the Liquidators (Mensheviks) drawing the threads of his argument into a consistent whole. *The May Day Action by the Revolutionary Proletariat* reaffirms Lenin's faith in mass strikes as vehicles of revolutionary mobilisation. The *Theses on the National Question* and the *National Programme of the RSDLP* affirm the right of national self-determination (with crucial qualifications) and reject cultural autonomy (pp. 243–51, 539–45).

Vol. 20, December 1913–August 1914

Contains important texts on the national question that were to be formative in later Bolshevik policy-making. *Critical Remarks on the National Questions* (pp. 19–51) locates the relative progressiveness of nationalism in the light of the changing nature and uneven development of capitalism that becomes ever more international in character. *The Right of Nations to Self-Determination* (pp. 395–455) is largely an account of past disputes within the RSDLP, the Conclusion (pp. 451–4) restates the difficult formula that the party supports the right to secede, yet insists on 'the unity of the workers of all countries'. Lenin rejects compulsory official language and cautions against the use of coercion in national questions (pp. 71–3). Numerous polemics against usual targets: Narodniks, Kadets, Liquidators; one new target discerned: *The Taylor System – Man's Enslavement by the Machine* (pp. 152–4).

Vol. 21, August 1914–December 1915

The preponderant themes throughout the volume are the analysis of the nature of the war and the formulation of the tasks of revolutionary social democracy in this transformed situation. Lenin's immediate reactions (pp. 15–19) were developed in *The War and Social Democracy* (pp. 27–34), his *Socialism and War* (pp. 297–338) and *Under a False Flag* (pp. 137–57), this last article is particularly significant for its account of a three-phase epochal development of capitalism, culminating in reactionary and militarist imperialism, sustaining itself through super-profits used to secure the support of a labour aristocracy – Lenin's most coherent account of the social basis of opportunism. Repeated analyses of the collapse of the Second International and treachery of its leaders,

Position and Tasks of the Socialist International (pp. 35–41); *The Collapse of the Second International* (pp. 207–59) again relates opportunism to imperialist politics and the absence of proper historical and theoretical method. *The Draft Resolution of the Zimerwald Left* (pp. 345–8) announces the bankruptcy of imperialism in war, and the approach of an epoch of social revolution. *Karl Marx* (pp. 46–79) is Lenin's fullest single account of the component parts of Marxism.

Vol. 22, 1915–16

Imperialism, the Highest Stage of Capitalism (pp. 187–304) is incomparably the single most important work of Leninism as an international ideology. It provided a Marxist explanation of the war and of the dominance of opportunism in the workers' movement. It justified Lenin's conclusion that capitalism had become moribund and bound to militarism, yet simultaneously had created the conditions for a transition to socialism through globalising its contradictions (though in an uneven fashion). It therefore created a theoretical justification for national democratic anti-imperialist revolutions in the periphery coinciding with socialist revolutions in the advanced countries. The 'Preface' to *N. Bukharin's Pamphlet Imperialism and the World Economy* pays scant homage to the main source of Lenin's ideas on monopoly capitalism and imperialism, and is more concerned to criticise Kautsky's theory of 'ultra imperialism' (pp. 103–7). Lenin continues his concern with the national question in two pamphlets, *The Socialist Revolution and the Right of Nations to Self-Determination* (pp. 143–56) and *The Discussion on Self-Determination Summed Up* (pp. 320–60). The latter adds little to earlier discussions, but the former is important for categorising three groups of countries at differing stages of capitalist development, in which nationalism has widely differing connotations. *Opportunism and the Collapse of the Second International* refines Lenin's earlier analysis that 'social chauvinism' and the treachery of socialist leaders has its roots in the politics and economics of monopoly capitalism, and that the time has come to sweep both away (pp. 108–20).

Vol. 23, August 1916–March 1917

Imperialism and the Split in Socialism (pp. 105–20) is an excellent, succinct statement of Lenin's position that closely relates his economic analysis of imperialism to his political analysis of the growth of opportunism and the collapse of socialism. *The Youth International* is a critical review of Bukharin on the state that concludes that he has obscured the distinction between Marxism and anarchism. *Lecture on the 1905 Revolution* (pp. 236–53) emphasises the importance of revolutionary struggle as an accelerator of class development and asserts that the Russian revolution 'is the *prologue* to the coming European revolution' (p. 252). Lenin greeted the news of the overthrow of tsarism with his *Draft Theses* (pp. 287–91), calling for the Soviets to be organised and the people to be armed, no faith in the government or any government of defencists; these themes are amplified in his *Letters From Afar* that effectively defined his theoretical and tactical stance up to the October Revolution (pp. 297–342). In the third and fifth letters he begins to develop, for the first time, his ideas on the

'Commune state' based upon a proletarian militia. *The Farewell Letter to Swiss Workers*, in which the radicalisation of the Russian revolution is presented as the prologue to a European Socialist revolution.

Vol. 24 April–June 1917

Lenin's *April Theses: The Tasks of the Proletariat in the Present Revolution* (pp. 21–6) condense the ideas of *Letters From Afar* (see above) into ten strident propositions that scandalised his Bolshevik followers. Lenin insists that the Soviets are the *only* possible form of revolutionary government' compatible with the 'Commune state', and he calls for the 'abolition of the police, the army and the bureaucracy' (p. 23); these themes are further elaborated in *The Dual Power* (pp. 38–41) and, particularly, in *The Tasks of the Proletariat in Our Revolution* (pp. 57–88) which is a eulogy to the theoretical propriety and actual practicality of building a commune state. So fundamental was this objective that Lenin insisted the party change its name to 'communist'. *A Proletarian Militia* (pp. 179–82) continues the themes of replacing the organs of repression of the bourgeois state as does his *Report on the Current Situation* (pp. 228–43), which is even more emphatic that there could be no other way to socialism, and that, in the era of international state monopoly capitalism, international action alone could be effective. *Inevitable Catastrophe and Extravagant Promises* (pp. 424–30) proposes a single state bank, workers' control over production, and universal labour service as the means to avoid threatening economic catastrophe (cf. pp. 513–15). Lenin's proposals for the *Revision of the Party Programme* encapsulate, in cryptic form, his theoretical account of Imperialism, analysis of the war, necessity for socialist revolution, and the economic, political, and administrative measures it will implement. It was the summary programme of the October Revolution (see particularly pp. 469–79).

Vol. 25, June–September 1917

The State and Revolution (pp. 387–496) is a close exegesis of the writings of Marx and Engels on the state and the distortions they had been subjected to by their followers. The epoch of militarist imperialism and state monopoly capitalism made it all the more essential to revive the radical imperative to smash the bourgeois state and create a state form of the commune type without a standing army, police or bureaucracy. The processes of administration, production and distribution had been so simplified that all could 'take part in the administration of the state' (p. 477). That this was intended as no mere theoretical project for a distant future is clear from Lenin's contemporaneous programmatic statements, popular brochures and speeches, as, for instance, in one of the lengthiest and most detailed of Lenin's programmes in the run-up to the October Revolution: *The Impending Catastrophe and How to Combat It* (pp. 327–69).

Vol. 26, September 1917–February 1918

Can the Bolsheviks Retain State Power? (pp. 90–6) emphatically restates the themes noted in Vol. 25 – the Soviets are a 'state apparatus' of the Paris-

Commune-type that dissolves the old state apparatus' and merges it with the armed people; this is made possible through the mechanisms created by monopoly capitalism (p. 108), in particular the big banks that will direct production and distribution and constitute 'nine tenths of the *socialist* apparatus . . . the *skeleton* of socialist society' (p. 106). Lenin asserts that 'we can at once set in motion a state apparatus consisting of ten if not twenty million people' (p. 114). This text, better than any other, brings together in fleeting synthesis Lenin's theoretical analysis of finance capitalism, theory of the socialist state, and faith in the transformative potential of mass participation in socialist practice; it is, in these senses, the most complex and coherent of all Lenin's writings. *Advice of an Onlooker* addresses the more mundane but vital business of treating insurrection as an art and codifies its five rules (p. 180), cf. *Marxism and Insurrection*, pp. 22–7. From mid-September onwards, Lenin calls on the Bolsheviks to seize power. His letters become ever more insistent, culminating in his *Letter to Central Committee Members* (pp. 234–5) on the eve of the October Revolution. The new government's Decree on Peace (pp. 249–53), Decree on Land (pp. 258–60) and its Regulations on Workers Control (pp. 264–5) were all drafted by Lenin. The *Theses on the Constituent Assembly* parade the most diverse pretexts to dissolve the body in which the Bolsheviks were in a minority (pp. 379–83). *How to Organise Competition* restates faith in the people to introduce effective accounting and control in production and distribution so long as 'stereotyped forms' and 'uniformity from above' are resisted (p. 413).

Vol. 27, 1918

Lenin's *Political Report of the Central Committee* (pp. 87–109) introduces a quite new, sober, almost sombre, tone – Russia is backward, little progress has been made to transform the apparatus or revive production, no army worth speaking of, world revolution a 'fairy tale' (p. 102) yet without the German revolution 'we are doomed' (p. 98); a period of disciplined retreat. *The Immediate Tasks of the Soviet Government* (pp. 237–77) reflects the new ambivalence. He clings on the one hand to the themes of *The State and Revolution* while simultaneously insisting upon the recruitment of bourgeois specialists, one-man management, large salary differentials, introduction of the Taylor system, close control of the press, 'the exercise of dictatorial powers by individuals' (p. 268), renewed insistence on '*iron* discipline while at work', and unquestioning obedience to the will of a single person, the Soviet leader (p. 271). *On the Famine* (pp. 391–8) drives home the message that desperate times demand dictatorial methods directed against the peasants and all opponents led by '*iron detachments* of the proletariat'. Lenin's draconian measures outlined in *Theses on the Current Situation* (pp. 406–7).

Vol. 28, 1918–19

The *Proletarian Revolution and the Renegade Kautsky* (pp. 229–323) is a counter-critique of Kautsky's *The Dictatorship of the Proletariat* and it is Lenin at his most relativist, maintaining that the *form* of government is secondary to its class objectives; he vindicates dictatorship 'based directly on force and unrestricted by any laws' (p. 236) as an essential component of the Marxist theory of revolution, preferable to *'moribund* bourgeois democracy' (p. 246). Like the Mensheviks, Kautsky fails to understand the significance of the Commune, or analyse the class basis of the Soviets, or comprehend the revolutionary potential of the peasantry. Lenin's *Report to the Second All-Russia Trade Union Congress* (pp. 412–28) emphatically restates his case that it is a choice between proletarian or bourgeois dictatorship. There is still (January 1919) the insistence that the great mass will, in and through the trade unions, be brought into the practical work of state administration, but this will take time because the workers are not 'cleansed of the filth of the old world' (p. 424). Lenin's *Theses and Report* to the First Congress of the Communist International (pp. 457–74) reviews the theoretical background of Soviet power and contrasts it with bourgeois democracy.

Vol. 29, March–August 1919

Achievements and Difficulties (pp. 57–88) is an unusually frank analysis, mainly of the difficulties and failings of the regime in international and internal affairs. His *Report of the Central Committee* and *On The Party Programme* recognise the gap between promise and performance in the construction of socialism, conceding that early decrees on workers' control were 'clumsy, immature and casual' (p. 154) and that the business of administration fell upon very few so that the Soviet apparatus is accessible to working people only in theory not in fact (p. 179). In part, this was attributable to the 'low cultural level' of the people and the insufficiency of capitalist development in Russia (pp. 182–3). *The Third International and its Place in History* (pp. 305–13) provides a potted history of the Internationals and a six-point summary of why it was Russia that inaugurated the socialist revolution and assumed leadership of the Third International. *A Great Beginning* (pp. 411–34) salutes the first *Subbotnik* (voluntary unpaid holiday labour), affirms the leading role of the urban workers, and defines communism as 'the higher productivity of labour' requiring discipline and exemplary production from the working class and the purge of adventurers from the party. He proposes to 'eliminate the word "commune" from *common* use' (p. 431). By July, Lenin concedes that the dictatorship of the proletariat is, in fact, dictatorship of the party (p. 535).

Vol. 30, 1919–20

Soviet Power and the Status of Women (pp. 120–3, cf. pp. 371–2) a rare and ill-developed foray. First mention of exhaustion of working class (p. 186). *The Constituent Assembly Elections and the Dictatorship of the Proletariat* (pp. 253–75), an important article vindicating Bolshevik strategy in a general way – country cannot be equal to town, nor peasants to workers; Bolsheviks disposed of preponderance of force in the right places (particularly the armed forces) and at the right time. Function of dictatorship of the proletariat – to win the majority to socialism through the use of state power to satisfy their economic needs. *Speech to . . . Water Transport Workers* sets more modest goals for state administrators – just equal to the British; Soviet power itself threatened by inefficiency 'let us frankly admit our complete inability . . . to be organisers and administrators'. The *Speech to the Third All-Russia Trade Union Congress* (pp. 502–15) is unrelievedly gloomy about the weaknesses of the proletariat and the general lack of organisation ability and discipline, in these circumstances: 'The talk of equality, liberty and democracy . . . is nonsense' (p. 506); 'We need more discipline, more individual authority and more dictatorship' (p. 514).

Vol. 31, 1920

Left-Wing Communism – An Infantile Disorder (pp. 21–118). Lenin's first attempt to project the Russian, Bolshevik and Soviet experience as valid and repeatable on a world scale. Takes issue with those on the left who confuse class with party dictatorship, emphasises the role of the RCP as *the* decision-making agency. The conditions for revolution specified (pp. 84–5, 94–5). The same universalisation of the Bolshevik model is implicit in the *Terms of Admission into the Communist International* (pp. 206–11). *The Tasks of the Youth Leagues* (pp. 283–99) is of interest for the assertion that the present generation can do no more than destroy the old, the next generation will build the new 'and will see a Communist society' (p. 299). Proletarian culture is not the denial but the culmination of prior cultural development; morality, however, 'is entirely subordinated to the proletariat's class struggle' (p. 291). *A Contribution to the History of the Question of the Dictatorship* (pp. 340–61) insists that both Marxist theory and practical experience confirm that the dictatorship is the only means by which to effect the transition to socialism. Dictatorship is starkly defined as 'authority untrammelled by any laws . . . and based directly on force' (p. 353). *Theses on Production Propaganda* (pp. 404–6) enjoins the media to reduce coverage of politics, to concentrate on production, to exhort rather than report. *Our Foreign and Domestic Position and the Tasks of the Party* (pp. 408–26) emphasises new tasks of economic reconstruction and centrality of constructing a single economic plan in which electrification is crucial ('Communism is Soviet power plus the electrification of the whole country', p. 419), referred to as 'the second programme of our party' (p. 514)). Notes difficulties of proletarian exhaustion, inadequate cultural level of the majority, prevalence of bureaucratic methods, and irresponsible criticism.

Vol. 32, 1920–21

In *On the Trade Unions* (pp. 19–42) and *Once Again on the Trade Unions* (pp. 70–107), Lenin argues against the incorporation of trade unions into state apparatus – they remain necessary to defend workers against bureaucratic distortions of the state. They are, however, unequal to the tasks of directing the administration because 'the proletariat is still so divided, so degraded, so corrupted in parts' (p. 21). Trade unions are, therefore, 'transmission belts' of the proletarian dictatorship or schools of communism (p. 98). Industrial democracy decried as dangerous and theoretically wrong: 'every kind of democracy . . . serves production' (p. 81). Lenin's *Summing-up Speech on the Report of the C.C.* is a bitter indictment of the Workers' Opposition group within the party attributing the prevalence of their views to the declassing of the proletariat (p. 199), in a situation of crisis unity is imperative and the lid must be put on all opposition. Lenin's later *Resolution on Party Unity* (pp. 241–4) bans the 'formation of groups with different platforms' (p. 241) and orders the dissolution of all such existing groups. His *Report on the Substitution of a Tax in Kind* (pp. 214–38) signified an abrupt reversal of the state monopoly of trade in grain and presaged the turn to the mixed economy of the New Economic Policy – the crisis of the economic system demanded concessions to the peasantry. *The Tax in Kind* (pp. 329–65) is a broader theoretical conspectus attempting to reconcile the market with state direction in a hybrid system that Lenin calls 'state capitalism', itself conceived of as a great advance over war communism and primitive, small-scale production and exchange.

Vol. 33, 1921–23

The New Economic Policy and the Tasks of the Political Education Departments (pp. 60–79) reviews the mistake of going over directly to communist production and distribution, since the proletariat is declassed and industry at a standstill (p. 65); order and discipline necessary in period of retreat; barbarism, bureaucracy, bribery and illiteracy are the enemies to be overcome. *The Role and Functions of the Trade Unions* . . . reiterates many of the themes of Vol. 32; no role for in management of factories (p. 189) yet must train masses 'in the art of managing socialist industry' (p. 190); mobilise mass behind state plans; and act as transmission belts of Communist Party leadership. *Political Report of the C.C. of the RCP* (pp. 263–309), a bleak assessment of the contemporary situation and future tasks; foundations of socialist economy not yet laid, communists lack ability to run economy and to trade; they do not even recognise 'that they must start learning from the beginning' (p. 275); 99% of communists 'unable to perform their duties' (p. 309). *On Cooperation* (pp. 467–75) co-operatives newly located as vital to the building of socialism and as *the* means of connecting the peasants to the proletarian state, but success of policy dependent upon reform of 'utterly useless' machinery of state and transformation of cultural level of peasantry (p. 474). *How We Should Reorganise the Workers' and Peasants' Inspection* (pp. 481–6), the centrepiece of Lenin's scheme to regenerate the 'utterly impossible, indecently pre-revolutionary' machinery of state by making all its agencies subject to the control of a high-powered and exemplary Workers' and Peasants' Inspectorate. 'Better Fewer but Better' (pp. 487–502), Lenin's last article, continues the critique of the 'deplorable' and 'wretched' state apparatus, in five years of bustle what has been created 'proved useless . . . or even futile, or even harmful' (p. 489). The worst organised of all is the Workers' and Peasants' Inspection (under Stalin) and it must imperatively be restructured and restaffed. The apparatus of state must also be reduced 'to the utmost degree of economy' (p. 501). Lenin ends with reflections on the international stalemate – capitalism failed to overthrow the socialist revolution but seriously stymied its development; in the long run, however, 'Russia, India and China, etc., account for the overwhelming majority of the population of the globe' (p. 500) but to prevail they must become civilised.

Vol. 34, Letters, 1895–1911

Two hundred items of Lenin's correspondence with Plekhanov, Akselrod and
Potresov – the establishment of *Iskra*, preparation of the Party Programme,
convocation of the Second Congress of the Party, and Lenin's resignation from
the editorial board of *Iskra* (p. 89). Letters to Bogdanov, Lepeshinsky,
Lunacharsky, Gorky and others, on organisational and tactical matters.

Vol. 35, Letters, 1912–22

Consists of 321 items, many to Gorky soliciting support, and many (the most
tender and solicitous of all Lenin's letters) to Inessa Armand. Shlyapnikov and
Koltontai are among his most frequent personal correspondents from 1914 to
1917. A letter to N. I. Bukharin (pp. 230–1) rejects his 'anarchist' orientation
on the state, but to Koltontai six months later (Feb. 1917) he concedes that
now he is closer to Bukharin than to Kautsky (pp. 286–7). Many cryptic
telegrams and notes of instruction on particular aspects of policy

Vol. 36, Letters and Documents 1900–23

Important letters particularly to Plekhanov and Akselrod on the formation of
Iskra in the period 1900–3. The newspaper report of the *Lecture on 'The
Proletariat and the War'* (pp. 297–301) gives a good indication of Lenin's
immediate reaction to the First World War and his *Preliminary Draft of the
April Theses* (pp. 431–2) is also important. His *On the Tasks of the People's
Commissariat for Justice Under the New Economic Policy* (pp. 560–5) reveals
the party's manipulation of the legal system and Lenin's insistence that 'model
trials' be conducted, with exemplary punishment (including shooting). By far
the most important document in this volume is Lenin's so-called 'Testament' –
the *letter to Congress*, his last communication to the party, dictated in
December 1922 and January 1923. Lenin reflects on the danger of a split in the
leadership of the party and undertakes a somewhat inconclusive survey of the
strengths and weaknesses of the major protagonists; on one thing he is certain;
that Stalin must be removed from his post as General Secretary. He concludes
that 'the relationship between Stalin and Trotsky is not a detail, or it is a detail
which can assume decisive importance' (p. 596). *The Question of Nationalities
or Autonomisation* (pp. 605–11) again censures Stalin for his spite and Russian
chauvinism over the matter of Georgian secession.

Vol. 37, Letters to Relatives, 1893–1922

Lenin sustained a regular, almost weekly, correspondence with his mother and
other members of the family. They disclose his careful concern for their health
and welfare oddly combined with matters of business – finance, obtaining of
books, liaison with publishers etc. There is rich detail about the daily life,
travels and infrequent diversions of Lenin's household.

Vol. 38, Philosophical Notebooks

Contains Lenin's annotations and reflections on particular philosophical works from 1895 to 1916. These are concentrated in two principal periods, 1908–9, when his main references were to Plekhanov and Deborin – used to prepare *Materialism and Empirio-Criticism* (see vol. 14); and 1914–16 when his main reference texts are those of Hegel. *On the Question of Dialectics* (pp. 359–63) is a resumé of Lenin's finding that dialectics, so neglected by other Marxists, is 'the essence of the matter' (p. 362).

Vol. 39, Notebooks on Imperialism

Largely consists of Lenin's notes, from a great variety of sources in German (by far the majority), French, English and Russian, compiled in the writing of *Imperialism, the Highest Stage of Capitalism* (see Vol. 22). They consist of substantial extracts from the huge literature covered, statistical tables and outline plans for chapters. Among the most interesting materials are the plans for articles and speeches towards the end of the volume, particularly pp. 734–42 and 754–61.

Vol. 40, Notebooks on the Agrarian Question 1900–16

More than any other Marxist theorist, Lenin consistently devoted himself to detailed study of the development of capitalism in agriculture. His interest in and proficiency with statistics is amply demonstrated on pp. 186–235 and pp. 295–405, but the more interesting materials are in the first part of the volume (pp. 29–70), which includes plans and outlines of most of Lenin's principal works on the subject in this period.

Vol. 41, 1896–1917

There is much contextual material (often brief notes, rarely exceeding a page in length) that is of value to the specialist. *The Replies to Plekhanov's and Akselrod's Remarks* . . . (pp. 53–9) demonstrate the strained relationships within the *Iskra* camp before the Second Congress. *Three Outlines for a Report on the Paris Commune* (pp. 113–22) demonstrates Lenin's unusual interest in the commune as far back as 1904. Drafts and plans for leaflets in 1905 (pp. 171–6), *Anti-Militarist Propaganda* . . . (pp. 204–7), *The Third Duma and Social Democracy* (pp. 209–16) and *Speech on the Organisational Question* (pp. 250–1) are among the more significant 'new' materials. *To All the Citizens of Russia* (pp. 262–6), written in 1912, is an unusually broad survey of international politics, war and tsarist foreign policy. Significant documents on the Bolshevik/Menshevik dispute (pp. 274–7, 308–10) extensive notes on the national question (pp. 313–23), socialism and the war (pp. 337–55), material on the Kienthal Conference (pp. 360–79), revision of the party programme in 1917 (pp. 418–24), and the only mention of his executed brother, Alexander (p. 430).

Vol. 42, 1917–23

Contains important material including the *Original Version* of Lenin's 1918 article 'The Immediate Tasks of the Soviet Government' (pp. 68–84), a letter to Chicherin on detailed preparations for the Communist International (pp. 119–21), instructions on film as a vehicle of propaganda (pp. 161–2 and 388–9), and, of particular importance, Lenin's lengthiest reflections on the necessity of coercion in revolution and the propaganda, economic, and coercive roles of the Cheka (pp. 166–74). Lenin's optimistic plans for economic co-operation with foreign capital are developed at length (pp. 175–80, 232–7, 239–48, 285–96), but he is forced to recognise that this pivotal policy in developing state capitalism bore no fruit (p. 426). His important drafts of the article 'How We Should Reorganise the Workers' and Peasants' Inspection' conclude the volume. In an Appendix, a *Re-registration Form for Members of the Moscow Organisation* is a characteristic piece of Lenin understatement that comes close to the comic; to the question 'What works of *Marx, Engels*, Lenin, *Kautsky* and *Plekanov* have you read?', Lenin replies: 'Practically all works (of underlined authors)'.

Vol. 43, Letters, notes, telegrams etc. 1893–1917

A great deal of day-to-day correspondence about the production, distribution and financing of *Iskra* and subsequent Bolshevik periodicals. Letters to figures within the Second International familiarising them with the split in the Russian party, particularly to the Secretary of the International Socialist Bureau, Camille Huysmans. There is a fawning encomium to August Bebel, full of luminous praise for the revolutionary rectitude and theoretical propriety of the German model (pp. 232–3). Shortly afterwards, however (pp. 253–4), he is moved to write a formal complaint to the Executive of the SPD for publishing an anonymous and slanderous article attacking all trends within the Russian party. Had he known that Trotsky was the perpetrator, his earlier critique of him (p. 222) would no doubt have been redoubled. Frequent letters on organisational and editorial matters to Kamenev, Zinoviev, Karpinsky and Inessa Armand. Writes to Gorter suggesting international journal to condemn the traitors to socialism (p. 453). Writes to Hanecki to facilitate plan for British authorities to grant safe conduct for Russian revolutionary emigrés to return to Russia (pp. 622–3). Letter to Radek on the formation of a Third International (p. 632, cf. 634–5).

Vol. 44, Letters, notes, telegrams etc. 1917–20

Notable mainly for the breadth of Lenin's concerns in co-ordinating almost all spheres of Soviet activity and his punctilious attention to detail particularly on military affairs, economic planning, electrification and scientific innovation, and issues of food supply. He even busies himself personally dealing with petitions from individuals to retain their accommodation. Few of the entries run to more than half a page; they are almost all highly context-bound and likely to be of interest more to the specialist historian than to the general reader. Some possible exceptions are his draconian proposals for requisitioning food from Ukrainian peasants – death sentences to be meted out to ill-defined 'rich peasants' in the event of non-fulfilment – Stalin to be in charge of the operation (pp. 406–8); and a letter illustrative of Lenin's technological 'short-cutism' on the hydraulic extraction of peat and administrative instructions for developing it (pp. 456–8).

Vol. 45, Letters, notes, telegrams etc. 1920–3

More than 800 items, mostly extremely brief and of passing significance. His letter to Ryazanov presages the establishment of the Marx/Engels Institute (pp. 80–1), February 1921 letter on the need for concessions to peasantry and the desperate food crisis (p. 89), trade with peasants stressed as vital to prevent collapse (pp. 94–5). Orders Zinoviev to attend to graves of Plekhanov and Zasulich (p. 138). Letters on the food and fuel crises, with precise instructions on retribution for non-compliance, Letter to Gorky imploring him to go abroad for treatment (p. 249). Letter to Rothstein, explaining that he himself is overworked and taking a cure (p. 255). Repeated complaints about inefficiency and red tape; detailed instructions and exhortations with regard to the building of electric power stations. To Unschlicht specifying no publicity for revolutionary tribunals: and shooting on the spot for terrorism (p. 454). Lenin to Stalin complaining of the diversion of personnel and energies to the Comintern (pp. 598–9). At the very end of the last volume are three brief letters enjoining Trotsky to take up the attack on Stalin over the Georgian affair (p. 607); reassurance to Georgian comrades that he is pursuing the matter (p. 608); and a letter to Stalin requesting apologies for having insulted his wife, on pain of severing relations with him (pp. 607–8).

Vol. 46, Index, Part 1

The first section contains an alphabetical listing of all Lenin's writings included in the *Collected Works*, including letters and notes. The second section is a Name Index that locates mentions of particular individuals.

Vol. 47, Index, Part 2

The whole of this volume comprises a Subject Index that is useful within the limits of the subjects thought appropriate by its Soviet compilers.

Appendix 3
Lenin's Principal Works by Topic

		Volume No.
General Theoretical		
1899	The Development of Capitalism in Russia	3
1916	Imperialism, the Highest Stage of Capitalism	22
Philosophy		
1908	Materialism and Empirio-Criticism	14
1914	Karl Marx	21
1915	On the Question of Dialectics	38
Political Strategy		
1905	The Stages, the Trend and the Prospects of the Revolution	10
1910	Strike Statistics in Russia	16
1916	Imperialism and the Split in Socialism	23
1917	The Tasks of the Proletariat in Our Revolution	24
1920	Left Wing Communism – an Infantile Disorder	31
Party Organisational		
1902	What Is to Be Done?	5
	A Letter to a Comrade on Our Organisational Tasks	6
1905	The Reorganisation of the Party	10
1907	Preface to the Collection *Twelve Years*	13
1920	Terms of Admission to the Communist International	31
1922–23	'Testament' – Letter to the Congress	36
Agrarian Programme		
1902	The Agrarian Programme of Russian Social Democracy	6
1906	Draft Agrarian Programme (Ch. 5 of Revision of Agrarian Programme of the Workers' Party)	10
1917	Decree on Land	26

Notes and References

Full title, place and date of publication is only given when a work is cited for the first time in the Notes. A bibliography of works cited is given at the end of the Notes for reference purposes.

Lenin's *Collected Works*, 45 vols (Moscow, 1960–70) is the principal source cited and this will be abbreviated to *CW*; references will give only the volume number in bold type, followed by the page number in plain type (V. I. Lenin, Collected Works, volume 12, p. 240 is rendered: *CW*, **12**, 240).

A similar notation is adopted for K. Marx and F. Engels, *Selected Works* (Moscow, 1962); this will be abbreviated to *MESW*.

Introduction

1. N. Harding, 'Lenin and his Critics: Some Problems of Interpretation', *European Journal of Sociology*, vol. xvii (1976).
2. E. Wilson, *To the Finland Station* (London, 1940) p. 390.
3. Consider, for example, the strident anachronism of the title of the book by A. L. Weeks – *The First Bolshevik – A Political Biography of Peter Tkachev* (New York. 1968).
4. This is a summary of the general position of Bertram D. Wolfe.
5. R. N. Berki, for instance, in his *The Genesis of Marxism* (London, 1968) p. 2, finds that Marx's thought has an underlying unity which can be rendered intelligible by being presented as the achieved "synthesis" of major perspectives and departures located in the European tradition'.
6. N. Harding, 'The Early Marx and the Decomposition of Marxism', *Studies in Marxism*, 1, 94.

Chapter 1

1. Edmund Wilson, in his influential *To the Finland Station*, first published in 1940, gave widespread currency to this view (see particularly p. 390 of the 1960 London edition). Similar accounts that disparage the importance of theory in Lenin's work were retailed in such influential texts as R. N. Carew-Hunt, *The Theory and Practice of Communism* (London, 1950), and J. Plamenatz, *German Marxism and Russian Communism* (London, 1954).
2. Almost all the widely-used Western texts on Lenin and Leninism give considerable prominence to the decisive impact of the Russian Jacobin

tradition. See, *inter alia*, A. B. Ulam, *Lenin and the Bolsheviks* (London, 1969) pp. 108–9, R. N. Carew-Hunt, *The Theory and Practice of Communism*, p. 166; L. B. Schapiro, *The Communist Party of the Soviet Union* (London, 1970) p. 4; R. Payne, *The Life and Death of Lenin* (London, 1964) p. 30; and S. V. Utechin, 'Introduction' to *What Is To Be Done?* (London, 1963) pp. 28–33. The most thorough attempt at an intellectual biography detailing the young Lenin's debts to the Russian Jacobins is in R. Pipes, *Revolutionary Russia* (London, 1968). Pipes' account is almost duplicated in R. H. W. Theen, *V. I. Lenin: The Genesis and Development of a Revolutionary* (London, 1974) pp. 38–42. A more recent variant on the theme of Russian Jacobinism ousting Marxism in Lenin's thought is D. Volkogonov, *Lenin, Life and Legacy*, trans. H. Shukman (London, 1994). More modulated and dispassionate accounts are to be found in L. Kolakowski, *Main Currents of Marxism* (Oxford, 1981) vol. 2, pp. 381–412; and the three volumes of R. Service, *Lenin: A Political Life* (London, 1985, 1991 and 1994).

3. Psycho-history features prominently in the accounts of Theen, N. Leites, *A Study of Bolshevism* (Glencoe, Ill., 1953), and E. V. Wolfenstein, *The Revolutionary Personality* (Princeton, NJ, 1967).

4. The one indispensable study of the variety of currents in the Russian revolutionary movement of the nineteenth century is Franco Venturi's *Roots of Revolution* (London, 1964). See also A. Walicki, *The Controversy Over Capitalism* (Oxford, 1969), and R. Wortman, *The Crisis of Russian Populism* (Cambridge, 1967).

5. Pipes and Theen make these claims particularly forcibly.

6. N. Harding, *Lenin's Political Thought* (vol. 1, London, 1977; vol. 2, London, 1981).

7. This was the title of one of the most coherent Russian Populist texts, challenging the very possibility of capitalism developing in Russia: V. V. (V. P. Vorontsov), *Sudby kapitalizma v rossii* (St Petersburg, 1882).

8. V. I. Lenin, 'What the "Friends of the People" Are and How They Fight the Social-Democrats', *CW*, 1, 133–332.

9. *The Development of Capitalism in Russia* comprises the whole of the weighty vol. 3 of the *Collected Works*. This crucially important text, the summation of seven years' continuous study, receives scant attention in the popular or academic literature on Lenin.

10. A brief summary of the progressive transformative role of capitalism in Russia is given in *CW*, 3, 598–9.

11. These were the themes of the programmatic statement '*Ob Agitatsii*' (On Agitation), written by A. Kremer and Iu. Martov first published in Geneva in 1896 but already adopted as the programme of the St Petersburg Marxists in early 1895. *On Agitation* is translated in the present author's *Marxism in Russia, Key Documents 1879–1906* (London, 1983) pp. 192–205, hereafter cited as Harding, 1983.

12. In G. V. Plekhanov, *Selected Philosophical Works* (London, 1961) vol. 1.

13. For rival interpretations of the role of the St Petersburg Marxists in these strikes see A. K. Wildman, *The Making of a Workers' Revolution* (Chicago, 1967) and R. Pipes, *Social Democracy and the Saint Petersburg Labor Movement, 1885–1895* (Cambridge, Mass., 1963).

14. The 'Manifesto' of the First Congress of the Russian Social Democratic Labour Party (RSDLP) is given in Harding, 1983, pp. 223–5.
15. Wildman, p. 83.
16. *CW*, **2**, 349.
17. A translation of the text of Kuskova's *Credo* as well as of the infamous lead article of the 'Separate Supplement' to issue No. 7 of *Rabochaya Mysl* can both be found in Harding, 1983, pp. 242–53.
18. *CW*, **5**, 443.
19. *CW*, **5**, 446. This lag of the leadership was persistent theme in Lenin's text, see pp. 397, 413, 435, 438, 444.
20. *CW*, **5**, 465.
21. *CW*, **5**, 502.
22. *CW*, **5**, 384.
23. *CW*, **4**, 368.
24. *CW*, **5**, 386.
25. Kolakowski, p. 389.
26. Quoted by Lenin, *CW*, **5**, 383.
27. For a brief summary of Plekhanov's account of the relationship between the intelligentsia and the working class, see Harding, 1971, pp. 49–52.
28. K. Marx and F. Engels, *Selected Correspondence*, D. Torr (ed.) (London, 1936) p. 316.
29. Ibid., p. 319.
30. K. Marx and F. Engels, *The Holy Family* (Moscow, 1956) p. 53.
31. *MESW*, **1**, 43.
32. Ibid., p. 46.
33. Ibid., p. 363.
34. *CW*, **5**, 443.
35. *CW*, **5**, 480.

Chapter 2

1. L. Trotsky, *1905* (Harmondsworth, 1971) p. 89.
2. It was only much later, in 1929,when he was already in exile, that Trotsky compiled a cohesive account of the theory of permanent revolution. See L. Trotsky, *The Permanent Revolution and Results and Prospects* (London, 1962).
3. *CW*, **9**, 29.
4. *CW*, **10**, 353.
5. *CW*, **10**, 181.
6. *CW*, **10**, 183.
7. See Note 14 above.
8. *CW*, **9**, 180–1.
9. A. Ascher, *The Mensheviks in the Russian Revolution* (London, 1976) p. 62.
10. Ibid., p. 22.
11. Ibid., p. 74.
12. L. Schapiro, *The Communist Party of the Soviet Union* (London, 1963) p. 82.

Chapter 3

1. C. E. Schorske, *German Social Democracy, 1905–1917* (New York, 1955, p. 83) The full Stuttgart Resolution is translated in J. P. Nettl, *Rosa Luxemburg* (London, 1969) pp. 269–70.
2. R. N. Hunt, *German Social Democracy 1918–1933* (Chicago, 1964) p. 9. See also the useful summary of the SPD's situation on the eve of the war, in E. Bevan, *German Social Democracy During the War* (London, 1918) ch. 1.
3. Hunt, *German Social Democracy*, p. 21.
4. Schorske, p. 5.
5. *MESW*, 1, 33–65. See, in particular, the ten-point programme, pp. 53–4.
6. E. Bernstein, *Evolutionary Socialism* (London, 1900) p. xii. This was the translation of Bernstein's collection of articles originally published in German in 1899 under the title *Die Vorrausetzung des Socializmus*.
7. Engels' so-called 'Testament' was written in March 1895 and published as the 'Introduction' to Marx's *The Class Struggles in France* (*MESW*, 1, 118–38).
8. *MESW*, 1, 130.
9. *MESW*, 1, 129.
10. *MESW*, 1, 135.
11. *MESW*, 1, 136.
12. Schorske, p. 19. Kautsky's initial reaction to Bernstein's analyses was quite mild. He even found them to be 'extremely attractive' (J. P. Nettl, *Rosa Luxemburg*, London, 1969, p. 95) and his eventual critique 'was tardy and hesitant'. See P. Good, *Karl Kautsky, Selected Political Writings* (London, 1983) pp. 15–31.
13. Bernstein, p. 102.
14. Ibid., p. 209.
15. Ibid., p. 49.
16. Ibid., p. 39.
17. Ibid., p. 145.
18. Ibid., p. 218.
19. Ibid., p. 221.
20. Ibid., notes to pp. 101–2.
21. Ibid., p. 100.
22. Ibid., p. 163.
23. Ibid., p. 151.
24. Ibid., p. 154.
25. Ibid., p. 160.
26. Ibid., p. 26.
27. Rosa Luxemburg's riposte to Bernstein was contained in a series of articles published in 1899 and issued as a pamphlet, *Social Reform or Revolution*. English translation in M. A. Waters, *Rosa Luxemburg Speaks* (New York, 1970).
28. Bernstein, *Evolutionary Socialism*, p. xxii.
29. Ibid., p. 202.
30. Ibid., p. 222.

31. Quoted in P. Gay, *The Dilemma of Democratic Socialism: Eduard Bernstein's Challenge to Marx* (New York, 1962) p. 80.
32. Extracts from the leading article of this 'Separate Supplement' are translated in Harding, 1983, pp. 242–50. An account of Lenin's controversies with native Russian 'revisionists' can be found in Harding, 1977, pp. 145–51.
33. *CW*, **4**, 275.
34. The title of a lengthy article written by Lenin at this time, *CW*, **4**, pp. 255–85.
35. Schorske, p. 23.
36. *CW*, **4**, 277.
37. Schorske, p. 24.
38. *CW*, **4**, 353.
39. The most distinguished theorist of syndicalism was the maverick Georges Sorel, whose book *Reflections on Violence* (London, 1961) was the most sophisticated vindication of syndicalist revolutionary practice. See, further, J. R. Jennings' excellent study *Georges Sorel* (London, 1985).
40. K. Kautsky, *Der Politische Massenstreik, Neue Zeit, 1910*. Excerpts in *Karl Kautsky, Selected Political Writings*, ed. and trans. P. Goode (London, 1983) pp. 53–73.
41. Ibid., p. 60.
42. Ibid., p. 72.
43. Quoted in B. D. Wolfe, *Marxism, 100 Years in the Life of a Doctrine* (London, 1967) p. 276.
44. Ibid., p. 280.
45. Ibid., p. 277.
46. S. H. Baron, *Plekhanov, The Father of Russian Marxism* (London, 1963) p. 324.
47. Wolfe, p. 282.
48. Quoted in M. Harrington, *Socialism* (New York, 1972) p. 75.
49. *CW*, **13**, 91.
50. *CW*, **13**, 92.
51. *CW*, **15**, 196.
52. *CW*, **15**, 194.
53. G. Steenson, *Not One Man! Not One Penny! German Social Democracy 1863–1914* (Pittsburg, 1984) p. 134.
54. Wolfe, p. 271.
55. Ibid., loc. cit.
56. Bevan, *German Social Democracy*, p. 21.
57. Schorske, p. 300.
58. Ibid., p. 288.
59. Bevan, *German Social Democracy*, p. 15.
60. Schorske, p. 292.
61. *CW*, **21**, 16.
62. *CW*, **21**, 18.
63. *CW*, **21**, 15.
64. *CW*, **21**, 18.
65. *CW*, **21**, loc. cit.
66. *CW*, **21**, loc. cit.

Chapter 4

1. S. P. Melgunov, *The Bolshevik Seizure of Power* (Santa Barbara, Calif., 1972) p. xv.
2. H. Shukman, *Lenin and the Russian Revolution*, (London, 1966) p. 177.
3. N. N. Sukhanov, *The Russian Revolution of 1917* (London, 1955) p. 273.
4. *CW*, **24**, 21–26.
5. Sukhanov, p. 289.
6. *CW*, **24**, 37.
7. *CW*, **24**, 67.
8. *CW*, **24**, 22.
9. *CW*, **24**, loc. cit.
10. *CW*, **24**, 21.
11. *CW*, **24**, 23.
12. *CW*, **24**, 25.
13. *CW*, **24**, 24.
14. *CW*, **24**, 23.
15. *CW*, **24**, 23.
16. *CW*, **24**, loc. cit.
17. Sukhanov, p. 287.
18. R. R. Abramovitch, *The Soviet Revolution* (London, 1962) p. 31.
19. Sukhanov, p. 287.
20. Ibid., p. 288.
21. Abramovitch, p. 30.
22. Tseretelli, quoted in Ascher, p. 93.
23. Ascher, p. 24. Among the Mensheviks only Martov was, at this stage, prepared to endorse the call for the soviets to seize power (see Ascher, pp. 101–2).
24. Ibid., loc. cit.
25. *MESW*, **1**, 44.
26. *CW*, **24**, 543.
27. *CW*, **24**, 32. Right up to, and even well after, the October Revolution, Lenin repeatedly insisted that, as far as *Russia* was concerned, the most that could be aspired to was a radicalised democratic revolution that prepared the way for a socialist advance. On this see further the present author's 'Lenin, Socialism and the State in 1917' in E. and J. Frankel and B. Knei-Paz (eds), *Revolution in Russia: Reassessments of 1917* (Cambridge, 1992) pp. 287–303.
28. *CW*, **24**, 73 (cf. pp. 193, 217).
29. *CW*, **24**, 242.
30. *CW*, **24**, 44.
31. *CW*, **24**, 306 cf. p. 240.
32. *CW*, **24**, 305, cf. p. 309.
33. *CW*, **24**, 459–60.
34. *CW*, **24**, 238.
35. *CW*, **25**, 19.
36. *CW*, **25**, 364.
37. *CW*, **24**, 53, cf. p. 194.
38. *CW*, **24**, 307.

39. *CW*, **24**, 504.
40. *CW*, **24**, 227.
41. *CW*, **24**, loc. cit.
42. *CW*, **24**, 40–1.
43. Melgunov, p. xviii.
44. Melgunov, p. 4.
45. *CW*, **26**, 84.
46. *CW*, **26**, 135–6.
47. *CW*, **26**, 145.
48. *CW*, **26**, 132. The quotation is from Marx's *Revolution and Counter-Revolution in Germany*.
49. *CW*, **26**, 23.
50. *CW*, **26**, 48.
51. *CW*, **26**, 69.
52. *CW*, **26**, 111–15.
53. *CW*, **26**, 106, cf. p. 130.
54. *CW*, **26**, 82.
55. L. Trotsky, *History of the Russian Revolution* (3 vols, London, 1967) p. 128.
56. Ibid., p. 129.
57. *The Bolsheviks and the October Revolution, Minutes of the Central Committee of the RSDLP* (London, 1974) p. 99. Hereafter, RDSLP, *October Minutes*.
58. Ibid., pp. 103–4.
59. Ibid., p. 108.
60. Anweiler, p. 192.
61. K. Marx, 'Contribution to the Critique of Hegel's Philosophy of Law: Introduction' in Marx and F. Engels, *Collected Works* [*MECW*] (London, 1975) vol. 3, p. 183.
62. Ibid., p. 177.
63. Ibid., p. 181.
64. L. Trotsky, *On Lenin: Notes Towards a Biography* (London, 1971) p. 74.
65. G. Lukács, *Lenin: A Study on the Unity of His Thought* (London, 1970) p. 13.
66. V. Broido, *Lenin and the Mensheviks* (Aldershot, 1987) pp. 14–15.
67. On the crucial role of the Red Guards in the October Revolution, see R. A. Wade, *Red Guards and Workers' Militias in the Russian Revolution* (Stanford, Conn., 1984) and the same author's 'The Red Guards: Spontaneity and the October Revolution', in E. and J. Frankel and B. Knei Paz, pp. 54–75.
68. *MESW*, **1**, 119–20. The insertion in square brackets is not in the original.

Chapter 5

1. *CW*, **22**, 187–304.
2. *CW*, 25, 363.
3. Georg Lukacs, *Lenin: A Study on the Unity of His Thought* (London, 1970) pp. 11–12. In Lukacs' account, 'Lenin did not make a single

326 Notes and References to pp. 115–42

practical decision in his whole life which was not the rational and logical outcome of his theoretical position.' Ibid., p. 42.

4. *MESW*, **1**, 37.
5. Ibid., p. 88
6. K. Marx, *Capital*, vol. 1 (London, 1938) p. 789.
7. *CW*, **22**, 240.
8. *CW*, **22**, 242.
9. *CW*, **22**, 193, cf. 300.
10. *CW*, **22**, 277.
11. The impact of Lenin's fellow Bolshevik Nikolai Bukharin upon the formation of Leninism in the crucial years 1914–17 has been generally underestimated. In Soviet commentaries it was wholly ignored after Stalin expelled Bukharin from the party and had him executed in 1936. It was Bukharin's study, *The World Economy of Imperialism* (published, with a foreword by Lenin, in 1914), which first convinced Lenin that capitalism had outlived its historical mission and had become degenerate. It was Bukharin too who led Lenin to conclude that the capitalist state had changed fundamentally in nature.
12. *CW*, **24**, 240.
13. *CW*, **24**, 403.
14. N. Bukharin 'K teorii imperialisticheskogo gosudarstva' ('Towards a theory of the imperialist state') in *Revoliutsiia Prava, Sbornik pervyi* (Moscow, 1925) p. 30. For a fuller account of Bukharin's impact on Lenin's analysis of the state see Harding, 1981 (pp. 94–8 and pp. 102–9); and Harding, 'Bukharin and the State', in A. Kemp-Welch (ed.), *The Ideas of Nikolai Bukharin* (Oxford, 1992), pp. 85–112.
15. *CW*, **28**, 462.
16. *CW*, **23**, 110, cf. 58 and 107.
17. *CW*, **21**, 146–7.
18. Most of the leading ideas about the role of the banks in the evolution of monopoly capitalism had been developed by Hilferding into a powerful Marxist synthesis in his book *Finanz Kapital* (Vienna, 1910, trans. and published in a Russian edition, *Finansovyi Kapital*, Moscow, 1914).
19. *CW*, **22**, 214.
20. *CW*, **24**, 235.
21. *CW*, **24**, 210.
22. *CW*, **24**, 196.
23. These ideas were first developed in Bukharin's article 'Towards a Theory of the Imperialist State', and they were further elaborated in his *Economics of the Transformation Period*, published in 1920.
24. *CW*, **23**, 43.
25. *CW*, **23**, 275–6.
26. *CW*, **23**, 297.
27. *CW*, **29**, 294.

Chapter 6

1. *CW*, **22**, 185–305.

2. *CW*, **22**, 213.
3. *CW*, **22**, 216.
4. *CW*, **25**, 346.
5. *CW*, **26**, 106.
6. *CW*, **26**, 90–136.
7. N. Bukharin, 'K teorii imperialisticheskogo gosudarstva', *Revoluitsiia Prava, Sbornik pervyi*, no. 25 (Moscow, 1925) p. 30.
8. K. Marx 'The Civil War in France', in *MESW*, **1**, 486–545. See also the even more virulently anti-statist drafts of the work published in the 1970 Peking edition, *The Civil War in France*.
9. *MESW*, **1**, 332.
10. *MESW*, **1**, 333.
11. *MESW*, **1**, 519.
12. *MESW*, **1**, 521.
13. *CW*, **24**, 170.
14. In his 'Notes in Defence of the April Theses' Lenin made the first identification of the soviets with the Commune of Paris: 'We must ably, carefully, clear people's minds and lead the proletariat and poor peasants forward, away from "dual power" *towards the full power* of the Soviets of Workers' Deputies, and this is the commune in Marx's sense, in the sense of the experience of 1871', *CW*, **24**, 32–3.
15. A. J. Polan, *Lenin and the End of Politics* (London, 1984).
16. *CW*, **32**, 274.
17. *CW*, **33**, 66.
18. *CW*, **29**, 559.
19. *CW*, **32**, 61.
20. *CW*, **28**, 461.
21. *CW*, **28**, 238.
22. L. Trotsky, *Terrorism and Communism* (Ann Arbor, Mich., 1961) p. 7.
23. N. Bukharin, *Economics of the Transformation Period* (New York, 1971) pp. 55–9; hereafter Bukharin, *Economics*.
24. *CW*, **29**, 437.
25. *CW*, **29**, loc. cit.
26. *CW*, **29**, 431.
27. *CW*, **29**, 447.
28. *CW*, **32**, 62.
29. *CW*, **32**, 21.
30. *CW*, **32**, 505
31. *CW*, **31**, 353.
32. *CW*, **31**, 238.
33. *CW*, **22**, 194.
34. *CW*, **28**, 301.
35. Anweiler, p. 248.
36. *CW*, **32**, 184, cf. 179.
37. *CW*, **32**, 184.
38. *CW*, **32**, 199.
39. *CW*, **31**, 45.
40. See, particularly, the scrupulous account given in Service, vol. 3.
41. *CW*, **28**, 268–9.

42. *CW*, **32**, 504.
43. *CW*, **32**, 27.
44. *CW*, **32**, 86, cf. 55.
45. *CW*, **32**, 495.
46. *CW*, **32**, 81.
47. I have developed these themes in 'The Marxist–Leninist Detour' in J. Dunn (ed.), *Democracy: The Unfinished Journey* (Oxford, 1992).
48. *CW*, **32**, 83.
49. *CW*, **29**, 510.
50. *CW*, **32**, 430.
51. *CW*, **31**, 514.
52. *CW*, **31**, 524–5.

Chapter 7

1. See, particularly, Lenin's last significant writings 'How We Should Reorganise the Workers' and Peasants' Inspection' and 'Better Fewer But Better', both in *CW*, **33**. For analyses of the significance of these last reflections on the party and state apparatus see M. Lewin, *Lenin's Last Struggle* (London, 1969), and 1981, chs. 14 and 15.
2. K. Marx and F. Engels, *Collected Works*, vol 1, p. 46.
3. Ibid., p. 43.
4. This was the introductory quotation to Plekhanov's first and seminal translation of Marx to Russian conditions, published in 1883 as *Socialism and the Political Struggle* (see G. V. Plekhanov, *Selected Philosophical Works*, vol. 1, London, 1961, p. 59).
5. *MESW*, **1**, 43.
6. See Note 26 to Chapter 1.
7. L. Trotsky, *Terrorism and Communism* (Ann Arbor, Mich., 1961), p. 10.
8. K. Marx and F. Engels, *Collected Works*, vol. 1, p. 217.
9. *CW*, **25**, 203–04.
10. *CW*, **28**, 108.
11. *CW*, **10**, 79.
12. *CW*, **28**, 284.
13. *CW*, **19**, 406.
14. 'Better Fewer But Better' was the title of Lenin's last article, March 1923, *CW*, **33**, 487–502.
15. *CW*, **28**, 254.
16. *CW*, **28**, 292–3.
17. *CW*, **31**, 207–8.
18. *CW*, **31**, 208.
19. *CW*, **31**, 210.
20. *CW*, **31**, loc. cit.
21. *CW*, **32**, 200.
22. *CW*, **32**, 252.
23. *CW*, **32**, 244.
24. *CW*, **32**, 505.
25. *CW*, **32**, 488–9.

26. *CW*, **32**, 21.
27. *CW*, **32**, 199
28. *CW*, **32**, 246.
29. N. Bukharin, *Economics*, pp. 106–7.
30. *CW*, **33**, 309.
31. *CW*, **32**, 492.
32. N. Bukharin, *Economics*, pp. 110–11.
33. Bukharin, 'K teorii . . .' Lenin initially rejected Bukharin's analysis of the imperative to destroy the all-embracing Leviathan of state monopoly capitalism, but by late 1916 he had clearly accepted it as the copestone of his strategy.
34. N. Bukharin, *Economics*, p. 69.
35. Ibid., p. 79.
36. *CW*, **31**, 514. Lenin looked forward to 'that very happy time when politics recede into the background, when politics will be discussed less often and at shorter length, and engineers and agronomists will do most of the talking' (pp. 513–14).
37. *CW*, **32**, 206.
38. *CW*, **32**, 99.
39. J. V. Stalin, *Works* 13 vols (Moscow, 1953) vol. 6, pp. 47–8.
40. *CW*, **33**, 496.

Chapter 8

1. K. Marx, *Economic and Philosophic Manuscripts of 1844* (Moscow, 1961), p. 74.
2. Ibid., p. 102.
3. *CW*, **23**, 43.
4. *MESW*, **1**, 38.
5. *MESW*, **1**, 37.
6. *CW*, **20**, 28.
7. *MESW*, **1**, 38.
8. *MESW*, **1**, 51.
9. *CW*, **22**, 150–1.
10. *CW*, **23**, 106.
11. *CW*, **23**, 110.
12. *CW*, **22**, 149.
13. *CW*, **19**, 243.
14. *CW*, **20**, 72.
15. *CW*, **20**, 34.
16. *CW*, **20**, 224.
17. *CW*, **20**, 32. cf. Lenin's 'Draft Theses on the National and Colonial Questions', written in 1920, that virtually repeats this formulation, *CW*, **31**, 145.
18. *CW*, **31**, 145.
19. *CW*, **20**, 282.
20. *CW*, **31**, 146.
21. *CW*, **31**, 149.

22. *CW*, **31**, 242.
23. *CW*, **31**, 243.
24. J. V. Stalin, *Works*, vol. 2, pp. 300–81.

Chapter 9

1. B. Shragin and A. Todd (eds), *Landmarks* (New York, 1972) p. 179.
2. Ibid., p. 143.
3. *CW*, **14**, 147.
4. *CW*, **34**, 361.
5. K. Marx, *Economic and Philosophical Manuscripts of 1844* (Moscow, 1961).
6. Kolakowski, vol. 2, p. 440.
7. *CW*, **14**, 41.
8. *CW*, **14**, 54.
9. *CW*, **14**, 145.
10. *CW*, **14**, 58.
11. *CW*, **14**, 123.
12. *CW*, **14**, 109.
13. *CW*, **14**, 123.
14. *CW*, **14**, 102.
15. *CW*, **14**, 46.
16. *CW*, **14**, 55.
17. *CW*, **14**, 27.
18. *CW*, **14**, 130.
19. *CW*, **14**, 84.
20. *CW*, **14**, 100.
21. *CW*, **14**, 130.
22. *CW*, **14**, 155.
23. *CW*, **14**, 190.
24. *CW*, **14**, 134.
25. *CW*, **14**, 103.
26. *CW*, **14**, 307.
27. Kolakowski, vol. 2, p. 451.
28. L. Althusser, *Lenin and Philosophy* (London, 1971) p. 56.
29. Ibid., p. 56.
30. *CW*, **14**, 326.
31. *CW*, **14**, 344.
32. *CW*, **14**, 125, cf. 341.
33. *CW*, **14**, 318.
34. *CW*, **14**, 339–40.
35. *CW*, **14**, 340.
36. *CW*, **14**, 341.
37. *CW*, **14**, 343.
38. *CW*, **14**, 358.
39. See for example, *CW*, **14**, 261.
40. *CW*, **14**, p. 120.
41. *CW*, **14**, 310.

42. N. K. Krupskaya, *O Lenine* (Moscow, 1971) p. 75.
43. See Chapter 2, Note 9.
44. K. Marx, *Capital*, vol. 1 (London, 1938), p. xxx.
45. Ibid., pp. xxx–xxxi.
46. K. Marx and F. Engels, *Collected Works*, vol. 1, pp. 25–105.
47. K. Marx and F. Engels, *Selected Correspondence*, p. 495.
48. K. Marx, *Capital*, vol. 1, p. xxx.
49. K. Marx, 'The Holy Family', *Collected Works*, vol. 4, p. 119.
50. Ibid., pp. 35–6, quoted by Lenin in *CW*, **38**, 26–7.
51. The one brief reference that I am aware of where Marx does appear to concede the operation of the dialectic in the realism of natural science is in a letter to Engels of June 22 1867: 'I refer to the law Hegel discovered, of *purely quantitative changes turning into qualitative changes*, as holding good alike in history and natural science', Marx and Engels, *Selected Correspondence*, p. 223.
52. K. Marx and F. Engels, *The German Ideology* (London, 1965) p. 38.
53. F. Engels, *Anti-Duhring* (London, 1948) p. 29.
54. Ibid., p. 158.
55. The negation of the negation, according to Engels, 'holds good in the animal and plant kingdoms, in geology, in mathematics, in history and philosophy (*Anti-Duhring*, p. 157). Engels' famous example of the qualitative transformation of water into steam is given on pp. 141–2. The example is clearly taken from Hegel's *Science of Logic*, quoted approvingly in *CW*, **38**, 123–24.
56. Engels, *Anti-Duhring*, p. 17.
57. Ibid., pp. 100–3.
58. Ibid., p. 101.
59. *CW*, **14**, 309 and 310.
60. *CW*, **38**, 221–2.
61. *CW*, **38**, 361.
62. On this highly important distinction, see, for example, *CW*, **38**, 201.
63. *CW*, **38**, 253–4, cf. pp. 296 and 361.
64. *CW*, **38**, 171.
65. *CW*, **38**, 201.
66. *CW*, **38**, 359.
67. *CW*, **38**, 139.
68. *CW*, **38**, 140.
69. *CW*, **38**, 283.
70. *CW*, **38**, 360.
71. *CW*, **38**, 362.
72. Engels, *Anti-Duhring*, p. 141.
73. *CW*, **38**, 123.
74. *CW*, **38**, 360.
75. *CW*, **38**, 284.
76. *CW*, **38**, 359–63.
77. *CW*, **38**, 195.
78. *CW*, **38**, 259.
79. *CW*, **38**, 109.
80. *CW*, **38**, 253, cf. p. 177.

81. *CW*, **38**, 212.
82. *CW*, **38**, 184.
83. *CW*, **38**, 342.
84. Marx and Engels, *Collected Works*, vol. 3, p. 183.
85. Ibid., p. 182.
86. *CW*, **38**, 218.
87. *CW*, **38**, 39.
88. *CW*, **38**, 276.
89. *CW*, **38**, 277.
90. *CW*, **38**, 180.
91. The term 'philosophical practice' is Louis Althusser's.
92. *MESW*, **1**, 46.
93. *CW*, **36**, 595.
94. Communist Party of the Soviet Union, *History of the CPSU (Bolsheviks) Short Course* (Moscow, 1938) pp. 105–31. Stalin's chapter, 'Dialectical and Historical Materialism', also appears in his book *Problems of Leninism* (Moscow, 1953) pp. 713–15.

Chapter 10

1. Among the more useful texts on Stalin and Stalinism are: R. V. Daniels, *The Stalin Revolution: Foundations of Soviet Totalitarianism* (Lexington, Mass., 1972); I. Deutscher, *Stalin: A Political Biography* (Harmondsworth, 1966); G. Gill, *Stalinism* (London, 1990); R. Medvedev, *On Stalin and Stalinism* (Oxford, 1979); L. Trotsky, *Stalin* (London, 1947); R. C. Tucker, *Stalin as a Revolutionary, 1879–1929* (London, 1974) and A. B. Ulam, *Stalin: The Man and His Era* (London, 1974).
2. *CW*, **36**, 594–5.
3. *CW*, **36**, 596.
4. *CW*, **33**, 481–6.
5. *CW*, **33**, 487–502.
6. *CW*, **33**, 490.
7. *CW*, **33**, 494.
8. L. Trotsky, *The Stalin School of Falsification* (New York, 1962) p. 72.
9. *CW*, **42**, 491.
10. *CW*, **45**, 608.
11. Foerster, the chief physician, had so instructed Lenin's secretaries. Lenin, for his part, 'had the impression that it was not the doctors who gave instructions to the Central Committee, but the Central Committee that gave instructions to the doctors', *CW*, **42**, 492–3.
12. *CW*, **36**, 596.
13. See M. Lewin, *Lenin's Last Struggle* (London, 1975) for a sympathetic account of Lenin's final conflict with Stalin.
14. R. Payne, *The Life and Death of Lenin* (London, 1964).
15. See Lenin's letter to Trotsky, 5 March 1923, *CW*, **45**, 607.
16. See Note 1 above.
17. I. Deutscher, *Stalin: A Political Biography* (Harmondsworth, 1966) p. 100.

18. Ibid., p. 109.
19. Stalin, *Works*, vol. 2, pp. 300–81.
20. In February 1913, Lenin wrote to Maxim Gorky: 'As regards nationalism I am fully in agreement with you that we ought to take this up more seriously. We have a marvellous Georgian who has set down to write a big article . . . for which he has collected *all* the Austrian and other materials' (CW, **35**, 84).
21. Abramovitch, pp. 276–77.
22. *CW*, **33**, 315.
23. The fullest account of the suppression of political opposition under Lenin is in L. S. Schapiro, *The Origin of the Communist Autocracy and Political Opposition in the Soviet State: First Phase, 1917–1922* (New York, 1955). See also R. R. Abramovitch, Ascher, and Broido.
24. Quoted in R Luxemburg, 1961, p. 57.
25. *CW*, **28**, 248.
26. The fullest analysis is in O. Radkey, *Russia Goes to the Polls. The Election to the All-Russian Constituent Assembly 1917* (Ithaca, NY, 1989). In December 1919 Lenin wrote a lengthy article, 'The Constituent Assembly Elections and the Dictatorship of the Proletariat' (*CW*, **30**, 253–75) which is an important codification of his strategy of revolution.
27. Luxemburg, 1961, p. 59.
28. Ibid., p. 62.
29. Ibid., p. 67.
30. Ibid., p. 72.
31. *CW*, **26**, 435.
32. *CW*, **26**, 440.
33. *CW*, **26**, 20.
34. RSDLP, *Minutes of the Central Committee*, pp. 48–9.
35. Quoted Anweiler, pp. 206–7.
36. *CW*, **28**, 417, cf. p. 431.
37. *CW*, **28**, 394.
38. *CW*, **27**, 219.
39. *CW*, **28**, 383.
40. *CW*, **28**, 335.
41. *CW*, **28**, 333.
42. Lenin himself refers to 'the morbid character of the question of the role and tasks of the trade unions' which had degenerated into factional struggle (*CW*, **32**, 54). In 'The Party Crisis' he called for the party to 'purge itself of the malaise' of endless debate: 'We must have the courage to face the bitter truth. The Party is sick. The Party is down with the fever' (*CW*, **32**, 43).
43. *CW*, **32**, 168.
44. *CW*, **32**, 244.
45. *CW*, **32**, 200.
46. See, for example, L. Trotsky, *The Revolution Betrayed* (New York, 1970). Trotsky's very readable autobiography, *My Life* (Harmondsworth, 1975) is coy in the extreme about his role in putting down the Socialist opposition in Russia and in smashing the Kronstadt revolt.
47. *CW*, **36**, 595.

48.   L. Trotsky, *Terrorism and Communism* (Ann Arbor, Mich., 1961).
49.   *CW*, **28**, 238.
50.   *CW*, **29**, 431.
51.   *CW*, **29**, 427.
52.   A. Nove, *Was Stalin Really Necessary?* (London, 1964).
53.   J. V. Stalin, *Problems of Leninism* (Moscow, 1953), pp. 713–45.
54.   Ibid., p. 720.
55.   Ibid., p. 718.
56.   *CW*, **30**, 476.
57.   *CW*, **30**, 516.

Further Reading

Writings by Lenin

There are many editions of Lenin's *Selected Works* and readers should be aware that the grounds for inclusion or exclusion of texts in such compilations frequently reflected political preferences as much as scholarly editorial concern. Similar strictures might, to a lesser degree, be directed at the one indispensable source for non-Russian readers, the *Collected Works* in 45 volumes (plus two volumes of indexes) produced by the Foreign Languages Publishing House, Moscow, 1960–70. This is, for the most part, a translation of the fourth (enlarged) Russian edition. Contemporaneously, however, Nikita Khrushchev had ordered the preparation of a fifth, and allegedly 'complete', edition in 55 volumes, the *Polnoe sobranie sochinenia* (Moscow, 1958–65). Part of the motive for this edition was undoubtedly political. Texts of Lenin that were critical of Stalin surfaced in Russian for the first time and were no doubt intended to legitimate Khrushchev's anti-Stalin campaign. The most important new material in the fifth Russian edition was presented in the Supplementary Materials and Letters that comprise Volumes 41–45 of the English language *Collected Works*. Scholars have long questioned the 'completeness' of the fifth Russian edition, and the post-Communist opening of the archives has confirmed the view that many of the more strident and brutal of Lenin's personal communications were withheld from publication. *A Guide to Lenin's Collected Works* appears as Appendix 2 in this book, pp. 300–16.

Writings on Lenin

General

The fullest political biography is Robert Service's scrupulously researched and balanced *Lenin: A Political Life* (3 vols, London, 1985–94). It is unlikely that this extensive and thorough work will be bettered for many years to come. Service acknowledges the importance of Lenin's theoretical preoccupations, but the bulk of his text is, understandably, directed towards contextual matters, personal and party affairs, and the concerns of practical politics. The present author's *Lenin's Political Thought* (2 vols, London, 1977 and 1981) remains the fullest account of Lenin's intellectual biography, presenting Lenin's structure of thought as more orthodox in its Marxism and more coherent in structure than had previously been allowed. The objective was to reconstruct the development of one man's ideas rather than (as in the present book) critically to engage an ideological position. Leszek Kolakowski's masterly study *Main Currents of Marxism* (3 vols, Oxford, 1981) places Lenin's contribution to the evolution of European Marxism and Volume 2 contains a concise and clear analysis of his thought. A. J. Polan's *Lenin and the End of Politics* (London, 1984) is, as the title suggests, a critique of Lenin's narrowly Utopian conception of politics which, the author insists, had a lasting and baneful effect on Soviet-style regimes. Moshe Lewin's *Lenin's Last Struggle* (New York, 1968) details Lenin's vain attempts to reform the party, restrain the bureaucracy, and break the power of Stalin.

Leninism

Stalin's 'The Foundations of Leninism' (1924) and 'On the Problems of Leninism' (1926) (in Joseph Stalin, *Leninism*, London, 1940) were the texts that defined Leninism to generations of communists. Among the better commentaries on Leninism as a mobilising ideology are A. G. Meyer's *Leninism* (New York, 1962) and M. Liebman's *Leninism Under Lenin* (London, 1975), which presents the incompatible dualism of Lenin's libertarianism and authoritarianism. David Lane's *Leninism: A Sociological Interpretation* (Cambridge, 1981) is broader than the title suggests and is useful for its discussion of the range of scholarly interpretative standpoints. Alain Besançon's *The Intellectual Origins of Leninism* (Oxford, 1981) locates the roots of Leninism as ideology in the 'contradictory compound' of faith and reason that was peculiar to the Russian intelligentsia, whereas Tony Cliff's four-volume *Lenin* (London, 1975–79) is a sympathetic account that credits Lenin with the creative development of Marxism but avoids serious discussion of difficult moments and texts. Dominique Colas's *Le Leninisme* (Paris, 1982) is a perceptive thematic examination, strong on exegesis of texts and psychological dissection. Georg Lukács' *Lenin: A Study of the Unity of His Thought* emphasises Lenin's capacity to articulate abstract theory in day to day political practice, whereas Rosa Luxemburg's *Leninism or Marxism* and *The Russian Revolution* (Ann Arbor, Mich., 1961) are critical Marxist analyses of Lenin on party organisation and as master of the Soviet state. An impressive account of how the marxian idea of human liberation mutated into despotism is given in Andrzej Walicki's *Marxism and the Leap to the Kingdom of Freedom* (Cambridge, 1995).

Biography

The range of biographical material is immense and its value just as variable. Soviet-produced versions (the anonymous but authoritative *Lenin: A Biography* (Progress Publishers, Moscow, 1983) is a typical example) presented Lenin as the paragon of personal virtues and progenitor of the successful policies of the Soviet state. The mirror-image of Lenin as depraved and demented in his pursuit and exercise of power comes, predictably, from post-Soviet Russian publicists such as Dimitri Volkogonov, *Lenin: Life and Legacy* (London, 1994). Alexander Solzhenitsyn, in his *Lenin in Zurich* (London, 1975) had earlier reduced Lenin to more human scale – a man with as much pettiness as grandeur, too frequently beset with migraines. Rolf W. Theen, *V. I. Lenin:*

The Genesis and Development of a Revolutionary (London, 1974), Robert Payne, *The Life and Death of Lenin* (London, 1964), and Nathan Leites, *A Study of Bolshevism* (Glencoe, Ill., 1953) were all, in their time, influential in depicting Lenin as driven by a lust for power and/or propelled by subliminal drives that were the *real* motivations of his thought and activity. More balanced accounts, that still read well, and more judiciously blend commentary and criticism, are Adam Ulam, *Lenin and the Bolsheviks* (London, 1969), Nina Gourfinkel, *Portrait of Lenin* (New York, 1972), Edmund Wilson, *To The Finland Station* (London, 1960), and Bertram D. Wolfe, *Three Who Made a Revolution* (Harmondsworth, 1966). David Shub's *Lenin* (Harmondsworth, 1966) remains a generally reliable short introduction.

Ancillary Materials

The interpretation of particular events or texts is often best grasped by looking at contextual material of a more specialised nature. The list here would be endless but among the more useful are: Abe Ascher, *Pavel Axelrod and the Development of Menshevism* (Cambridge, Mass., 1972); Samuel Baron, *Plekhanov, The Father of Russian Marxism* (London, 1963); Stephen Cohen, *Bukharin and the Russian Revolution* (New York, 1971); Isaac Deutscher, *Trotsky*, 3 vols (Oxford 1954, 1959, 1963) (vol. 1, *The Prophet Armed*; vol. 2, *The Prophet Unarmed*; vol. 3, *The Prophet Outcast*). See also the same author's *Stalin: A Political Biography* (Oxford, 1950); Israel Getzler, *Martov: A Political Biography of a Russian Social Democrat* (Cambridge, 1967); Leopold Haimson, *The Russian Marxists and the Origins of Bolshevism* (Cambridge, Mass., 1955); John Keep, *The Rise of Social Democracy in Russia* (London, 1963); Baruch Knei-Paz, *The Social and Political Thought of Leon Trotsky* (Oxford, 1978); Richard Pipes, *Social Democracy and the St Petersburg Labour Movement* (Cambridge, Mass., 1963); Alan Wildman, *The Making of a Workers' Revolution* (Chicago, 1967); R. Craig Nation, *War on War: Lenin, the Zimmerwald Left, and the Origins of Communist Internationalism* (London, 1989).

Bibliography of Works Cited

More comprehensive, specialised bibliographies can be found in Volume 2 of the present author's *Lenin's Political Thought*, and Volume 3 of R. Service's *Lenin, A Political Life*. The works cited in 'Further Reading' themselves contain further bibliographical guidance.

Abramovitch, R. R. *The Soviet Revolution* (London, 1962) .
Althusser, L. *Lenin and Philosophy* (London, 1971).
Anweiler, O. *The Soviets* (New York, 1974).
Ascher, A. *The Mensheviks in the Russian Revolution* (London, 1976)
Baron, S. H. *Plekhanov, The Father of Russian Marxism* (London, 1963)
Berki, R. N. *The Genesis of Marxism* (London, 1988)
Bernstein, E. *Evolutionary Socialism* (London, 1900)
Bevan, E. *German Social Democracy During the War* (London, 1918)
Broido, V. *Lenin and the Mensheviks: The Persecution of Socialists under Bolshevism* (Aldershot, 1987)
Bukharin, N. *Imperialism and World Economy* (New York, 1929)
Bukharin, N. *Economics of the Transformation Period* (New York, 1971)
Bukharin, N. 'K teorii imperialisticheskogo gosudarstva' in *Revoliutsia prava, sbornik pervyi*, no. 25 (Moscow, 1925)
Carew-Hunt, R. N. *The Theory and Practice of Communism* (London, 1950)
Communist Party of the Soviet Union *History of the CPSU (Bolsheviks) Short Course* (Moscow, 1938)
Daniels, R. V. *The Stalin Revolution: Foundations of Soviet Totalitarianism* Lexington, Mass. (1972)
Deutscher, I. *Trotsky* (3 vols) (Oxford, 1954, 1963, 1969)
Deutscher, I. *Stalin: A Political Biography* (Harmondsworth, 1966)
Engels, F. *Anti-Duhring* (London, 1948)
Frankel, E., J. Frankel and B. Knei-Paz *Revolution in Russia: Reassessments of 1917* (London, 1992)
Gay, P. *The Dilemma of Democratic Socialism: Eduard Bernstein's Challenge to Marx* (New York, 1962)
Gill, G. *Stalinism* (London, 1990)
Harding, N. (1976) 'Lenin and his Critics: Some Problems of Interpretation', *European Journal of Sociology*, vol. xvii.
Harding, N. (1977, 1981) *Lenin's Political Thought*, (2 vols: vol. 1, *Theory and Practice in the Democratic Revolution*; vol. 2, *Theory and Practice in the Socialist Revolution*) London.
Harding, N. (ed.) *Marxism in Russia: Key Documents 1879–1906* (London, 1983)

Harding, N. 'Lenin, Socialism, and the State in 1917', in E. Frankel, J. Frankel and B. Knei-Paz *Revolution in Russia: Reassessments of 1917* (Cambridge, 1992a)

Harding, N. 'Bukharin and the State', in A. Kemp-Welch (ed.), *The Ideas of Nikolai Bukharin* (Oxford, 1992b)

Harding, N. 'The Marxist–Leninist Detour', in J. Dunn (ed.), *Democracy: The Unfinished Journey* (Oxford, 1992c)

Harding, N. (1994) 'The Early Marx and the Decomposition of Marxism', *Studies in Marxism*, vol. 1.

Harrington, M. *Socialism* (New York, 1972)

Hilferding, R. *Finanz Kapital* (Wien, 1910)

Jennings, J. *Georges Sorel: The Character and Development of His Thought* (London, 1985)

Kautsky, K. (ed. P. Goode) *Selected Political Writings* (London, 1983)

Kolakowski, L. *Main Currents of Marxism* (3 vols: vol. 1, *The Founders*; vol. 2, *The Golden Age*; vol. 3, *The Breakdown*) (Oxford, 1981)

Kremer, A. and I. Martov 'On Agitation' in N. Harding (ed.) *Marxism in Russia.*

Krupskaya, N. K. *O Lenine* (Moscow, 1971)

Kuskova, I. D. 'Credo' in N. Harding *Marxism in Russia.*

Leites, N. A *Study of Bolshevism* (Glencoe, Ill., 1953)

Lenin, V. I. *Collected Works*, 45 vols, London. 1960–70 (*CW* in Notes, pp. 319–34.) For particular titles and their location, see above, Appendix 2, *Guide to Lenin's Collected Works* on pp. 300–16.

Lewin, M. *Lenin's Last Struggle* (London, 1969)

Lukács, G. *Lenin: A Study on the Unity of His Thought* (London, 1970)

Luxemburg, R. *The Russian Revolution, Leninism and Marxism* (Ann Arbor, Mich., 1961)

Luxemburg, R. 'Social Reform or Revolution', in M. A. Waters (ed.), *Rosa Luxemburg Speaks* (New York, 1970)

Marx, K. *Capital*, trans. S. Moore and E. Aveling (London, 1938)

Marx, K. *Economic and Philosophic Manuscripts of 1844*, also known as 'Paris Manuscripts' (Moscow, 1961)

Marx, K. and Engels, F. 'The Holy Family' in *Collected Works*, vol. 4.

Marx, K. and Engels, F. *Selected Correspondence*, D. Torr (ed.) (London, 1936)

Marx, K. and Engels, F. *Selected Works*, 2 vols, Moscow. 1962 (*MESW* in Notes).

Marx, K. and Engels, F. *The German Ideology* (London, 1965)

Marx, K. and Engels, F. *Collected Works* (London, 1975–)

Marx, K. and Engels, F. *The Manifesto of the Communist Party* in *MESW*, 1.

Medvedev, R. *On Stalin and Stalinism* (Oxford, 1979)

Melgunov, S. P. *The Bolshevik Seizure of Power* (Santa Barbara, Calif., 1972)

Nettl, J. P. *Rosa Luxemburg* (London, 1969)

Payne, R. *The Life and Death of Lenin* (London, 1964)

Plamenatz, J. *German Marxism and Russian Communism* (London, 1954)

Pipes, R. *Revolutionary Russia* (London, 1968)

Plekhanov, G. V. *Socialism and the Political Struggle and Our Differences*, in G. V. Plekhanov, *Selected Philosophical Works*, vol. 1 (London, 1961)

Polan, A. J. *Lenin and the End of Politics* (London, 1984)

Radkey, O. *Russia Goes to the Polls – The Election to the All-Russia Constituent Assembly 1917* (Ithaca, NY, 1989)
Russian Social Democratic Labour Party *The Bolsheviks and the October Revolution. Minutes of the Central Committee of the RSDLP* (London, 1974).
Schapiro, L. S. *The Communist Party of the Soviet Union* (London, 1970)
Schapiro, L. S. *The Origin of the Communist Autocracy* (New York, 1955)
Schorske, C. E. *German Social Democracy 1918–1933* (Chicago, 1964)
Service, R. *Lenin: A Political Life*, 3 vols: vol. 1, *The Strengths of Contradiction*; vol. 2, *World in Collision*; vol. 3, *The Iron Ring* (London, 1985, 1991, 1995)
Shragin, B. and A. Todd (eds.) *Landmarks* (New York, 1972)
Shukman, H. *Lenin and the Russian Revolution* (London, 1966)
Sorel, G. *Reflections on Violence* (London, 1961)
Stalin, J. V. *Problems of Leninism* (Moscow, 1953a)
Stalin, J. V. *Works*, 13 vols (Moscow, 1953b)
Steenson, G. *Not One Man! Not One Penny! German Social Democracy 1863–1914* (Pittsburg, Penn., 1984)
Sukhanov, N. N. *The Russian Revolution of 1917* (London, 1966)
Theen, R. H. W. *V. I. Lenin: The Genesis and Development of a Revolutionary*
Trotsky, L. *Stalin* (London, 1947)
Trotsky, L. *Terrorism and Communism* (Ann Arbor, Mich., 1961)
Trotsky, L. *The Permanent Revolution and Results and Prospects* (London, 1962a)
Trotsky, L. *The Stalin School of Falsification* (New York, 1962b)
Trotsky, L. *History of the Russian Revolution*, 3 vols (London, 1967)
Trotsky, L. *On Lenin: Notes Towards a Biography* (London, 1970a)
Trotsky, L. *The Revolution Betrayed* (New York, 1970b)
Trotsky, L. *1905* (Harmondsworth, 1971)
Trotsky, L. *My Life* (Harmondsworth, 1975)
Tucker, R. C. *Stalin as Revolutionary 1879–1929* (London, 1974)
Ulam, A. B. *Lenin and the Bolsheviks* (London, 1969)
Ulam, A. B. *Stalin: The Man and His Era* (London, 1974)
V. V. (Vorontsov, V. P.) *Sudby kapitalizma v rossii* (The Fates of Capitalism in Russia (St Petersburg, 1882)
Venturi, F. *Roots of Revolution* (London, 1964)
Volkogonov, D. *Lenin, Life and Legacy* (London, 1994)
Wade, R. *Red Guards and Workers' Militias in the Russian Revolution* (Stanford, Conn., 1984)
Walicki, A. *The Controversy over Capitalism* (Oxford, 1969)
Weeks, A. L., *The First Bolshevik – A Political Biography of Peter Tkachev* (New York, 1968).
Wilson, E. *To the Finland Station* (London, 1960)
Wolfe, B. D. *Marxism, 100 Years in the Life of a Doctrine* (London, 1967)
Wolfenstein, E. V. *The Revolutionary Personality* (Princeton, 1967)
Wortman, R. *The Crisis of Russian Populism* (Cambridge, 1967).

Index

agrarian question 85–6, 283, 284,
314; *see also* peasants
Akselrod, P. B. 36, 46, 282, 283,
284, 313, 314
Althusser, L. 225, 238
anti-socialist laws 54–5
Aristotle 288
Armand, I. 297, 313, 316

Babushkin, I. V. 23
Bakunin, M. A. 17
Bebel, A. 53, 54, 60, 73, 315
Berdyaev, N. 219
Bergson, H. 220
Bernstein, E. 58–66, 67, 283, 304–5
Bloody Sunday 38
Bogdanov, A. A. 49, 86, 220–2, 248,
287, 304
Bolsheviks: emergence of 36–7, 285;
in 1917 83, 99–106; and
Communist International
183–8; chronology of 290–94
bourgeois politics 9–12, 33, 44, 45,
65, 151–2, 167, 175–8, 262–3
Bukharin, N. I.: on imperialist
state 46–7, 189; and
proletarian state 190–2;
anticipated Lenin 202–3; and
dialetic 240; and redefinition
of socialist project 123, 129,
246, 255, 256, 257, 258–9, 260,
289, 294, 307, 313

capitalism in Russia: Populists
and 19–20, Lenin's analysis
of 18, 22–3
Cheka 258, 293, 315; *see also* terror
Chernov, V. 80

Chernyshevsky, N. G. 219, 226
Chkeizde, N. S. 80, 81–2, 101
commune *see* Paris Commune
commune state 85, 92, 291, 307–9,
310
Communist (or Third)
International 295, 296, 297,
298, 310, 311
consciousness: Marx, Kautsky and
Lenin on 32–6; Lenin
on 171–4, 181–2, 273
Constituent Assembly 38, 80–1,
102, 250–3, 281–2, 293, 310
Constitutional Democrats *see*
Kadets

Dan, F. I. 47, 100, 109
Danton 102
Deich, L. 36
democracy: Engels and 58–9;
Bernstein on 61–2; Lenin
and 9–10, 150–1, 166–9, 170–1,
175–8, 188, 196, 250–6, 274–5,
277, 311
Democratic Centralists 254, 255
Deutscher, I. 218
dialectics: Bernstein and 60–1;
Engels and 228–9, 236; Marx
and 227–8, 232; Lenin and
229–42, 314; Stalin and 240
dictatorship 154–9, 161–3, 261–3,
277, 309–11
Dietzgen, J. 225, 226
Dreyfus, A. 72
Duma 39–41, 72, 80, 286, 303, 304

Emancipation of Labour
Group 282, 283

341